JOURNAL FOR THE STUDY OF THE OLD TESTAMENT SUPPLEMENT SERIES

73

Editors

David J.A. Clines

Philip R. Davies

THE SOCIAL WORLD OF BIBLICAL ANTIQUITY SERIES

7

General Editor

James W. Flanagan

Almond Press

Sheffield

DAVID'S SOCIAL DRAMA

A Hologram of Israel's Early Iron Age

JAMES W. FLANAGAN

The Almond Press · 1988

The Social World of
Biblical Antiquity Series, 7

Published by Almond Press
Editorial direction: David M. Gunn
Columbia Theological Seminary
P.O. Box 520, Decatur
GA 30031, U.S.A.
Almond Press is an imprint of
Sheffield Academic Press Ltd
The University of Sheffield
343 Fulwood Road
Sheffield S10 3BP
England

Typeset by Sheffield Academic Press
and
printed in Great Britain
by Billing & Sons Ltd
Worcester

British Library Cataloguing in Publication Data

Flanagan, James W.
David's social drama: a hologram of Israel's
Early Iron Age.—(The Social world of biblical
antiquity, ISSN 0265-1408:7)—(Journal for
the study of the Old Testament supplement series,
ISSN 0309-0787:73)
1. Israel, ancient period
I. Title II. Series
III. Series
933

ISBN 1-85075-201-X
ISBN 1-85075-202-8 Pbk

CONTENTS

ILLUSTRATIONS

Preface

If this book accomplishes its goal, it will first, enrich the understanding of ancient Israel's early Iron Age, especially the processes of state formation that the Bible attributes to David; and second, contribute to the development of social scientific analyses of biblical antiquity. The thesis, if one can be summarized, is that the "Israel" of the time was transitional and in the betwixt and between religiously, socially, politically, economically, and ecologically and that tradition casts David in a mediator's role in each of the domains.

In terms of content and method, the volume must be read for what it is: an attempt to advance an emerging subspecialty within biblical studies (social world studies) by investigating a period that has left comparatively little solid "historical" information. Many sections are merely restatements of long-held positions; some incorporate opinions that might be rejected if they were forced to stand by themselves; and others raise doubts about conventional truisms in biblical studies. As a result, new hypotheses are offered about the emergence of Yahwist centralization and state on the one hand, and on the other about the metaphors available to biblical historians for understanding and describing the remote past.

As hypotheses, these, like every other historical reconstruction and approach, are subject to immediate review and revision. Hence, the description of the David figure and the social world of Iron Age I are offered as tentative but informed portrayals. They are meant to add perspectives and invite others to continue investigations on David and the Iron Age.

Arrangement of the Volume

Because of the number of disciplines involved, the history of the problems addressed, and the fact that distinct types of information must be examined separately before a cohesive image can be discussed, the volume is unusually complex. The approach necessitates evaluating and re-evaluating similar issues in several chapters. In the Introduction I cite briefly many of the issues that are taken up individually in later chapters so that readers may see from the beginning the purpose and direction taken in the study. The preliminary overview is useful because David, the volume's central topic, does not move to center stage until Chapter 4.

Chapter 1 discusses the traditions of scholarship that have contributed both to the malaise in biblical history and to the beginnings of solutions. The problems biblical historians have left unresolved offer room for new proposals, and a general familiarity with the recent issues and approaches helps to situate social world studies. I use "social world studies" as a label for the social scientific analyses of ancient Israel championed in America and making inroads in Britain, Europe, and Israel. A brief summary of recent works in social world studies is included for non-specialists who may not be familiar with trends in present-day biblical studies.

Chapter 2 develops a holographic model by summarizing several comparative sociological studies. Distinctions made in those studies are applied in later chapters. The review includes works by anthropologists Edmund Leach, Marvin Harris, Roy A. Rappaport, and Ladislav Holy and Milan Stuchlik. In later chapters, I also draw on the work of Jack Goody, Ernest Gellner, Victor Turner, Michael Meeker, and several others.

In summarizing anthropological studies, I have chosen to retain the terminology used by the authors and to refrain from offering comparative examples taken from the biblical tradition even though they might guide the reader through the labyrinthine world of social scientific jargon. The temptation to "translate" has been resisted for two reasons. First, each study reflects the ethnography of one or more societies and, while the authors generalize from those specific instances, it would be unwise to assume that individual phenomena match others in ancient Israel. Second, most of the authors have not understood themselves to be saying exactly what the others were saying. Hence, their choice of terminology has been intentionally diverse. To force one's vocabulary on another's concepts would do injustice to both. Therefore, in the first round I let the authors speak for themselves as clearly as they can through my summaries.

The archaeological and literary information pertaining to David are presented in Chapters 3 and 4. Here again I have tried to be restrained, in effect, saying less rather than more about the history of the period. Part of the bewilderment about David, it seems to me, is caused by claims that exceed available information. By trying to fill the gaps in our historical knowledge, students of the Bible have turned their imaginations into highly creative forces. It is time to look again, to report only what is found, and to distinguish that from our own retelling of the story. What is found and admitted into evidence will of course remain the object of debate because no definitive history can be written.

The material world and archaeological record are sketched in Chapter 3; the written record is reviewed in Chapter 4. The purpose for the ordering will become clear as we progress, especially in the discussions of Rappaport's systemic ecology approach.

Chapter 5 develops the hologram model and concludes the representation of Iron Age I. Archaeological and literary images are integrated holographically, ritual studies are applied, and a hologram of Iron Age I is proposed.

Three appendices are added. The first presents material and archaeological information to supplement Chapter 3. The additional information would be cumbersome and somewhat repetitious if placed in the main body of the text. Some readers may find it useful while others may be satified with the general overviews and conclusions stated the chapter.

The second appendix contains information about Abdul Aziz Ibn Saud, the founder King of Saudi Arabia. The material, which supplements information in Chapter 5, helped me understand the processes and motives that led to statehood in Saudi Arabia and by analogy in ancient Israel. Some of the information is based on personal interviews with former members of Ibn Saud's court and has appeared only in prepublished form (Flanagan, 1982). By presenting it separately here, I hope to make the story more fully available than could be done in Chapter 5. Appendix III contains Saulide and Davidic genealogical charts and lists that are discussed in Chapter 4.

Acknowledgements

The queries, criticisms, guidance, and urgings of my family, students, teachers, and colleagues over the years have shaped my thinking and expression more than they or I will ever know. To each, I express my gratitude.

Such clan and communal supports means that individuals who are named represent others who for reasons of space must remain anonymous. The volume is dedicated to my most caring and loyal friend, my sister, and our parents, who both died during this writing. They stand for my extended family including my sister's family, Irene Oberholser, and Josephine and Loddy Gruca who shouldered many burdens that were rightly mine so that I could spend lengthy periods in England and the Middle East.

My interest in the enigmatic David figure goes back to graduate student days and the influence of John L. McKenzie. His encouragement continues unfailingly. The influence of George Mendenhall and David Noel Freedman, traced to my days at the University of Michigan, is visible in Chapters 1 and 4. Michigan also introduced me to Roy A. Rappaport who in turn directed me toward Jack Goody and Cambridge University. Professor Goody generously introduced me to the world of anthropology, the Faculty of Social Anthropology, the Friday seminars, and the gatherings at the bar in King's College. In the mix, Sir Edmund Leach stood out (figuratively as well as literally) because he, like Goody, was asking hard questions about the Bible and voiced interest in my project. Conversations with them, and later with Ernest Gellner, greatly influenced my approach. To these as well as the President and Fellows of Clare Hall, Cambridge, the Master and Fellows of St. Edmund's House, Cambridge, and James Sauer, first as Director of ACOR in Amman and later as President of the American Schools of Oriental Research, I owe a special debt of gratitude. The same applies to the Principal and staff of Wesley House, Cambridge, who warmly welcomed me as a resident, and to Bernadette O'Flynn, Fellow of St. Edmund's and Assistant Registrary of Cambridge University, who assisted my arrival and continued to facilitate many arrangements in the University and Cambridge community.

ASOR trustee Gough Thompson introduced me to Sheikh Mohammed Almana of Al Khobar, Saudi Arabia. The Sheikh's hospitality and conversations at Almana Hospital have been invaluable for understanding the richness of Middle Eastern life. My curiosity about his hero, King Ibn Saud, arose independently of interests in antiquity, but I have come to see the usefulness of the King's life for social world studies.

My views on David and the early Iron Age continue to be shaped by conversations with David Gunn and Paula McNutt. Without their help and comments, this work would not have been begun or finished. The same can be said for Margaret Almond Gunn, co-founder of Almond Press. David Hopkins, Keith Whitelam, John L.

McKenzie, Sir Edmund Leach, Jack Goody, Elizabeth Bellefontaine, and Philip King kindly read parts or all of the manuscript at various stages of completion. James Holub, Jan Brocci, and Jean Harte ably assisted with bibliography and preparation of the manuscript. To Jean I owe first access to President Franklin D. Roosevelt's log that is cited in Appendix II. Completion of the manuscript was expedited by the comments of Kathleen McCrone and the editing of Ann Johnston of Paris who sharpened many arguments and forestalled many embarrassments. David Clines, Philip Davies, and the staff at Sheffield Academic Press took personal interest that exceeded the professional responsibility of publishers.

Finally, I thank my departmental colleagues at the University of Montana, Alexander P. Madison of the UM Printing Services, and the members of the Society of Biblical Literature's Sociology of Monarchy Seminar for their generous encouragement.

Research for the book was supported in part by grants and fellowships from the National Endowment for the Humanities (Centers and College Teachers Programs), the University of Montana Research Council, the American Schools of Oriental Research Fellowship Program, the American Center for Oriental Research (Amman), St. Edmund's House, Cambridge, and Clare Hall, Cambridge.

Credits

I am grateful to the following publishers for permission to use illustrations and maps that have appeared in other works: Cambridge University Press for the use of Figure 33 from Meeker, 1979: 199; Methuen & Co. for the use of Figures 12, 13, 15, 16, 17 and 37 from Fisher, 1978: 14, 15, 401, 405, 61 and 40 respectively; Arizona University Press for use of Figure 9 from V. Turner, 1985b: 293; Eisenbrauns for use of charts and lists from Flanagan, 1983a: 39-44; and the *Bulletin of the American Schools of Oriental Research* for use of Figures 18 and 19 from Stager, 1985: 2; and Sauer, 1986: 2, respectively. I also thank Paula McNutt for drawing Figures 1, 23, 24, 25, 26 and 38.

J.W.F.
Atlanta, Iowa
Summer 1987

With gratitude to my sister

Mary Patricia Holub

and

in memory of our parents

James P. and Agnes Durham Flanagan

To See a World in a grain of Sand,
And Heaven in a Wild Flower,
Hold Infinity in the palm of your hand,
And Eternity in an hour.

William Blake

Abbreviations

ANET	James B. Pritchard (ed.). 1969. *Ancient Near Eastern Texts Relating to the Old Testament*. 3rd edition. Princeton: Princeton University.
EA	El Amarna Letter, cited from J.A. Knudtzon. 1915. *Die El-Amarna Tafeln*. Leipzig: Hinrichs.

Introduction

Demise of Confidence in the Bible as History

For the past several centuries, the Bible has been submitted to criticisms and comparisons that have threatened its life as a historical document. The text has been divided according to forms, traditions, redactions, settings, and sources by scholars using critical methodologies in attempts to recover original expressions and unravel the Bible's development. Similarly, comparisons with non-biblical literatures and societies have made the Sacred Book host to invasions of information from Mesopotamia, Egypt, Anatolia, and Greece that swept in with artifacts, rituals, and myths in order to explain the origin and meaning of difficult passages.

Although the techniques were intended to enable the reconstruction of events as they happened in the ancient Near East, the effect was paradoxical. As the past was more fully illuminated, some of it disappeared. Also, the presumed bases for orthodox doctrines were threatened. Each comparison, it seemed, further eroded the shrinking confidence in Israel's uniqueness as well as the historical accuracy of its literature.

The process continued until some critics, disillusioned with the standard criticisms and anxious about the ability of these methods to achieve their stated goals, turned to structural analysis, New Criticism, canonical criticism, deconstructionist theory, and other Bible-as-literature approaches in efforts to understand and save the book's religious meaning. These offered fresh theories for retaining the literature's value while avoiding or by-passing questions of Israel's history.

Much was at stake for the historian, including the question of "the same and the other" described by Augé (1982: 14). Were Israel and the Bible the same as other Near Eastern cultures and literatures and therefore only delayed replicas, or were they unique and therefore truly incomparable? Did comparisons with other societies perhaps betray an underlying common pattern, single experience, or unconscious structure that would mean Israel's religion was only a cultural mutation of others before or beside it in history? Or were such questions themselves irrelevant?

In the beginning, of course, the questions were not posed as matters of critical theory nor couched in Augé's terms. Instead, long-held assumptions about authorships and dates began to collapse under the weight of comparative and critical information. First to go was the biblical holograph, i.e., the belief that the Pentateuch and other books were autographs written by historical individuals whose names appear in them. Theologians were compelled to wrestle with theories of inspiration while critics, their senses whetted, probed further into the history of texts and searched for the events behind them.

Criticism continued unabated until the historical foundations for the creations and falls in Genesis 1-11 were eroded, the ancestral traditions were threatened, and the Conquest was placed in serious doubt. Efforts to reconcile old beliefs with new information forced scholars to appeal to categories such as "mythopoeic" and "metahistorical" in efforts to explain the relationship between history and religious meaning. And eventually, settling pastoralists and revolting peasants were substituted for the invading nomadic foreigners previously credited with bringing Yahwism to the Promised Land.

By comparison, the period of Israel's United Monarchy seemed historically unassailable: it was the high ground where the Bible, extra-biblical texts, and archaeology came together to present a reliable picture (cf. Soggin, 1984; Miller and Hayes, 1986). There, it was thought, criticism and comparison could affirm real events and personalities. Critics presumed that literacy and monarchy had left behind Iron Age texts and monuments that provided biblical historians with solid "factual" information. The biblical texts were early and therefore reliable; archaeological information, though not abundant, was sufficiently unambiguous; and the institution of kingship was widely known and easily compared. Israelite kings would be more clearly understood with each scholarly endeavor and the passage of time.

But the synthetic logic did not hold. Soon the kings were having their day in court until the historical David in particular was being put on trial.

Four reasons for the lapse of confidence regarding David and the monarchy can be cited. First, studies on the pre-Davidic periods, especially by Mendenhall and Gottwald, shifted focus from exogenous to endogenous causes for Israel's emergence and began to expose monarchy as alien to primal Yahwist religion. Consequently, the motives for establishing Israelite kingship were questioned. Explanations for the deep-seated tensions that the institution caused within the religious community were proposed. As a result, attention was drawn toward religious struggles within the Yahwist community, and Israel was no longer portrayed as completely and actively united in its movement toward centralization.

Secondly, the setting of the Davidic stories came under attack after half a century of relative certainty. For example, the extent, purpose, and date of the Court History in 2 Samuel were reviewed (cf. Whybray, 1968; Van Seters, 1976; Würthwein, 1974; Veijola, 1975; Langlamet, 1976; and Conroy, 1978). More than others, David Gunn's treatment (1978; cf. Chapter 1 below) challenged conventional wisdom regarding the narrative's historical value. Earlier and on grounds other than Gunn's, I had argued for distinguishing the so-called "Court History" from the "Succession Narrative" (Flanagan, 1972). I sought to revise Leonhard Rost's claims: 1) that the latter was a single composition written to explain Solomon's succession and 2) that it extended from 2 Samuel 9-20 through 1 Kings 1-2. On the basis of themes and chiastic structure, I identified a substrata that related only to David and to his problems in maintaining paramountcy. This I called the "Court History," a narrative limited to 2 Samuel 9-10, 13-20. I proposed that the unit was revised to include stories of Solomon's rise which transformed it into a "Succession Narrative." In this volume, I retain the thematic distinction between the story of David's court and the story of Solomon's succession, but for reasons other than those offered in 1972 (cf. Chapters 4 and 5). In any case, interpretation of these and other Davidic stories changed and contributed to the spreading loss of confidence in biblical history.

A third reason came from archaeology. Confidence in Davidic archaeology was fading quickly as excavations failed to yield signs of centralization that could be firmly dated to the early 10th century. At best, archaeologists could affirm that dramatic social change had occurred between the end of the Late Bronze Age and the beginning of Iron Age II. The change, it was thought, must have been associated with David and Solomon. But in spite of this, because the science of archaeology was no longer tied to historical studies, the discipline began to assign a diminished role to literary information generally and the Bible particularly. Like literary studies that moved away from history, archaeology pushed beyond space-time systemics in the direction of synchronic, social, and cultural issues. Biblical archaeology as it had been known soon fell into disarray.

Finally, behind each of these changes was a renewed, growing concern for epistemology, historiography, and philosophy of history. As biblical criticism embraced secular criticism and archaeology sought more from its companion social sciences and the hard sciences, the chasm between the traditional sources used by biblical historians and the history they were trying to comprehend widened. The journey from one to the other that had previously required a leap of faith now demanded a similar "leap of history" as theological uncertainties were joined by doubts about the reliability and validity of historical sources and methods.

These issues must be examined as we proceed. There are, however, two additional concerns: 1) the question of the ancient mind and what qualities it found in David. Why, if he was historical, did it make him a legendary figure; or, if he was legendary, what historical processes led so many to think of him as historical? And 2) in light of the changing attitudes outlined above, how can we approach the social world of Iron Age I as biblical historians and still retain intellectual respectability? Is it possible to avoid accusations of literalism on the one hand and fantasy on the other?

Other Reasons for Re-examining the History of David

In earlier studies I proposed, largely on the basis of texts in the books of Samuel and Chronicles, that chieftaincy was a more appropriate analogue than kingship for understanding David's early historical role (Flanagan, 1981). Now (in Chapters 4 and 5) I insist rather that the image of David in the texts is, in a sense, that of a paramount chief and not of a king. The earlier study was one part in a larger re-evaluation of David that I set forth in separate studies on the Davidic capital (1979), biblical genealogies (1983a), and ritual (1983b). I became increasingly suspicious of claims made about the "United Monarchy." In spite of the chronological distance between the stories of David and Ibn Saud, the similarities between the relationships of elements in each instance suggested either that the biblical image of David and Almana's biography of Ibn Saud (1980) were alike, or that the persons behind the stories shared common social roles, or both.

Considering such questions drew attention to the obvious methodological issue: how can we validly draw comparisons between such widely separated periods and cultures, and if we can, how can the comparisons be controlled?

I did not review archaeological information in these studies. Gradually, I became convinced that the pattern of archaeological information from ancient Syro-Palestine (i.e., mounds of material from some regions and periods interspersed with a paucity of it from others, especially in places and times associated with the David stories) tells more about the early Iron Age than was previously recognized. The pattern is itself a type of information, as are the apparent discrepancies between it and the claims made by the biblical writers. I sensed the need for an approach to Iron Age history that separated *analytically* archaeological information from literary information in order for each record to speak independently. Biblical historians usually spoke of "correlating" the records, but this prevented separate disciplines from presenting their own interpretations before confusing them with claims from another.

Finally, the concurrent turning away by literary critics from historical questions was beginning to cause a schism in biblical studies. A widening gulf separated those who viewed the Bible critically but as having referential value for knowing historical events and authors' intentions from those who chafed under the weight of historical questions. The rift threatened to divide the field into two disciplines. I decided to address the issue directly.

The environment forced me to question my own assumptions as well as other historians' reconstructions of the period. General interpretations of Israelite history and texts pertaining to monarchy, as well as judgments about historical details and individual texts, came under review. The common assumption that Israelite monarchy began with David, or possibly Saul, controlled the way that long- and short-term history were interpreted. If the sources were approached without presupposing a monarchical ethos, many details, I believed, would be interpreted differently, and a substantially different picture would emerge.

Approach to the Study

In spite of arguments against eclecticism (e.g., Harris, 1979: 287-314), the approach taken here is eclectic and interdisciplinary. I accept Goody's assertion that the nature of available information and the type of questions brought to an investigation necessarily determine how research must proceed (1982: 5-8). It is safe to predict, therefore, that others would take a different approach to the topics treated here. It is also important to note, however, that an eclectic approach makes it possible to integrate insights and information from a wide variety of studies where a methodologically invariable approach does not. Such flexibility is necessary for interdisciplinary inquiry.

The study draws primarily on literary, archaeological, and comparative sociological methodologies, and to a lesser degree on philosophies of history and science. These are combined in a historical investigation on a single period. No effort is made to generalize about social phenomena on the basis of the specific historical case. Thus, the work differs from that of a comparative sociologist.

For me, literary studies on the Bible have awakened sensitivity 1) for the relationship between texts' meanings and historical occurrences (i.e., for detaching historical meaning from other textual claims); 2) for the polyvalence of texts; and 3) for finding meanings beyond and in the structure of texts. These more than the specific interpretations of literary critics are visible in the chapters that follow. A literary approach necessarily differs sharply from a historical investigation. For example, the former's interest in readers' response and its propensity for "filling the gaps" in a text are valid interests, but they do not necessarily pertain to historical inquiry. Determining which literary insights are useful historically and devising an approach that suits both sets of interest is one reason for the emphasis placed on modeling in this volume (cf. Chapter 2).

Throughout, "comparative sociology" is used, again after Goody, as an apt label that includes anthropology and sociology (two subfields in the overarching discipline) and social as well as cultural anthropology (Goody, 1982: 7-8; *pace* Leach, 1982: 27-41). Most references, however, are to anthropology, whether social or cultural.

Drawing disciplines together demands balance, restraint, and introspection. The task is especially delicate here because each discipline is undergoing fundamental re-evaluation simultaneously. Therefore, we risk bringing the disciplines together at points where they are individually weakest, or we chance hiding the epistemological problems in one discipline behind those troubling another. This, I contend, is what has happened in studies on the early Iron Age and is what stands behind the need for a new approach to Davidic studies, one that offers new models and metaphors for ancient history.

The models, metaphors, and analogies evolved as I reflected on specific historical questions and juggled partially incongruent information and images from several disciplines. In search for a way to describe the relationships among textual, archaeological, and anthropological information about David, I happened upon holograms and holography. The technology and the images it produces seemed to characterize my situation. Making holograms, like reconstituting history, requires a great deal of trial and error. When the process is successful, images emerge; when unsuccessful, nothing can be seen. When successful, the image remains invisible until illuminated. The image seen varies with the perspective of the viewer. The image is not in the holographic plate but beyond it. These and other qualities make the processes and images a useful basis for a hypothesis about the work of biblical historians and the history they recover.

Models and Modeling

Generally, models are hypotheses that simplify complex situations by allowing noise to be sorted from information. Which is noise and which information depends on the frame of reference of the model (cf. Clarke, 1978: 31).

In the pages that follow, a number of types of models are mentioned, described, or applied. I believe my uses fall into two broad categories: first, models that assist in the investigation of history (i.e., models of methods), and second, models that are a society's (either the actor's or observer's) comprehension of itself. The former, as research designs, illustrate how a research topic is structured and addressed, i.e., how investigators apply their skills, integrate information, organize descriptions, sort explanations, etc. The latter, as mental constructs, are peoples' conceptions of their actions, their reasons and explanations for their actions, and their notions about their environments, natural and cultural.

The second type may be either participants' (insiders, natives) or investigators' (scientists, outsiders) conceptions. The one is held by members of a sociocultural group; the other is held by non-member observers of the group. We shall see in Chapter 2, however, that problems arise because, when the conceptions are reported by the observers, both descriptions are really views held by observers. Both are conceptions held in the observers' world, but one is of their own world and the other is their impressions of alien actors' conceptions.

As we proceed, several additional types of each will be discussed. However, because models (especially the first type above) are "designed," "constructed" or "built," sometimes in stages, several preliminary remarks about model building as it pertains to the research design used here are appropriate.

R. Harré uses the term "model" ". . . to signify a real or imagined process which behaves similarly to some other thing or process or which is similar in some way other than its behavior" (Harré, 1972: 174). His definition is very close to his description of analogy and in fact links the two concepts:

> An analogy is a relationship between two entities, processes, or what you will, which allows inferences to be made about one of the things, usually that about which we know least, on the basis of what we know about the other. If two things are alike in some respects we can reasonably expect them to be alike in other respects, though there may be still others in which they are unlike (Harré, 1972: 172).

Additional connections should be noted. First, the fact that a model is a representation of something else means that the model and its referent are analogous, i.e., in varying degrees similar or dissimilar, or that they share the same similarities and dissimilarities simultaneously. Secondly, theories are often nothing but descriptions of models that in turn are representations of analogies. Third, an analogy may be positive, neutral, or negative depending on the balance between the similarity and dissimilarity of the things compared. Fourth, in the sciences, if something is known only on the basis of a model, it may not be possible to identify a negative analogy. In other words, it may be impossible for a researcher to demonstrate with models how the things compared are dissimilar. But even in instances where a strong negative analogy co-exists with neutral and positive analogies, according to Harré, analogies are still useful. A negative analogy only means that the model is expressing a new kind of entity or process different from the one it is modeled on, and not that the analogy is erroneous or useless (Harré, 1972: 174–175). We might ask whether the last assertion applies only to science, rather than to history and social science where scholars are customarily concerned about the dissimilarities as well as the similarities in comparisons. In any case, the claim suggests that practitioners in the "softer" disciplines need not feel insecure about their failure to establish "scientific" explanations. Their self-doubts rest on false assumptions about scientific certainty.

It is common for models to be modeled on other models, and for unknown processes to be modeled. For example, laws of electrical conduction were first explained by two suppositions. Scientists supposed that electrons behaved like molecules in gases and then by reasoning on a second level that a swarm of confined molecules behaved like a container full of gas (Harré, 1972: 178). In this way a two-step model was constructed to explain two levels in the behavior of electrons.

The second stage stratum is important in models aimed at describing causal mechanisms. Although rare, an ideal theory contains a description of something known (a model) that is capable of standing in for its unknown counterpart and also allows for the double analogy just mentioned, i.e., for modeling of models. The second are hypothetical mechanisms conceived as causing the phenomenon being examined. Causal knowledge tends, therefore, to be stratified. The facts are set out and their patterns and structures described first, and then the underlying causal mechanism is imagined or described. To penetrate both strata requires "disciplined imagination" (Harré, 1972: 179-180).

Modeling theory has been applied in conceptions of "black boxes" and "translucid (or gray) boxes." In black box theory, the box is an imaginary mechanism that conceals its inner workings. Observers can see the box and note inputs and outputs, but can only hypothesize about the causal factors that transform the former into the latter. The black box concept is closely related to gray box or translucid box theories developed within philosophy of science and widely applied in the hard and social sciences.

> Both scientific theories and their referents have often been likened to devices in the form of boxes with external dials that can be manipulated. The dials correspond to the 'external' variables representing observable properties, such as the size and direction of motion of visible bodies; the pieces inside the box correspond to the 'internal' or hypothetical variables, such as elastic strain or atomic weight. If, in order to run the box, only the dials have to be manipulated, we have a *black box* theory ... If, in addition to the handling of the dials representing the external variables, we are required to meddle with a hypothetical inner mechanism described

> with the help of 'internal' variables (hypothetical constructs), we are confronted with what may be called a *translucid box* theory. Black boxes theories are also called *phenomenological*; and translucid box theories may be called *representational* (Bunge, 1964: 235).

Black box theory focuses on the behavior of systems, especially inputs and outputs, whereas translucid theory attempts to explain the constitution and structure of systems and to establish links between the inputs and outputs (Bunge, 1964: 236). As we shall see, these are precisely the tasks anthropologist Edmund Leach assigned respectively to archaeology (black box) and anthropology (translucid box) in a lecture to archaeologists (cf. Chapter 1).

The relationship of the two types of theory is important. Black box theory can provide explanations and prediction, but it cannot offer interpretation of data. For that a mechanism must be postulated, as we have seen in the two strata of models and analogies. But any number of representational theories (translucid boxes) are compatible with any given phenomenological theory (black box) (Bunge, 1964: 249).

This means that black box theory is a first step in the construction of theory and is superseded or supplemented by a second step, translucid box theory. The former is less complete than the latter; the latter lends itself to greater variety. In sum, black boxes are built to provide global theories, whereas translucid boxes are employed to explain black boxes and therefore to interpret reality (Bunge, 1964: 252-253).

These distinctions will become clear as we proceed and move beyond them with a holographic model. Here it is sufficient to note that one use of the term "model" applies to the research design, i.e., the manner of investigating, used in examining Davidic history. Texts, archaeological information, and comparative sociology are integrated according to a model described in Chapter 2.

Archaeological Dates

Throughout the volume, the archaeological chronology and terminology developed by William Foxwell Albright and refined by Paul Lapp are used. Only the historical periods between the Early Bronze Age and Iron Age II are examined:

—Early Bronze Age		3300-1950 B.C.E.
—EBIA-C	(3300-2900 B.C.E.)	
—EBII	(2900-2700 B.C.E.)	
—EBIII	(2700-2300 B.C.E.)	
—EBIVA-B	(2300-1950 B.C.E.)	
—Middle Bronze Age		1950-1550 B.C.E.
—MBI	(1950-1750 B.C.E.)	
—MBII	(1750-1650 B.C.E.)	
—MBIII	(1650-1550 B.C.E.)	
—Late Bronze Age		1550-1200 B.C.E.
—LBIA	(1550-1500 B.C.E.)	
—LBIB	(1500-1400 B.C.E.)	
—LBIIA	(1400-1300 B.C.E.)	
—LBIIB	(1300-1200 B.C.E.)	
—Iron Age I		1200-918 B.C.E.
—Iron IA	(1200-1000 B.C.E.)	
—Iron IB	(1150-1000 B.C.E.)	
—Iron IC	(1000-918 B.C.E.)	
—Iron Age II		918-539 B.C.E.
—Iron IIA	(918-721 B.C.E.)	
—Iron IIB	(721-605 B.C.E.)	
—Iron IIC	(605-539 B.C.E.)	

Because this scheme necessarily mixes chronological periods with cultural distinctions, confusion and debate have arisen. Iron I is the most important period for this study. Iron IA is a regional designation for the temporal era following the collapse of Late Bronze IIB civilizations. Biblical and Near Eastern historians interested in ancient Israel have identified IA almost exclusively with "Israelite," tying the chronological phase to a specific culture and implying that they were synonymous. The ethnic identification is now known to be too restrictive because an Iron IA phase has been found in "Ammonite," "Moabite," and "Edomite" regions of Transjordan where it can be distinguished from the so-called "Israelite" occupation (Ibrahim, 1978; Sauer, 1982: 76, 82). In addition, the label could apply to any civilization yet to be discovered if it were to share the same temporal and material characteristics. Unfortunately, however, because of the confusion of Iron IA with "Israelite" in secondary literature and archaeological reports it is now difficult to distinguish the categories even for analytical purposes.

In Lapp's sequence, Iron IB overlaps IA chronologically and refers to remains associated with the "Sea Peoples," a heterogeneous group known in the Bible as "Philistines." In this case, blending cultural and temporal meanings under a single heading, Iron IB, has not raised the religious concerns associated with IA. But as with "Israelites," we must not assume too quickly that either "Philistines" or "Sea Peoples" connotes ethnicity, nor that Iron IB remains imply the presence or dominance of a politically homogeneous group (Mendenhall, 1973: 143-144).

Iron IC, the period customarily referred to as the "United Monarchy," presumably included the time of David and his successor, Solomon. Because information from the first half of the 10th century is meagre and the boundary between it and the second half is difficult to define archaeologically, scholars have been unable to indentify firm, explicit, and universally accepted archaeological criteria for dividing the century. Thus, the eras attributed to the father and son have often been combined in archaeological as well as biblical studies. In fact, the coincidence of biblical images of David and early 10th century archaeological materials is itself problematical. Dating David to the period rests on relative chronologies that fix Iron II according to events in Egypt and that count backward by assigning reigns of approximately 40 years each to David and Solomon as suggested by 2 Sam 5:4 and 1 Kgs 11:42 (cf. Bright, 1981: 195 n. 25). Hence, in this volume, we join in the speculation by assuming that the years depicted in David's stories are set between approximately 1000 and 961 B.C.E., and in Solomon's from 960 to 922 B.C.E. (Albright, 1969: 232; 1945: 16-22). We must begin somewhere, and we do so by hypothesizing that the social world envisaged by the tellers of the David stories and in Iron Age I correspond at least in part positively.

To avoid additional confusion, readers should note that many modern authors use different labels for the same archaeological sequence. For example, many use IA and IB, IIA and IIB to correspond to our IA, IB, IC, and IIA. Although the individual phases often span the same sets of years in alternative chronologies, there IIA equates Lapp's IC, and IIB is his IIA. Therefore, in several alternate schemes, the Davidic era constitutes the first part of Iron IIA, Solomon's is either the second part of IIA or IIB.

I
PROLEGOMENA TO A HOLOGRAM OF THE EARLY IRON AGE

Chapter 1

DEVELOPMENT OF SOCIAL WORLD STUDIES

A. *Demise of David's History*

Overview of the Biblical David

The Bible presents David in a panorama of scenes stretching from his youth to his old age. In the representation, he captures Jerusalem during life's middle years and sets about building the most expansive federation of alliances in ancient Israel's history. He pushes Jerusalem's influence to its zenith, pacifies the entire eastern end of the Mediterranean, and unites it under his sole political authority.

Few before or since have achieved what David reportedly accomplished in a relatively short time. No one else has done it without help from a major exogenous military power. On the contrary, because the territory forms a corridor between sea and desert at the juncture of the Eurasian and African land masses, it has typically hosted foreign conquerors who marched into and through it for their own gain leaving in their wake the alien cultures and social orders whose remnants are still visible today.

The true limits and exact nature of paramountcy in the first half of the 10th century B.C.E. may never be known [Figure 1]. The type of terrain, the character of Iron Age leadership, and the social class of followers attributed to David, to say nothing of the paucity of material and written records resulting from these factors, militate against it. In Iron Age I some boundaries were probably perpetually undefined because, as in other pre-industrial tribal societies, access to resources was as important as formal control over them. Additionally, like several modern Middle Eastern nations, the geographical limits of a leader's dominance could not be precisely delineated where subjects in outlying regions continually relocated or changed allegiances according to mood, marriage, weather, war, and other variables. Hence, it may be better to think of access to territory and subjugation of peoples rather than of control or governance of lands.

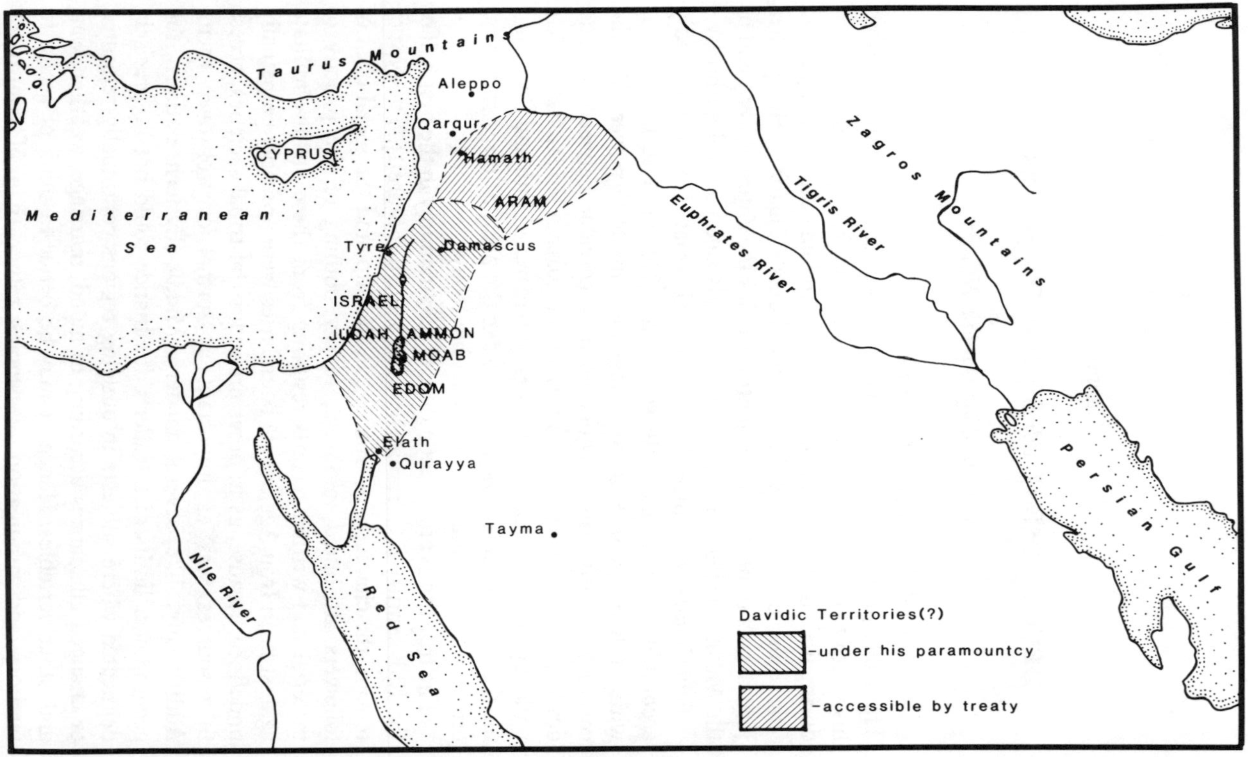

Figure 1: Territories Commonly attributed to David's Control

Accepting the Bible's claims as an accurate description of the Davidic arena assumes that the stories point to historical referents in Near Eastern life. Biblical historians who make the assumption commonly describe David's power as stretching from Anatolia to Egypt. Boundaries are set at the Mediterranean sea on the west, the Syrian desert and Wadi Sirhan on the east, the Euphrates river and Amanus and Taurus mountains on the north, and the Brook of Egypt, the Sinai wilderness, and the Gulf of Elat/Aqaba on the south (Bright, 1976: 194-197; Aharoni, 1979: 276-277; Cross, 1973: 262; Soggin, 1984: 54-63). Such estimates rest almost exclusively on biblical claims that David subdued the peoples of Judah, Israel, Edom, Moab, Ammon, and Philistia and arranged alliances with Phoenician and Aramean (Syrian) leaders who agreed to live peaceably with him.

Although historians have become increasingly skeptical of so expansive a description (Miller and Hayes, 1986: 180-185), it offers a convenient starting point for a study of David. The eastern Mediterranean world is the stage envisaged in David's drama, and its wadis, plains, plateaus, and hills are where information regarding him or his tradition must be sought.

Appeal of the David Myth

The David myth, as the tradition has been called, spread rapidly. Whether its beginnings were set in the dimness of the early Iron Age as is commonly thought or were later, the prominence and tenacity of the Davidic tradition within Israelite, Jewish, and Christian religions testifies to its influence. Diverse communities appealed to it for enjoyment, inspiration, wisdom, and legitimacy until David's stature increased, his fame spread, and Western cultures appropriated his authority for every kind of religious and political claim. The usage finally established his era as a pivotal epoch in world history.

Enthusiasm for the David figure is easily understood. All available information suggests that the early Iron Age throughout the Near East was a transitional period characterized by exceptional social traumas and internal political turmoils caused when international forces withdrew and left Syro-Palestine in a power vacuum. Freed from outside forces, inhabitants were swept up in a swirl of competing religious, military, political, and economic currents. The legendary David stood in the storm's eye. He sensed his advantages more keenly than others did theirs, and by design and coincidence succeeded in exploiting the disturbances for his own and his deity's gain.

Many myths with origins in David's biblical image have been embellished by artists, writers, and theologians during the past three thousand years. Not surprisingly their works show a fascination for the hero's complex personality as well as his political acumen and statecraft. Their favorite image is the shepherd boy who left pasture for palace, became a revered warrior, and lived to be an aged king who retained his pastoral ways. Their variations on the shepherd-lord theme spring from the Bible's paradoxical portrayals so that poets, novelists, and dramatists have heightened but have not created the mysteriousness.

The paradoxes are remembered as much as specifics about the David figure. Indeed, the enigmas are what capture attention. Shepherd and lord, saint and sinner, outcast and victor, the biblical David and his reincarnations in arts and letters contain ironies and ambiguities that stretch human imagination (Gosselin, 1976). As a result, his story numbers among the classics because it provides a variety of "patterns to think or imagine one's way through a peculiar human concern" (Frontain and Wojcik, 1980: 1). The story possesses what, in other contexts, Gadamer describes as "a kind of timeless present that is contemporaneous with every age" (1975: 256). It has "a particular mode of being" that resists historical criticism because "... the binding power of its validity that is preserved and handed down, precedes all historical reflection and continues through it" (Gadamer, 1975: 255, 257).

Thus, the story is a metaphor snatched up by tradition to be used and reused. Ignoring this, biblical historians have suggested widely ranging dates and settings for the biblical accounts of David, particularly the books of Samuel. However, scholarly attempts to excavate the way back to history by working through layers of literary overburden until an "authentic" historical original is reached have failed and our interest is not in saving them.

The David story is a unified "myth-history" (Leach, 1969: 81). Even its early forms would be compatible with a number of historical settings and circumstances. In trying to determine the character of Iron Age IC society, therefore, the search is in a sense for a classic Iron Age situation that gave rise to the classic stories. Such a quest includes little hope for vivid, detailed recreations of historical personalities and events which escape a classic's grasp. Because contemporary written records like those available for other periods are lacking for Iron Age IC, there can be no appeal to contemporary literatures from outside Israel for direct references either to David or his accomplishments. Indeed, were it not for the Bible, history would not know of him at all. Whether an accident of reporting, preservation, or discovery, the silence drives home the fact that we have only religious testimonies about David, and we lack independent, non-Yahwist witnesses regarding his existence and conduct.

Developments in Biblical Criticism

The character and scarcity of information affects not only the vision of Davidic "history" but also the ways historians approach the Iron Age. In the Introduction above, we pointed to the growing disaffection with critical methods that drain narratives of their vibrance and drama by assigning every opposing view to a separate literary unit. Critics' attention has been drawn to the books of Samuel and, as we have seen, especially the Court History in 2 Samuel 9-20 and to reactions to the critical 1926 study of Leonhard Rost. There, the document was identified as an eye-witness account and "an historical narrative which rushes along with the excitement of a drama [that] is based on actual events. . . " (Rost, 1982 [1926]: 104). Gerhard von Rad went so far as to label it the earliest "historical writing" and extended the claim by asserting that the history of David's rise in 1 Samuel 15—2 Samuel 2 is also early and predates the Pentateuchal Yahwist (J) source (von Rad, 1962 [1957]: 48-62; 1966 [1958]: 166-204). If the connection between history and literature could hold anywhere, these early critics thought, it would hold in the Court History and the books of Samuel. Although restoring pre-critical literalist belief in the historical accuracy of the biblical record was not the goal, finding literary settings proximate to the events reported in the texts seemed to alleviate worries about the Bible's reliability and to advance theologians' understanding of Israel's historical consciousness.

Athough Rost's views were controversial from the beginning, the basic claim for a thematically unified historical narrative was accepted while other details of his argument, especially the literary limits of the single-authored work, were questioned. As newer literary approaches emerged, his fundamental assumptions about historicity and history writing were also challenged (cf. Ball, 1982).

The challenge to this and other "historical" texts is plotted by John Barton who outlines the trend in critical theory toward literary studies (1984a; 1984b). He suggests that two important assumptions have developed. First, is the assumption that theories behind biblical criticism pertain to "literary competence," not to critics' certainty or skepticism about historical realities, i.e., criticism aims to elucidate texts not reconstruct history. Second, divergent approaches do not all strive to achieve the same goal (Barton, 1984a: 11-16; 205). Critical methods are theories about the ways texts are capable of having meaning as much as they are techniques for producing fresh interpretations. Methods are codified theories and therefore logically subsequent to intuition about meaning.

> Texts are perceived as having certain sorts of meaning—or, just as interestingly, as failing to convey meaning—by reading them with certain vague expectations about genre, coherence and consistency, which are either confirmed and clarified, or disappointed and frustrated. Then reading begins again, this time with a sharper focus; and at the end of the process there emerges a distinct impression of what the text means, together with an explanatory theory as to how it comes to mean it. But the theory—which, when codified, will become source analysis or redaction criticism or whatever—is logically subsequent to the intuition about meaning. It may lead to useful insights into other texts, when they are approached with a similar frame of mind, and so may greatly shorten the quest to understand them; but it can never be a technique which can always be used with the assurance that it will yield correct results (Barton, 1984a: 205).

Therefore, the issue is not whether insights behind earlier criticisms were wrong and should be abandoned, but whether obsession with them has turned them into "pedestrian 'methods'" (Barton, 1984a: 206).

Barton's studies call attention to the wilderness or "hornet's nest" (Gunn, 1984: 113) between events and text. He follows H. W. Frei's interpretation of the differing reactions to the rise of historical criticism in the German- and English-speaking worlds, and sees G. E. Wright's Biblical Theology movement in America as an attempt to integrate the responses (Frei, 1974: 180, 167-281; Barton, 1984a: 161-162). Both camps viewed the Bible as a witness to history rather than as narrative text. Liberal Anglophones, however, sought to reconstruct events as they happened, using the text as evidence the same way other historians use primary sources. Germanics, on the other hand, searched for the ideas communicated by the text, formulated systematized biblical theologies, and presented histories of Israelite thought.

According to Barton, Wright fused the two concerns by using archaeology to combine historical facts in the Bible with the Hebrew world-view and distinctive modes of Israelite thought. Whether Wright's Mighty Acts of God approach used archaeology indirectly as a witness to texts, as Barton implies, or directly as a discrete source for establishing "facts" is a question we must eventually address. In any case, the break-up of "Biblical Archaeology" and the emergence of social world studies in American scholarship are linked to the collapse of the synthesis, the rise of new literary approaches and New Archaeology, and the turn toward comparative sociology in biblical studies.

Literary Foundations Crumble

The onslaught against Davidic history has come from two directions and has had far-ranging effects. Almost at once, literary and archaeological specialists have lost confidence in their ability to recover the biblical past. A summary of several important studies will illustrate the problems that haunted early investigators and forced them to take new paths.

For the Bible, I choose studies by David Gunn (especially 1978) and Edmund Leach (especially 1969; 1982; 1983a). The choice does not imply that the works are either paradigmatic or typical—Leach's in fact would be considered exceptional by most biblical critics. However, Gunn's works on David (1978) and Saul (1980), seen in retrospect, marked a turning point in the direction of studies on the books of Samuel because they challenged presuppositions and piqued scholarly curiosity. Moreover, his thought represents development within the discipline and Leach's insights from outside; both initially stirred considerable comment; and both raise specific questions that are important for this study. Leach also offers a bridge to other disciplines used in social world studies because he has placed similar concerns before archaeologists and anthropologists as well as biblical specialists; and Gunn's recent writings (not reviewed here) illustrate the movement of one drawn increasingly away from historical interests toward literary studies. Therefore, the focus the writings of these individuals bring to the discussion, rather than agreement or disagreement with their conclusions, guides the selection.

Gunn on King David's Story

Early on, Gunn shunned labels and critical schools and preferred to speak simply of "literary approaches" to the Bible. With the passage of time, he has become increasingly "reader oriented" and interested in theoretical as well as theological concerns (cf. Gunn, 1987). His background and publications make clear, however, that his interests developed in part from work in classics, especially Homeric studies, and in part from exposure to literary criticism. Both prepared him to seek traditional narrative patterns in the Bible.

In his monograph on the David story, Gunn sets out to demonstrate that the Succession Narrative is a traditional story written for purposes of serious entertainment that, as he explains later, challenges one to self- or social-reassessment (1978: 61-62; 1980: 11). Patterns within the narrative suggest close proximity to oral traditional composition and place its writing "not far from an oral stage of transmission, though its precise relation to oral story-telling is impossible to determine" (1978: 61). The composition's genre causes him to challenge previous characterizations such as history writing, political propaganda, and didactic or wisdom literature. Each is inappropriate for the content and form; each misleads readers' expectations; and each misstates the author's intention (1978: 19). Moreover, none of the forms can explain the story's longevity (1980: 12).

Arguments favoring an early date of composition are for him unconvincing because the signs of traditional composition, the subject matter, and the narrative's motifs seem to require a longer development than Rost and others allow (Gunn, 1978: 30-34). While he posits no exact date, settings "a few generations . . . perhaps more" after the events (1978: 33), or "sometime in the period of three or four hundred years after the death of David" (1978: 87), or even as late as the exilic period are acceptable (1978: 30). Gunn wants only to "stress how hypothetical is the nexus between the text and the generally accepted setting" (1978: 34).

It seems in his early work that Gunn does not explicitly reject critics' presupposition that genre, date, and setting are entwined. Where he differs is in his insistence that history is not necessarily at risk if a new interpretation and later date are proposed because "serious entertainment" can include the retelling of historical information no matter when or where the story is told (1978: 62). This, however, merely restates forcefully the old insistence that criticism of ancient literature and ancient history are related but distinct enterprises. Therefore, Gunn calls standard literary and historical critics back to their individual tasks and carefully puts distance between his approach and the redactional hypotheses of Würthwein, Veijola, and Langlamet (1978: 115-118).

Gunn rejects Rost's succession theme both as a criterion for determining the boundaries of the Succession Narrative and as an interpretation of the text. Already moving toward a final form reading, he attaches material in 2 Samuel 2-4 and 6 to the Succession Narrative, and offers a rich and intricate interpretation that exposes several "levels" of meaning within the text.

> The story tells how David gained the throne (which was given to him), how it was taken away from him but restored, though somewhat uneasily, and how finally he himself gave it away, or alternatively, as we are invited to see it, how it is again, but now successfully, taken from him. But it is not only the story of the kingdom and David the king. It is also a story of David the man... political and personal spheres of his life were interrelated... The action concerns the gaining, displacement and bequeathal of status or authority, themes which come to concrete expression in specific political and personal forms...
>
> This is the work of no propagandist pamphleteer nor moralizing teacher: the vision is artistic, the author, above all, a fine teller of tales (1978: 110-111).

By denying that the narrative's author intends to write history, Gunn opens the text to multiple meanings, various readings, and numerous uses while retaining controls over his interpretation, controls that he feels emerge from within the narrative itself. The stratagem does not drain the narrative of its historical content even if the storytellers lack historical interest, but it forces readers to think about important distinctions: 1) what the historical situation may have been, 2) what the text says or could say in the ancient world, and 3) the use an ancient or modern reader might make of it. Genre, date, literary boundaries, themes, and interpretation are all tossed up for review. Historical referent, author's intention, text, and reader are separated analytically and their relationships realigned. Historians are forced to abandon approaches that view ancient texts and modern interpretations as mere restatements of past "facts."

Although in later comments he warns against mixing literary studies with historical questions as is done by calling the Succession Narrative a "Court History" (as some Americans do!), his writings - it seems to me—retain their usefulness for historical studies (Gunn, 1984: 109-113). He links the Succession Narrative's genre to the passage of time and proposes several possible settings, authors, and audiences. He does not object to historical content as much as to treating the Bible as a historical source in a modern, Western sense of the word.

Leach on Solomon's Legitimacy

Sir Edmund Leach, a structural-functionalist convert to structuralist anthropology, influences biblical studies directly through his own interpretations of biblical texts and indirectly through his manifold contributions to anthropology. The extent and nature of his contributions to the former can be debated as can many of his conclusions about biblical topics, but it is agreed that he raises important, relevant points and applies his interpretations consistently across several disciplines (cf. Clements, 1984: 307). His concerns strike at the heart of historical and comparative inquiry where they cannot be dismissed as an outsider's observations. Instead, in pushing them to the fore he argues authoritatively that biblical historians and literary critics face the same epistemological issues as are confronted in other disciplines. Biblical specialists, archaeologists, and comparative sociologists share fundamental methodological questions pertaining to literary analysis, historical inquiry, and cross-cultural comparisons (Leach, 1969; 1983a).

To raise specific, detailed historical questions about the Bible, according to Leach, is to persist in misunderstanding the nature and purpose of biblical literature and to risk distorting the book's meaning (1983a: 8-12). For him the Bible is not quite fantasy, but certainly no more than a sacred tale whose meaning lies in the use religious groups make of it rather than in the history it may or may not have recorded. He is concerned not with author's intentions or with finding *the* correct interpretation. There is no *correct* interpretation.

Like Gunn, he favors final-form readings. The Bible must be read in its entirety to discover the meanings that a piecemeal or "excavative" (cf. Alter, 1981: 13) approach misses. Even dividing the text according to genres is misleading because "text is text" and can only be understood as a whole and by recognizing that sections are structural transformations of each other (Leach, 1983b: 92-93).

Because the motives of the Bible's compilers are religious, the argument goes, readers must be satisfied with the limitations this implies instead of pressing toward more and more conjectural history. History is not the writers' motive, and sequential, chronological history is probably even alien to their understanding (1983a: 23). Thus, by accepting the religious value of the Bible, its synchrony can be grasped and by using methods adopted from structuralism and literary criticism, its meanings can be exposed.

Interest in the Bible arises from Leach's quest for a widely known, readily available myth that can be used to demonstrate structuralist methods and illustrate the processes of human thought. Hence, his curiosity follows from his anthropology. He is primarily concerned with stories rather than texts, but because the stories are now imbedded in texts, the texts are of concern (1969: 32; 1983b: 96). Their patterns and structures tell something about the storytellers and their world. But again, the entire text, not just segments, must be looked at if the structural relationships that now tell the story are to be found.

Leach is consistent and unrelenting. While passing through several editorial hands, the texts are encoded with many patterns. Those that survive, however, come from the final editor's mind. Thus, knowledge of those who thought and told the story before is irretrievably lost, buried beneath the structures imposed by their successor, and to try to recover them would be like trying to "unscramble an omelet" (1983a: 23).

By comparing myth and history, Leach seems to deny the validity of using the Bible for historical investigations. In fact, he proposes that anthropology's contribution to biblical studies is to show that "... no part of the Bible is a record of history as it actually happened. ... the whole of the Bible has the characteristics of mytho-history. ... The similarity [between the Bible and the mytho-history of contemporary societies] is a matter of structure and not of content" (1983a: 21). Moreover, in the Bible the state of things is justified by "'myth', that is to say tales about the past which had a sacred or religious quality (after the fashion of the Christian Bible), rather than by legislative enactments or precedents recorded in historical documents" (1982: 144). Myth and history both serve mythical functions in the scriptures because they must justify the doctrines of the religious community (1969: 54, 81). And, denying Levi-Strauss' distinction between "cold" (preliterate) and "hot" (literate) societies that presume differing views of the past, Leach believes that mythical structure extends even to the chronological sequences in the Bible (1969: 56, 65, 79), because biblical writers do not view the past as a sequential chronology (1983a: 23).

Specific doubts about a historical David are equally negative and long-standing in Leach's writings (1969: 34). When discussing the boundary between legend and history, he notes that most people assume Moses, Saul, and David to have been real people who existed between 1250 and 1000 B.C.E.

> Personally I find this most implausible. There is no archaeological evidence for the existence of these heroes or for the occurrence of any of the events with which they were associated. If it were not for the sacredness of these stories their historicity would certainly be rejected (Leach, 1983a: 10).

In light of these statements, should Leach's work be considered in a discussion of Iron Age history? The answer is affirmative, not only because of the reasons already cited, but also because, stripped of their rhetoric, his statements show his goals in studying the Bible to be in one sense the same as those that motivate historical critics. He seeks to understand the mentality and worldviews of ancient people, in this case, of the writers who have given the texts their present forms. Like other critics, Leach searches for a context in which to read texts, i.e., the life settings of final editors or redactors. Knowledge of history guides his quests. Solomon's legitimation he reads against the background of "ancient Jewish culture" that appears to mean the "arguments about endogamy and exogamy, legitimacy and illegitimacy as operative in the thought processes of Palestinian Jews of the third century B.C." (1969: 26). However, it is their world, not Solomon's, that now appears in the stories.

Texts, Leach insists, regardless of their date, are records of views held in their time even though their contents are not literal ciphers for past historical events. The historical stricture includes both the fictitious past portrayed in the texts and specific historical details (but not the general course of history) occurring at the time of writing or editing. Neither can be determined by reading biblical texts. For methodological reasons, Leach refuses to take the leap of history that would allow him to identify the contents of texts with real life sequences in the past. He is simply uninterested in biblical history as the phenomenon is commonly understood.

Two additional concerns of Leach may be mentioned. In the first place, for him, myths, mytho-history, and mythopoeic texts encode the synchronic tensions and contradictions confronted in human life. These are the "story" in the texts. That is one reason why structuralist approaches that emphasize binary opposition, reversals, and transformations are appropriate for biblical analysis. In a sense, the media, message, and manner of interpretation are at one because they focus on the same human phenomena—tension, drama, and contradiction. Thus, a story does not have a beginning, middle, and end. It is like a dream. Its structure is metaphoric, so the beginning refers to the end and vice versa (1983b: 98). Later we shall see that this description brings Leach very close to describing the biblical text as a hologram.

Second, and related to the first point, Leach favors Victor Turner's analysis of van Gennep's "rites of passage" as a way of thinking about the transitions in biblical texts (1983a: 24; 1983b: 99-107). The rites' tripartite structure of separation, liminality, and reaggregation, he asserts, underlies biblical myth.

We shall return to these points later when considering holography and ritual as metaphors and heuristic aids for understanding our task. Like Leach's approach, they address relationships among historical occurrences, the encoding of texts, and the decoding of them in another age. We shall see that others, including Victor Turner and Roy A. Rappaport, who approach the epistemological questions raised by Leach from different perspectives, also turn to ritual as a way to bridge the gap between our understanding and others' views of their own worlds. At this point, however, we must turn to the broader bases supporting Leach in his positions.

Leach arrives at his positions, in part at least, because of his attitudes toward human diversity, culture, history, and cross-cultural comparisons. He is interested in culture and generalization rather than cultures and comparisons (Leach, 1977: 1-4). The former lead to understanding humanity by penetrating to the human level; the latter, because they compare social structures, lead to "collecting butterflies," i.e., classifying and organizing things according to type and subtype. The distinction is important because it discriminates between what is fundamentally human and what on other levels are abstractions, ideologies, or structures that are at least one step removed from their human basis and therefore are not the true subject matter of anthropology.

Because the possibilities for human diversity are limitless, Leach distrusts cross-cultural comparisons based on social organizations and is especially chary of conjectural histories based on them. He warns anthropologists against being "counterfeit historians" who waste their time trying to reconstruct the past or predict the future (1982: 49). Against Pitt-Rivers and Morgenstern, he rejects homology, i.e., drawing ethnographic parallels, as a historical tool. Not only are comparisons among cultures hazardous especially when drawn from widely separated civilizations, and the risks not worth the uncertain rewards, the practice is, he claims, rooted in a concept of cultural patterning that cannot be established without contemporary documentary and archaeological information (1983a: 18-20).

On the surface at least, Leach's claims seem to be directly opposed to the goals and approaches of social world studies, including those proposed in this volume. Our work, however, is neither a response to structuralism nor an attempt to apply its insights and methods to the history of Israel. Instead, it recognizes the validity of the issues raised by Leach and others and attempts to draw upon the social sciences for information and approaches for understanding the past and problems standing in its way. Accordingly, we heed the warnings addressed to comparative sociologists. They are the practitioners who try to comprehend a people's total way of life that plays itself out in "an endlessly repeated social drama" (Leach, 1982: 130).

The part of the warning that applies directly to social world studies pertains to several important distinctions. Anthropological investigators must be careful to distinguish their own worlds and views from those of their subjects, and they must distinguish between what their subjects do and what they say they do.

> This distinction between the roles in a drama and the actors who play the roles corresponds to the fact that the data of field research must always be looked at in two dimensions. The observer must distinguish between what people actually do and what people say that they do; that is between normal custom as individually interpreted on the one hand and normative rules on the other.
>
> When they come to write up the results of their research different anthropologists will, for doctrinal reasons, give very different weight to these two major aspects of the data, but, in the

> field, the anthropologist must always pay attention to both sides. He must not only distinguish behaviour from ideology, he must also take careful note of just how they are interrelated (Leach, 1982: 130).

The contrasts draw attention to investigators' needs to distinguish their own views from their subjects', to discriminate between the subjects' social lives and cultural roles, and to study the relationships between the pairs on either side of each equation. For example, investigators must distinguish between their subjects' behavior and ideology. Leach also emphasizes that anthropological research has two discrete phases: field work followed by analysis and interpretation. These can be diagrammed in a way that allows his view to be compared with others [Figure 2].

Figure 2: Research Research Design Outlined by Leach

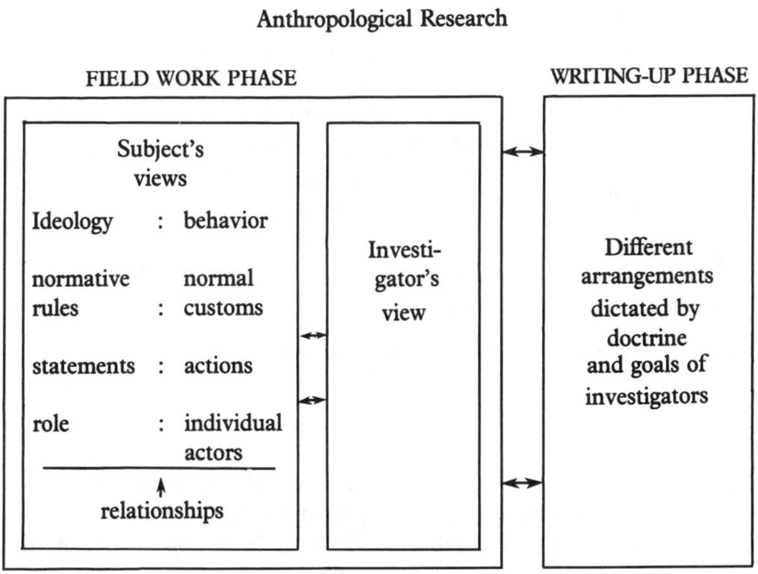

We shall return to these points in Chapter 3.

Davidic Archaeology

When faced with few or problematical written sources, biblical historians customarily turn to archaeology for additional information.

However, for the time alleged for David, the maneuver has met with only qualified success. Two reasons have already been suggested. Archaeological information from the period is meagre, at least the type collected according to the research designs of the past; and epistemological problems confront those who would supplement the archaeological record with literary or ethnographical evidence.

Leach's criticism of the epistemological problems within historical archaeology is relevant. He includes archaeologists in his indictment against conjectural history. He warns that they should be wary of their ability to know the past, 99.9% of which is irretrievably lost. Thus, their principal contribution, he claims, is their role as debunkers of anthropological speculation (1982: 50).

It would be easy to dismiss Leach's views because of his apparent preference for monumental, public types of information that are outdated by today's archaeological standards. Nevertheless, in an interesting way, he links historical archaeologists' problems to the differences between archaeology and anthropology and therefore raises questions for social world studies. He cautions archaeologists to use ethnography carefully. As expected, they are warned to be conscious of the limitations human variety imposes on their conclusions (1973: 764, 770), particularly when stressing subsistence and economic systems while neglecting the rituals and beliefs where anthropologists find the symbolisms that are important for understanding the workings of society (1973: 768).

To illustrate his concerns, Leach appeals to a black box model like that discussed in our introduction.

INPUT ——————→ "Black Box" ——————→ OUTPUT

X Y

$$y = F(x)$$

In this instance, X and Y represent the observable features, and F unobservable possible mechanisms within the black box that might explain how X is transformed into y. It is the F, i.e., what goes on in the black box which for us is the social world, that comparative ethnography is usually expected to explain. But because the variety of possibilities cannot be predicted cross-culturally, Leach doubts whether the contents of the black box can ever be known with *reasonable certainty*. He is not opposed to informed guesses, but he insists that they be recognized for what they are.

Leach goes on to contrast the goals of anthropologists with those of archaeologists. The former do not face the black box problem because they can visit the society under study and observe the social processes first hand (1973: 766). Again he diagrams the foci of the two disciplines [Figure 3]. They are the different points where the disciplines intersect with the human processes that transform an environment culturally (Leach, 1973: 767):

Figure 3: Contrasting Emphases of Archaeological and Anthropological Research as Described by Leach

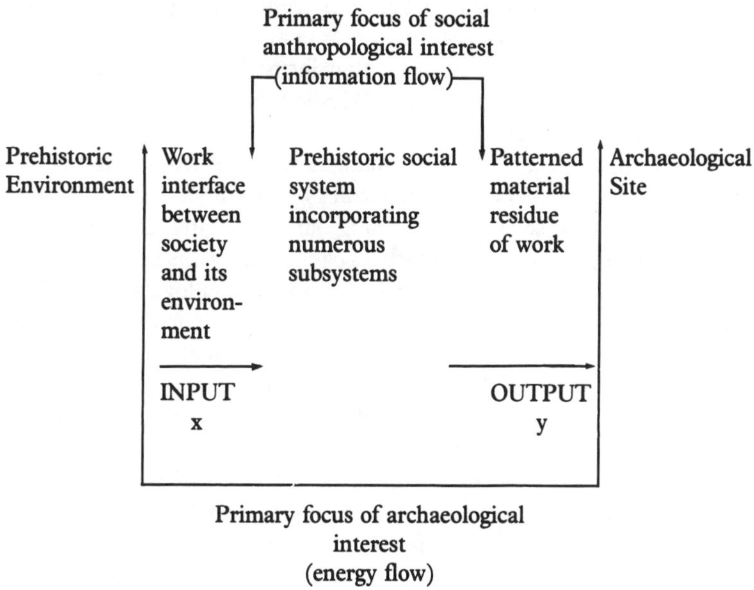

Therefore, as in literary studies, according to Leach, archaeologists using anthropology face problems when integrating diachronic with synchronic information. In archaeology, the movement away from history—or, more exactly, toward synchronic studies and toward anthropological modeling of archaeological data—has not been completely successful. We shall return to the problems the changes create in Davidic studies, but first we must examine briefly the trend and its causes.

New Trends in Archaeology

Many of Leach's worries are shared by professional archaeologists. There, new, processual, analytical, theoretical, and scientific archaeologies, as they are called, began in the 1960s and 1970s to develop theories and methods that in some ways lessen interest in diachronic history and in accumulating similar data from more and more sites. Inspired by a desire to escape from idealistic and impressionistic views of the past, theoretical archaeologists turn away from history and literature in the direction of science. The shift affects Near Eastern archaeology on two levels. First, discoveries such as radio-carbon and thermoluminescence dating, trace analysis, etc., introduce objective measures that enable archaeologists to free themselves from the diffusionism that formerly tied their discipline to the histories of Egypt and Mesopotamia where diachronic schemas are firmly established.

The second effect of the new dialogue with the sciences has a still more profound effect on archaeology and archaeologists. The association with science is refining and changing the questions brought to the field, and it greatly expands the means of interpreting information in the material record. Statistics, analogical reasoning, and model building make epistemology and disciplinary independence central concerns. The debates sparked by individuals such as Clarke (1978; 1973), Binford (1962; 1968; 1972; 1977; 1983), and Flannery (1972) have raised issues both in prehistoric and historical archaeology that remain largely unresolved (Wylie, 1985: 93-95).

The differences between the two effects are important for understanding the specific character of today's Near Eastern archaeology. Most field reports boast interdisciplinary teams and projects, yet the endeavors are often merely multidisciplinary attempts to answer long-standing historical questions. While multi-disciplinary historical investigations are valuable, merely to add staff from science departments is not to redefine the archaeological enterprise. The former may help to shed light on literary claims, but to redefine the discipline requires addressing the epistemological relationship between such claims and other sources of information.

The late David Clarke's early description of new archaeology is indicative of changes within the discipline.

> To recapitulate, archaeology can be redefined as the discipline concerned with the recovery, systematic description and study of

> material culture in the past. Archaeology is a discipline in its own right, providing a framework within which the entities and processes of archaeology act one upon another. The entities, processes, aims, procedures and concepts of archaeology have a validity of their own in reference to the archaeological frame and despite their generation by—and partial correlation with—former social and historic entities (1978: 12).

For Clarke, sites have lives of their own. Archaeological data are observations based on the specific and contextual attributes of artifacts (1978: 18) that are studied for their static and dynamic qualities, for repeated similarities and regularities, and for developing predictive models and hypotheses (1978: 20). Clarke defined the last:

> Essentially, models are hypotheses or sets of hypotheses which simplify complex observations whilst offering a largely accurate predictive framework structuring these observations—usefully separating 'noise' from information. Which aspect is noise and which counts as information is solely dependent upon the frame of reference of the model (1978: 31).

Models are of three kinds, according to Clarke: iconic, analogical, and symbolic or mathematical. The second, the kind most often used in social world studies, are "tantalizingly dangerous" because by them historical, anthropological, or abstract situations are transferred to archaeological situations (1978:33). His concern corresponds to Leach's fears about the epistemological problems associated with using anthropological materials for interpreting archaeological data. Realizing the dangers has caused archaeology to lose its innocence (Clarke, 1973: 6-18).

Not every change brought about by the new approaches can be counted an unqualified success. Nevertheless, the processual and social studies they inspire expand archaeologists' interests beyond ever more refined chronologies and typologies, tracing cultural diffusion, and accumulating monumental and public data. The discipline is turning toward general explanations for human behavior, social processes, and relationships among humans and artifacts, in sum, toward understanding the lives and cultures that once gave meaning to the ancient remains uncovered by the modern archaeologist.

It would be wrong to identify all the developments in theoretical archaeology since the 1960s and early 1970s with new archaeology and to fail to distinguish their impact on prehistoric studies from their effects on historical studies. In the first instance, the early 1970s mark an advance beyond the early emphasis on theory and epistemology to another stage where processual studies and examinations of social change come to the fore. In the second case, where new archaeology continues to aid prehistoric studies directly, in historical processual studies closer relationships among archaeology, anthropology, and history perpetuate earlier problems.

Impact on Syro-Palestinian Archaeology

Although interest in the new questions is documented in the writings of some early Near Eastern archaeologists (e.g., Albright, 1957: 112-115), theoretical archaeology's impact on knowledge of Syro-Palestinian society during historical periods is less than on European, British, and American civilizations. Reasons for the lag frequently pertain to politics in the Middle East and in modern universities, two domains where boundary lines enjoy inordinate sanctity. Both are theaters of comedy and tragedy that carve up the world according to politics, culture, viewpoint, and chronology so that information from one area is often inaccessible in another.

Another reason for new archaeology's delay in affecting Levantine studies resides in the nature of theory building. Archaeological and social theorists are more interested in functionalist generalizations than in history or, as they might say, pseudo-histories. They see themselves as scientists called upon to explain synchronic relationships rather than as historians expected to identify and interpret diachronic sequences in civilizations even though processual studies are central to their interests. Likewise, they have been forced to present their data in forms acceptable to scientists with whom they are now in constant dialogue. As a result, like their anthropological colleagues who seek generalizations, they prefer to study primary, i.e., pristine, societies where exogenous influences are minimal. Because ancient Israel is a secondary, literate society repeatedly swept across by the tides of outside civilizations, it does not offer the laboratory conditions preferred for scientific theory-building. So theoretical archaeologists turn away.

A third reason for ancient Israel's isolation must be mentioned even though its major cause is largely eliminated. The popular impressions that many excavations are biblically motivated religious quests which attract only participants who share directors' beliefs and aspirations is harmful. Consequently, the projects are not judged to be legitimate scientific inquiries, and archaeologists uninterested in the Bible ignore them and their reports. The situation produces a sad irony: enthusiasm for biblical historicity, biblically named sites, major battles, monumental splendor, and Israelite dominance repels archaeologists who would be most helpful in clarifying the history of the Hebrew scriptures' and their greatest hero, David.

These comments cannot be directed exclusively or against all archaeologists who work in biblical regions. On the contrary, it must be remembered that in spite of popular perceptions, many early "biblical" archaeologists shared the basic motives of their contemporary classical and historical peers. Each sought to illumine ancient literatures and documents by comparisons with material records, and each brought literalist and diffusionist presuppositions of their day to the field. It was these more than a biblical link that affected progress.

Regardless, association with texts, linguistics, and comparative philology made it easy to assume that the spread of customs and institutions could be traced in the same way that languages and literatures are, and that both pairs pass from culture to culture with similar formal and functional changes. While the presupposition proved useful in resolving many historical questions, we now know that language and other social phenomena do not always travel in tandem. Nevertheless, such assumptions reinforced convictions that Israel's history had unfolded as described and for the reasons reported in the Bible. The reasons were usually not visible in the material record, so according to the theory of the times, biblical literature was welcomed in the field as a historical control over archaeological interpretation. Whenever the written and material evidence could be reasonably reconciled, especially if both records suggested similar foreign contact or comparable social evolution, certainty was assured.

Archaeology and the Bible

Barton's remarks about Wright's "Acts of God" approach and the difference between American and German scholarship have been cited above. The two sides addressed biblical history from different starting points and spawned two schools of historical thought. One is identified with Albrecht Alt and his student Martin Noth; the other with William Foxwell Albright and his student John Bright. The differences and their consequences need not detain us. However, the mounting pressures arising from those bases and attempts to reconcile them with emerging archaeological information plagued Wright until his death. Late in life, he wrestled with "What Archaeology Can and Cannot Do" (1983a [1971]) and inveighed against "The 'New' Archaeology" (1983b [1975]).

Wright's answer to his own queries suggests that the view implied in Barton's comment above, namely that Wright saw archaeology as a direct aid for reading the Bible, may be wrongly attributed.

> What archaeology can do for Biblical study is to provide a physical context in time and place which was the environment of the people who produced the Bible or are mentioned in it.... It then is used along with other critically assessed data, where it exists, in order to form [hypotheses] about the how, why, what and when of cultural, socio-political and economic affairs... (Wright, 1983a: 69).

His assessment of the relationship between textual and archaeological information is clear. His failure was in expecting one to illumine the other as if either or both contain history or are history.

> These [texts] must be interpreted by all the means of literary analysis available to us. Then we must reconstruct the archaeological and ecological context as best we can both in the given area and in the widest possible context. Only then can we examine the question as to whether the one illumines the other, or whether a reasonable hypothesis can be reconstructed which best explains what we know at this time.... Conversely, archaeology, dealing with the wreckage of antiquity, proves nothing in itself. It must be analyzed in a variety of ways, and then with all other data available, not in a pure vacuum mistakenly called by some 'science.' Its meaning in the overall picture of a cultural continuum is expressed by interpretation (1983a: 71-72).

Wright became increasingly wary of the new archaeology that he saw developing under the influence of Lewis Binford in America and David Clarke in Britain. "Testable propositions" and "valid scientific criteria" seemed to him inappropriate for archaeology, naive applications of scientific method, or both (1983b: 80-83). He saw the approach as an attack on the humanities and history but failed to recognize his own confusion of cultural and ecological systems.

> For myself, I remain unabashedly a humanist. I was trained in the humanities, and only humanists in the true sense can in the end make any sense out of the seeming chaos of human cultural systems, synchronically or diachronically. I believe archaeology is far too restricted when treated as a discipline in and of itself, whether by those who presume to be pure scientists, or by those who belong to other wings of anthropology or fine arts. In my opinion, archaeology must use all of the science that it can, but in the final analysis it is dealing with human beings, and therefore it can never be anything other than one among the several branches of cultural and humanistic history (1983b: 85-86).

Wright's strong personal commitment to the book that occupied much of his life led him to defend its relationship to archaeology. This caused a tunnel vision that affected his reading, not of the past, but of his contemporaries' writings. Because of his influence in Near Eastern archaeology, an acceptance of cross-disciplinary research designs (a design that incorporates information from several disciplines) yet a rejection of true interdisciplinary approaches (those that integrate the disciplines and disciplinary models as well as the information collected by them) as proposed by theoretical archaeologists meant that advances in Syro-Palestinian history were postponed, and needless debates about biblical archaeology ensued. What has fallen behind more than anything else are the overviews and perspectives needed to integrate increasingly specialized approaches in order to study biblical history. Attempts to provide these also have a long-standing tradition, and to it we now turn.

B. *Social World Studies*

While disillusionment with historical quests was contributing to the development of new interests in the Bible and Near Eastern archaeology, widespread intellectual concern for biblical history and historical method continued. Treating the Bible as literature and as the conveyor of myth and separating archaeological questions from curiosities that were spawned by biblical questions forced historians to re-evaluate their access to antiquity.

Rethinking the historical enterprise invites difficulties and disagreements in resolving specific questions about the past. For many, especially in America, the route has been toward the social sciences and sciences where they find models and metaphors for understanding and interpreting the humanistic information available in texts and traditions. Social world studies as they are pursued today are the heir and outcome of those ventures.

Nineteenth-Century Evolutionists

The roots of these interests and of social scientific studies of biblical antiquity are traced at least to the second half of the 19th century when Darwinism and humanism began influencing studies of the Bible. The Enlightenment a century earlier suppressed infallible biblical claims about the origin and universality of the human race, so intellectuals began to examine the book according to the same scholarly principles as were applied to other ancient documents. They began to expose the historical development of Israel's religion and, with new methods, compared the Bible to religious developments among non-biblical peoples and to literatures from other ancient societies. Modern biblical studies as we know them today had begun.

Every list of influences on social scientific studies of ancient Israel must mention Julius Wellhausen (1844-1918) and William Robertson Smith (1846-1894). Although each approached the Bible's development from his own perspective and made differing but substantial contributions to the field, the two shared much in common. They were friends and professional associates at a time when German and British scholars largely ignored each other's accomplishments, and both eventually fled theological studies to become Arabists.

The spirit of an age influenced by the schematic, positivistic patterns of history that Hegel, Comte, and Spencer fostered affected Wellhausen and Smith who were seeking a new basis from which to read the Bible (Albright, 1957: 89; 1966: 136-39). Their milieu offered reasons for asserting that all civilizations including ancient Israel's passed through identical stages of social and religious evolution. Consequently, they thought, primitive forms of Israelite religion could be recovered—along with one's personal, ancestral, primitive religious past—by studying contemporary primal groups where earlier stages of evolution were still manifest. The parallels would reveal their own and pre-Israelite origins.

In some ways, the evolutionary schemes appeared alien to biblical doctrine. In others, they confirmed the universality and diffusion of the human race and so reinforced the Bible's claims about creation. This paradox as well as the intellectual excitement of the late 1800s encouraged biblical scholars to find layers of development within the biblical text and to penetrate to the earliest stages of biblical history.

Wellhausen and Smith each erred by adopting the artificial, *a priori* evolutionary schemes of their day and by misinterpreting important information, but their insistence on the comparative method was sufficient to alter biblical studies and to help in establishing anthropology as well. The fact that Wellhausen's work is better known among biblical scholars and Smith's among anthropologists, even though in 1885 the latter wrote the preface to the English translation of the former's *Prolegomena to the History of Israel*, indicates a historical fission of disciplines rather than a difference in objectives.

The social scientific character of Smith's work wins it a place on the stage of current interpretation even though many of his conclusions are no longer helpful. Where Wellhausen shunned comparative ethnographical resources, Smith incorporated them in ways that are similar to those employed in social world studies.

Smith's personal story is as fascinating as it is tragic. The aspects that pertain directly to our study are his mastery of diverse cultures and languages, his extensive travels in the Middle East where he collected ethnographic analogues used in biblical interpretation, and his attempt to bring living examples of desert life up against biblical stories where they could illumine its content. Through his writings, especially his encyclopedia entries on "Bible" and "angels," he won a trial for heresy in the Free Church of Scotland, a loss of his teaching position, and a refuge in Cambridge and the safety of Oriental Studies. He succumbed to tuberculosis at the early age of 48.

The concepts embodied in Smith's work are summarized by Beidelman (1974: 29-68). There we can easily see the 19th century presuppositions that must be avoided in current social world studies. Smith's belief in an evolutionary process in society and intellectual consciousness, together with his commitment to cultural relativism and a developmental process, forced him to accept historical and anthropological analysis of the Bible as the most valid approach. He felt that mastery of sundry skills that others would consider beyond the capacity of a single individual should not dissuade the biblical scholar. Etymology, archaeology, geography, and skills in technology were basic (Beidelman, 1974: 32). The litany convinced Smith that a good biblical scholar needed the same abilities and sensitivities as a good historian or anthropologist.

The comparative emphasis in his positivism, which is similar to that found in modern interdisciplinary biblical studies, has endured better than the details of his arguments or his specific cross-cultural comparisons. Like Wellhausen, Smith stressed the relationship between the evolution of groups and the development of their intellectual and moral life. Contrary to others, he insisted that ritual preceded myth, that primitive religion was not a system of beliefs with practical applications, and that religious institutions were older than religious theories. His greatest contribution, though, was his emphasis upon the social basis of belief and values i.e., that deities and humans form "a single natural community" (Beidelman, 1974: 66).

We must note what others have apparently ignored, namely, the coincidence of Smith's personal ecclesial struggle, his empathy for the religious values that he thought paralleled the Bible but had survived among the Bedouin without ecclesial custody, his experiences in pre-industrial societies, and his Renaissance curiosity for and appreciation of issues that affect humanity across its cultural spectrum. So equipped, he sought to save biblical religion from isolation and stagnation. He paid attention to the juncture where biblical religion intersected the rest of human life. He fought to retain the connection and remained a convinced but argumentative believer until his death.

Spreading Interest in Israel's Social Life

A full treatment of Smith's influence on social scientific biblical studies would include discussion of the field's classical figures such as Max Weber, Emile Durkheim, Adolphe Lods, Antonin Causse, Sigmund Mowinckel, Johannes Pedersen, and others. The most obvious heir of Smith, however, was his student at Cambridge, Stanley A. Cook (Leach, 1983a: 13-20).

Writing in 1927, Cook advocated a continuation of Smith's method, but with more careful attention to historical data. He abandoned Smith's general evolutionary scheme in favor of individual cultural systems because he thought that relating and evaluating elements in a society according to their presence in a cultural pattern was methodologically more sound than stringing them together according to a generalized scheme of evolution.

By the 1930s, the concept of cultural patterning surfaced in the so-called Myth and Ritual School, represented in Britain by E. O. James and Samuel H. Hooke. These scholars were influenced by Frazer and especially by A. M. Hocart, an anthropologist who published a comparative study of kingship in 1927 and a treatment of myth in 1935, the latter in a volume edited by Hooke. Hocart had argued that social institutions such as kingship and New Year's festivals must always be considered as constituent wholes that correspond to a limited number of ideal types. Hocart rather than Frazer, Leach argues, was responsible for the cultural pattern concept Hooke found so appealing (Leach 1983a: 16).

The assumption that ancient Israel conformed to the cultural pattern of ancient Babylon and Egypt and therefore shared common features with them enjoyed popular appeal. It quickly led scholars to interpolate pieces of history missing in one society from the extant records of another as if they were building up a mosaic or a composite photo from transparency overlays. In doing so, they raised a serious question of historical method that continues to divide scholars. It is this that is at the root of the tendency to make David's image conform to that of ancient kings.

The British scholars' assumptions forced homology to the fore. Hocart described the controversy as a battle between convergence and divergence—whether societies had evolved from a common origin or whether the pressure of need had forced several societies to adopt common forms (Hocart, 1927: 1-6). Convinced by the analogy between natural and human history, he chose the former.

Following Smith's arguments that ritual lay beneath myth, Hooke and James insisted that rituals could be reconstructed on the basis of shared cultural patterns if the myths were known. But when the question was reopened in 1958 in a volume edited by Hooke but influenced by Henri Frankfort, the answer seemed less certain. Substantial differences between cultures had been discovered in the interim, making a piecemeal reconstruction highly risky. Frankfort's own volume on kingship, for example, devoted only a brief section at the end to Israelite kingship, and much of that was spent cautiously pointing out the differences rather than the similarities between Israel's monarchy and those of Egypt and Babylon (1948). Interestingly, Frankfort seemed to prefer chieftaincy status for David but failed to exploit his preference.

As noted, a tradition of biblical scholarship paralleling the sociological tradition emerged out of the Wellhausen literary-historical critical school, and the two branches of scholarship continued to influence one another. European scholars meticulously analyzed the text while they searched continually in other societies for oral and literary forms that could guide their criticism. Albrecht Alt and his student, Martin Noth, for example, were among those who combined these interests with a mastery of biblical archaeology and geography, knowledge of extra-biblical literatures and institutions, and a sense of ancient Israel's place within world history. Their work was rigorous and influential.

Beginnings of the Albright School

Frankfort's reluctance to press diligently for comparisons among societies sharing the same cultural patterns was affected by developments within several disciplines. History of religions, archaeology, and anthropology were all wary of the patterns. History of religions was developing rapidly as a discipline around Frankfort at Chicago, and he recognized the need for greater methodological rigor and caution. But by 1934, William Foxwell Albright had given his cautious approval to the British school of comparative religion (1964: 152-156), and by 1940 he had developed his own methodology published in his classic, *From the Stone Age to Christianity*.

A variety of factors places Albright among the founders of social world studies. Biblical history was his central interest, but he stretched the biblical world to include all territories between Spain and India and Russia and South Arabia—regions matching the horizons of his own interest and competence (Albright, 1966: 13). Best known for his mastery and development of philological and archaeological disciplines, his writings also reveal an insatiable appetite for the methodological questions raised by comparative scholarship. His treatments of the philosophy of history and his attempt to formulate his own philosophy surfaced repeatedly. This interest, it seems, has been largely neglected by most of his students and others who appeal to his authority.

The lives and interests of Robertson Smith and Albright were remarkably similar. Both were ministers' sons who suffered physical impairment. Like Smith, Albright's Renaissance brilliance—in his case as a linguist, philologist, archaeologist, and historian—transformed the nature of Near Eastern studies in his day by setting the advances of the past generations on a new methodological foundation. His energy and talent coincided with fortunate timing that enabled him to weave a meaningful fabric out of threads leading from a number of disciplines that were individually in disarray. And for him, archaeology was what evolutionist philosophy had been for Smith. It was the whole cloth, the integrating discipline to be used primarily as a backdrop for sound interpretation of the Bible. Finally, the Bible was the topic central to his interest and, in his judgment, to the history of the world (1964: 291).

Archaeology for Albright was really a number of disciplines encompassing the study of language and literature as well as artifacts. The interpretation of data uncovered in excavations necessitated drawing comparisons between time periods and across cultural boundaries. These could be placed, as it were, on a grid where space and time lines intersected to give a context for interpreting finds. The methodological problems raised by such comparisons inspired Albright to propose a philosophy of history that in his judgment was neither instrumentalist nor functionalist, at least not in the same manner as for others who wore the labels in his day (1964: 178-79).

He rejected the instrumentalism influenced by John Dewey that treated individual social concepts and forces as independent factors. To ignore the possibility of a relationship between them defied his experience, even though instrumentalism would have enabled him to propose modifications in society without worrying about the overall effect the changes might induce on other aspects of a social unit. Although his care for improving the human condition, especially of minorities, could have led him in this direction, the solution seemed wrong, and so was avoided.

But neither did he subscribe to the rigid Malinowski-type functionalism that claimed social phenomena were so closely entwined that tampering with one would risk the survival of the whole. Although this view of human life was useful for explaining a phenomenon by determining its function, it could neither explain social change nor offer a basis on which to propose improvements in society, both topics that Albright considered important.

Albright described his position as intermediate. The claim is clearer, however, than his description. He taught that all social structures were *organismic* rather than organic in nature, and that each had its own distinct characteristics and definite life cycle (1964:

179). Social structures exhibited great variety in space, time, and function, and were usually bound together in larger, less stable organisms. Albright's theory explained, for him, the stability in and similarities among societies while allowing the flexibility needed to explain historical changes that occurred when new cultures emerged from a collision of heterogeneous bodies. He illustrated the process clearly in a single remark that also describes the image of biblical David: "A single innovator has often fashioned powerful new social and cultural structures from miscellaneous materials at his disposal, choosing his building elements more or less eclecticly" (1964: 180).

A resolute "positivist" by self-description, Albright qualified his claim by insisting that he suited the description "*only in so far as positivism is the expression of the modern rational-scientific approach to physical and historical reality*" (italics his; 1964: 140). He accepted the label "evolutionist" as well, but again with qualification. His organismic evolution was neither mechanical nor melioristic as the *a priori* evolutionary schemes of Hegel and Comte had been. He described organismic evolution somewhat negatively. It was not unilineal progress, or merely a series of abrupt mutations, or an organic development. It had more or less definite configurations and patterns. The historian's task was to find, describe, and interpret their definite, purposeful, structural relationships in societies by comparing successive organismic phenomena.

His view on the periodization of history was admittedly influenced by Lucien Lévy-Bruhl's description of "primitive" and "civilized" humanity (1957: 7, 122, 168-69). Lévy-Bruhl distinguished the two groups by their pre-logical and logical thinking, respectively. Albright offered "proto-logical," "empirico-logical," and "logical" stages in the progression of thought to replace Lévy-Bruhl's classifications and to serve as a framework for organizing the history of the ancient Near East (1964: 52-53, 66-73). He felt that his close attention to archaeological information governed the scheme and therefore saved him from the arbitrary, subjective synthesis of history that had haunted schema of earlier evolutionists and positivists. His views on progression and the superiority of the Graeco-Roman civilization at the time of Christ led him to offer a five-stage diagram to explain the relation of undifferentiated, differentiated, and integrated cultures that stretched from Early Paleolithic times to the present. He viewed history not as a unilineal chain of related occurrences, but rather as a continually changing, complex web of interacting patterns, each of which had its own structure. By comparing successive states, the direction of change could be detected (1957: 3).

By rejecting functionalism (1964: 47-49), Albright was left to explain the proper use of analogy for reconstructing history (1964: 73-75). For him, anthropology provided more useful integrating paradigms for history than did mathematics or biology as long as the anthropological principles were correct (1957: 119). Historians of antiquity would find anthropology helpful because of the similarities between "primitive" peoples who were the subject of both disciplines. Yet, in spite of his positive attitude toward anthropology, Albright appears to have been little influenced by and little interested in exploiting it. The reasons for this no doubt reside in the fact that the discipline was itself only beginning to make an impact upon American scholarship when Albright was at the height of his career and the fact that he spent most of his professional life in Jerusalem and at The Johns Hopkins University where anthropology as a discipline held little force.

Albright's views on analogy are interesting in light of what has followed in biblical studies and the social sciences. He demonstrated that analogy had been used throughout the proto-logical, empirico-logical, and logical stages of civilization (1964: 74-75). This he thought proved that using known human models for interpreting lesser-known phenomena was legitimate at each stage of history as long as the analogies were truly comparable (1966: 5-13). The persistence of human nature guaranteed an analogy's validity provided the function as well as the form of the two phenomena compared positively. This could be checked by requiring that the analogies point to a stochastic, i.e., probability, model.

Analogy had also played a role in earlier evolutionary theories as the theorists shifted away from homology, i.e., the recognition of homologues, similar forms, or counterparts in two cultures. To the 19th century evolutionists, analogies consisted mostly of examples within the physical and biological sciences. Although Albright cautioned against the use of analogy by individuals who had little knowledge of the paradigms' limitations, he encouraged study of their use for social sciences and humanistic disciplines, as well as for the natural sciences. He believed that analogy had to be used to achieve a historical understanding of the Bible because it was *not* primarily a historical record and because archaeology was a means of establishing the matrix for biblical events. Because a single analogy could not solve a historical problem, the comparison of artifacts and language traditions made possible by archaeology provided the basis for historical analogy.

As with Smith, Albright's personal and professional lives impinged on his intellectual views. His interest in minorities, his long years in the Middle East, his physical handicaps, his insatiable appetite for languages, and his interest in finding a firm, non-ecclesial base for reading the Bible compare closely to aspects in Smith's career. But he enjoyed a physical stamina Smith lacked, and most importantly, he was far removed from the 19th century form of evolutionism.

Also like Smith, some opinions that were helpful in his day have lost their cogency. If one were to cite an area where scholarship has advanced beyond Albright's thinking, it would be in the understanding of sociopolitical processes. He understood well individual peoples, regions, and periods in antiquity, and many of his descriptions have withstood the test of time. But like others of his day, he had greater difficulty in describing changes inside or across the boundaries of separate units. Although his emphasis on space-time systemics advanced the state of scholarship enormously, it has continued to prevail, especially among members of his "school," at the expense of processual and relational studies.

Mendenhall on Covenant and Peasant Revolt

Despite Albright's insistence upon expertise both in languages and archaeology, most of those he trained chose to concentrate on one or the other. Although many of his students have sustained a surprising breadth of interest regardless of their choice, George E. Mendenhall has been the most successful in combining dual literary and archaeological inquiry with a continuing curiosity about analogies and methodologies drawn from other social sciences.

In 1954, Mendenhall published two articles that provide the basis for his later work. In one (1970a [1954]), he proposes first (against the Wellhausen School), that the covenant at Sinai marks the origin of the Israelite religious community and second, that covenant contrasts sharply with law. Covenant creates a religious community whereas law always depends on a monopoly of force to impose it. Furthermore, by drawing distinctions between continuity and discontinuity in cultural traditions and between the form and function in cultural elements, as suggested by Albright, Mendenhall situates the early Yahwists within the context of ancient Near Eastern societies without forcing them into an ethnic, national, or kinship identity. For Mendenhall, the Yahwist religion bonded the new group and established a radical discontinuity with Late Bronze Age ideologies, even though the group borrowed existing literary and legal forms to express its new freedoms and responsibilities. He demonstrates that form and function can be differentiated if one is sensitive to the context and intentionality of religion.

In the second article (1970b [1954]), Mendenhall expands these insights. He argues that the early Yahwists borrowed a common ancient Near East covenant formula and fitted it to their new religious intentionality by transforming its function. Following Korosec's work on Hittite suzerainty treaties, he alleges that the same treaty form was used in ancient Israel and is evident in the Bible. He identifies it in covenantal texts, even in passages where one or more elements of the Hittite formula are lacking. Mendenhall insists that the form of the treaty is continuous with the Hittite model, but that its function is totally transformed. In Hittite culture, suzerainty treaties link the peoples' interest to those of their civil-political overlords.

Among the Yahwists, the formula expressed the unity of the community with its deity, Yahweh, who did not rely upon earthly overlords or notables as mediators. In effect, the deity displaced political centralized monopolies of force that were relegated to the status of pagan elements incompatible with the new religious faith. It is important to note that Mendenhall's interpretation portrays the people as vassals according to both ideologies. But unlike those in Late Bronze Age states, the Yahwists' vassalage was to a deity rather than a political suzerain.

Like his teacher, Mendenhall feels the need for external criteria to check historians' reconstructions of Israel's religious past (1970b: 25). Also true to Albright, he demonstrates both a sweeping grasp of ancient Near Eastern studies and a functionalist's concern for the historical context of specific events, personalities, and institutions. By drawing upon legal as well as Near Eastern studies, he proves the usefulness of Albright's approach for uncovering Israel's earliest religious meaning. He accomplishes this, however, without explaining precisely what his criteria are or how one can identify religious meaning without slipping into the idealist's subjectivity that has plagued theologians and biblicists since the 19th century.

Mendenhall's claims for Israel's religious uniqueness struck sympathetic chords in American scholarship, but to many in America and elsewhere his insistence on the antinomian, anti-centralist, and even anti-urban character of the early Yahwistic community sounds either too much like Colonial America or Reformation Protestantism. No one has suggested that Mendenhall is imposing midwestern American Lutheranism on ancient Israel, but the contrasts he frequently drew in his earlier studies between the authentic, early Yahwist faith and later decadent forms of institutional religion might have been exploited by critics if he had not soon stated the theory behind his historical methodology.

In 1961, Mendenhall addressed this topic directly. His study begins by calling attention to the dissolution of general assent among specialists concerning the origins and history of biblical religion. Without assuming credit for his own part in creating the malaise, he identifies three factors that helped dismantle the synthesis produced by the Wellhausen School: the exhaustion of source analysis as the primary method of reconstructing history; the introduction of new data and methods; and changes in mood among angry scholars and general populations since World War I (1961: 33).

Mendenhall alludes to new data and new controls offered by archaeological discoveries, increased knowledge of the processes of transmitting writing and of cult-borrowing in the ancient world, and new linguistic criteria for dating portions of the biblical text more precisely. The new methods were adopted principally from linguistics, anthropology, and archaeology, which developed rapidly since 1920, and from the pioneering work of Max Weber that was beginning to exert its influence anew within biblical studies.

The new spirit Mendenhall senses after World War I emerged, he claims, for two reasons. First, the *a priori* evolutionary schemes that permeated Wellhausen's scholarship were finally laid to rest by new information showing that Israel's origins were not at the sophisticated, cosmopolitan end of a cultural evolutionary spectrum, but rather were embedded in the destruction layers and chaotic collapse of an ancient, material and political Golden Era of the Late Bronze Age. Yahwism, therefore, cannot be viewed as a continuation or enhancement of the values that had supported the former prosperity.

The second reason for the new mood was associated with world events. By abandoning the Old Testament as irrelevant, Mendenhall claims, modern Christian theologians and politicians had fallen victim to self-deception that led to Nazism, the Holocaust, and extreme secularism. Guided by the fallacy that modern is better and ancient is primitive, they failed to identify the tension and contradiction between religious values and social control, a theme that Mendenhall touched in his covenant studies and would explicate some years later (1975b).

According to Mendenhall, the absence of an adequate hypothesis to replace Wellhausen's is a major problem. Earlier, he sought a remedy by proposing a five-phase scheme of historical development similar in some ways to that offered by Albright. He labeled the phases "praeparatio," "creative period," "adaptive period," "traditional period," and "period of reformation." These provide a framework for Israel's history that allowed him to demonstrate how forms (and structures) might continue across temporal and geographical boundaries while functions change or cease. The scheme explains, for example, how the Bronze Age ancestral traditions that were pre-Yahwistic came to be incorporated in Israelite tradition during the monarchical period. The resulting tensions between "appropriate" and "intolerable" accommodations that divided the ancient community could now be detected and the dynamics of history recovered.

Mendenhall continued to expose such tensions. He proposed that tension between land-holding aristocracies and unclassed peasant groups (*'apiru*) caused a widespread peasant revolt at the end of the Late Bronze Age. For him, this offers an explanation for the so-called "Hebrew Conquest" (1970c [1962]). His hypothesis about the Settlement has had a profound, lasting impact—especially in the United States—on historical reconstructions of Israelite and early Iron Age history. Previously dominant views of Israelite nomadism, the character of the Hebrew tribes, the contrast between religion and politics, and the spread of Yahwism are all clarified while older views are discarded. The "ideal models" that included sedentarization of nomadic tribes and massive military conquest are challenged by the peasant revolt model. It must be noted that, unlike some who appeal to his hypothesis for their own reconstructions, Mendenhall admits that his proposal leaves some questions unresolved, and he suggests further lines of inquiry for exposing relationships between seemingly unrelated pieces of information.

Mendenhall continued to examine and test his hypothesis in studies on the monarchy (1975a) and the conflict between religious values and social control systems (1975b). His fullest review was *The Tenth Generation* (1973), a compilation of essays covering a broad range of topics on ancient Near Eastern history and religion. Several are important for our discussion of the emergence of state in the early Iron Age.

In his treatment of thesis and method, Mendenhall pulls together material scattered throughout his earlier writings and reasserts the methodological bankruptcy of approaches that rely exclusively on form criticism, nomadism, and ethnicity. For him, methods grow out of the nature of the evidence and begin with critical examination of widely held assumptions (1973: 4). Hypotheses are necessary when evidence is minimal, as in the Bible, but these should be consciously adopted in order to avoid uncritical conclusions. Because all history is comparative, analogies must be used (1973: 6, n.21), but whenever possible these must be derived from the ancient Near East rather than from modern or post-biblical societies. He insists that every society is unique even though the forms of behavior in any society cannot be unique. They may be similar because of borrowing. Consequently, the study of history or religion requires delving "beneath the forms of language, organization, and behavior to their functions: the sum of their relationships to other aspects of society and, above all, to the hierarchy of values upon which the social solidarity ultimately depends" (1973: 6). Because no form can have identical functions in two societies, cultural borrowing does not negate the uniqueness of either loaner or borrower.

Mendenhall's functionalism leads him to propose a single analogy for understanding the operation of myth in ancient societies. In his estimation, myths function as ideologies to identify and promulgate the legitimacy of existing power structures. Therefore, Israel's religion, manifested in covenant, contrasts with the myths of its neighbors even when their literatures share common forms. Here, cultural discontinuity enters again and the radical newness of Yahwism is reasserted.

The primacy of religion, in Mendenhall's estimation, is clearly evident because religion is the basis of Israelite solidarity and therefore the creator of a people (1973: 16). In fact, the biblical revolution forces a redefinition of the term religion. He proposes a "voluntary submission to the will of God defined in ethical terms that [are] binding beyond any social or territorial boundary" (1973: 24-25).

In Mendenhall's writings, the original covenantal community seems to be the "true" Israel. Monarchy, therefore, with its accompanying revival of laws, wars, social stratification, taxation, conscription, and general monopolizing of force, constitutes a return to the paganism of the Late Bronze Age when, among other things, the kings claimed divine prerogatives and sought control over aspects of life that were rightfully within the deity's domain.

When analyzing tribes, state, and monarchy, however, Mendenhall draws attention to anthropological studies on cultural evolution such as those of Elman Service. While he is disposed to Service's 1962 statement of a four-stage evolutionary pattern, he is careful to point out that no individual stage exactly parallels a phase in the development of Israel's society. For him, Israel's uniqueness extends to this process, a view that recalls again the distinctions between form and function, continuity and discontinuity (1973: 175-177). Fictive kinship, the function of common ancestors, genealogies, and the role of ritual are aspects of ancient Israel that he feels Service helps to illuminate.

Israel's social process, however, included devolution as well as evolution, the former occurring when the city-states of Canaan disintegrated at the end of the Late Bronze Age. For Mendenhall, the dissolution was accompanied by the emergence of a new ideology, i.e., Israel's religion, which was radically opposed to the ideology of the former society. The resulting tension constituted a basis for the continuing conflict that lasted throughout the remainder of Yahwist history.

Mendenhall's contributions are many. Although he is best known for his innovative hypotheses that pertain to the transitional Late Bronze/Iron Age era, his influence has also been felt through the broad sweep of his theories' application. Because of his personal ability to manage, sort, and organize vast amounts of information from ancient Near Eastern languages and archaeology, he demonstrates that the revolutionary character of early Yahwism and its radical stance against centralized monopolies of force constitutes the religion's fundamental tenet. Mendenhall's work helps biblical specialists to follow the tortuous course of Israelite affairs by probing to the origin of the problem—the covenantal beginnings of the religious tradition.

His ideal models of covenant and rebellion have been the subject of controversy since they were first proposed. There are several reasons why his critics' ardor has not subsided with the passage of time. First must be the fundamental revision that his hypotheses require in ancient Near Eastern history. These threaten the truisms of many schools of thought. Next are the honest, informed disagreements about his interpretation of key biblical texts and historical events. But finally, Mendenhall has also added to the controversies by continuing to press more and more data into his hypotheses' molds, thereby creating impressions of singularity and repetition. Yet, despite controversy and dissent, his hypotheses continue to influence American scholarship on the Settlement and to provide a basis for investigating the methods and problems that accompany studies on Israel's early history.

The reconstruction proposed in this volume owes a great deal to Mendenhall's insights and arguments. Here, however, greater use is made of modern comparative materials, and less is said about the discontinuity between Yahwist and non-Yahwist groups and centralized and uncentralized sociopolitical forms. The boundaries, it seems, may not have been as clear or as stable as they first seemed.

Wilson on Biblical Genealogy

The opening toward social sciences, especially anthropology, has continued to expand as biblical scholars in America, Europe, and Israel seek fuller understanding of ancient Israel's religion and culture (cf. Rogerson, 1978). After Mendenhall, several of the earliest attempts to illumine biblical history were studies on biblical and ancient Near Eastern genealogies by Abraham Malamat (1967; 1968; 1973a) and Robert R. Wilson (1975; 1977). Both were successful in explaining the form and function of biblical texts by demonstrating that the genealogies conform to patterns found in other societies, mainly ancient civilizations and modern African groups.

Wilson has been explicit about his method of applying anthropological material in his examinations of genealogies (1977: 13-16), Israelite prophecy (1980: 14-16), and biblical sociology (1984). He tries to avoid two flaws in William Robertson Smith's work by outlining guidelines for interpreting the Bible anthropologically. Smith's studies, he feels, were marred by his use of uncritical sources and his willingness to force biblical material into a mold created from extra-biblical data. A highly artificial reconstruction resulted from mixing bits of information in a distorted portrait of Israel's past.

In his first book, Wilson recommended four guidelines for using anthropological data, plus two more for connecting its use to interpretations that used form-critical methods. In his second and third books, the two sets are combined as guidelines for using comparative materials drawn from anthropology and sociology: the substance of the list has not changed, but the boundary line marking the area for comparison has. What had previously encircled anthropology is stretched to include the two subdisciplines in comparative sociology.

Wilson suggests: 1) that comparative material must be systematically gathered by trained social scientists; 2) that it must be properly integrated in its own context before being applied to the Bible; 3) that it must be drawn from a wide range of societies in order to avoid the risk of using atypical materials; 4) that the data but not the interpretative schemas of social scientists should be used; 5) that the comparative material must be truly comparable; and 6) that the biblical material must control the interpretation. For Wilson, the last requirement establishes the relationship between the two forms of information.

> The comparative material is simply used to form a hypothesis which is then tested against the biblical text. The exegesis of the text itself will confirm, disprove, or modify the hypothesis. In this way comparative data can be used to broaden the horizons of the interpreter by suggesting new hypotheses and to assess the value of hypotheses previously advanced (1984: 29).

Wilson argues that his cautious, constructive approach enables him to draw upon anthropological data that might "provide clues" for illuminating meagre biblical evidence (1980: 14). He is careful to insist, however, that the anthropological material should not be used to fill gaps in our knowledge of ancient society, a point he drives home by insisting that if the texts fail to provide sufficient evidence to support or deny a hypothesis, the question must be left open (1980: 16). A hypothesis may say more than the text says, but it cannot say less.

Wilson's application of his method to concrete biblical data reveals that he believes in a dialectical relationship between theory and data that his description tends to blur. His methodological statements suggest that anthropology and biblical exegesis should be applied, as it were, sequentially, with anthropology being used to formulate hypotheses and at the end to decide finally on proof or denial. Biblical exegesis is applied in between to link the hypotheses to the text. In practice, the separation of phases is not clear. He employs biblical and anthropological data dialectically to construct a portrait of ancient Israelite life.[1]

Gottwald's Historical Cultural Materialism

To date, the most complete attempt to apply and refine Mendenhall's peasant revolt hypothesis has been Norman K. Gottwald's lengthy study, *The Tribes of Yahweh: A Sociology of the Religion of Liberated Israel, 1250-1050 B.C.E.* (1979). The book was welcomed by biblical specialists as a serious, innovative endeavor to examine the social processes that shaped Israel during the tribal period. By appealing to sociological and anthropological research, Gottwald analyzes the social world of ancient Israel and sets Israel's religion in the context of its politics and economics.

In the preface, Gottwald outlines the procedural steps he follows in examining Israel's history (1979: xxii-xxiii; cf. 1985: 20-33). First, the recognized methods of biblical studies—the standard criticisms, history, and history of religion—are used "to assemble the most reliable information about the rise of Israel." Second, social-scientific methods are applied to the body of data and theory derived from the first step. Here, Gottwald seeks "to delineate and to conceptualize early Israel as a total social system." Third, specific aspects of the social system identified in step two (namely, pastoral nomadism, tribal confederation, and peasant revolt) are examined. Finally, an "explanatory social theory" is introduced to explain change in Israelite society.

In the final step, Gottwald proceeds in two phases, first using a structural-functional model in order to demonstrate the relationships among elements in Israel's social structure, and then using a historical-cultural-material model to explain the changes accompanying Israel's emergence from the "imperial-feudal Canaanite society." Environmental and technological aspects of society, such as metallurgy, agricultural methods, and water systems, are brought in during this final phase of investigation because they pertain to the materialist model used by Gottwald.

Gottwald's study focuses on pre-monarchic Israel—a historical period prior to the one central in this study. Although his investigation overlaps ours there is no need to summarize his conclusions here. My indebtedness to his work—which set the discipline on a new course by forcing it to rethink old issues and recast old questions—will be clear as we progress.

It is important, however, to anticipate differences in the approach taken by Gottwald and the one followed here. Statements about eclecticism and method made in the Introduction already indicate that these differences do not imply clear choices between correct and incorrect ways to proceed. The choices are dictated, at least in part, by the nature of the information, the character of the questions brought to the subject matter, and the research design and goals of the investigator.

By beginning his study with a description of an ancient Israel based largely on biblical texts as they are reconstructed by means of the standard criticisms and methods, Gottwald risks creating the cadaver he ultimately dissects. He seems to seek first an "original" historical entity (Israel) in the Bible's text-images by means of excavative methods. Then by applying his model(s), he appears to trace the entity's (or images'?) development along paths suggested by the model. The distinction between the history of Israel and the history of Israel's literature is blurred again. Likewise, Albright's insistence on the value of language traditions and the primacy of archaeology properly understood and executed are ignored. For Gottwald these are of secondary importance (1979: 25).

Gottwald wrestles with the classic problem of stable state versus sequential change and with the epistemological problems that accompany the historical reconstructions of rapidly changing societies that are undergoing multilinear development. By dividing his book into two all-encompassing sections that separate synchronic (Parts I-VII) from diachronic (Parts VIII-XI) investigations, he admits the methodological problems and attempts to bypass them by first establishing the history of the Israel to be investigated and then contrasting Israel with her neighbors. A different ideology, together with its accompanying economics (or vice versa), he feels explains Israel's difference and the processes that brought it about.

Treating the literature first and the techno-environmental and techno-economic features last is the opposite of what one expects in a materialist analysis. We might ask why Gottwald does not begin with the material culture even though by doing so he would be raising other questions about the evolutionary schemas championed by Hegel and Marx. Here the dilemma all historians of Israel face becomes clear. The material culture associated with early Yahwist Israel cannot be distinguished from Canaanite culture on the basis of material information alone. Only the Bible, the sole literary record of the new ideology and religion, is available to guide the historian who sorts elements and artifacts on the basis of belief. Gottwald elects to rely on that record for "reconstructing" early Israel. In doing so, he risks begging his fundamental question: what type of society was the tribal Israel in which the new religious belief arose?

Although Mendenhall sharply criticizes Gottwald's view and distinguishes it from his own (1983), together their studies are a convenient departure point for an investigation of the rise of David. Their analyses of the structure and function of tribal Yahwism, as well as their descriptions of the unsettled social conditions, the diversity of peoples, and the deteriorated economy when Yahwism claims to have first flourished in Canaan, aptly depict the opening scenes in the literature that portrays David's social drama. Likewise, their ability to build on their methodological predecessors provides a basis for understanding and describing social world studies.

Agenda for Social World Studies

This abbreviated review of scholarship demonstrates that historical studies of the Bible continue to wrestle with the causes of disillusionment that frustrated earlier biblical quests. Interest in literary studies of the Bible and in ahistorical archaeology have in fact helped by tearing away the thin veil of disciplinary and multidisciplinary integrity that had long shrouded methodological problems and unfounded historical assumptions. Social world studies have helped expose both and are developing approaches to cope with them.

Social world studies do not offer a single method or theory in the usual sense of the terms. Their dependence on standard biblical methodologies, archaeology, and comparative sociology make them derivative and eclectic in ways that defy methodological purity. They comprise an approach—in fact, many approaches. These seek to illumine hidden and overlooked information in ancient material and written sources. This means, in effect, that they endeavor to formulate hypotheses and to understand less known ancient societies by illuminating them with comparative information from better known ancient and modern societies. The "better knowns" are drawn from general and theoretical social studies, from ethnographies and ethnologies of societies with ecologies similar to those in the ancient world, and from ancient societies investigated by similar approaches. Processes, dynamics, transformations, and metamorphoses as well as static phenomena are used. Social world studies treat every society as unique, but the comparisons inject pragmatism, positivism, and Missouri-style "show-me-ism" that both expects and suspects consistencies in human behavior.

The approach assumes that the ancient past is neither an idealized dream world whose characters and events float uncontrollably through the minds of historians, nor a physical reality that can be recovered, photographed, described, and assigned to museums where it stands as proof of "life then" for future generations to admire nostalgically. In two ways, social world approaches aim at the in-between. On the level of modern investigating, the studies spark imagination and control speculation, spur intuition and discipline reflection (cf. Ziman, 1978: 185). They rest on the assumption that knowledge of history requires imagination, but disciplined imagination, and that critical thinking is aided and made less arbitrary by integrating archaeology, literatures, and cross-cultural comparisons of the kind Leach finds highly risky. Social world proponents know that neither positive nor negative correlations among samples constitute "proof" that two societies are or are not twins. The studies distinguish between images of the past and images from the past, between literary and archaeological sources of information, and between ancient sources and interpretations based on modern societies.

The efforts also depart from earlier worries on two important, closely related points. First, social world studies accept homologues and analogues in historical reasoning. Hypotheses are formed on the basis of comparative information, and they are used in efforts to interpret the past adequately. "Adequately" is used here instead of "truly" or "correctly" because historians' interpretations are not scientifically testable assertions. They are hypotheses that offer plausible explanations, guide further reflection, and are subject to constant revision.

The second in-between is implied in the first but frequently passes unobserved. Texts and tells that serve as testimony to past social worlds are partial or fragmentary sources of information. And yet, entire social worlds produce and are encoded in each. Historians attempt to reconstitute holistic images of the past on the basis of the partial information. The sources, therefore, stand between observers and the past observed. Wilson understates the issue when he places the sources in the past and speaks of the gap of history that separates readers from the biblical text (1984: 4). Instead, two gaps exist. One divides investigators from their sources. The other stands between the sources and the ancient societies they represent. In this sense, the ancient sources are, as Binford suggests, modern phenomena.

The ancient social worlds seen in the sources are not contained there but are antecedent worlds that produced the sources. The distinction does not lessen the concerns raised about comparisons, but it makes the issues more clear. Regardless of the worries methodological purists might have about comparing several societies, ancient historians cannot escape the problem. Following Rappaport (1979: 87), every mode of analysis has limitations, but to abandon all analyses is to be left either with nothing, because everything is rejected, or with an undifferentiated everything. Stated positively, every use of ancient sources for purposes of history engages presuppositions about the ancient world and makes attempts to situate partial information within the framework of antiquity. That frame is itself hypothetical and dependent on some image of society. Social world studies identify explicitly the character and location of the controlling image and the worlds on which it is based. This does not solve the epistemological problems, but it allows readers to measure the coherence of the hypotheses, the sources, and the ancient social world.

The object of comparison in this study of Iron Age I is the world or worlds associated with the figure David. The circumstances that caused ancient material remains to be what they are, the images created by and within the biblical stories, and the impressions that influenced the storytellers are important aids for hypothesizing about life in the 10th century B.C.E. But each in itself is a reconstruction and hypothesis that partially coheres and partially contrasts with the others. Consequently, a social world study of the social world of David will not be able to choose one over the other and make it the "historical" image. A modern reading is yet another perspective, but one that is immediately open to reinterpretation.

The pitfalls, therefore, are not the ones suggested in archaeological and anthropological debates, i.e., forced choices between the world-views of scientists or humanists. Neither are the difficulties caused solely by the variety and unverifiability of human historical realities.

Instead, investigators' tensions reside in the anxiety and self-criticism they feel when they look at the past, or at other human beings, and try to understand and explain. As historians, they are anxious to avoid purely pedestrian quantitative descriptions on the one hand and widely fanciful speculations on the other. How to achieve a reasonable balance and how to communicate it to others causes methodological anxiety and debate.

Taking Stock of Social World Studies

The agenda for a social world study of Iron Age I can be summarized succinctly.

1. Obervers' ideas, viewpoints, and perspectives are distinct from those that influenced the ancient sources. And the latter are only partial sources of information about ancient life. Hence, historical images of the past are hypotheses, subject to continual revision.
2. Neither the Bible nor Iron Age archaeology offers the interpretative framework for understanding the other. To read in the Bible the explanations for archaeological information that are in turn used in reading the Bible makes the conclusions predictable. In spite of risks from human diversity, comparative information affords new openings and controls. Epistemological problems remain, but the combination of categories of information illuminates the problems and makes them manageable.
3. Modeling, analogy, and metaphor become central concerns in historical studies of biblical antiquity. Recognizing the tentativeness of historical interpretations shifts the focus of investigations away from details toward macroscales and holistic approaches which examine the relationships and relativity that join observers' models and ancient aspirations and actions on the one hand and the disciplines that study them on the other.
4. The social world of biblical antiquity becomes the object of biblical historians' quests. Reconstituting ancient society from partial information in order to understand the religions of the past is not the same circle that dizzied earlier biblical historians and archaeologists. Social world critics know from the outset that their sources of ancient information are

> of two related but distinct kinds (material and textual), and that each was shaped by a combination of factors that are now only partly visible. The social world in which religion resided is not immediately observable; it stands "beyond" the sources. Neither source, individually or jointly, describes or is the exclusive medium through which ancient religion traveled. Religion arose in, was influenced by, and in turn shaped ancient societies. It eludes direct observation, but it bound ancient domains together and linked disparate peoples. It was at the same time everywhere and alone nowhere in antiquity. Thus, moderns must tease their understandings of it out of all available information. All aspects of society must be considered.

How this can be accomplished leads to models, metaphors, and holograms, the topics of the next chapter.

Chapter 2

HOLOGRAPHIC MODEL FOR A SOCIAL WORLD STUDY OF IRON AGE I

Developing a model for a social world study requires that we identify a means for sorting information and for reintegrating it in order to depict life in Iron Age I. Here we draw upon holograms and the technology of holography, theories and methods used in anthropological research, and ritual studies. We begin by describing holography and by borrowing from it metaphors and models that are used in our approach. Next, we suggest dividing information according to ontological categories that are used by anthropologists. Finally, we propose a holographic model for integrative social world studies based on the technology and separations.

A. *Hologram as Metaphor and Model*

Holography is a laser-based, vibration-free technology used to encode visual information on an opaque or transparent plate in a way that allows three-dimensional images to be reconstituted (Abramson, 1981; Saxby, 1980; Kasper and Feller, 1985). A laser beam—a highly coherent monochromatic radiation, a single-phase beam of light—is split in two when it passes through a partially silvered mirror known as a beam splitter [Figure 4]. With a system of filters, mirrors, and spreading lenses, the two portions are directed onto an emulsion-backed plate that captures their amplitude and phase. One portion, the object beam, is diffracted off an object; its waves are thrown partially out of phase by the contours of the object. The other portion, the reference beam, falls directly, unaltered, and in phase onto the plate. The wave patterns of the two portions interfere to produce a wave front of partially coherent and partially incoherent (i.e., cancelling) crests and troughs. The fringe pattern of constructive and destructive interference, as it is called, is encoded so that when the plate (the hologram) is struck by an illuminating beam, the pattern, and hence the object's image (also called a hologram), is reconstituted. The illumination produces a realistic, three-dimensional image as if the object were there. The image appears to be suspended in space either behind or in front of the plate.[2]

Figure 4: Technical Process of Constructing a Hologram

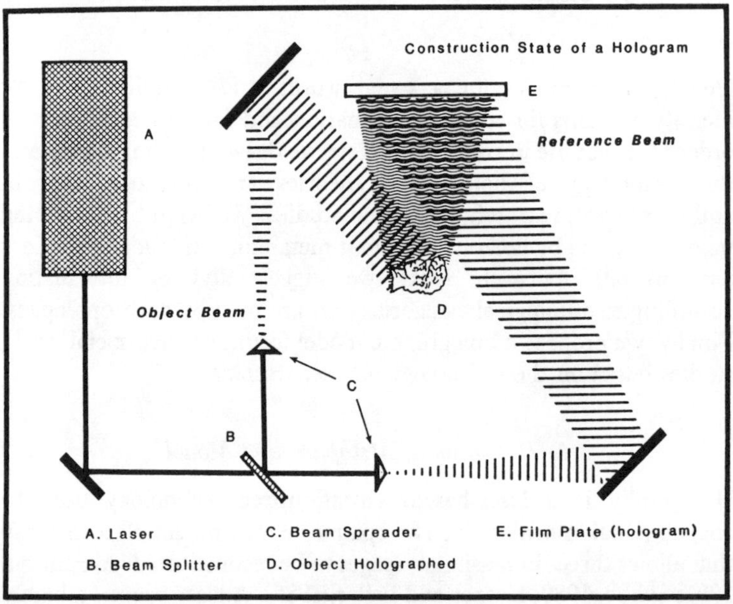

Holography depends on part-whole, whole-part relationships. Although a whole object is holographed, only partial information is actually encoded on the plate. But, on the basis of the partial information, the whole object reappears when the hologram is illuminated. Moreover, the coherence of the object and reference beams must be only partial. If the crests and troughs of the two beams are either totally congruent or totally incongruent, no interference pattern, and therefore no image, is encoded and none can be reconstituted.

Social World Analogies

The technology of holography and holograms offers analogies that are useful for social world studies. The stages in the process of holographic encoding and illuminating, as well as the holographic image, are metaphors and models for several aspects of a social world approach.

First, holography is a metaphor for the processes and relationships that constitute a social world. Here, the relational theory of metaphor applies. The theory assumes that metaphors involve more than simple comparisons of two items. Relational theory emphasizes that relationships within each of the two items are related to each other. The separate sets of relationships are drawn out and illuminated by the metaphor.

The components of a social world can be separated analytically into several groupings: 1) ideas, opinions, aspirations, and motives; 2) physical and material resources; and 3) social norms and systems. But the constituent statements and beliefs, the physical settings, and the social conventions are, in a sense, only the surface of a social world—information about that world—and not the real, meaningful "world" that biblical historians seek. To peer beneath the surface or into the midst of these phenomena exposes the relationships among the constituent elements and hence their meaning.

Such meanings more than their consequences are the subject matter of social world studies. The full meaning ("meaningfulness") existed once upon a time when it accompanied a particular relationship of the components on a particular occasion. But part of the significance of the historic moment passed immediately from sight and is now knowable only through its effects. The effects and the relationships among them bear information about the past that can be studied in attempts to perceive former meanings. Because the past and its meaning cannot be fully regained, such perceptions are hypotheses or hypothetical reconstructions.

To state the matter in other words, in historic moments, human agency and ecological resources come together in the context of and in reciprocity with contemporary systems and norms in order to make things happen. The processes and the connections among the elements at work are the realities biblical historians seek. They are the subject matter that lurks beyond and is pointed toward by questions like, "Who did it?" "When did it occur?" "What happened?" and "Why?" To know what was said, to reconstruct the scene, and to understand the social context and norms is to be in possession of the so-called "facts." But by themselves, these are the information and bases that historians must reach beyond in order to gain understanding.

In order to penetrate beyond thoughts and statements, beyond geosphere and biosphere, and beyond customs and conventions the links and processes in a social world must be addressed. Each of these is past; they are history; they are holographic. Therefore, history is a hologram.

Secondly, it follows that historians' portrayals of the past are also holograms because they reconstitute past meanings. They are more than attempts to recover the "facts." Settings, scenes, sensibilities, and statements are important because they bear information and because at a given time they stood in a particular relationship to each other. But reconstructions of the relationships and what they stood for—more than knowledge about effects and products—comprise the focus of a biblical historian's view. Thus, biblical historians seek the holograms that existed in the past, and they offer holograms of the past, but their holograms are in the present.

Third, the technical processes of holography are a model for a social world research design. This includes using literary and archaeological disciplines to examine the information in ancient artifacts (e.g., texts and tells) and using information drawn from comparative sociology to illumine the ancient information and the relationships among individual sources of information. As we shall see, the process of making holograms from master holograms (the functional equivalent of making photographic copies from negatives) can also be used as a model for the two-step process required to combine disciplinary analyses in interdisciplinary studies.

With these analogies ordered 1-3-2, i.e., metaphor—model—metaphor, the path biblical historians follow becomes apparent. They move from an ancient social world to a study of the social world to an image of a social world of antiquity. The past is a hologram, the research design is modeled on holography, and the image of the past is a hologram. Thus, the journey is from subject matter (and metaphor) to discipline (and model) to subject matter (and metaphor).

Relational Aspects of the Technology

Four technical aspects of holograms are important for understanding the sequence and the relationship among the items in the metaphors and model. Each is connected to the whole-part-whole phenomenon that links an object that is holographed, a holographic plate, and a hologram image.

First, as holograms encode entire objects in partial information so that images of the whole object may be reconstituted, so entire social worlds are "remembered" in fragmented ancient sources, and by means of comparisons, the worlds' multidimensional images are reconstituted from the partial information. Like holograms, the partially cohering and partially interfering pattern of information in ancient sources is actually what makes historical reconstructions possible and necessary. Without the pattern, historians either would be reduced to knowing very little (total incoherence—which would force them to trust a single source) or they would be strongly tempted to accept ancient interpretations by simply paraphrasing biblical sources (total coherence—again trusting a single source). Unfortunately, one or other of these substitutions is often made in biblical studies. However, when the information pattern that unites and divides the sources is allowed to stand, and the pattern illuminated, life-like "images" can be reconstituted. These, like holograms, are holistic images reconstituted from partial information and from information sources that are only partly coherent with each other.

Second, and related, is a technical phenomenon that allows entire images to be reconstituted from each portion of a holographic plate. Because every point of light from the object is spread across the entire surface of the holographic plate, when the plate is broken or divided, each part retains the whole image but lacks perspectives contained in the larger plate. The effect is like looking through a partly shuttered window. Although viewers standing away from the window see only a portion of the scene framed by the entire window, they can move closer in order to widen their scope and see the entire scene as if the shutter were open. The closer they move, the more perspectives they gain. With holograms, the entire original image is contained in each portion and can be reconstituted from every piece. Only perspectives are lost when the plate is divided, not access to the total scene.

Historians employ the same "technology," although sometimes in reverse fashion. Their holistic images are reconstituted on the basis of partial information. When additional information becomes available, only rarely does it cause historians to discard an entire historical framework. In most instances, it clarifies the image or, as they say, adds perspectives that have been missing. It figuratively expands the size of the "window" onto the past. But the analogy is appropriate even where no new information is discovered because biblical historians, like viewers looking through a shuttered window or small hologram, try constantly to peer beyond the limits of the information in order to gain a view of a bigger scene.

The third and fourth aspects of the relationships pertain to the quality of the image. In holograms, the image is both real and elusive. What viewers see is not an image in the holographic plate in the same way that a photo is an image on photographic paper. With holograms, viewers do not actually see the plate or anything on its surface. Instead, when the illuminating beam strikes the interference pattern encoded in the plate, the beam reconstitutes one of the original light waves, usually the object beam. Thus, the light that was actually diffracted off the object when the hologram was made is reconstituted. In other words, because the light reconstituted by the illuminating beam is the actual light that was diffracted from the object, viewers see the "original" object (the original light) rather than an image of the object (as would be the case in a photo). Viewers see what they would see if the object itself were there. The object is not present, but in a forceful three-dimensional way, it seems to be. The image is simultaneously rich and powerful, distant and elusive. It causes ambivalent feelings of warmth, beauty, vibrance, dimensionality, and proximity on the one hand and on the other inaccessibility, the beyond, the past, and "here and not-here" qualities.

This spreading of information and the resulting dimensionality gives rise to another analogy with history. The information about the ancient social world that is encoded in the sources is spread holistically across the entire "plane" of the sources. Leach argues as much for texts (1983b: 98). The same is true of archaeological remains because each artifact, typology, or site, in a sense, represents with varying degrees of clarity an entire social world. As a result, each partial source of information contains holistic information but offers only a limited perspective on the whole.

Finally, like holograms, historical images are invisible, or more exactly not there, until illumined. For social world studies, the illuminating beam is comparative sociological models that contain relationships like those encoded both in and between the ancient information sources. The interferences between verbal claims and material information tell stories of their own that have parallels in other societies. Hence, information from those societies can be used to illumine the patterns left in ancient sources. The image reconstituted is the image viewers would have seen in the past, but it depends on their ability to recognize relationships that without the comparisons would go unnoticed. Therefore, it is the relationships as much as the information that is illumined.

In sum, history (the past) is a hologram; histories are holograms, histories and holograms are images of the past but, technically, not from the past.

Interdisciplinary Two-Stage Holographic Model

Before discussing holographic technology further, we may recall remarks made in the Introduction about black boxes, translucid boxes, and two-stage modeling. Applied to biblical studies, Robert Wilson's analysis of biblical genealogies can be interpreted as a relatively uncomplicated example of stratified black and translucid box modeling (1975; 1977; 1984).

Wilson lays out the biblical genealogical materials showing the patterns, contradictions, and inconsistencies within them. Alongside the biblical material, he places genealogies from other archaic and primitive societies and demonstrates the patterns in them. Using the extra-biblical examples in order to build a black box model, he claims the patterns to be analogous to those in the Bible. Next, he establishes that the social organizations and processes in the extra-biblical model-groups caused the patterns. Finally, the extra-biblical social processes are used as translucid box models from which Wilson hypothesizes that similar social processes caused the patterns in the biblical genealogies.

The example draws on relatively uncomplicated biblical materials, less complicated in some ways than biblical narratives, and it draws information from only two disciplines rather than three as we must use. Relatedly, in the example Wilson does not directly address the epistemological problems confronting the social sciences. As a result, the application illustrates how distinguishing social forms from social processes allows investigators to move toward causal explanations, but it does not address the problems of the relationships among material and textual sources.

A second illustration can be drawn from material already cited. If G. E. Wright had reversed the order of inquiry implied in his statement on archaeology's capabilities (1983a), he might have used literary information as a translucid box in order to offer plausible interpretations for the black boxes established by archaeology. Instead, he posited literary analysis as a first step and establishing the ancient ecology via archaeology as a second. He thereby confused issues by mixing stable (ecological) and highly variable (notional) information. He left himself open to claims that he used archaeology to interpret the text. Had he proposed working the other way—as indeed he may have done in actual practice—by applying translucid box theory to a given historical case, any number of interpretations drawn from ancient literature or from various archaic and primitive societies could have been tried, until a case was built either based on a combination of models or, with negative analogies, constructed anew from them and from his subjects' differences. It is important to note that the order of presentation in most archaeological reports—literary and documentary information first, material information second—implies a similar reversal. We cannot be sure, of course, that the research does not proceed in the opposite direction, moving from archaeology to literature or dialectically back and forth, but the usual format suggests otherwise.

Wilson and Wright each used only two of the three information sources needed here. The inclusion of a third adds a level of complexity by requiring that relationships 1) between two ancient sources and 2) between ancient and alien (either ancient or modern) information must both be examined before 3) a plausible causal explanation can be offered. In order to accomplish 1 and 2, we continue to appeal to holography; for 3, we will eventually turn to ritual studies.

Studies that are truly interdisciplinary require a two-stage model, one for gathering and interpreting information in each discipline, another for combining that information in an integrative fashion. The way that composite holographic images are made from multiple exposures of a single master hologram or from several masters exposed simultaneously serves as our model [Figure 5].

In order to make composite holograms, several first-stage master holograms are illuminated simultaneously or serially so that a second generation or double exposure hologram is produced. In this process, the laser beam is split into three or more parts, i.e., at least two object beams and one reference beam. Instead of diffracting off objects, however, the object beams pass through the master holograms, projecting their pseudoscopic images onto a plate where the

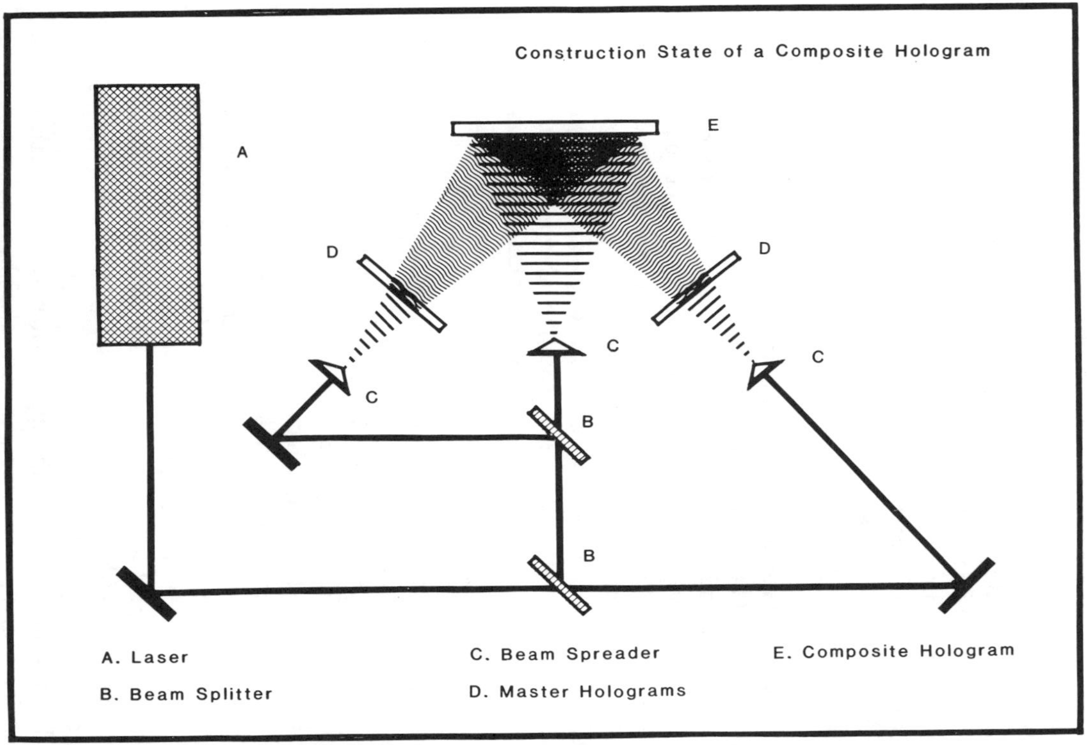

Figure 5: Technical Process of Constructing a Composite Hologram

reference beam interferes with them. The pseudoscopic images from the master(s) are encoded as parts of a composite information source. When the composite hologram is lighted by an illuminating beam, viewers can see one or other image or both—actually a composite of both—depending on their angles of vision, i.e., their perspectives. The same encoding techniques could be continued through additional generations of images, but the composition would eventually become so complex that computer analysis and enhancement would be needed in order to sort and view any of the images.

Analogies with social world studies are easily found. In the case of David, for example, literary assertions about Davidic monarchy and archaeological information that bears no trace of him present contrasting images of Iron Age centralization. Both images are firmly rooted in valid but separate sources. The contrasting images must be allowed to stand in a composite image where David the king and David the non-king can both be seen depending on viewers' perspectives. However, when viewers stand where they can "see" both images, a third image of David the chiefly mediator comes into sight. Hence, adjusting either the archaeological or literary image in order for it to cohere completely with the other is unnecessary and wrong because it distorts the information, reduces the perspectives on Iron Age I, and obscures the "real" composite image that appears beyond the sources. Thus, the relationship between the images makes the hologram interesting and true to life when illuminated.

In this instance, textual and archaeological sources and disciplines formulate images separately. In social world studies which draw eclectically on a number of approaches, the disciplinary studies can also be conceived holographically. But we must insist again that literary and archaeological studies are disciplines in their own right. Their insights and conclusions are independently valid without being integrated by comparative historians. Hence, pre-interdisciplinary, i.e., disciplinary, studies can be understood as the first phase in making historical holograms. Individual disciplinary "masters" are created first and then used in making second-level composite interdisciplinary holograms.

By this we do not deny the appropriateness of comparisons in the first level, disciplinary stage. In fact, disciplines seem anxious to become interdisciplinary although the desire in many instances is more for pushing back rather than stepping beyond disciplinary boundaries. The ventures are often cross-disciplinary more than interdisciplinary. As we shall see, at the disciplinary level of inquiry, literary and archaeological information differ according to the ways that sociocultural phenomena impinge on human subjects and is transmitted by them. Information comes through notions and statements on one hand and through actions on the other. In this sense, interdisciplinary social world studies are charged more directly with integration, illumination, and interpretation than with accumulation of new information. Disciplines have responsibility for collecting information according to analytical models, interpreting the models systemically, and hypothesizing about social processes. Interdisciplinary, i.e., holographic, models are charged with integrating those hypotheses and their information in order to create holistic hypotheses (holograms) about antiquity. Rightly, therefore, interdisciplinary models are derivative and dependent upon the disciplines they use.

Advantages of a Stratified Holographic Model

1. By modeling the separation and integration of sources of information as well as the relationship among the corresponding disciplines, neither literary studies nor archaeology is reduced to an ancillary role.
2. By distinguishing information encoded in antiquity from the comparative sociological information that illumines it, the latter is assigned a clearly heuristic role that prevents it from being confused with ancient biblical and archaeological information.
3. By placing images outside or beyond the sources, literalism is avoided; historical information is distinguished from historical interpretations.
4. Partial or incomplete sources can be used because their images are recognized for what they are and are not confused with definitive comprehensive reconstructions.
5. The boundary line between excavative and non-excavative biblical studies is respected. The difference between texts-as-texts and texts-as-referents-for-events is accepted and included in the research design.
6. The presuppositions of investigators and the bases of their comparisons (illuminations) are made explicit so that they can be weighed and evaluated by others.

7. Multiple "histories" are possible because images depend on the questions and perspectives of investigators.

B. *Anthropological Guides to Social World Studies*

The second major step in the construction of a holographic model is to separate the categories of information used in social world studies and assign each to the disciplines discussed above. In this, we follow the example of social scientists who respond to charges of subjectivity by describing their models' subjects exactly and by making their approaches explicit. They establish analytical cases and identify and describe categories of information. Thus, for purposes of analysis, temporal and spatial boundaries are drawn around subjects, and distinctions within the boundaries are explained. A slice of time and patch of territory, as it were, are lifted out of larger contexts, but with explicit knowledge that investigators are dissecting and compartmentalizing life solely for the purpose of analysis. The goal is not to isolate frozen, motionless segments of humanity, nor to fall back upon space-time systemics. Instead, the intent is to establish analytical models that in turn can lead to systemic models where operating relationships among the parts can be studied (cf. Rappaport, 1979: 52). The analytical models are used to collect data and organize information according to categories; the systemic models examine how the categories relate and interact. It is the latter properly executed that saves the approach from falling motionless onto a Cartesian grid (cf. Flanagan, 1987: 23-24).

The following sections examine the works of several anthropologists. I seek to demonstrate that epistemological problems are not restricted to certain schools or approaches. Cameo-like summaries allow the authors to speak for themselves and readers to judge the validity and usefulness of individual approaches.

Leach's Call for Analytical Clarity

Leach's call for analytical clarity cited earlier introduces many of the distinctions we must explore (cf. Fig. 2, p. 45). The series of dichotomies illustrates the cultural and social phenomena that must be sorted out at different levels.

Ideology : : Behavior
Norms : : Custom
Statements : : Actions
Role : : Individual actors

These distinctions and relationships were discussed in Chapter 1. They are expressed differently by other anthropologists.

Harris' Emic and Etic Domains

Cultural materialist Marvin Harris' dual distinction of emic and etic, and mental and behavioral domains in sociocultural fields of inquiry is one of the fullest, most explicit, and most widely quoted approaches to epistemological problems in anthropological research. Borrowing from linguistics, Harris conceives a strategy that would identify and compensate for an investigator's and subject's sharply differing viewpoints. He refuses to assume that one is objective and the other subjective because such a dichotomy implies true and false views of reality. Right and wrong are for him improper categories.

He proposes an emic/etic distinction. Research in the emic mode "attempts to acquire knowledge of the categories and rules one must know in order to think and act as a native...," while "... etic operations involve the measurement and juxtaposition of activities and events that native informants may find inappropriate or meaningless ... because they are derived from science" (Harris, 1979: 32). We should note that in both approaches the observer remains the investigator, i.e., even in "emic research" it is the investigator who is trying to reconstitute the view of the actor. As a result, the emic view is a description drawn out by the investigator, not actually the view of the native subject.

Harris distinguishes mental and behavioral fields within each domain [Figure 6] (1979: 38).

Figure 6: Harris' Domains within the Sociocultural Field of Inquiry

	Emic	Etic
Behavioral	I	II
Mental	III	IV

The behavioral field represents all the activities that constitute the behavioral stream: body movements, environmental effects of the movements, etc., and is the domain of operations. In Harris' view, the emic behavioral stream can be described without knowing what the actors are thinking. The mental field, on the other hand, is the thoughts and feelings that humans experience in their minds. Establishing this presents greater difficulties for Harris' materialist theory.

Harris further distinguishes the major aspects of society that he groups under three rubrics: infrastructure, structure, and superstructure. In his grid, diagrammed above, these constitute etic behavioral components of sociocultural systems (II). Paralleling them are mental components which he groups together and describes as "mental and emic superstructure" (1979: 54). These are attitudes or statements about behavior which could either be elicited from participants or inferred by the observer.

Several observations apply to our study. First, the grid is useful for identifying discrete analytical domains, especially for separating the emic (actors') views from the etic (observers'), and the emic mental from emic behavioral, i.e., what people think and say they do from what they actually do.

Second, Harris' difficulty in separating etic mental (what observers think) from the emic superstructure (what the actors believe) suggests that analytical categories are not as easily separated as the grid implies. Harris knows this and attempts to answer the charge that all emic mental claims (III) are in fact etic mental (IV), but his answers are not as direct as those he offers on other issues. He leaves readers with knowledge about "what the observer thinks the actor is thinking," but with no criteria for separating the two according to his cultural-material method.

Third, in Harris' strategy speech acts constitute a special category of information with its own problems for bridging the emic-etic gap. Communication is, he says, the very stuff of which mental and emic superstructure is made, so speech cuts across the boundaries dividing his categories and domains (1979: 55). He suggests that the difference between the emic and etic meanings of an utterance is the difference between the conventional meaning (what the observer hears) and the deeper psychological significance the utterance held for native speakers and hearers (what the participants mean) (1979: 43). But in the final analysis, Harris offers little help in solving the emic mental problem. "Clearly anthropologists should use the etic approach to mental life sparingly and should not attempt to override every emic explanation with an etic alternative" (1979: 40). After arguing for the integrity of social scientists and for their ability to correct and refine their views of the emics of actors as evidence is accumulated, he asks, "What is the alternative?" (1979: 45). Applied in biblical interpretation, his complacency reopens the old exegesis/eisegesis dilemma and then leaves it unresolved.

Fourth, the role of informants, the native participants who act as the vital link between the worlds of actors and observers, is significant. Informants live in two worlds and, according to Harris, their statements can be either emic or etic depending on whether they are couched in the natives' categories or those of the observer. Here again Harris leaves investigators to their own devices. He offers no means of determining which framework controls an informant's statements at a given time. The problem, we might observe, is analogous to the hermeneutical question in biblical studies and is addressed in part at least by our hologram model.

Harris' anthropology has influenced biblical studies especially through Gottwald's book on Yahwist tribes (1979). While Harris' critique of idealist strategies that define social and cultural phenomena exclusively from an etic perspective is helpful, his approach leaves little room for the influence ideologies and beliefs exert on the material world. In sum, his distinctions are valid, but it is not immediately apparent how each can be equally useful for solving problems in Davidic history. As Leach observes in other contexts, we need not assume *a priori* that ideological factors—religion being an important one—do not contribute to the shaping of events.

Rappaport's Cognized and Operational Models

Roy A. Rappaport, a systemic ecologist, describes the distinction between an actor's and observer's worldviews as the difference between cognized and operational models that parallel Harris' emic/etic distinction (1979: 97-98; 1984: 337-340). Cognized models are descriptions of peoples' knowledge of their environment and their beliefs concerning it. They are, according to Rappaport, the equivalent of Harris' emic domain. Operational models, the etic equivalent, are descriptions of the same ecological systems but expressed in accordance with the assumptions and methods of the objective sciences (Rappaport, 1979: 97). As with Harris, both exist in the minds of the observers (1984: 338-340). Thus, field anthropologists must record both, keeping several notebooks for describing each separately.

Again the models do not differ in accuracy. In fact both may contain some of the same elements but will rarely be totally identical. For example, notions of a supernatural being may have a place in a cognized model but not in an operational, scientific model. The difference is important for Rappaport because of his notion of culture and because it allows him to include religion—a topic central to his interests—in his descriptions of society while remaining faithful to scientific inquiry.

Cognized models, while not scientific in the modern sense of the word, should be regarded as "parts of populations' distinctive means for maintaining themselves in their environments" (1979: 98). The description is very close to his definition of culture and sets his approach apart from a materialist's:

> *For purposes of ecological formulations*, cultures or their constituents may be regarded as *properties* of populations. In this view, culture is not analogous to animal populations but is, *in part*, analogous to the distinctive means by which populations or other species maintain their environmental relations. It is important to emphasize, however, that to say that a population's means for meeting its needs are cultural is surely *not* to say that cultures are mere instruments in the service of organic phenomena. Far from being merely instrumental, cultures have, as it were, needs and purposes of their own; some are material and some may be at odds with the organic needs of the populations in which they occur. That the cultural properties of human populations can be inimical to their organic properties is as inherent to this view of the relationship between cultural and organic phenomena as is the recognition that aspects of culture are properly regarded as instrumental. Indeed, the contradiction, perhaps inevitable, between the cultural and biological is, in my view, the most important problem of an ecologically aware anthropology (italics his; 1979: 62).

Other approaches, in Rappaport's view, have confused culture with psychological, biological, and inorganic orders of phenomena (1979: 59). Consequently they have used cultures as "referent units" in anthropological formulations. In contrast, he insists that

> ...cultures and ecosystems are not directly commensurable.... An ecosystem is a system of matter and energy transactions....

> Culture is a category of phenomena distinguished from others by its contingency upon symbols. A culture consists of the cultural phenomena distinguishing a particular group or category of people from others (1979: 59-60).

The task of sound analysis, Rappaport says, is to integrate cognized and operational models in order to describe the effects that behavior acted out according to cognized models has on the ecology represented in the operational model. The components are similar to those confronting biblical historians [Figure 7]. The integration makes it possible to assess adoptiveness of behavior and even of the ideology that informs the behavior.

Figure 7: Rappaport's Cognized and Operational Models

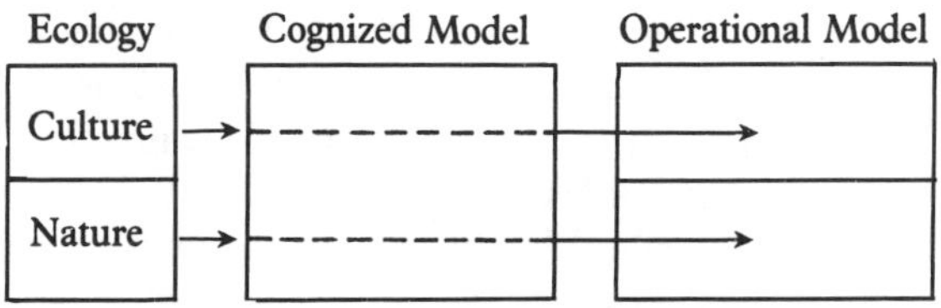

Rappaport's plan retains the emic/etic distinction, but forgoes the difference between behavioral and mental in favor of ecology/nature and culture. The change does not affect an ecologist's work as much as it might others', especially those who apply the categories to projects that are not strictly ecological. One reason is the relationship between a model and its real life setting in Rappaport's analysis. When he describes his models' content as they apply to a specific society, the content falls out according to a nature/culture distinction, it would seem, along lines similar to, but also different from, Harris's behavioral/mental categories (cf. Fig. 6). When investigators examine the ecology and ecosystems—that might be crudely described as the physical environment and all the organisms, including human, acting upon it—the actors' notions and their settings emerge. But, according to Rappaport, the representations in cognized models are what regulate an ecosystem, rather than vice versa as a cultural materialist would hold (1979: 116).

Although Rappaport does not state the matter in precisely these terms, his culture/nature distinction appears to be part of the operational model and not part of the cognized model. This does not come as a surprise. The difference between modern and alien worldviews is in fact part of the problem anthropology and history are designed to address. That many peoples fail to divide their worlds according to the categories used in Western scholarship hardly requires explanation. Such peoples customarily relate to their world in a closer, more integral, and personal way that does not acknowledge social scientists' separate, isolated compartments of life. This does not necessarily imply that they are more sensitive to ecological limits, but it offers one reason for distinguishing the cognized from the operational model. The distinction is an analytical tool for recognizing alien worldviews, for assigning our own categories, and reciprocally for identifying the seams and divisions among our categories that prevent us from seeing the world as others see and experience theirs.

The commonplace religion/politics dialectic illustrates the difference. Investigators of primitive and pre-industrialized societies insist that theocratic societies do not distinguish the domains according to categories embedded in our Western industrialized worldview. When we sort religious from political phenomena in primitive societies, we impose our analytical distinction on the subjects. Noting this is another way of recognizing the need for operational and cognized models.

Rappaport's Use of Systemic Models and Ritual

While tight and accurate descriptions and taxonomies of other societies, their viewpoints, beliefs, and cultures are essential for social and historical analysis, they are only a first step toward understanding another era or culture or the processes in them. The summaries indicate that others do not see things as modern scholars do, and that what they treat as a single phenomenon includes what analysts assign to several domains. But we also need a way to grasp how the domains relate, integrate, and interact. In short, analysts would like to understand how cultures and ecosystems function together. Not to know is to remain ignorant of the peoples they set out to understand in the first place.

In answer, Rappaport offers systemic models to explain his analytical models. For systemic models, he turns to ritual, "the prescribed performance of conventionalized acts manifestly directed toward the involvement of nonempirical or supernatural agencies in the affairs of the actors" (1979: 28), and "a form or structure. . .[which is] the performance of more or less invariant sequences of formal acts and utterances not encoded by the performers" (1979: 175). His discussions of rituals' role do not lend themselves to easy summary:

> Ritual among the Tsembaga and other Maring, in short, operates as both transducer, 'translating' changes in the state of one subsystem, and homeostat, maintaining a number of variables which in sum comprise the total system within the ranges of viability....
>
> Religious rituals and the supernatural orders toward which they are directed cannot be assumed *a priori* to be mere epiphenomena. Ritual may, and doubtless frequently does, do nothing more than validate and intensify the relationships which integrate the social unit, or symbolize the relationships which bind the social unit to its environment. But the interpretation of such presumably *sapiens*-specific phenomena as religious ritual within a framework which will also accommodate the behavior of other species shows, I think, that religious ritual may do more.... Indeed, it would not be improper to refer to the Tsembaga and the other entities with which they share their territory as a 'ritually regulated ecosystem,' and to the Tsembaga and their human neighbors as a 'ritually regulated population (Rappaport, 1979: 41).

Rappaport moves beyond ethnography to generalize about ritual. For him, "ritual is not simply an alternative way to express certain things, but [it is apparent] that certain things can be expressed only in ritual.... I take ritual to be *the* basic social act" (1979: 174). Ritual is 1) formal, 2) performance, and 3) an efficacious mode of communication (1979: 178-179). Its messages are indexical and canonical, i.e., both immediate and enduring. The indexical message communicates the current status of participants while the canonical expresses the regularity, propriety, and durability in words and acts spoken or performed before. The two sorts of information are mutually dependent because rituals transmit an indexical message that cannot be transmitted in any other way, and canonical messages are without force and sense unless accompanied by indexical messages (1979: 182).

Religious conceptions are logical entailments of the ritual form according to Rappaport (1984: 410), and using concepts from cybernetics, he links them to societies' adaptive processes (1979: 145-172). The association allows him to relate synchronic and diachronic aspects in a society's evolution and to include notions of sanctity and the sacred. Thus, the ecosystem and culture—including its religious aspects—are recognized as a functional and evolutionary entity.

We shall return to Rappaport's treatment of ritual later, but these brief remarks indicate ritual's significance for analyzing social structures and changes, for relating persons' notions with their actions, and for sensing ideological shifts in times of upheaval. Rituals encode the meanings that are at work in a society and express and mediate their transformations. Rituals are regulators rather than the regulated:

> The ritual cycle is a sacred structure within which productive and reproductive activities (ecological, biological, and social) proceed, and in terms of which social, political, and ecological relations are defined and given meaning (1984: 410).

Holy's and Stuchlik's Actions and Notions

Ladislav Holy and the late Milan Stuchlik take up the same methodological and epistemological problems, but shift the emphasis toward 1) the ontological status of the phenomena studied, 2) the relationship between a society's norms and an individual's conduct, and 3) the continual process of group formation, realignment, and dissolution (1981; 1983). Each is examined within two frameworks: the folk model and an action/notion dialectic similar to the behavioral/mental dichotomy suggested by Harris.

Like others, they complain that by discarding folk models as poor or false, scholarly explanations often substitute anthropologists' (i.e., derived) models without weighing their dubious validity. The problem, according to them, stems from a failure to distinguish the categories of information in a folk model and an unwillingness to consider the relationship between the categories as always problematical.

Echoing the concerns of Leach, Harris, and Rappaport, the fundamental issue for them is the confusion and uncertainty about the ontological and epistemological status of phenomena studied by anthropologists. The phenomena actually constitute two qualitatively different kinds of data, namely, things that exist "on the ground" and things that exist "in people's heads." The former are observable; the latter unobservable. The former constitute the domain of action and are identified with social structure; the latter belong to the domain of notions and are assigned to an ideational system, i.e., a culture (1981:

4). They differ not in the degree of "facticity," but in the mode of the domains' existence and the quality of their manifestation in social life (1983: 21). Therefore, data from both cannot be perceived as a unitary concept, but must be discriminated according to the kind of phenomenon referred to and modeled in the data.

Ontological Distinctions

"on the ground"	: :	"in people's heads"
actions	: :	notions
observable	: :	unobservable
social structure	: :	culture (ideational system)

An example of the confusion illustrates its practical consequences. Some anthropologists hold that segmentary lineage systems are sets of notions, ideas, or myths in participants' minds and therefore cultural. Others claim that, in addition to being notions, they are patterns of social processes and ways that social members organize their activities in the domain of actions and so pertain to social structure. The impasse is caused, according to Holy and Stuchlik, by representing social reality as a unified system consisting of undifferentiated notions and actions (1983: 14).

They propose to solve the problem not only by distinguishing notions from actions but also by stressing the problematical relationship between them. Regardless of the apparent compatibility of actions and notions, their relationship is always problematic and the object of investigation. They admit that they are speaking of analytical distinctions only, and that in practice notions and actions overlap and cannot be fully separated. The most one can do in research, they claim, is to assign priority to one or the other domain according to the circumstances uncovered during the investigations. It is this difference that biblical historians have neglected to their own regret.

The domains of notions and of actions are parts of a folk rather than derived model. The domain of notions is "a separate, self-contained and self-explanatory world of strictly 'cultural' phenomena unrelated to anything else" (1983: 22). The "meaning" of this domain, as with Rappaport's cognized models, concerns the "modes through which people make sense in and of their worlds" (1983: 24). Arguing against the view that culture determines meaning, the authors insist that a symbol's meaning is ascribed to it by actors. Diversity demonstrates the point. The same symbol can have different meanings for different people or at different times. Such differences become obvious in periods of rapid, profound cultural change when differences emerge among peoples sharing a single culture (1983: 30). This is one reason why anthropologists must recognize the provisional nature of their concepts and be willing to abandon their definitions in the course of analysis (1983: 33).

In some ways actions pose the greater epistemological problem because they cannot be examined in isolation from notions. Unlike Harris, Holy and Stuchlik refuse to separate the domains because doing so would mean surrendering to tiring descriptions of physical movements. For them the difference between a movement and an action is the presence of notions. So ethnocentrism plagues the study of actions when anthropologists erroneously assume that actions form objective reality and wrongly believe actions can be explained more objectively by researchers' notions than by actors'.

At first glance, linking notions and actions in this way seems to contradict Holy's and Stuchlik's own warning against translating the relations and structures of one domain into the other directly, as if the relationship were unproblematical. If researchers must assume that actions mean what the actors say they do, there is little reason to fuss about the distinctions. The anthropologists argue, however, that the matters are sorted out at the time of analysis and explanation when researchers decide whether the actors' notions are true or false (1983: 37). Then the domain of an actor's notions must be given the same status as the anthropologist's explanatory model and judged accordingly.

The point need not delay us, but—if this is a fair rendition of their views—Holy and Stuchlik seem to be stymied by the same problem confronting Harris' emic mental category. How do investigators render objective judgments about their subjects' notions?

Holy and Stuchlik move the discussion beyond individually held notions and actions to collectivities of people. As members of a group, inhabitants of a social world share two types of knowledge that relate differently to the domains of notions and actions [Figure 8]. First, members share knowledge of the state of affairs, i.e., of what people do and why they do it, and second, knowledge of what to do and how to do it. In other words, they share theoretical and practical knowledge, or in Holy's and Stuchlik's terms, representational and operational models (1983: 51).

Figure 8: Holy's and Stuchlick's Domains of Notions and Actions and their Folk and Investigators' Models

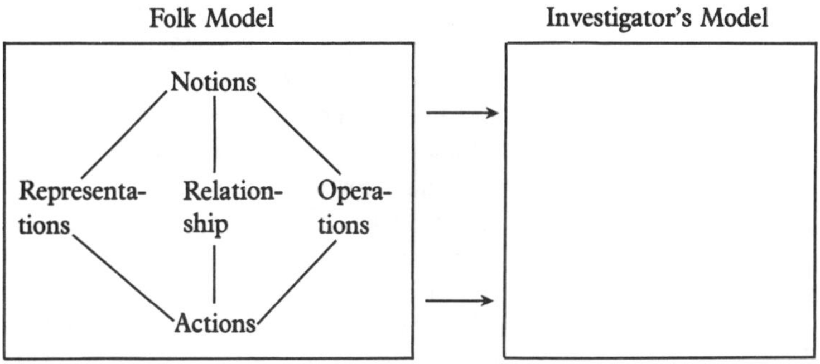

The distinctions are important—as with Harris' mental and behavioral domains—because peoples' notions of their totality, their ties, and what is expected of them, i.e., their "formal structure," often have little to do with actual interaction, i.e., with "social organization," where different relationships emerge.

When studying social processes, Holy and Stuchlik propose, investigators observe that an actor's notions—an individual's knowledge—are constantly being restructured. This shifts interest away from individual knowledge toward the structures of knowledge made public by the people who hold it (1983: 44). No two persons' knowledge is identical, and knowledge is not held equally by all members of society. Instead, possession is related to social position, first because the type and quality of knowledge depends on a person's access to its sources, and second because social position must be corroborated and may be manipulated by displaying certain types of knowledge. Shared knowledge—"knowledge of society"—is held collectively by members who share notions and the principles for organizing them (1983: 49). It forms a continuous chain of shared, overlapping bits of information held in models.

But this does not mean that society or our view of it is necessarily shattered into useless bits of individuality. Researchers are not interested in private notions as private, but in public notions, i.e., in the role that privately held notions play in the process of social life. Likewise, because verbal statements can be distinguished from actions, both can be used as sources of information about notions. Thus, although representational models should be viewed as social or cultural theories that are never fully expressed because only the parts relevant to a specific situation are stated by individuals at any one time, full models can be constructed from observed actions and isolated statements made in various situations (1983: 56). In short, the observer can infer the general model from personal observations and from actors' statements. Here, I propose, is where biblical historians of Iron Age I stand in reference to information from the past. As with holograms, the whole is reconstituted from a part.

Holy and Stuchlik maintain that representational models play an important generative role in processes of interaction, especially in situations such as newly emerging states where individuals have to manipulate several separate models simultaneously (1983: 100). Again the authors return to their lineage example. They observe that segmentary lineage structure is not a model that actors use in actual political processes, but an ideology or representation of an enduring form of their society. They reject Salzman's claim that a segmentary lineage is "a social structure in reserve," a framework for when territorial interests are temporarily suspended (1983: 102; Salzman, 1978a; 1978b: 626). Instead, they prefer the view that lineage ideologies are flexible. Lineages assume invariance and uniformity in the constitution and relations of different units, but allow internal differentiation, cohesion, and development according to circumstances, and they tolerate rationalizing of departures as consistent with the system (1983: 103; Smith, 1956: 65-66).

> By ideologically defining any political action as if segments in balanced opposition, and not as an affair of particular individuals, the notion of the segmentary lineage structure allows for the emergence of men entrusted with considerable authority and wielding great political power. As long as political leadership remains personal and does not become institutionalized into an office, it can be accounted for within the given ideology, and the ideological dictum of egalitarianism can be upheld in spite of considerable political inequality on the ground (Holy and Stuchlik, 1983: 103).

The issue is controversial and need not be decided here, but we should note what is at stake for us. Restated, the questions would be: do genealogies reflect what happens or what people think, hope, or want others to think happens in circumstances where inheritance and succession are at issue? For example, do the genealogies of David's family that in contrast to Saul's show movement toward centralization also convey resistance to the process? Are they both transducers and homeostats as Rappaport suggests for rituals? In any case, representational models are more general than operational models and, when disturbed by opposing normative rules, can come into conflict either with other representational models or with operational models. In such situations, Holy and Stuchlik assert, behavior which is congruent with societies' norms does not need to be legitimized. Incongruence does. In those instances, behavior at odds with societies' norms is made meaningful by invoking a shared representational model such as a genealogy (1983: 105).

Holy and Stuchlik illustrate the point by citing a dispute over succession to tribal headship (1983: 105-106). When succession fell to one whom some considered outside the legitimate line, the representational model, in this case a lineage, was invoked by portraying the individual as being part of a legitimate lineage. The effort succeeded in demonstrating that the successor was actually legitimate by linking the specific normative rules used in a concrete situation to the transcendant values and notions of the society. In other words, the operational model that was outside the norm was interpreted as fully consistent with the ideology in the representational model. As suggested above, the case should be recalled when we examine the tensions that accompany centralizing the government in ancient Israel where we shall see conflict between several representational models and between them and operational models.

Because actions can be observed and verbal statements about them heard, operational models can sometimes be more readily known than representational models. It must be remembered, however, that statements are also actions and are usually made for a purpose. As a result, they must be examined both for their content and for their purpose. Purposeful statements remain useful for knowing the broader representational model because they connect statements made in varied situations and expose the "logic in use" within a society (1983: 58).

But identifying an operational model can also be problematical. In most situations, interactions are complex and actors seldom occupy only one social identity at a time. Thus, "appropriate action is defined by combining the role entailments of the component social identities" that must be determined on a case by case basis (1983: 69).

Holy and Stuchlik go on to question the common definition of "group."

> [Ordinarily] . . . the concept of 'group' is seized upon in many analyses assuming a congruence between actors' representational models and their interactions . . . [and] usually refers to a plurality of individuals bounded by some principle(s) of recruitment and by a set of membership rights and obligations (1983: 111).

Against this, they again demand that a distinction be made between the domain of social processes and the domain of actors' notions. They want to focus on social life in the making, life as a process not as a form. Reminiscent of Leach, their agenda calls for seeing people as individuals rather than as fulfillers of statuses.

Citing examples of warfare in a stateless society, they argue that the makeup of warring contingents always varies according to proximity of relationships and other factors, so that a fighting group cannot be described in terms of other groups, whether a local or kinship group. As with others (cf. Verdon, 1980; 1981; 1982), Holy's and Stuchlik's groups are purposeful, goal-oriented collections. They are differentiated from categories. Categories engage in no activities. Who does what with whom in groups becomes important. Thus, the idea of permanent discrete groups is at the notional level and is a model that the members or anthropologists or both have of a society. Only as an analytical concept, can a "group" be defined in terms of the ideology of membership (1983: 113).

> . . . no actual task group, i.e., two or more people engaged in a concrete set of interactions, can safely be assumed to be homologous with any 'permanent' or enduring groups which we, as observers, define as component units of the society; neither can it be assumed that individuals enter such task groups strictly in function of their membership of those component units. This situation does not change even when the permanent groups are conceived of as such by the actors themselves, as well as by the observer (1983: 115).

By describing groups in singular, purpose-oriented terms, Holy and Stuchlik again raise methodological questions that they answer by appealing to their distinctions between domains. They assume that the relationship between behaving individuals and the structures of society is not intrinsic and therefore is problematical. The existential status of the two domains and the specific relationship between them demand study in each case. A "social world" is not composed of "things" but is a set of intersubjectively shared notions (1983: 116).

Before proceeding we should observe that the emphasis Holy and Stuchlik place on the processes of group formation and deformation is consonant with Rappaport's interest in ritual. The perpetual regroupings, at least the major ones, that occur in society can be expected to be mediated by rituals. It is Leach, however, who recognizes rituals' usefulness for interpreting biblical texts. While he seems to avoid claims about their relationship to historical events, he feels that the synchrony in texts, the reversals, the sense of *communitas*, and the self-contradictions contained in them parallel the patterns in Victor Turner's rites of passage (Leach, 1982: 24; 1983b: 97-109).

Turner's Ritual Processes and Social Dramas

The agreement among different schools of anthropological thought regarding rituals' importance for understanding the relationship between the domains of notions and actions leads directly to the processual anthropology of the late Victor Turner (V. Turner, 1957: xvii-xviii, 91-94; 1974: 32-45; 1977; 1985a [1969]; 1985b). Under certain conditions, Turner labeled the phenomena "social dramas," the concept and term adopted here to describe life in Iron Age I.

While working in Zambia, Turner observed disturbances in Ndembu village life where individuals, parties, or entire groups were in apparently ceaseless conflict with other individuals, factions, or communities. As he became convinced that the tensions related to the paradigm shifts societies undergo periodically, he sought a measure and a metaphor that would enable him to gauge and describe the transformations he was witnessing. For the former, he settled on censuses and genealogies. Through them he could detect actual realignments among contesting parties and could document the social changes in a way that offered him controls over his interpretations. For the latter, the concept of "social drama" provided the key.

> Through the social drama one can sometimes look beneath the surface of social regularities into the hidden contradictions and conflicts in the social system. The kinds of redressive mechanism deployed to handle conflict, the pattern of factional struggle, and the sources of initiative to end crisis, which are all clearly manifest in the social drama, provide valuable clues to the character of the social system (1957: xvii).

It remained for Turner to test his analytical tool on the interdependencies in a variety of cultures including literate historical societies. There the patterns observed in real life among the Ndembu would have to be recreated from history, art, literature, ritual formulas, and other types of information that distanced observers from subjects.

Works on ritual and pilgrimage continued to refine a method of processual analysis that included the relationships among ritual, symbol, and paradigm, as well as social drama (1974; 1977; V. and E. Turner, 1978). The influence of theoretical formulations found in Arnold van Gennep's 1909 *Les rites du passage* was evident from the beginning (van Gennep, 1960 [1909]). The French folklorist recognized that ritual "epitomizes" the movements and transitions in status encountered in society. Human life is filled with experiences of passing from one territory to another, between statuses, even from one age group to the next. Profound feelings accompany transitions such as birth, puberty, marriage, and death. Van Gennep discovered that rites of passage frequently accompany these periods of life-crisis.

The rites that symbolize and mediate transformations have three phases, each with its own rituals. The first is the rite of separation whereby individuals first move from an original aggregated position or condition in which structures and relationships are known and defined. The separation gives way to a liminal, marginal condition where persons feel that they are on a threshold of space and time between former and future worlds. The final phase follows and includes a rite of reaggregation whereby new statuses are achieved and roles are again defined and stabilized. In a sense this move is back into the secular sphere from the state of religious suspension experienced during the passage. For van Gennep, the transitions' liminal stage—the phase of marginality between periods of established status—is crucially important for the "process of regenerative renewal" (cf. V. Turner, 1977: 66-67).

According to Turner, culture is processual. It is a flux and flow that assigns meaning to the natural world in which it resides. Meaning can be assigned in many ways including speech, ceremony, and ritual and "is often stored in symbols which become indexical counters in subsequent situational contexts" (1977: 63). Turner therefore described "processual analysis" or "processual symbolic analysis," as it has come to be called, as,

> ... the interpretation of symbols operating as dynamic systems of signifiers (the outward forms), their meanings, and changing modes of signification, in the context of temporal sociocultural processes (V. and E. Turner, 1978: 243).

In other words, processual analysis is a study of fluid and indeterminate processual units and what appear to be regularized situations and temporal structures by looking at them through the symbols that store their meaning (1974: 42).

When using processual analysis Turner did not displace or deny other forms of cultural investigation such as structural-functional analysis. Instead he emphasized the dynamics of change within social structures. Here "structure" assumes the meaning found in British rather than French anthropology, referring to social rather than cognitive phenomena. Therefore, social structures are,

> ... the patterned arrangements of role sets, status sets, and status sequences consciously recognized and regularly operative in a given society and closely bound up with legal and political norms and sanctions (V. and E. Turner, 1978: 252).

Thus, processual analysis focuses on the dynamics of social morphology or, stated otherwise, it examines the dramas accompanying fundamental social change.

Such changes include shifts in paradigms, especially root paradigms. The first are sets of socially sanctioned rules that generate sequences of social action and, as is often more important, specify what actions must be excluded. For Turner, they exist as "cultural models in the heads of the main actors." Here it is important to note that Turner accepted the cognitive quality of paradigms but denied it to social structures. This distinction, one that we have seen before, is important for understanding the function of rituals.

Root paradigms go beyond social relationships to include outlooks, patterns of belief, and goals of humankind that inform the relationships. This is true even when only the relationships are consciously grasped. Therefore, root paradigms are cultural models existing in the minds of the actors, but also they "reach down to the irreducible life stances of individuals," emerge in life crises, and are held as axiomatic, matters of life and death (1974: 64; V. and E. Turner, 1978: 249). As an example, Turner cited the Christian death-resurrection paradigm so important for a number of historical figures. In many cases it is so alien to other paradigms that the conflict leads to martyrdom. In episodes of such extraordinary tension, the dramatic quality of daily life is easily recognized.

It is in this metaphorical sense that Turner introduced the notion of social drama. The dramas are aharmonic or disharmonic units of social life arising in times of conflict. They are contrasted with social enterprises, the harmonic processual units. Together the two represent sequences of social events that have structure even though it may not be recognized by the participants at the time of the events. Social dramas and rites of passage are closely related because the latter often occur within the former [Figure 9].

Typically, social dramas have four phases: 1) breach, 2) crisis, 3) redressive actions, and 4) reintegration. Here again the influence of van Gennep's tripartite scheme is apparent (V. Turner, 1974: 38 42).

Breaches between individuals or groups in the same social system occur when by dissidence or deliberate non-fulfillment one party publicly disregards a crucial norm held by the other or previously held by both. Because the disruptive deed is performed by an individual acting altruistically as a representative of a group, whether the group knows it or not, the act is not criminal. Still, the action serves as a "symbolic trigger" which sets the social drama in motion.

A phase of mounting crisis follows. Then the wound is either treated and confined to a small portion of society or it will spread to "world-wide" proportions. If allowed to escalate, secondary crises are apt to be provoked, causing lasting cleavages in social relations. Crises are liminal times when the future of the society as it has existed hangs in the balance.

Redressive action follows as the offended party attempts to limit the crisis. Formal and informal mechanisms are brought into play by the leaders or representatives of the aggrieved group. Their measures vary in type and complexity depending on the groups in conflict, the nature of the offense, the severity of the crisis, and other factors. At the time of redress, escalation of the crisis with an accompanying state of liminality can occur again. In fact, the redressive action may be raised from a personal, to local, to a higher level as the defenders of the established paradigm attempt to contain and reverse the conflict. Consequently, at each step, the parties waver between resolution and further revolt. This is an example of the marginality Turner characterized as "betwixt and between." Such escalations

Figure 9: **The Relationship between Social Drama and Ritual Process as Depicted by Victor Turner**

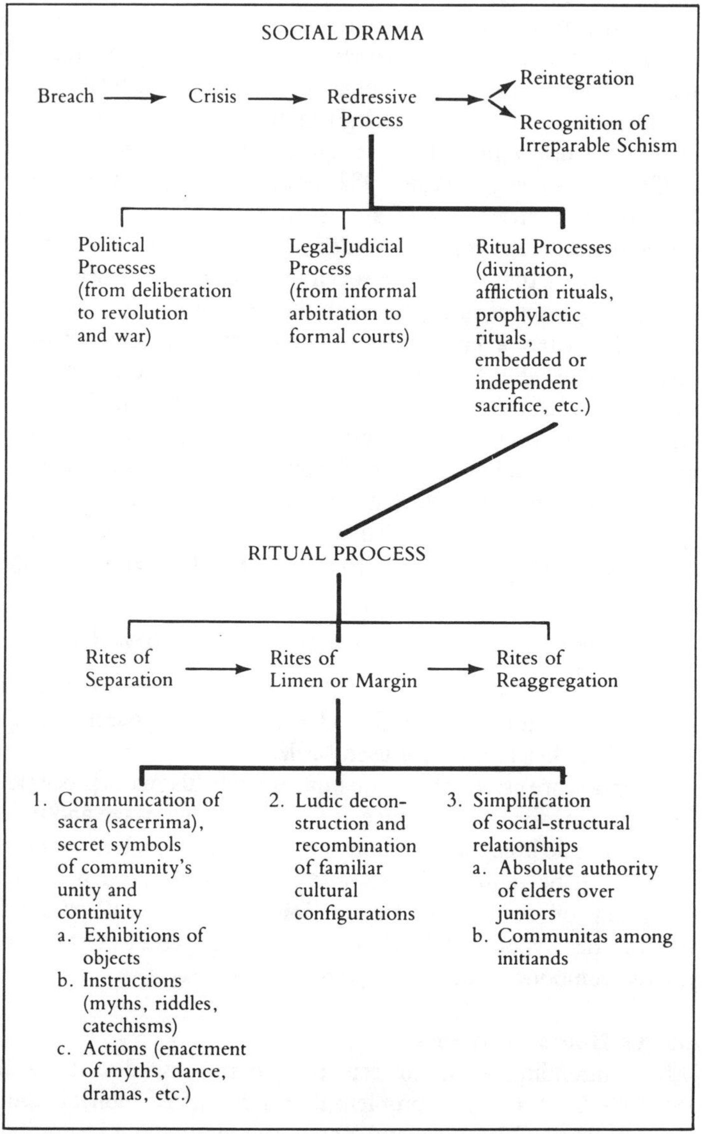

will be important in later discussions of segmented societies (cf. Chapter 5).

Reintegration may entail either rejoining the disturbed social group to the former unit or recognizing the fission and legitimating the irreparable schism. In either case, a new order must be established with new balances of power, new formal relationships, new statuses, and new bases of legitimation.

Turner's work is important for analyzing political processes and the effects of ideology (Augé, 1982: 64). He identified two types of interconnected rites: rites of status elevation and rites of status reversal that together mark and index the sequential and hierarchical transformations that constitute social change. Augé's observation is relevant: "... rites of status reversal intervene at strong moments in public life, when a chief is installed or dies, during periods of interregnum or when terrible scourges threaten a society as a whole" (Augé, 1982: 65). Thus, Turner helped to link symbolism and ideology in a way that rephrases the problem anthropologists confront when studying power. Because symbols teach people to accept their own place, ideology exists in symbolism (Augé, 1982: 65). We shall see later that Turner's interpretation also helps in understanding the tensions and their effects in the early Iron Age.

C. *Holographic Model for Illuminating the Iron Age*

The relationship between holograms and the general distinctions modeled in the anthropological studies is already apparent. Rituals and ritual studies also play a useful role.

Holograms are essentially static images while history is processual. To compensate for the difference, it is helpful to envisage and model a sort of mobile hologram. Rituals serve this purpose, but the bridge to them will be more easily crossed if it is introduced by a brief description of several of David Bohm's theoretical proposals, including his hypothetical holomovements that connect static and dynamic components of reality (1965; 1980).

Bohm's Holomovements

Without intending to do so, scientist Bohm aims directly at the space-time Cartesian-grid problem that has plagued biblical studies since Albright's, Wheeler's, and Kenyon's monumental beginnings.

> In Bohm's view . . . Scientific laws and theories are abstractions and idealizations that hold true only to a certain degree of approximation within limited domains. Scientific progress is not identified with convergence toward some absolute truth, but consists in the proposal of new theories, often based on radically new conceptual frameworks, which reveal the limitations of older theories, suggest new kinds of experiment and establish new criteria of relevance (Curd, 1981: 58).

For Bohm, the irony of scientists trying to understand the wholeness of entities on the basis of their parts is ludicrous. Consequently, he redefines the relationship between wholes and parts according to what he calls implicate and explicate orders and explains them by several analogies (Bohm, 1980: 145-147, 149-150).

In order to illustrate that wholeness is flowing movement Bohm describes an experiment. A drop of insoluble dye is placed in a glycerine fluid encased between two glass cylinders. When one cylinder is rotated slowly, the dye becomes first a streak and then disappears within the liquid. When a second droplet is added and the process continued, the result is repeated.

If the cylinder is rotated the same number of turns in the opposite direction, interestingly, the droplets, first the second and then the first, are reconstituted. This illustrates, according to Bohm, that what initially appears to be a random state of diffusion or mixture is actually a hidden implicit or "implicate" order that endures the rotations. The dye maintains its integrity within the body of fluid even though it appears to be intermixed.

Bohm believes the same kind of order pervades the universe. When that order evolves into a form that can be seen, as with the dye, an implicate order becomes explicate. Thus, for him, implicate and explicate orders are merely different expressions of the same order. Implicate orders are not made up of parts but are orders in which things "enfold" one another. Thus, the unmanifest, implicate orders provide the ground for the manifest, explicate orders we see and identify.

Bohm's second analogy, like our own, is borrowed from holography (cf. Fig. 4, p. 78). He finds photographic analogies for science too limited because of their emphasis on part-to-part relationships. Thinking of science as "photographing" exaggerates the impression that scientists can gain knowledge by acquiring more and more details of information. This deceives researchers into seeking ever more powerful figurative lenses that will allow them to observe ever smaller parts so they can gain ever greater knowledge of the wholeness of a phenomenon.

Bohm wants an analogy that offers insights into wholes the way lens-photography encourages analyses of parts. The technology of holograms and holography serves him by retaining whole images in parts. This offers a basis for arguing that holograms can model the relationship between implicate and explicate orders, i.e., between the fundamental movement and its manifestations.

Bohm expands the imagery by speaking of holomovements, holofluxes, and photographs of movements (Bohm, 1980: 150-157). Again, he turns to wave theory where waves carry enfolded in their implicate orders the various orders that are unfolded in the explicate order. Thus, he argues, the whole movement of the universe carries the implicate order that becomes explicate in the world we see. Even history and events are merely ripples whose meaning depends on what lies below (Weber, 1982: 97).

The partial/totality analogy extends to the relationship between human unconsciousness and consciousness, the latter an explicate manifestation of the former's implicate order (Bohm, 1980: 210). Bohm argues that perception, in his case in science, is comparable to the way relatively invariant features in an environment are abstracted in order to create maps. In memories, as in maps, invariables are picked out and stored until used to condition later perceptions. Thus, for example, cartographers record curves in roads but not variables such as a tree near a corner or a crack in the concrete because these are apt to change and will be of no use for further perceptions. Likewise, when a friend is seen after years of separation, the "face," i.e., the person or map, is recognized first. Only afterward is notice taken of specific variables such as the graying hair, thickened waist, or sagging jowls. If we fail to recognize a person we know, Bohm argues, it is not because the individual is an illusion or on account of some other thing "out there." It is because of problems with the relationship between the old map stored in memory and the present appearance of the person. The relationship to the wholeness, not only to individual parts, has been lost.

In the social sphere, rituals incorporate many of the relationships Bohm attempts to make explicit in scientific perceptions of physical realities. As primary social acts, as metaphors for fundamental social change, and as regulators—transducers and homeostats—of human relations, rituals contain and manifest underlying, enfolded representations, structures, and processes. These unfold and become visible in social actions, but especially in the primary acts. Because rituals stand at, encode, reveal, and effect intersections of canonical (traditional) and indexical (current) social indicators, they are the intersections of diachronic and synchronic components in societies. Status reversals and elevations (synchronic relations) and social change (diachronic relations) intersect as well as relationships between beliefs and actions. Terence Turner insists correctly that there is a reciprocal as well as iconic concurrence between social contexts and ritual situations. Ritual behavior constitutes a "controllable, unambiguous, orderly pattern of action" that is an effective mechanism for "reordering the uncontrollable, ambiguous, or otherwise dangerous aspects of a situation" (T. Turner, 1977: 60). Rituals constitute microcosms of macrocosmic processes of change and homeostasis and therefore are parts that bear wholes. They are both implicate forms of explicate orders and explicate forms of implicate orders because they encapsulate as well as expose structures and processes in societies.

In our model, holomovements and rituals (and ritual studies) at once belong to the illuminating phases of holography. Rituals, however, as referents also play a peculiar role in the encoding process of our holograms by offering both the setting and the mechanism that incorporate representations and operations (to use Holy's and Stuchlik's categories) and produce ancient texts (and to a lesser degree the ancient tells). Later we shall see that V. Turner demonstrates that the rituals within social dramas are the settings in which texts are produced (V. Turner, 1980). The texts, therefore, encode the tensions, liminalities, and dramas present in the social world. As illuminators, though, as in Rappaport's systemic models, rituals also expose processes imbedded (implicate) in the static information encoded (explicate) in texts and recovered (made re-explicate) during research. Like the classical David, they are microcosms of life, but are holomovements where he is the hologram. Both are maps imbedded in the religious consciousness of the ancient Yahwists and the subconsciousness of their traditions.

Our models and metaphors, both for a social world approach and for the world approached, cannot overcome all epistemological problems and doubts. Scientific uncertainty and discovery (Ziman, 1978: 185), inferring analogically (Wylie, 1985: 107), and modeling

(Harré, 1972; Bunge, 1964) all suggest that historians, like others, must live with questions and not be unduly constrained by hypotheses, methods, and interpretations. Imagination, intuition, empathy, and chance, as Ziman demands for scientists, must be given some rein. The approach, analogies, and metaphors, therefore, can only channel research energies toward critical problems and offer suggestive approximations for historical realities. Certainty, if it comes, will reside not in the models but in the viewers who may enjoy passing confidence gained from consensibility and consensuality, i.e., agreement and acceptance (cf. Ziman, 1968: 28).

Our approach has roots in the studies cited thus far, and it selects language and imagery from them. But it does not jerrybuild random pieces of earlier approaches. That would go beyond tolerable eclecticism to insensitivity for the seriously argued nuances in the studies. Instead, our debt is principally for the studies' explicating of problems faced in social world studies and for their analytical distinctions that help in surmounting those problems.

Drawing the Analogies

Social world studies and their distinctions act like beam splitters in holography. Domains are separated so that they can be clarified and eventually reintegrated according to other relationships. In turn, the new relations can be illumined in order to see different holistic images. The split beam is the social world of the David/Iron Age. Its representations are separated from its operations, its notions from its actions. Correspondingly, its literary information is separated ontologically from its archaeological remains. The relationships between each pair, as in their reintegration, are analogous to relationships in better- or otherwise known societies. Life in the world of the actors is always distinguished from the impressions of it in the minds of investigators. The latters' images of the former are holograms and holomovements, i.e., reasonable images of the life investigators would see if they were seeing the real life. The images are whole and explicate orders reconstituted from the partial information, the implicate orders preserved in texts and tells that are made explicate by comparisons. [Figure 10]

The diagram elucidates distinctions within the ancient world and sources of ancient information. It identifies the illuminating light that comparative sociology throws on the relationships between the domains and the feedback loop connecting images in antiquity to

Figure 10: Relationships in Social World Studies

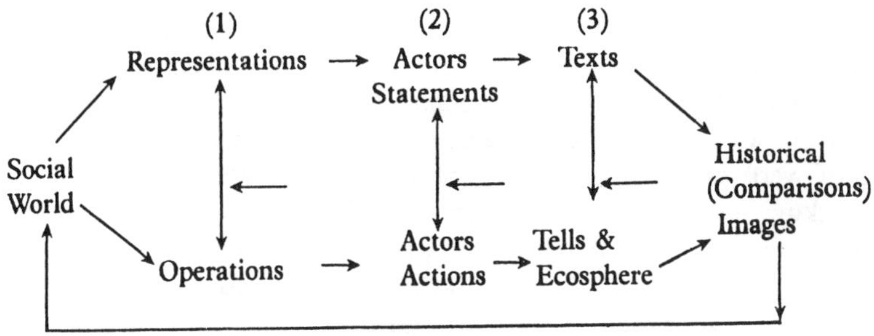

those derived from antiquity. The loop recalls the need for emic/etic, operational/cognized, or actors/observers distinctions.

Adding a fourth rank and distributing the others along the path of research locates the representations/operations in the ancient social world, moves the ancient sources to the position of mediators or informants, and attaches and assigns responsibilities to the principal disciplines used in analyzing ancient information. It again distinguishes and reconnects actors' and investigators' models [Figure 11].

Figure 11: Model for a Social World Studies Research Design

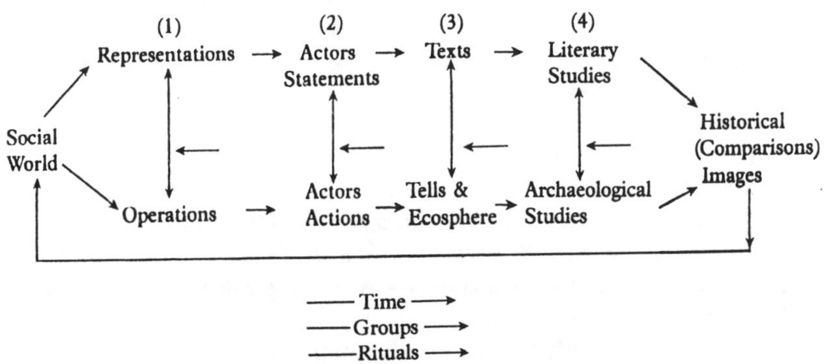

In these models, textual/literary studies are primarily responsible for ancient information from the domain of notions and archaeology is responsible for the physical, material world (Rappaport's nature) and the domain of actions. Comparative sociology—where comparable relationships can be viewed—illuminates relationships between domains and within the worlds behind them. The division of labor is obvious. Literature reflects the notions and ideas, what people in the past were thinking and saying or what others claimed they were thinking and saying. These claims and the way that oral traditions and texts are transmitted are appropriately examined within the field of literary studies. Archaeology customarily exposes and examines material information as well as human actions on the physical environment. Comparative sociology illuminates relationships between the two domains that several of our authors warn are always problematical. Representations and operational models in the social world encoded in the sources are therefore exposed by the illumination.

Several cautionary notes are in order. First, the continual social ebb and flow demanded by operational definitions of groups may not always be detectable in remote historical societies. This is one of the handicaps imposed by distance, the passage of time, the dominance of elites, and other factors that militate against the kind of day by day, issue by issue information investigators would need in order to detect every operation and hence every group. The hindrances dictate the level of detail that can be expected in an investigation. General, large-scale, long-duration trends—in the Braudelian sense—will be more apparent than those involving fewer people, shorter time, or more limited issues. The social world model includes group formation and deformation as an ongoing process in research, but it does not overcome completely the elitism that has plagued biblical history since the beginning.

Secondly, the boundaries separating the disciplines must not be imposed too rigidly. Here our two-level model assists. On the first disciplinary level where the boundaries are maintained, they are not meant to be barriers that exclude one discipline from another's territory or prohibit conversations across disciplinary lines. On the contrary, information about one type of data can depend on information in another, and the disciplines used in social world studies share some data in common. For example, actions reflect notions; archaeology yields information about notions, ideologies, and symbols; and stories in texts are sometimes set in physical space and time. Hence, wooden, inflexible assignments are not intended.

What then is proposed by the model? That in the first-stage model, phenomena in ancient Near Eastern societies can be separated and sorted *for analytical purposes*, and disciplines' priorities can be identified according to the phenomena, subject matter, and data they focus on most directly. By recognizing this, investigators begin to realign many important issues. For instance, the old worry that makes biblical literature the interpreter of Syro-Palestinian archaeology can be discarded without discarding either the Bible or the archaeology.

Assigning priorities does not prevent a discipline from studying phenomena that for it are secondary. Instead, the disciplinary, pre-interdisciplinary stage and the subsequent interdisciplinary stage structured in our holographic model enable one discipline to defer to the other. Each discipline must be allowed to "do its own thing." For example, literary and archaeological studies must each collect, assemble, analyze, and interpret its own information and offer a plausible explanation of the data as seen from the discipline's perspective. Later such master images can be integrated and reinterpreted when the disciplinary reconstructions are compared and combined in the second-level interdisciplinary stage of investigation. There, the investigators' models, not the actors', will be juggled and reshaped in order to make a plausible replica (a hologram) of the actors' models and world. This is similar to the process recommended by Rappaport, Leach, and others who emphasize that the order of information in final reports depends on the interests and goals of the investigators.

The divisions are also practical. They allow researchers to proceed without compelling them to force their views into a common mold. Biblical/archaeology as a term and concept in this model is recognized as holographic. By identifying it as the integration of two integrating disciplines, historians are absolved of responsibility for making all ancient information coincide and interlock in an artificial, mechanistic spatial-temporal matrix of analysis. Differences between sources are not immediately unsettling because the relationships between the domains (and disciplines) are always considered problematical. Conversely, apparent concatenations and convergences of information deserve as much scrutiny in light of general and particular patterns of social behavior as do instances where circumstances initially appear contradictory. Every relationship must be examined before it can be assumed to be understood. Furthermore, although an interdisciplinary approach does not impose disciplinary straitjackets, it requires special disciplinary integrity. The consumptive intellectual greed that tempts disciplines to turn themselves into psuedo-interdisciplinary fields is controlled. The difference between a discipline incorporating information from other fields and integrating the disciplines suggested by our distinction between "cross-disciplinary" and "interdisciplinary" is maintained.

A third cautionary note follows from this. The disciplinary interpretations to be integrated are formed in analytical and systemic processes such as Rappaport recommends. Comparative sociology plays a role in disciplinary analysis, but it is subsidiary and ancillary to literary studies and archaeology which individually draw upon comparisons for interpreting their specific kind of data. Thus, the primary role for comparative sociology as a discipline in social world studies is at the second-level interdisciplinary stage where the comparisons illuminate the images of the past generated separately by the other disciplines. In a sense, therefore, the second stage is a second systemic stage where disciplinary systemic models are integrated.

This is another way of calling attention to the distinction between information that comes from ancient Israel and comparative information drawn either from other ancient societies or from modern ethnographies. For biblical historians, the former is data to be interpreted; the latter are heuristic devices aiding interpretation.

Finally, rituals viewed as anthropologists describe them play an important part among peoples and sources that are defined as innately religious. Thus, in the process of model building, rituals have a place at the disciplinary and interdisciplinary stages of research.

II

MAKING A HOLOGRAM OF THE EARLY IRON AGE

Chapter 3

DOMAIN OF ACTIONS: ARCHAEOLOGICAL IMAGES OF THE EARLY IRON AGE

In this chapter, analytical and systemic archaeological models are developed for Iron Age I. In addition to the reasons already cited, they are necessary because, compared with other social sciences, archaeology can recover only partial information about the societies it studies. Models expose, and in a sense compensate for, the scarcity of information by enabling observers to determine both the ecological goal ranges of Iron Age I and the extent of human interaction with ancient ecologies. Following Rappaport, goal ranges are the carrying capacities of an environment, i.e., the range of states that allow a society to continue in existence (Rappaport, 1979: 99). The actual goals a society sets for itself, however, are controlled by reference values. They are cultural and are the values societies prize and organize around. Although goal ranges can be identified scientifically by observers, they may or may not have been known and adhered to by the ancients themselves. When values that are disproportionate to the goal ranges are ignored, societies become maladaptive and self-destructive. Hence, ecological ranges and cultural values are intrinsically linked but must be determined by independent means in order to avoid confusing the one with the other.

Archaeological analytical models serve another purpose by allowing analysts to identify and control levels of information. By measuring and relating differing scales of detail, movements back and forth between inductive and deductive approaches can be regulated. This restrains the usual scholarly tendencies both to generalize on the basis of information from a few ecological niches and to infer local behavior from generalized patterns. Our hologram model compensates for differences of scale by making movements among them explicit and part of the model itself. In the Middle East, where access to information is limited by political circumstances, the need to be explicit about the level and range of data is exceptionally important. To generalize about ancient Israel, for example, on the basis of information drawn exclusively from highland Canaan fosters distorted impressions.

In the description that follows, we move from geological and geographical aspects of Near Eastern ecology (Rappaport's nature) toward social phenomena (his cultural domain). We presume that the domains interact continually in ways that affect all aspects of life.

A. *Geographical Setting*

The eastern end of the Mediterranean has experienced stress at every ecological level and during every epoch of prehistory and history. Today the area continues to be subject to geophysical, societal, and cultural movements that make it a major interface where East, West, North, and South meet to form a single intercontinental zone (cf. Drysdale and Blake, 1985: 12-33).

The territory depicted in the David stories spans approximately 565 km north to south and 120 km west to east, and lies roughly between 20 and 40 degrees north latitude. At least two dozen soil types are scattered over a relief that reaches from heights of +1725 m and +2815 m in Edom and on Mt. Hermon respectively down to -396 m at the northern bank of the Dead Sea. The area is rimmed on the south, west, and north by the coasts and banks of the Gulf of Aqaba, the Mediterranean, and the Euphrates respectively, and on the east and southeast by the sands of the Great Syrian Desert.

The area's long history of social and political turmoil was preceded by geological transformations of even greater proportions. These and later changes have been aptly described by modern geographers, and I draw heavily on their work, especially Fisher's (1978; cf. also Beaumont, Blake, and Wagstaff, 1988; Baly, 1974; 1987; Drysdale and Blake, 1985; Aharoni and Avi-Yonah, 1977; Rogerson, 1985; Orni and Efrat, 1973). My reliance upon their primary investigations and my indebtedness to their syntheses will be apparent as we proceed.

Geomorphology

According to plate-tectonics theory, in Triassic-Jurassic eras approximately 200 million years ago, drifting continental plates coalesced to

Figure 12: Geological Development of the Tethys Sea Embayment

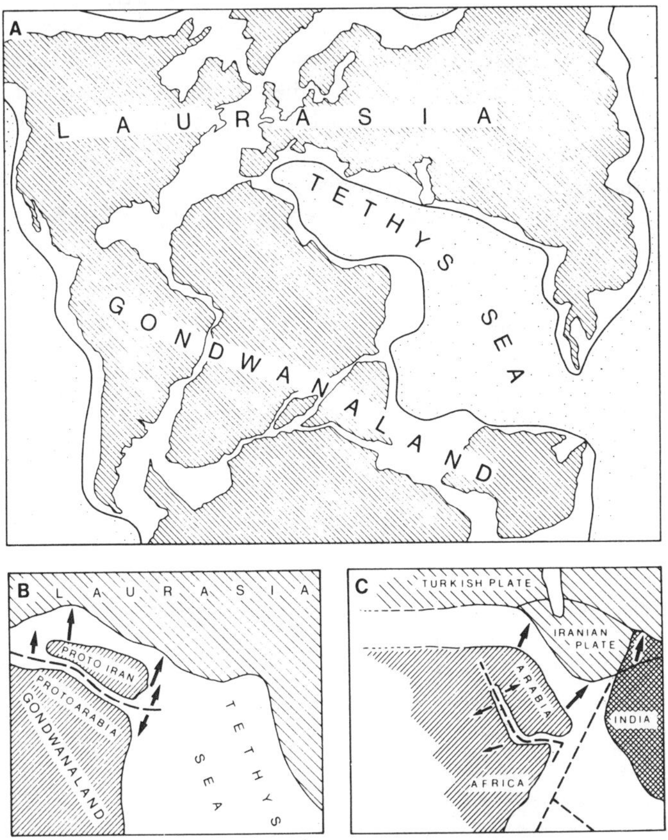

form the world's two major land masses [Figure 12]. A northern (Laurasia) and a southern (Gondwanaland) land lobe rested beside the Tethys Sea, a body of water that filled the modern Mediterranean zone, stretched across the present-day Middle East, and joined the waters of today's Indian Ocean. Most of Europe and Asia originated as parts of the northern lobe, separated by the sea from Africa and Proto-Arabia that were formed from the southern lobe.

Approximately 65 million years ago, the great sea receded, the lobes shifted, and the Arabian plate broke away to move to its present position northeast of Africa. Other smaller land units formed as Iranian, Turkish, and Aegean plates that eventually came to rest between the more massive African and Eurasian plates [Figure 13]. These two land areas formed the bases for separate systems of production and reproduction identified by Goody (1976). According to geomorphologists, the pressures of the Arabian plate impinging on the others caused the relief at the eastern end of the Mediterranean basin, the Zagros mountains in Iran, and the rift system that reaches from the Orontes valley in Syria, through the Biqa valley in Lebanon, the Jordan River valley, the Wadi Arabah, the Red Sea, and the Gulf of Aden.

Figure 13: Formation and Movement of Middle Eastern Tectonic Plates

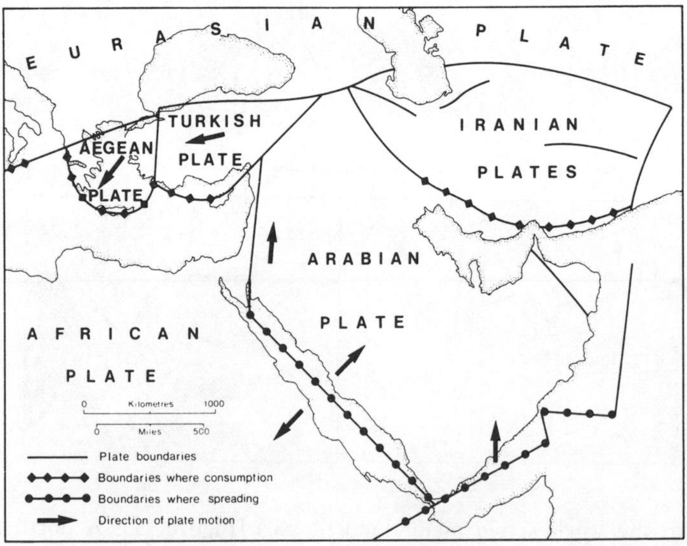

The description suggests that structurally the Middle East is two major zones (Fisher, 1978: 17). One comprises the region's central and southern parts including modern Libya, Egypt, Sudan, and the

Arabian peninsula. These are mainly continental plate areas now divided only by fault structures that were caused by spreading, as in the Red Sea, or colliding, as in the Jordan valley system. The second zone comprises areas where the moving African and Arabian plates produced extreme folding, as in present-day Turkey, Syria, Lebanon,

Figure 14: Geographical Subregions in the Northern Levant

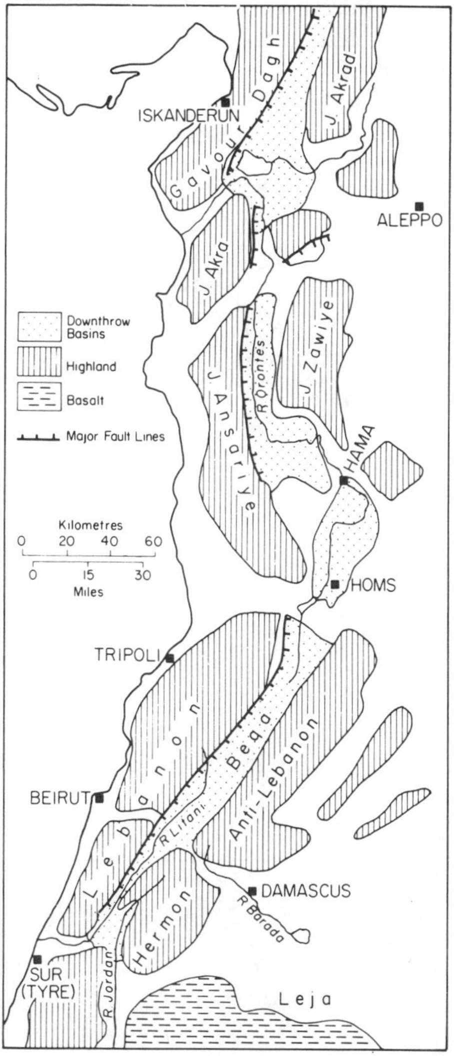

and Israel. Therefore, on this scale, the major zones divide geomorphologically along predominant E-W axes, and the now prominent N-S profiles are consequences of northerly movements by the large E-W oriented land masses [Figures 14 and 15]. The beginnings of the J- or S-shaped border of the Fertile Crescent can be seen in the division that places Syria, Lebanon, and highland Israel in one area and the southern and eastern zones of the Negev, Arabah, and Transjordan in the other.

David's drama as described by most biblical writers was staged primarily in the second, i.e., northern and western, structural zone. Nevertheless, the biblical sources suggest that it also reached into the Negev and into the southern and eastern Transjordan regions of the

Figure 15: Geographical Subregions in the Southern Levant

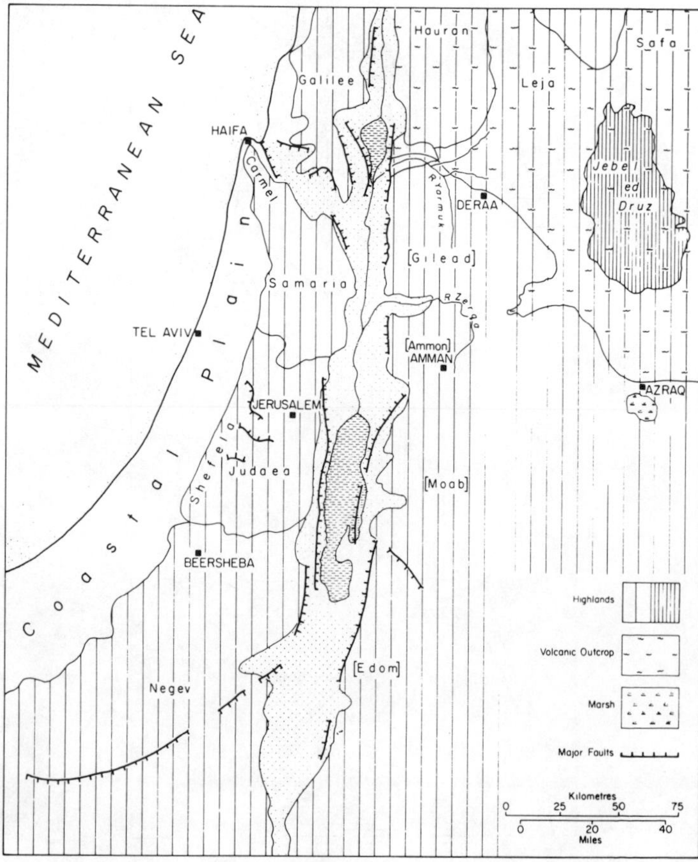

first zone. In fact the stories remember much of the early drama as occurring along and back and forth across the structural boundary. Because of the movements and social weaving David supposedly made across the geomorphological lines, initial attention must be given to both areas as well as to the depressions and fault structures marking the edges of the tectonic plates.

The plate interfaces caused prominent fault and scarp structures on either side of the N-S Jordan valley system and in the numerous minor cross-faults that align at right angles to it. These structures left strikingly different ecological niches within relatively small geographical areas. Many affected migration and production patterns.

Baly (1987: 12) emphasized the complexity of the region when he called attention to two oblique geographical matrices caused by geological depressions forming separate but superimposed lattice patterns on the surface [Figure 23, p. 189]. The N-S axes of the Mediterranean coastline, coastal plains, highlands of Palestine, Jordan valley, and Jordan plateau tend to obscure a second series of NNE-SSW lines that intersect the first obliquely. Nevertheless, the orientation of the Biqa valley between the Lebanon and Anti-Lebanon ranges parallels another line that extends from the Gilead region in Transjordan to the upland region near Beersheba in Cisjordan. Similar depressions that on first glance seem to extend W-E actually run NW-SE to intersect the NNE-SSW axes perpendicularly.

The matrices share several major depressions. Four extend from the coastline, through the rift system, and into the centers of the continental plates. Aquatic and aeolian erosion filled some with sand, like the Wadi Sirhan, and widened others, like the Jezreel valley, until both could be used as routes to the interior eastern steppes. The corridors affected history by facilitating E-W movements back and forth across the structural interstices.

The northernmost corridor extends from the Mediterranean near the mouth of the Orontes river, through the Amuq plain, the Aleppo basin, and the Euphrates valley. This is actually the major fault between the former Eurasian and African land masses and coincidentally marks the northern reaches of territories discussed in the David stories. The second passage is the Tripoli-Homs-Palmyra depression that reaches inland from the coast between the Jebel Ansarieh in Syria and the Lebanon range, through the regions of Homs and Palmyra, to the mountains of Persia. The third, part of the NW-SE matrix, connects the Bay of Acco with Lower Galilee, Lake Tiberias, and the Yarmouk valley in Transjordan. This depression includes part of the plain of Esdraelon and Jezreel valley system that play an especially important role in the agricultural, economic, and military development of the interior during the Iron Age. The southernmost depression extends along a W-E line from the Gaza region on the Mediterranean coast to Beersheba where it turns southeast to cross the base of the Dead Sea before continuing into the Wadi el-Hasa in Transjordan.

Geographical Zones (cf. Appendix I)

Attempts to delineate further the area's geographical zones have ranged from simple outlines of coastal, highland, and interior regions to enumerations of thirty or more separate sub-regions. The differences in scale are caused by the combination of geological and hydrological variety and disunity on the one hand and the region's recognized geographical, climatic, and cultural unity on the other. For our analytical model, a compromise scheme of seven zones that exemplifies the complexities affecting Iron Age history while avoiding meticulous, technical, and detailed descriptions is sufficient [Figure 24, p. 190].

Although the characteristics of each zone are important for our analysis, they are already familiar to most readers. For that reason, only a brief description is provided here with fuller information relegated to Appendix I.

The seven zones are:

Zone 1: Northern Syria from the Mediterranean to the Euphrates, south to the Tripoli-Homs-Palymra depression. The area includes the coastal Mediterranean region, the mountainous Jebel Ansarieh, Jebel Akra, and Gavour Dagh areas, the Orontes valley, the Ghab and Amuq, Jebel Zawiyeh, the fertile northern Syrian plateau, and the eastern desert.

Zone 2: The Lebanon Range, the Anti-Lebanon, the Hauran, Jebel Druze, and Leja. Again, the region extends from the coast to the desert interior and includes mountainous areas, a river valley (Litani), fertile plains, and desert zones. In the southeastern portion is the basalt desert formed by volcanic eruptions.

Zone 3: The uplands of Palestine. Although the area is commonly described as the "highlands of Canaan," it comprises several geomorphological zones including the Shephelah.

Zone 4: The Negev. This southern region in Cisjordan forms a frontier that separates the highlands and coastal areas to the north from the Sinai in the south.

Zone 5: The coastal plain. The zone stretches from Turkey to the southern Gaza strip and varies in width. In Cisjordan, the zone includes areas that are fertile and prosperous, such as the Plain of Sharon, and others that are little more than sand dunes, such as southern Gaza.

Zone 6: The Jordan trough. This zone comprises the Dead Sea region and the Jordan valley. Temperatures are hot, and the borders are lined by rugged clifts and deep wadis.

Zone 7: The eastern plateaus of Transjordan. The fertile areas that receive sufficient rainfall for cultivation give way quickly to the Great Syrian Desert and the Wadi Sirhan whose surfaces range from flat, silty gofs to rugged badland buttes and hills.

Soils

Recent research has shown that the soils result from interaction among complex factors including climate and human activity. Although there is disagreement regarding the processes and nomenclature for types, A, B, and C soil horizons are generally distinguished here and elsewhere. C horizon soils represent parent soils from which A and B horizons derive. The A horizon soils develop when soluble compounds and finely divided insoluble materials are removed by seepage and other erosive processes. B horizons are formed by the materials carried and deposited by those processes. Therefore, A horizons are eluvial soils caused by solubles leaching downward, and B horizons are illuvial soils formed by evaporation.

Middle Eastern soils are also classified broadly according to zones. Typically, true desert soils, arid steppe soils, sub-arid area soils, and sub-humid area soils are differentiated. Although allowance must be made for changes stimulated by human and environmental agents, today's variety is probably similar to that of the Iron Age. The denuding of surface soils in hilly areas by deforestation, grazing, and erosion have affected the composition of soils and societies in the region since antiquity (cf. Rogerson, 1986: 58-63).

Desert soils are found in the eastern reaches of Syria, in Transjordan, the Negev, and on the southern Mediterranean coast. For the most part, the desert has ermolithosol (hard pavement) surfaces rather than dynamic, semi-static, or static ergesol (sand dune) surfaces. Some ermolithosol areas are suitable for cultivation in spite of the sturdy crusts formed by salt efflorescence. Where loess-type soils have been formed by wind deposits of fine sand, silt, clay, and organic matter, and where non-saline water is available, the desert may be cultivated.

Besides the desert zones where seasonal pastoralism and very limited cultivation coexist, the most prominent type of soils are the brown and yellow-brown stoney soils and *terra rossa* soils found in semi-arid and semi-humid areas. The stoney types range from silty clays to clay loams. The latter have a heavy texture with high (50-70%) clay content and high moisture retention that makes them good for agriculture but susceptible to erosion and rapid run-off when heavy rainfalls seal surface pores.

Two additional soil features in the Middle East are hard-pan crusts and infill and bench soils. The former are layers of concrete-like soil on or beneath the surface, varying from a few centimeters to four meters in depth. The pan must be broken up or penetrated before vegetation will grow. The latter, found in hilly topography, are flat patches of arable land surrounded by barren or uncultivatable surfaces. They are often reddish or brown and have relatively high silt, clay, and humus content.

Climate

It is generally assumed that Near Eastern climates have not changed substantially since the early Iron Age. Hence, in the midst of so many factors dividing the area, climate stands as a major unifying force defining the region and contributing to its ways of life (cf. Fisher, 1978: 3). Still, in spite of the broadly integrating pressure it brings to Near Eastern cultural and religious expressions, weather varies significantly from north to south and from the coast to the mountains, steppes, and plateaus. The tension between unifying and segmenting forces can be seen in two sets of meteorological determinants. Atmosphere and seasons affect the entire area in long cycles; temperature and rainfall are felt immediately and with great variance in daily living.

a. *Heat Exchange and Seasonal Patterns*
Because local conditions are controlled by area- and world-wide climates, to contrast only coastal, highland, and inland zones and to sort them according to N-S lines is to leave distorted impressions. Although rainfall generally diminishes and temperature generally increases as summer follows winter and if measured from coast to interior, a consistent pattern of uniformly striated N-S zones paralleling those in the terrain cannot be found. Instead, global factors result in numerous highly localized weather zones.

Because heat exchanges between lower and higher altitudes over the Middle East are part of the continuing world-wide process (Fisher, 1978: 43), the recognition of high and low pressure gradients, jet streams, and continuously forming and dissipating fronts in upper zones has forced re-evaluation of meteorological phenomena at lower levels. Now, studies indicate that the Mediterranean area lies between two weather systems, i.e., a hot Sahara and a cooler southern-central Europe climate. These cause an exceptionally deep (5 km) southwesterly monsoonal air current above the sea that becomes thinner over Arabia. Jet streams above the air current move westwardly from November to March but eastwardly at other times.

During the summer, a low pressure zone protrudes over the Arabian Gulf and northward towards Iraq and Syria, causing a low pressure center over Cyprus that lasts the entire season and affects wind patterns throughout the eastern Mediterranean. The center pulls prevailing southwesterly winds toward Syro-Palestine producing sea breezes as far inland as Palmyra, Damascus, and Amman. The swirl is northerly, Eurasian, dry, and at lower levels warmed by the surface.

Winter patterns differ. The subtropical jet stream increases in velocity and settles above the southern Mediterranean coast. The lower-level depressions that are created move from the Atlantic to pass over Europe, the Mediterranean, or North Africa on their way east. Similar depressions form in the Mediterranean basin and eventually affect the lee depressions in Syro-Palestine.

The Mediterranean, therefore, has its own winter weather system. Fronts may cause dry cloudless weather, and shallow depressions may produce rapidly changing conditions. Fronts moving off the sea pass either northeast toward Asia Minor or southward toward the eastern basin and Iraq bringing rain to both coastal areas and interior.

b. *Temperature and Rainfall*

The chief consequences of these features are high summertime temperatures, wide diurnal and annual temperature ranges, and occasionally rapid changes in weather. In addition, clear summer skies allow great amounts of heat to radiate from the sun to the earth during the day and from the earth to the atmosphere at night so that the area is one of the warmest on earth, even warmer than equatorial zones where cloud cover slows radiation.

In these conditions, ground altitude also affects climate greatly. The coastal mountains limit the sea's tempering effect to a narrow littoral strip, and the absence of soil and vegetation cover as well as the presence of basin-like structures in much of the interior contribute to heat-exchanging radiation.

On a macro scale, dominant surface winds throughout the year are from the W-SW. The direction explains why drier air coming from

Figure 16: Annual Temperature Ranges in the Middle East

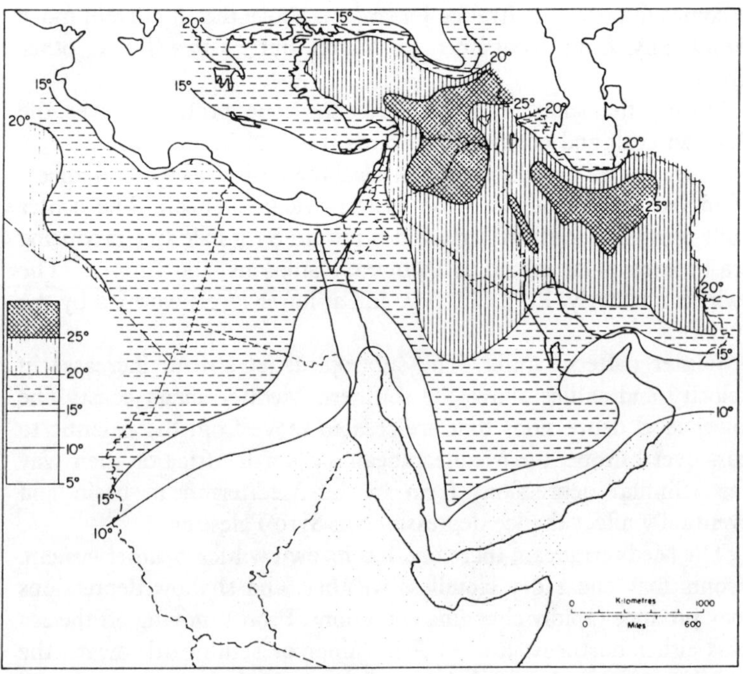

Figure 17: Annual Rainfall in the Eastern Mediterranean Basin

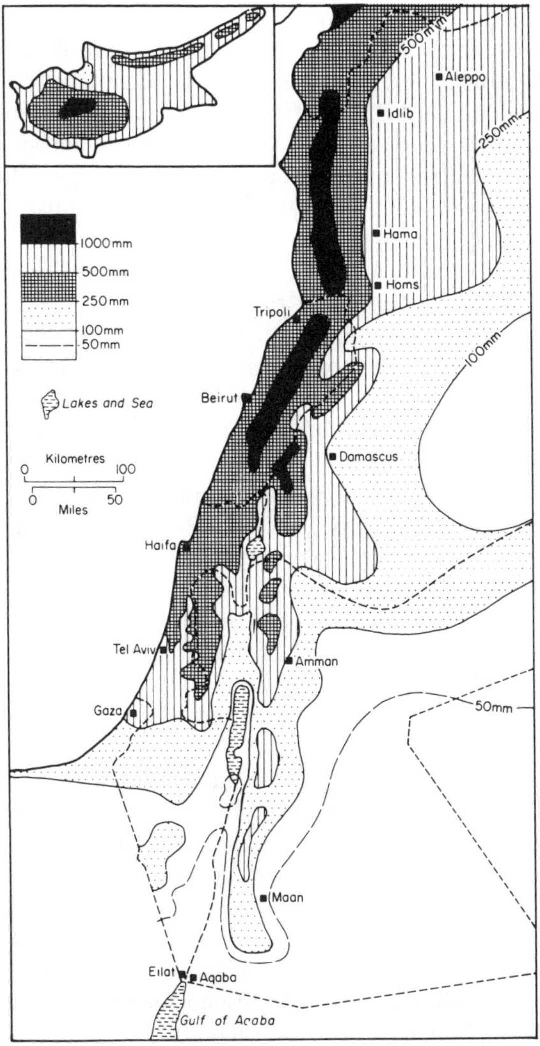

Africa strikes the southern regions of the eastern Mediterranean basin while moisture collected over the sea affects the north [Figures 16 and 17]. As a result, the coastal region experiences mild winters, moderate summers, abundant rainfall, and relatively high humidity. In this climate, August, the hottest month in many zones, is cooler in the south than in the north where mountains trap the humidity by blocking the eastward air flow.

Coastal rainfall varies from approximately 750 mm annually in Syria and Lebanon to 355 mm in the Gaza region, both well above the 200 mm limit needed for cultivation. January, the rainiest month, brings precipitation comparable to sections of Europe but accumulating with greater intensity during fewer days. Heavy dew, another source of moisture, is perceptible along the coast on as many as 250 nights annually.

The contrast between the coast and mountain zones a few kilometers away is striking. In the winter, snow, heaviest on the Lebanon peaks, is common in the higher mountains. Seasonal diurnal temperatures range approximately 6-8 degrees C. lower than on the coast, with a 5-6 degree C. spread between the northern and southern mountainous and highland areas. Rainfall is abundant and heavy. For example, the Jebel Ansarieh and Lebanon mountains enjoy 1000-1250 mm annually, Galilee approximately 700 mm, and the Cisjordan highlands approximately 500-600 mm. Again, however, the quantities accumulate during relatively few days. Mountainous areas in Syria and Lebanon receive measurable precipitation on 80-85 days annually while in the south the number falls to 40-60 days. The totals are only 5-10 days more than in corresponding coastal zones, but the distribution affects greatly the kinds of agriculture and residence patterns the inhabitants have developed throughout history.

In the steppe zones east of the mountains and hills, rainfall diminishes sharply in part because the relief controls precipitation more there than in more temperate zones. Lee sides of upland areas are substantially drier than the west sides. Thus, the Amuq, Ghab, Biqa, and Ghor valleys and basin zones have their own distinctive climates. Although near to upland areas, these narrow depressions have either moderate or deficient rainfall and are relatively hot in the summer and cold in the winter. At Jericho, for example, openness to the sun during January, the coldest month, causes temperatures to average 14 degrees C., while during August, the hottest month, averages range near 27 degrees C. and temperatures as high as 50 degrees C. have been recorded. Annual rainfall, however, is only 125 mm and evaporation rates are high, reaching as much as

4000 mm (4m!) annually at the Dead Sea nearby (Fisher, 1978: 419).

Because of their western exposure, the Anti-Lebanon and northern Transjordan highlands enjoy heavier rainfall than the valleys to their west. The advantage vanishes quickly, however, in the semi-arid steppes to the east where the orientation of isohyets and isotherms compare positively with the geomorphological patterns discussed above. In northern zones where mountains and highlands are separated from deserts by steppes, rainfall and temperature lines generally extend N-S, but in the south and east, they follow a J-shape interior line roughly paralleling the orientation of the Mediterranean coast. The eastern desert encroaches on the Cis- and Transjordan south. The areas south of Ma'an, Hebron, and Gaza are within the rainshadows of Africa and the Sinai and consequently are true desert regions. The demarcation between steppe and desert, therefore, becomes elliptical or semi-circular as it sweeps south and westward and unites the dry eastern and southern zones and separates them from the more moist western and northern sections of the eastern Mediterranean basin. The pattern is similar to the geomorphology in that it unites areas on either side of the central rift system, and the demarcation follows approximately the same line as that separating the two major geo-structural zones. Structure and climate, therefore, link the eastern desert ecologically to southern Judah and the Negev.

An important exception surrounds the Dead Sea. There an interruption in the isolyths' smooth curves is caused by patterns that unite the area immediately surrounding the sea. During all seasons, rainfall on either side of the sea and at its northern end approximates that in the desert regions. As a result, isolyths drawn from Transjordan turn sharply northward, pass through the Jordan valley and southward in lines through or near Jerusalem before turning westward again toward the Mediterranean. Therefore, it is not only the southern Negev that shares precipitation with steppe and desert zones east of the rift. Territories in Judah, the northern Negev, the northern and southern Ghor, and portions of the Jordan valley do as well. This pattern, we propose, must be considered when reviewing the movements and migrations described in the David stories.

Diurnal and annual rainfall variations and temperature ranges can be extreme not only in the steppe region, as meteorologists have suggested, but in all areas along the borders between desert and non-desert areas marked by the isohyets. Places on the steppes, like

Aleppo for example, commonly receive frost and snow during the winter but have summertime temperatures exceeding 30 degrees C. Diurnal ranges in wintertime average 10 degrees C. and in the summer 17 degrees C. Rainfall varies from 250 mm to 450 mm annually.

Circumstances are even more complex and less predictable than these figures imply. Two reasons are the usual annual rainfall cycle and frequent exceptions to the cycle. As suggested above, rainfall is normally distributed unevenly throughout the year. The former rains of early autumn arrive in mid- or late October. The main rains come, according to region, in January, February, or March. After a lull, the latter rains fall usually in April or early May.

While the cycle is generally predictable, even minor variations in the times and intensities of precipitations affect growing cycles. They also render mean averages deceptive or useless for estimating agricultural strategies. In any case, deviations are common and may occur in several consecutive years. Using Jerusalem between 1920 and 1962 as a sample because data is available and because the city has one of the highest "average" rainfalls in the region, Frick (1985: 106) observes that "a cycle of three or more consecutive years with thirty percent or more negative deviation occurs *twice* even within the relatively short span of forty years [emphasis his]." He concludes that most of ancient Cisjordan was in a medium risk agricultural environment.

Vegetation

Plants as well as humans have responded to the complex conditions (cf. Zohary, 1982: 28-35; Fisher, 1978: 86-98). In order to survive, Middle Eastern vegetation developed growing cycles that are completed during the cooler, rainy season, and some developed deep or extensive root systems that compensate for lack of moisture. Other plants responded by developing structural means of reducing water loss so that they can continue to grow during the hot arid seasons. Thick outer layers on stems and trunks, thick leaves, reduced leaf surface, or thick hairy coatings typify this group. Examples include cork oak, evergreen oak, olive trees, thorn bushes, and hyssop.

Today's agriculturalists cope with the environment by regulating and mixing the natural responses. Wheat, barley, and millet are planted in the autumn to ensure maturation in the late spring or early summer, and vines, tubers, and bulbs are cultivated that cope by spreading or sinking roots to absorb surface dew or reach lower levels of moisture. It is not unusual to find olive trees, grapevines, cereals, and vegetables planted together in a single field in order to utilize limited land resources, spread the risk of crop failure, and add variety to the diet.

Distribution and types of natural vegetation no doubt differed during the early Iron Age, but the choices then as now were determined by the climate. The Sinai and eastern regions of the Great Syrian Desert marked the northern and western edges of Saharo-Sindian vegetation that spreads throughout northern Africa and the Arabian peninsula. To the north and west along the S-shaped Fertile Crescent, there was a Irano-Turanian vegetation zone and on its inner fringes and along the coastline a Mediterranean vegetation zone.

On a macroscale, these zones divide Mediterranean, steppe, desert, and mountain forms of vegetation [Figure 25, p. 191]. Mediterranean vegetation is relatively restricted but is important for the history of David's territories. Vines, cereals, and olive and fruit trees are typical commodities, but various shrubs, evergreens, and herbs are also found. In the spring, assorted bulbs fill the region with their colorful flowers.

The zone is best know for its *maquis* or *macchia*, a dense covering of evergreen oak, myrtles, and broom with a thick undergrowth of thorn bushes and shrubs. Two degenerate forms—garrigue and phrygana—survive. The former grows in thinner soils capable of supporting its dwarf bushes and thorns. Interspersed with bare patches of rock or soil, garrigue is common in the eastern Mediterranean basin today. Phrygana, on the other hand, consists mostly of thorn bushes and is found in deeper valley bottoms where it often restricts passage.

Although steppe vegetation is greatly influenced by climate, predominantly Irano-Turanian types have developed there. Carob, juniper, and terebinth trees, Christ thorn, wild plum, and wormwood scatter the lower mountain slopes of the steppes. No trees are found today in the more arid true steppes, but many grasses and flowers flourish during the spring, only to disappear quickly in the early summer. These areas have historically been home for pastoralists even though relatively minor fluctuations in annual temperature and rainfall can affect grazing conditions disproportionately.

In the deserts, dry and saline conditions produce Saharo-Sindian vegetation. Camel thorn, tamarisks, and plants that can complete their growing cycle in a few weeks are found there. In the spring, however, this zone has an abundance of flowering grasses that can support grazing for a few weeks or months depending on the temperature and region.

The mountains of the Mediterranean basin have their own distinctive type of woodland growth. Native evergreen oak, carob, and pine grow at altitudes as high as +1000 m above sea level. Cedars, maples, firs, valonia oak, and Aleppo pine are found at higher elevations.

Summary

Several general observations summarize the physical setting of the Middle East during Iron Age I. First, the eastern Mediterranean's geography, geology, geomorphology, and meteorology each show W-E orientations. These are as prominent as the area's more visible N-S surface orientations. The combination made it possible for peoples to move back and forth across the central rift system with as much frequency and purpose as they moved north and south along it, the coastline, highland ridges, and valley floors.

Second, the S- or J-shaped Fertile Crescent that sweeps from the Euphrates valley through the eastern Mediterranean basin to northern Africa includes many different ecological zones. These are marked and transected by geographical corridors. The four principal W-E depressions especially facilitated movement between coast and interior. Pastoralists today still follow them where possible in their annual migrations. They follow the green line westward (and northward) from the desert to the hills and valleys west (and north) of Aleppo, Hama, Damascus, Amman, and Beersheba.

A prominent feature in each ecological strip is the oscillating boundary area between pastoralist and agrarian environments that separates the steppes and plateaus of the Syrian desert, Negev, and Sinai from the uplands on the east and west banks of the rift systems. The valleys, highlands, mountains, and coasts north of the Gaza region fall within the fertile, agricultural crescent where weather, soil, and terrain favor labor-intensive agriculture and small-mammal grazing. The line generally separates these cultivated areas from others that can support only pastoralism or at times semi-pastoralism.

Third, as implied in the first and second observations, the rift system, especially the Jordan valley, must be viewed as a center among other geographical features rather than as a border and marginal zone. While the valley's depth, the deep ravines emptying into it, and the contrasting altitudes of upland zones on either side make the depression seem like a boundary between east and west zones, measured by geology, meteorology, or ecology it stands at the middle and as a meeting point of the eastern Mediterranean basin's geography.

Fourth, exceptional changes in terrain, elevation, moisture, soil, and vegetation occur within constricted areas. The variety creates microenvironments with the potential for supporting vastly differing economies, residential strategies, and life styles in close proximity to each other and within very restricted geographical areas. Therefore, studies of social and cultural phenomena in the areas, especially factors pertaining to their unification, must be cautious about generalizing on the basis of information taken from only a few ecological niches. Furthermore, to unify the area successfully and for an extended period necessitates satisfying or controlling groups and individuals who are accustomed to and depend on such diversity.

B. *Archaeological Occupation Patterns*

The diversity in the physical setting for the David stories requires that the extent of Iron Age occupation and the varied cultural developments in individual zones be investigated [Figure 26, p. 192].

Temporal Setting for David's Drama

As we noted in the Introduction, the dates for the Davidic period are problematic, and the end of Iron I is more easily defined archaeologically than its beginning. These factors in themselves say something about the period's sociopolitical processes. Iron IC in Syro-Palestine appears to have culminated in a Jerusalem-based centralized polity that was stable enough to construct monumental architecture and defense systems such as those represented by the gate and fortification systems at Gezer, Hazor, and Megiddo; the temple in Jerusalem is another example. The archaeological period of their construction is presumed to have ended following a succession struggle that led to a post-Solomonic Schism in ca. 922 B.C.E. The Egyptian pharaoh Shishak invaded (920/918 B.C.E.), leaving signs of his destructive path in the gates, cities, and towns as far away as the Esdraelon and Jordan valleys.

This *terminus ad quem* may be tentatively accepted for our model. We are proceeding on the assumption that the setting for David's drama preceded a successor's more highly centralized reign and ended well before the Great Schism and return of outside powers to the region. This does not imply, however, that the subsequent developments were divorced from events in early Iron IC or in earlier IA.

Our analytical model begins at the archaeological end of the Late Bronze Age when Syro-Palestine was caught in a pincher movement that placed it in the center of Mediterranean, Anatolian, and Egyptian pressures pushing from the sea as well as overland from the north and south (cf. Ward and Martin, 1964: 15, 20). The turmoil has often been described:

> The Late Bronze period in Syria-Palestine ended with widespread upheaval in the Levant at the end of the thirteenth century BCE, with the break-up of the Mycenaean world and the displacement of the 'Sea Peoples'; the fall of the Hittite Empire; the collapse of the Mitannnian (Hurrian) Kingdom; the resurgence of Assyria; the yielding of the Kassites to the Second Dynasty of Isin in Babylon (a bit later); and the expansion of the early Aramaean peoples. . . . While LB traditions in Palestine continue into the twelfth century at sites like Megiddo, Bethshean, Shechem, and Gezer, other sites like Hazor and Bethel show a virtually complete stratigraphic and ceramic break (*contra* Franken) (Dever, 1977: 91).

The relative degree of cultural continuity and discontinuity remains a topic of debate, even for Dever (cf. Gonen, 1984: 70). However, all descriptions depict a scene where relatively prosperous societies were disintegrating, especially along the Mediterranean coastal plains. The causes of the decline, although important for history, are at the beginning edge of our model and for the most part are beyond the scope of our investigation.

Occupation Sequences in the Analytical Model

In the attempt to establish reasonable taxonomies, i.e., accurate analytical chronological orders, analysts usually organize Iron I into a series of sequential periods and phases. The normative typology and dating was set by William F. Albright in his excavations at Tell

Beit Mirsim (Albright, 1932; 1938; 1943). According to his reading, destruction debris from a LB II city (Stratum C2) rested under a thin layer of pits and other occupational materials containing Iron IA pottery (Stratum B1); he dated the latter, comprising pre-Philistine but not LB remains, to the 12th century. Above that stratum was a deeper layer of Iron IB (Stratum B2) occupation that he associated with the Philistines and—using Lapp's nomenclature—it was in turn covered by Iron IC materials (Stratum B3). Stratum B3 represented a new tradition of pottery with hand burnishing over red slip. Albright attributed the ceramics to the Israelite monarchy. He interpreted the sequence culturally by assigning LB II to the Canaanites, IB to the Philistines, and the one between, IA, to the early Israelites (Albright, 1932: 53-58, 74; 1943: 38).

The chronology and typology lifted Near Eastern archaeology into a new age. Although both have been continually refined and Albright's interpretations challenged, his fundamental observations regarding the overall archaeological course of Near Eastern history still remain normative. They have, however, led to Procrustean efforts to make them fit all subsequent excavations and surveys. For one thing, although material remains at Tell Beit Mirsim and elsewhere do suggest some devastating intrusions and long gaps in occupation, many transformations signalled by the archaeological record seem to have been metamorphoses rather than abrupt changes. Ceramic typologies often evolved (or devolved) gradually and in concert with other indicators. Hence, conquest, settlement, and revolt hypotheses regarding the LB-Iron I transition have each been criticized for failing to do justice to the complexity and diversity of the information (cf. Lemche, 1985: *passim.*)

Re-evaluation of Tell Beit Mirsim

A recent re-evaluation of the Tell Beit Mirsim materials confirms the need for caution. Raphael Greenberg (1987) finds greater continuity between LB and Iron I than formerly believed, and suggests that significant political and social upheaval is not apparent until Iron IC (Stratum B3).

> In the first part of Iron I the Canaanite forms of Stratum C2 continued to appear. These were soon joined by new forms and techniques, still strongly rooted in the Canaanite tradition, though differing from the Tell Beit Mirsim Late Bronze Age material. Only in the tenth century do we see that the character of the pottery

> changed, becoming indistinguishable from that of the other regions of Judah incorporated in the Israelite Monarchy (Greenberg, 1987: 76).

Greenberg insists that the first phase of Iron I lacks similarity with contemporary settlements in Cisjordan such as 'Ai, Raddana, Giloh, and Tel Masos—all presumed by Greenberg to be "Israelite"—and that the second phase is not demonstrably "Philistine" (Greenberg, 1987: 76). Both factors suggest a continuing "Canaanite" presence similar to that found in northern valleys of Cisjordan. They also identify local traditions linking the site to the area but distinguishing it from other "Israelite" regions.

> It is thus clear that what has been termed above "late Late Bronze" is more a cultural distinction than a chronological one; for the "late Late Bronze" of southern Canaan is contemporary with, if not later than, the "early Iron I" of the presumed Israelite settlement sites. While this mid-12th century phase seems, at Lachish, to predate the Philistines, there is no reason to assume that its pottery styles could not have survived the destruction of that site to coexist with Philistine pottery (Greenberg, 1987: 78).

Greenberg's claims regarding "new forms," "the character of the pottery," and "cultural distinction" and his use of ethnic categories are conflicting and confusing, and they betray an uncritical use of the archaeological vernacular that continues to plague Near Eastern studies. Nevertheless, his thesis is meritorious and convincing. His argument, together with information from other sites, can be used to counterbalance the presuppositions that have dominated the field since Albright.

The last word has not been spoken, but two tentative conclusions may be drawn. First, although archaeologists since Albright have sorted information according to his periods and phases, his taxonomy did not establish a universal, serial, temporal sequence that should be expected at all sites. At Tell Beit Mirsim, Albright sifted the noise of his day from the information available at the time. Such first-effort diachronic clarity was needed, but the analytical distinctions must not be interpreted too rigidly. Stratigraphy does not always imply that groups represented by upper and lower strata were successive or their relationships entirely hostile. On the contrary, in many areas, indeed at many sites, especially where there is no interval between layers, several typologies surely coexisted in symbiotic or synchronic relationships before one gave way to the other. The proposition should not be disregarded because of zealous quests for "pure" unmixed strata and loci in excavations. In material remains, "cultural" differences can seldom be traced with full certainty to distinctive ethnic identities. Regionalism, for instance, may account for variety, especially in areas as diverse as the eastern Mediterranean basin.

The second conclusion goes beyond the issue of ethnicity. The lengthy span of time allowed for the cessation of the Late Bronze Age and the beginning of the early Iron Age, i.e., the several centuries between 1200 and 1000 B.C.E., suggests less uniformity among the generations of successive populations than archaeologists are wont to report. Several radical sociopolitical transformations did occur as Mendenhall, Boling, and others argue (cf. below), but to assume naively either that different typologies always reflect ideological differences (as pointed out above), or conversely that common, long-standing typologies represent universally shared ideologies, is to deny the possibility of human diversity. A ceramic typology may survive many shifts in opinion and ideology. Archaeology is better suited for detecting long-term and economic changes than short-term and ideological shifts. Therefore, although Albright's categories continue to serve as a general guide to chronology and topology, by themselves they are not shakeproof foundations for reconstructing sociopolitical or religious history.

Re-evaluation of Occupational Sequences in Transjordan

In light of the re-evaluation of stratigraphical and typological sequences in Cisjordan, Rudolph Dornemann's (1983) interpretation of cultural developments in Transjordan adds breadth and balance to portrayals of Iron Age I. Dornemann develops a firm ceramic typology by arranging sites serially according to the dates of the finds, usually ceramic but including other artifacts. For the Iron Age, his study moves from the Jebel Nuzha tomb, to Madeba tomb A, Irbid tombs A, B, and C, Deir 'Alla, Balu'a, Aro'er, Dhiban, and finally the western Wadi Arabah and Timnah. Finds from numerous other sites as far away as Tarsus and the Amuq were compared, but the controlling site is Dornemann's own excavation at the Amman citadel.

The significance of the changes he proposes becomes apparent when they are compared with earlier analyses of sites such as Deir

'Alla. Excavations at Iron Age Deir 'Alla near the confluence of the Jordan and Zarqa rivers are published in a series of preliminary and final reports (Franken, 1960; 1961; 1962; 1964; 1969; Franken and Ibrahim, 1977-78). The excavator, H. J. Franken, dates a LB temple on the basis of an imported Egyptian faience vase bearing a cartouche of Queen Tauosert (1205-1194 B.C.E.) and on a Carbon-14 test (1190 B.C.E. +/– 30 years) (Franken, 1969: 19-20). Because no signs of a defense system or ordinary dwellings are found in remains of the period, Franken hypothesizes that the site is a cultic center, and because a fissure in the mound extends up to the level of the destroyed temple but not above it, he credits the building's destruction to earthquake. Although his interpretation has been controversial, it may be supported by new information found elsewhere, e.g., at Ras Shamra, where natural disasters caused some destruction either instead of or in conjunction with human agents at the end of LB II.

Above the Deir 'Alla temple, Franken dates several phases of occupation to the 12th, 11th, and 10th centuries. During Iron IA, according to Franken, the site continues to serve as a sanctuary in spite of differences between the former and the new occupants. Some pottery traditions derived from the LB Age continue but with noticeable deterioration in technique and with additions to the repertory (Franken, 1969: 20). The absence of domestic houses and the presence of furnaces, metal droppings, and burnt clay suggest, according to Franken, seasonal summer occupation by itinerant metalworkers during Phases A to D, "the first Iron Age" (Franken, 1969: 21).

Phase A is probably Philistine, i.e., Iron IB (Rast, 1978: 5), or inhabited by peoples who trade with them (Franken, 1969: 20), or home to local populations who imitate Philistine (or more probably Syrian) wares (Dornemann, 1983: 168). Whatever the case, local itinerants seemingly continue to live in the vicinity during Phases A-D until they are driven from the site by new settlers who build a small town during the transition between Phases D and E (Franken, 1969: 45). The transition is peaceful and occupation continuous. However, even though the new peoples draw upon the same pottery traditions as the itinerants, their ceramics develop differently from their predecessors'. The new occupation must last from the 11th to 10th century, a settlement Franken labels "the second Iron Age" (1969: 21). No wheel-burnished pottery is found in these levels, i.e., E through L. Dates for the last two Phases, J and L, are set respectively at approximately 1050 B.C.E. and tentatively the last quarter of the 11th century which would place the next phase, Phase M, within the timeframe assigned to David (Franken, 1969: 245, 246). Rast, however, following Lapp, dates Phases A-D to between 1125 and 1050, and E-J between mid-eleventh and late 10th century "tying in with the third phase of Iron I" (Rast, 1978: 5). These differences of interpretation place the "Davidic" materials in a state of uncertainty.

Although pottery from the important Phases M and N is not included in Franken's Iron Age volume, several helpful comments are made. In a limited way, they can guide our interpretation. Phase M shows a reorienting of village layout and is probably separated from L by a short interval. In any case the interval is less than that between M and N which starts Period III (Franken, 1969: 62-63). In later publications, however, Franken seems to move the date of Phase M down so that it is more in line with Rast's suggestion (Franken, 1976: 12).

As later seasons clarified earlier impressions, Franken saw fewer signs of Philistines, but he always limited them to Phases A-D. In his later reports, however, he remains convinced of the presence of smelters, transient metalworkers, and at least one phase of building activity during or near the period we identify as early Iron IC. At this site, therefore, typological development oscillates more than a typical IA, IB, IC sequence can explain. Early IC appears to be a phase in the development of a settled population that draws on several ceramic traditions that preceded it.

Dornemann's interpretation can be read against this background. He divides the Transjordan area into ten distinct districts: 1) Irbid, 2) northern Jordan valley, 3) southern Jordan valley, 4) northern hill country of Gilead, 5) southern hill country of Gilead, 6) Amman district, 7) area north of the Wadi Mujib, 8) area between the Mujib and Wadi el-Hasa, 9) area between Wadi el-Hasa and the southern desert, and 10) the Arabah. The variety among the regions contributes in part to Dornemann's decision to forgo strict Iron I and II divisions in favor of a "Sequence I" and "Sequence II" that avoid assumptions about the periods' uniformity (Dornemann, 1983: 166).

Sequence I comprises the first two centuries of the Iron Age, i.e., 1200-1000 B.C.E., while Sequence II belongs primarily to Iron II but extends into Iron III (according to Albright's scheme of Iron I, II, and

III). However, because the introduction of red wash and burnish decoration on ceramics is a major indicator of change in Transjordan, Dornemann moves away from Albright by marking the transition from Iron I to II at 1000 B.C.E. as Lapp did earlier (Dornemann, 1983: 26). Therefore, Dornemann's sequences relate only broadly to his own archaeological periods.

> The [sequences'] information clustered in Iron I and the end of Iron II. The pottery of the tenth century, the end of Iron I, is considerably different from that which preceded it in Iron I; it shows more of a continuity with the pottery of the first centuries of Iron II (Dornemann, 1983: 166).

The implications are clear. Either a firm typology for Transjordan Iron Age wares is not set, or regional diversity accounts for some differences in chronology—meaning that various ecological niches have their own specific sequences. Both seem to be the case. Therefore, although an archaeological topology based on the Tell Beit Mirsim excavations is useful for defining the broad stages in typological metamorphoses during the LB/Iron I period, it is inadequate for discriminating detailed local processes in diverse ecological zones in Transjordan. Moreover, the complexities on the one hand set Transjordan and Cisjordan apart historically, but on the other require the areas to be weighed together when conclusions about Iron Age I are drawn.

> It does not seem that the Jordan Valley was ever consistently associated with the region to the west or that to the east. This status probably changed from period to period and future research must be oriented not to generalizations, but to understanding separately the situations existing at different times. It is understandable that at most times the Jordan Valley formed a distinct unit in the way in which influences from east and west were combined here. Future research must take this into consideration (Dornemann, 1983: 170 n. 1).

This view confirms the basis for re-evaluating Franken's Deir 'Alla dates and interpretations.

> The C-14 date for the end of the L.B. cella, 1180-1160 B.C., fits well with the 1205-1194 B.C. date for Queen Taousert. . . . If a decade or two are allowed for the attempted L.B. resettlement, a date of roughly 1165 B.C. seems a good approximation, though it is longer than the excavators allow. This requires a slightly later date

> for Phases A to L also. Phases A to D must be kept within the twelfth century and we should follow the excavators' lead in staying close to the estimate of a century for Phases E to L. Thirty-five to forty years for Phases A to D should be sufficient if not too long. The estimates of Phases E to L has been stretched only slightly, allowing around 120 years so that Phase L would end about 1000 B.C., which is also what the excavators suggest. In this way, the similarity of types and other parallels that have been noted seem to mesh with the greatest satisfaction (Dornemann, 1983: 44).

To illustrate his point, Dornemann cites two manufacturing techniques found in cooking pots at Deir 'Alla. Type 1 dominates Iron Phases A-D but declines through E-L. Type 2, a continuation of a LB technique, is not used in Phases A-D, but reappears in Phase E and becomes more frequent in Phases K-L. "The disappearance and eventual reappearance of type 2 cooking pots mean that this type must have continued in use elsewhere in the meantime" (Dornemann, 1983: 41). Thus, the oscillation between ceramic innovation and traditionalism and the reappearance of forms suggest that the zone is awash with movements of peoples who sometimes reject and sometimes accommodate the ways of those around them.

These and other factors lead to the conclusion that archaeologists must at times be satisfied with identifying orientations instead of causes and origins. The archaeological record often indicates the direction peoples are "looking" even when it may not demonstrate immediate historical causation. For example, the Solomonic Stratum VIII at Tell er-Rumeith shows signs of a Palestinian orientation while later strata are oriented toward Syria, suggesting that the primary relationships between the occupants and the outside world shifted (N. Lapp, 1975: 114; Dornemann, 1983: 156). Or again, the ceramic continuity among "Ammonite," "Moabite," and "Edomite" finds (and "Israelite," if Ibrahim's estimation [1978] of Sahab wares is added) in Iron Age I illustrates that local differences may be caused by chronological rather than "cultural" discontinuities. This is the thrust of Dornemann's reasoning when he is finally forced to assume "a basic Palestinian orientation of the ceramic materials in the tenth century."

> The past designations of Edomite, Moabite, and Ammonite painted wares can no longer be substantiated and, though new distinctions may arise as a result of increased information, it is necessary for the

> time being to be content with the documentation of features which demonstrate a common tradition in Transjordan. . . . A chronological difference may actually provide the basis for these distinctions rather than a regional difference. . . (Dornemann, 1983: 172).

Effects upon Interpretations of other Sites

Such re-evaluations are only beginning to affect the interpretation of other previously excavated sites [Fig. 26, p. 192]. Here, we apply the more flexible and varied framework to sites in three regions that are important for Iron Age archaeology. The sites are chosen for their location rather than because they are "typical," a category that according to our description is nearly meaningless. As suggested below and in Appendix I, the collared-rim jar—a primary indicator for Iron IA—in Cisjordan is concentrated between the Jezreel valley and the Beersheba depression, the third and fourth corridors identified in our geographical survey. In light of that, Taanach on the northern edge of the central highlands, Tel Mevorakh on the coastal plain, and Tel Masos near Beersheba in the northern Negev, together with very brief summaries of several sites that have become standards in "Biblical Archaeology" are reviewed.

At Taanach, a LB I city is destroyed and not reoccupied until the end of LB II or beginning of Iron I (Rast, 1978: 3). Iron I is divided into two periods separated by an occupational gap. The first contains two subphases, while the second, lasting a century or more, also has two main phases and many subphases of reuse.

Using Albright's terminology instead of Lapp's, Rast identifies the occupational sequence as Iron IA (ca. 1200-1150 B.C.E.), IB (1150-1125 B.C.E.—not the Sea Peoples IB), a gap, IIA (1020-960 B.C.E.), and IIB (960-918 B.C.E.). His outline offers a coherent picture. IA seems to continue from LB I and therefore corresponds to a pre-Philistine phase at other sites (Rast, 1978: 6). His IB lies above IA but contains no Philistine wares. The break at the end of IB suggests that the site is abandoned during most of the 11th century. After the gap, a new pottery repertory connected with the second period and distinguished by hand burnishing begins to emerge. That and changes in architecture point to new settlers during a phase that corresponds to a third and post-Philistine phase elsewhere. Rast notes that his IIA is characterized by the sparse architecture of a smaller settlement. This marks the modest beginnings of an occupation that becomes more impressive during IIB. Hence, there are two subphases within our Iron Age IC as found at Bethel. Equally important, however, is the fact that Taanach remains "Caananite" until Period II. This means much of Iron I is "Canaanite." Like Megiddo, the site probably did not become "Israelite" until the time commonly attributed to David (Rast, 1978: 15, 55).

A second sample is Tel Mervorakh. However, because the excavator, Ephraim Stern, relies heavily on the biblical stories of David and Solomon when reporting the findings, it is difficult to distinguish excavated material information from impressionistic interpretations based on literary claims (cf. Stern, 1978). In any case, he interprets the site south of Dor as Canaanite until it is destroyed by invading Sea Peoples, probably the Tjeker, in the 13th century (Stratum IX). The latters' culture terminates before the earliest Iron Age settlement (Stratum VIII). Somewhat surprisingly the excavator assigns Mevorakh's earliest Iron Age occupation to the post-Tjeker period that marks the beginning of David's time (Stern, 1978: 76).

Stratum VIII, belonging to the late 11th and early 10th centuries, is greatly disturbed by rebuilding during the Solomonic period (Stratum VII). A small center, a few ashlar pillars—the type commonly associated with the four-room house—and a number of late collared-rim pithoi comprise the principal finds in Stratum VIII (Stern, 1978: 66-67). Except for one jug decorated in Phoenician style, the pottery is local. Virtually no Cypriote ware is present. The parallels are to Iron IA groups at other sites, but they date to the very end of the period (Stern, 1978: 70). This confirms, for Stern, the opinion that Strata VIII and VII are separated by only a brief gap and that VIII dates to the transition period between the 11th and 10th centuries.

Stratum VII dating to the late 10th century Solomonic period is dominated by a single large four-room building, L-130, that is an administrative center standing in the center of a large courtyard (Stern, 1978: 46). Materials from the earlier Stratum VIII are reused, and a paved stone floor from the earlier structure is covered with Nari limestone (Stern, 1978: 47). The late 10th century ceramic repertory includes axe-rimmed cooking pots that continue LB traditions into Iron II (our Iron IC). Hand-burnished red slip ware, black-on-red Cypro-Phoenician ware, and Cypriot and Phoenician bichrome ware are mixed with a host of local types. The stratum is of relatively short duration and is followed by a long gap that allows Stern to affix a definite 10th century date.

As might be expected, the excavator's interpretation suggests a Sea Peoples' occupation between Canaanite and Davidic phases, credits David with ending their occupation, and assigns humble architectural remains to his time. The last are presumably demolished and replaced by larger structures built according to the same model during Solomon's era. Stratum VIII pottery contains few signs of trading but does indicate continuation of some LB forms, while Stratum VII introduces a mixture of imported and continuing local wares.

The third site is Tel Masos. It is one of four Iron Age sites explored in the Arad/Beersheba area and is apparently occupied in the Chalcolithic period and again from the late 13th century to the end of the 11th century (Aharoni et al., 1974; 1975; Fritz, 1975). Attention is drawn to settlement patterns and a series of four-room houses that include several that are substantially larger than others (cf., Frick, 1985: 159-169). The larger dwellings are thought to be either public buildings or the residences of chieftains (Aharoni et al., 1975: 100). The few IB sherds at the site are in one such house in area H, and it also contains an abundance of imported, Phoenician-type pottery comparable to wares found in Megiddo VIA. These suggest that the Stratum, IIb belonging to the mid-11th century, is a time of expansion, social stratification, and incipient political centralization. Frick proposes, in fact, that the site is re-established at that time because population pressures force agriculturalists from highland areas into marginally arid zones, and that Tel Masos becomes an administrative center for surrounding villages such as Tel Esdar (Frick, 1985: 168).

Without determining its cause, we may conclude that the site is a new Iron Age foundation where Iron IC represents an unbroken continuity with IA culture. Simultaneously, the site manifests signs of trading with coastal and more distant areas toward the end of the 11th and beginning of the 10th century.

Each of the three sites is in a different area of Cisjordan, exhibits its own peculiar occupation sequence, and suggests two continuous but distinguishable phases or subphases in Iron Age IC, the second always the more developed architecturally. Combined with other excavations and surveys, the sites present Iron IC both as a companion of continuing LB, IA, and IB traditions and as an amalgamating heir to all of them. No universal pattern of LB/Iron I discontinuity and continuity pervades the area, and no single date for the transitions from LB can be set. In some places IC develops early and immediately from preceding peoples, while in others it marks either a later development or a return to abandoned sites after a considerable gap. Variety in chronological and typological schemes, even at single sites, is common.

Survey of Occupation in the Geographical Zones

Appendix I describes the geography of our seven zones [cf. Fig. 24, p. 190]. Here we observe trends and patterns of occupation cited by archaeologists. Although detailed, specific conclusions about individual locales and sites must be avoided for the reasons already cited, overall trends and trajectories can be determined.

a. *Zones 1 and 2: Syria and Lebanon*

Northern and southern Syria extends across the first two zones examined geographically above. The regions apparently experience a steep decline in population between the MB and LB Ages. Surveys and excavations suggest that the trend continues into Iron I when imported wares are replaced by technically inferior, local productions.

In Syria, the transition from the LB to Iron Ages is set at ca. 1200 B.C.E. and associated with the turmoils sweeping the Mediterranean basin. However, diminished LB traditions continue under the influence of new populations (cf., e.g., Riis, 1948: 192-203; Fugman, 1958: 146-149, 273-276). At Hama, two phases of Iron Age remains are dated to 1200-1075 B.C.E. and 1075-925 B.C.E., corresponding roughly to our IA and IC. During the first phase, iron jewelry and implements begin to appear in tombs and occupation levels, and by the end of the second, red polished monochrome ceramics characteristic of the new period emerge (Fugman, 1958: 275). The Amuq plain may be influential as an origin of the red-slip burnishing that became the hallmark of IC occupations after 1000 B.C.E. in Cis- and Transjordan (Rast, 1978: 21).

At many Syrian sites, traces of LB sedentary populations are either followed immediately without an interval by painted ceramics similar to those of Iron IB in the south, or the sites are destroyed and/or abandoned. In most regions, however, Iron IA and IC type artifacts comparable to those farther south are scarce, suggesting different patterns of sociopolitical dominance. The northern Orontes valley surveyed by an American team in 1979 is an example. Although 103 sites are recorded in the El Ghab and Er Rouj regions, statistically the MB population level declines sharply in LB I and II and does not recover until the Hellenistic period. The survey yields only five "possible" Iron I sherds. In spite of the pattern, however, conclusions about cultural trends in the area remain tentative because excavations locally at Tell Qarqur are discovering extensive Iron II monumental architecture that is not inferred by the survey.

South of Damascus in Zone 2, the early Iron Age is the only pre-Roman period missing in the eastern areas of southern Syria's Hauran region (Braemer, 1984: 224). West of a line extending southward from Damascus to a point a few kilometers east of Der'a, among more than 125 Hauran sites only one is a new Iron Age foundation (Tayyibeh), one a MB site occupied again in the Iron Age but not during the LB period (Der'a), and two continue from LB into the Iron Age ('Ashtara and Sheikh Sa'd).

To the west in the Biqa between the Lebanon and Anti-Lebanon ranges, MB occupation also decreases toward the end of the period but begins to recover gradually in LBI, LBII, and Iron I. Nearly 150 MBIIA and MBIIB sites are recorded, but none from MBIIC. For LBI there are 31, LBII 44, and Iron I 65 (cf. Marfoe, 1979: 31).

b. *Zones 3, 4, and 5: Cisjordan*

The quality of life in LB Cisjordan when the region was recovering from the devastation at the end of the MB Age remains a matter of dispute (cf. Gonen, 1984: 61; Liebowitz, 1987: 16-18). Although LB artistic and cultural glories can be cited, population seems to have declined during the LB period before it rose again [Figure 18].

In excavated areas, 54 MB sites decrease to 24 in the first century of LB but climb to 56 by the period's end in the 13th century. Survey totals, however, show a drop from 272 MB to 101 LB sites, i.e., a 63% decrease (Gonen, 1984: 63-66). Although sites from both periods are scattered throughout Zones 3, 4, and 5, LB populations shift toward coastal regions and major trade routes, and site size decreases so that by the end of LBII the surface area under urban occupation is only 45% of that in MB. The notable exception is LB Hazor which comprises 840 dunams, or in other words, 40% of all the land under settlement in Cisjordan (Gonen, 1984: 68).

Only 17 out of 77 MB sites are occupied throughout LB. However, new cities serve as ports along the northern Mediterranean coast and as strongholds throughout southern areas, especially inland on the coastal plain and Shephelah where Egypt's influence continues (Gonen, 1984: 69). Few of the LB cities are fortified. Coupled with the cessation of imported wares and a general decline in the quality of local pottery at the end of the period, the changes signal a break-up of urban life.

The patchwork pattern of continuing and discontinuing occupation during the transition from LB to Iron I compares favorably with that noted in the re-evaluations cited above. Cultural metamorphoses are more gradual, more mixed, and less interrupted than previously thought. LB traditions continue at some sites such as Tell Keisan, Tell Qiri, Yoqne'am, Megiddo, Bethshean, Shechem, and Gezer, but are interrupted at others (Mazar, 1985: 62). Like Heshbon, cities such as Arad, Jericho, 'Ai, Dan, and Gibeon are either unoccupied or scarcely occupied during the LB period but inhabited in Iron I (Kochavi, 1985: 55).

Little is known archaeologically of Upper Galilee during these periods. Qedesh is its only LB site, and not a single collared-rim jar, a principal indicator of Iron IA on both sides of the rift, is found there. Lower Galilee, in fact, seems to be the northern border for the jar's dispersion which, in Cisjordan, is used primarily from the Jezreel valley to Hebron but rarely north of the valley and seldom if ever in Upper Galilee or the northern Negev. Although the vessel has a counterpart in the Galilean pithoi that evolved from a LB type found from Hazor to Ugarit, the collared-rim jar is most prominent in central and highland areas on either side of the Jordan and at cities such as Megiddo and Sahab (Mazar, 1985: 68-69).

LB populations favor the Shephelah, lowlands, and coastal areas, i.e., fertile, level, well-watered food-producing subregions, and seaport areas conducive to trade. Iron I sites, on the other hand, dominate the highlands and remote areas where access is difficult. Although Iron I settlements are found in western Galilee between the coastal strip and the high mountains of Galilee and further south in the Shephelah, the extraordinary increase in the highlands of Zone 3 remains the most striking feature of the new age. One hundred and fourteen Iron Age sites, 97 of them new foundations, replace 23 permanent LB highland settlements (Stager, 1985: 3-4). Like the MB/LB succession, the Iron I sites are substantially smaller than

Figure 18: Late Bronze and Iron Age I Sites in the Cisjordan Highlands

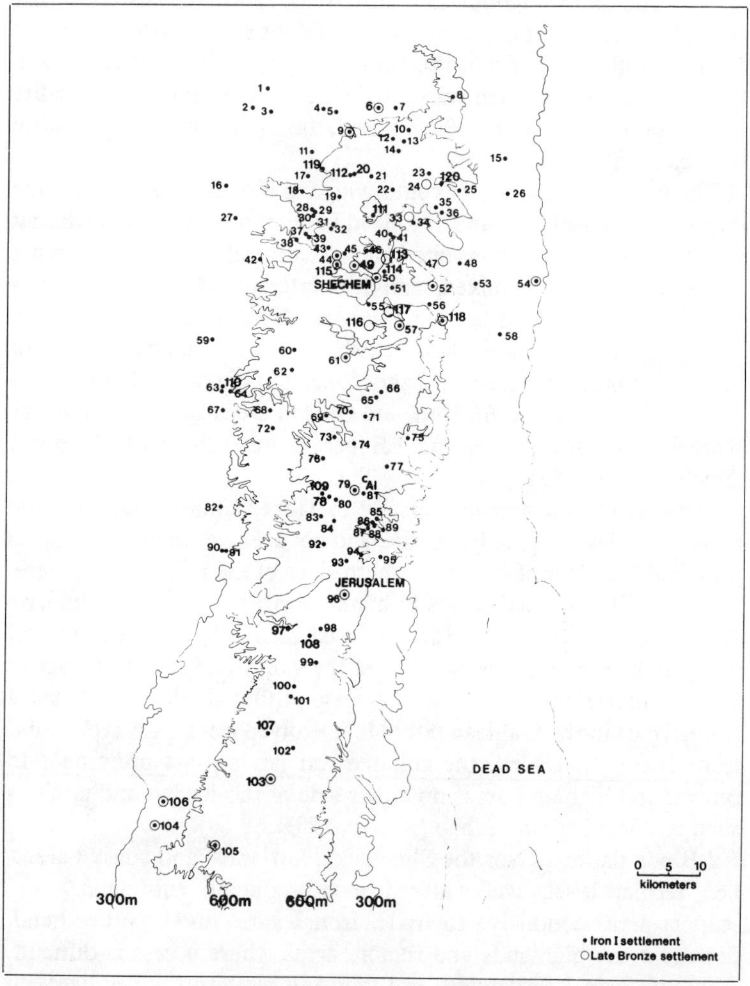

Distribution map of Iron I (dots) and Late Bronze (circles) settlements in the central highlands of Palestine from Khirbet Rabūd in the south to Jālbūn in the north. The shaded area indicates terrain that lies 600 m or more above sea level. The surveys of the Israelis (Kochavi 1972), Campbell (1968), Sapin (1968–69), and Stager were used to compile the list of settlements. Douglas Esse, Research Associate at the Oriental Institute, drew the contour map at 300-m intervals and located the settlements on it.

Iron 1 and Late Bronze Age Site List by Number and Size*

1. Kh. Barta'a
2. Kh. el Aqābe
3. Kh. Mas'ūd (0.25)
4. Tell el-Masalle
5. Tell el-Muhafar
6. Kh. Bal-āme (9.0)
7. Kh. Abū Ghannām (0.2)
8. Jālbūn
9. Tell Dôthān (Dothan) (6.0)
10. Kh. Tannīn (0.5)
11. #41 (Israel Survey) (3.5)
12. Kh. Anāḥūm (1.0)
13. Kh. esh-Sheikh Safīryyān (0.7)
14. ez-Zabābide
15. Tell el-Hamme (0.5)
16. Kh. Shuweikāt er Ras (2.5)
17. er-Rāme
18. Kh. el-Farīsiyye (0.5)
19. Jaba'
20. Sānūr
21. Kh. Kheibar (3.5)
22. Kh. el-Hājj Ḥamdād
23. Kh. Salḥab (0.3)
24. Kh. edh-Dhuq
25. Kh. el-Kureibat (0.1)
26. Kh. Tell el-Hulū (0.2)
27. #99 (Israel Survey) (1.5)
28. #94 (Israel Survey) (1.5)
29. Kh. Qubūr esh-Sheikh (0.1)
30. Kh. el-Bāb (0.1)
31. #113 (Israel Survey) (0.2)
32. Kh. Shureim (0.1)
33. Tell el-Far'ah (N)
34. Kh. Burj el-Fari'a (0.5)
35. Kh. ed-Deir (1.0)
36. Kh. 'Einūn (0.8)
37. Kh. Kūsein es-Sahel (S) (0.2)
38. Kh. Qarqaf (2.0)
39. Kh. el-Barbariyye (0.7)
40. Kh. el-Minūniyye
41. Kh. Mayyāse (0.15)
42. Rās el-Burj (0.3)
43. Kh. Kafr Farāt (0.3)
44. Kūmen (1.5)
45. Jebel Ajram
46. 'Asira esh-Shamāliyya
47. Tell Miskeh (0.4)
48. Bab en-Naqb (1.0)
49. Tell Sūfan (1.0)
50. Tell Balatah (Shechem) (5.0)
51. Kh. Ibn Nāsir
52. Kh. Shuweiha (0.2)
53. Kh. Marāh el-'Inab (0.4)
54. Kh. es-Sālih (0.4)
55. Kh. en-Nabī (0.5)
56. Kh. Ṭanā el-Fawqā
57. Kh. el-'Urmeh (1.2)
58. Tell es-Simādi
59. Kh. Ahmad el-'Awde (0.3)
60. Kh. et-Tell (3.0)
61. Tell Abū Zarād (1.2)
62. #198 (Israel Survey) (0.2)
63. Kh. Sarsara (0.3)
64. Deir el-Mīr (2.5)
65. Kh. er-Rafīd (0.7)
66. Seilun (Shiloh)
67. Kh. ed-Duwwār (0.5)
68. Beit Rīmā
69. Kh. el-Mushraqa (3.0)
70. Kh. 'Alyāte (0.7)
71. Kh. et-Tell
72. Kh. Tibne (1.5)
73. Kh. Ṭarfein (2.0)
74. Burj el-Bardawīl
75. Kh. Marjame
76. Kh. Bīr Zeit
77. et-Ṭaiyibeh
78. Kh. Raddana (0.8)
79. Beitīn (Bethel)
80. Bas eṭ-Ṭāhūneh
81. et-Tell ('Ai) (1.1)
82. Ḥ. Tittora
83. #7 (Sapin Survey) (0.75)
84. Tell en-Nasbeh (3.75)
85. Kh. el-Askar
86. Kh. el-Hāra el-Fawqā
87. Tell Maryam†
88. Mukhmas (Michmash)
89. Kh. ed-Dawwāra
90. Yālū
91. Tell el-Kôkah (S) (0.5)
92. Bīr Nebâla
93. Tell el-Fūl
94. Rās Dhukeir
95. Kh. Abū Musarrah
96. Jerusalem (5.0)
97. Kh. el-Yahūd
98. Giloh (#7 Israel Survey) (0.6)
99. Kh. el-Khawkh
100. Rujm es-Sabīt
101. Kh. Umm et-Tala' (0.75)
102. Kh. Ras et-Tawīl (2.0)
103. el-Khalil (Hebron) (5.0)
104. Tell Beit Mirsim (3.0)
105. Kh. Rabūd (6.0)
106. Tell 'Eitun (6.0)
107. Kh. et-Tubeiqeh (Beth-zur) (1.0)
108. Kh. Judūr
109. 'Izbet Ṣarṭah
110. Deir Ballūṭ
111. Yāsīd
112. el-Kirbeh (0.2)
113. Kh. Kefr Kuz
114. 'Askar
115. Beit Dajan and Ras ed-Diyar
116. Beit el-Khirbeh
117. Kh. Shurrāb
118. Kh. Tānā et-Taḥta
119. 'Ajje
120. Tayāsīr

* Size is given in hectares.
† Iron 1 occupation has not been confirmed by subsequent surveys.

their LB predecessors, but their greater density offsets the decrease and results in a sharp statistical rise in Iron I highland population.

The increased density affects inter- and intrasite composition. LB cities frequently guard the major N-S and W-E trade and communication routes so that Hebron, Jerusalem, Bethel, and Shechem extend along the N-S watershed of the anticline, and similar sites are scattered across W-E routes in Galilee and elsewhere (Hopkins, 1985: 158-159). Although occupation continues at some of these in the Iron Age, sites in Zone 3 are frequently removed from transportation and communication routes. Inhabitants prefer the isolation and protection of ecological niches that have marginal agricultural potential and require labor-intensive cultivation. The rationale explains many sites: Tel Esdar stands in a semi-arid zone of the Arad basin; Giloh lacks good soil and water sources; and 'Izbet Ṣarṭah rests on an stone outcrop near Nablus. Tel Masos, not far from its satellite Tel Esdar, is near the waters of the Wadi Beersheba but in a high-risk rainfall zone (Frick, 1985: 167). Other protected sites dot the Peqi'in valley in Upper Galilee, the central highlands near Nablus, and the Judean hills (Hopkins, 1985: 160-163).

Strategies to make the zones economically viable for extended families are developed. Athough neither terrace farming nor lime plastered cisterns are inventions of the Iron Age, they open new areas to agriculture. Iron Age terraces can be firmly dated at 'Ai and Raddana where they convert the steep and sometimes nearly barren hilltops and slopes into flat, step-like cultivation areas that produce olive trees, vines, and cereals (Stager, 1985: 6). Usually lying below villages that are set at higher elevations, the terraces help to retain moisture, prevent erosion, and make sedentary cultivation possible.

Hopkins (1985) is certainly correct, however, in challenging interpretations that place too much emphasis on cistern and terracing technologies as explanations for the increased agriculture in highland zones. He presents a more complex picture, one that takes into account diversity among ecosystems, labor resources, and risk-spreading strategies. He links the density of the small Iron IA sites to suggestions that some are inhabited only seasonally or are secondary habitations for disparate peoples, including sedentaries, whose principal residences were at nearby primary sites (Hopkins, 1985: 163). The suggestion may find support in A. Mazar's (1985: 62) assertion that the "Bull Site" southeast of Taanach is an open cultic place in the 12th century where regional peoples shared rituals.

The proximity of sites, as well as the presumed relationship among seasonally occupied and secondary and primary sites, suggests specific behavior patterns and recalls Marfoe's analysis of the Lebanon Biqa (Marfoe, 1979). Inhabitants' ability to travel by foot between villages within an hour or so would allow considerable interaction without centralization. The same impression is derived from intrasite village plans that compensate for the absence of public fortification systems. The two-, three-, or four-room pillared houses typical of the period on both sides of the Jordan are often spatially distributed in clusters and compounds protecting central open areas (Stager, 1985: 17-23). In fact, the houses themselves appear to replicate the village plan by having small, open, central courtyards. In any case, although entry to the dwellings is not always from the courtyard side and unattached houses are sometimes constructed with small spaces between, the pattern helps defend inhabitants from unwanted intruders (cf. Shiloh, 1978).

Pillared houses from the 14th century excavated at Tel Batash (Timnah) demonstrate that the form is in use during LBII and carries over to Iron I (Mazar, 1985: 68). Iron I types are found not only in the highlands, but also at Tell Keisan, Megiddo, Tel Abu Hawam, Tell Qasile, Tel Sippor and Tel Sera' in Philistia, and at Sahab and Khirbet el-Medeiyineh in Transjordan (Mazar, 1985: 68). Therefore, like the collared-rim pithoi, the form is used in a wide area bridging both eastern and western zones and falling between the Esdraelon and Beersheba geological corridors discussed above.

The types of buildings at Iron I highland sites show some variation from contemporary LB urban centers. Domestic architecture displaces public structures that reflect the earlier era's social stratification (Stager, 1985: 23). The same domesticity explains the abundance of large pithoi and storage jars and cooking pots that sometimes account for as much as 80% of the entire ceramic assemblages. The percentages are dictated by subsistence economies where storage of food and water are primary concerns (Mazar, 1985: 68). But some minimal ranking according to affluence is suggested by unequal house sizes at Raddana and in the south at Tel Masos where one or more slightly larger dwellings amid nucleated clusters seem to be homes of leading families in lineage systems or of emerging chiefdoms (Stager, 1985: 23; Frick, 1985: 159-160).

Most Iron IB ceramics are found on the southern coastal plain and Shephelah [Fig. 26, p. 192]. They are best attested at Tel Ashdod,

Tel Miqne, and Tell Qasile, but they are also inland, in the Jezreel and Jordan valleys, and as far north as Dor and Akko on the Cisjordan coast, Dan in the rift, and Ras Ibn Hani on the Syrian coast (Bounni et al., 1979a; 1979b: 246, 280-282). Traces or more are scattered throughout the southern portions of Zone 3 north as far as Bethel and south to Tel Masos. In Zone 4, sites concentrate near and eastward from Tell Qasile in the modern Tel Aviv area and along the Gaza littoral from Tel Mor to Tell ez-Zuweyid.

The roots and influences of the IB peoples are diverse. At Ibn Hani, for example, a new wave bearing Mycenaean IIC:1b ceramics arrives after the destruction of a LB city. Elsewhere, the Mycenaean wares are mixed with both LB and Iron I strata (Dothan, 1985: 166, 175). Sites such as Ashdod stand on military and commercial routes from Egypt. Recent excavations at Tel Miqne, possibly Ekron the northern city in the Philistine pentapolis and the largest Iron Age site in Cisjordan, place its founding ca. 12th century B.C.E. and relate Iron IB forms closely to Mycenaean and other wares.

> The shapes and decorative motifs of Philistine pottery were a blend of four distinctive ceramic styles: Mycenaean, Cypriote, Egyptian, and local Canaanite. The dominant traits in shape and almost all the decorative elements were derived from the Mycenaean repertoire and point to the Aegean background of Philistine pottery (Dothan, 1985: 169).

Iron IB burial customs are also an eclectic fusing of indigenous funerary customs and tomb architecture with Aegean and Egyptian elements. Rock-cut chamber tombs and anthropoid clay coffins are the most prominent indicators. Chamber tombs at Tell el-Far'ah are built on the Mycenaean model of stepped passageways leading to a rectangular chamber where shelves cut into the rock hold the deceased and goods. One tomb has two anthropoid coffins, human-sized ceramic "jars" like those found in Egypt encasing human remains. Such coffins usually date to the LB Age and are earlier than the IB peoples (Dothan, 1985: 172). For example, the cemetery at Deir el-Balah contains 40 coffins from the LB Egyptian period while LB/Iron I 13th-11th century Levels VII-VI in the northern cemetery at Bethshean have 50. A small number of IB sherds are found with the later coffins, and five of their lids have distinctive applique headdress, one with vertical fluting identical to feathered headgear worn on the Medinet Habu reliefs of Rameses III in Egypt. The evolution indicates that the coffins belong to the Sea Peoples.

Ironically, Iron Age IC is the most problematical period in these zones. Although its distinctive red burnished ware is found stratigraphically above both IA and IB levels, most architecture from the period is attributed to the end of the 10th century B.C.E. rather than its beginning. The so-called Solomonic gates and accompanying remains at Megiddo, Hazor, and Gezer are well known, and we have already observed the "Solomonic" levels at Tell er-Rumeith and IC ceramics elsewhere in the highlands and Jordan valley of Transjordan.

Excavations at the City of David in Jerusalem demonstrate occupation during most periods from Chalcolithic to medieval times, but materials that can be firmly dated to the first half of the 10th century are few (Shiloh, 1984: 25). The stepped stone structure in Area G is above 14th-13th century LB remains and below later architecture dated to the 9th-6th centuries (Shiloh, 1985: 454). The excavator assigns the structure to the 10th century B.C.E. and describes it as a retaining wall and podium built to support a citadel contructed above.

Stratum 16 contains a massive substructure rising in two main terraces that provide an immense artificial surface possibly belonging to a podium of the LB Canaanite-Jebusite city (Shiloh, 1984: 26). Shiloh hypothesizes that the acropolis of the City of David is fixed on the LB stratum so that the site serves David as it had earlier occupants (Shiloh, 1984: 26). Shiloh assumes the terraces to be a supporting wall for a superstructure rising above the eastern slope. Instead of rebuilding the supporting walls of Stratum 16, he hypothesizes, the Iron Age planners lay their own supports against the slope. Eventually, as Kenyon's excavations show, public and royal installations are built above the supports, but these are not in place until later in the 10th century.

We are left, then, with clear information for periods before and after the first half of the 10th century, but with few indicators that can be certainly assigned to the time between. It is now clear that some traditions dating from before continue without interruption through the first half of the century, but the effects of events in the period are not easily detected. The situation suggests reuse and renovation rather than innovation and initiation.

Figure 19: Transjordan Archaeological Sites

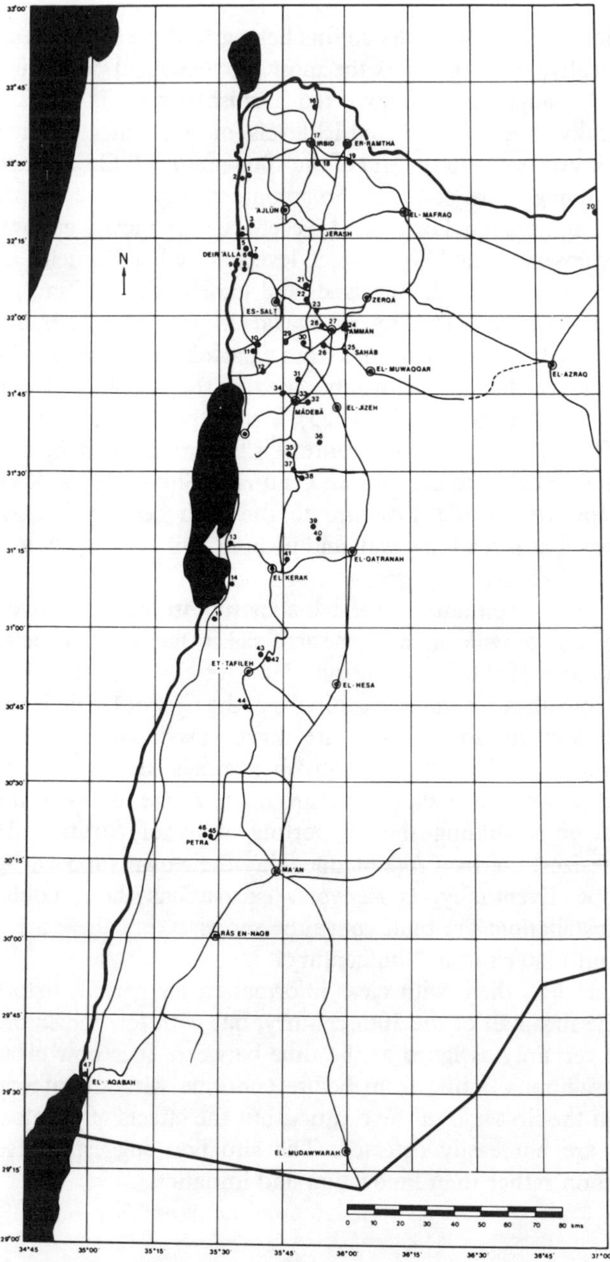

Map of western Transjordan, showing locations of relevant archaeological sites (Sites 1–47, see Site Lis
system is only approximate. Dots (•) indicate archaeological sites; dots in circles (⊙) represent sites of moder

SITE LIST

1. Ṭabaqat Faḥl (Pella)
2. Tell el-Ḥayyât
3. Tell el-Ḥandaqûq North
4. Tell es-Saᶜîdîyeh
5. Tell el-Mazâr
6. Tell Deir ᶜAllâ
7. Tell el-Ḥandaqûq South
8. Tell Umm Ḥammâd esh-Sharqî
9. Qaṭâret es-Samrâ
10. Tell Nimrîn
11. er-Rashîdîyeh West
12. Tell Iktanwah
13. Bâb edh-Dhrâᶜ
14. Numeira
15. eṣ-Ṣâfî
16. Quweilbeh (Abila)
17. Tell Irbid
18. Tell el-Ḥuṣn
19. Tell er-Rumeith
20. Jâwâ
21. Beqᶜah Valley
22. Tell Ṣâfûṭ
23. Tell Sîrân
24. ᶜAmmân Airport "Temple"
25. Saḥâb
26. el-Meqâbelein
27. ᶜAmmân (Rabbah of the Ammonites; Philadelphia)
28. Rujm el-Malfûf North
29. ᶜArâq el-Emîr
30. Khirbet el-Ḥajjâr
31. Tell Ḥesbân (Heshbon; Esbus)
32. Jalûl
33. Mâdebâ (Medeba)
34. Khirbet el-Mekhayyaṭ (Nebo)
35. Khirbet Iskander
36. Khirbet el-Medeiyineh Themed
37. Dhîbân (Dibon)
38. ᶜArâᶜir (Aroᶜer)
39. Khirbet el-Medeiyineh North
40. Khirbet el-Medeiyineh South
41. Ader
42. Khirbet Abû Bannâ
43. Khirbet Mashmîl
44. Buṣeira (Bozrah)
45. Ṭawilân
46. Umm el-Biyârah
47. Tell el-Kheleifeh

c. *Zones 6 and 7: Jordan Trough and Transjordan*

Transjordan explorations have linked the south to the pattern in Cisjordan and the northern zones [Figure 19]. Surveys in the Jordan and Arabah troughs, the associated wadi and river systems, and the eastern plateaus have clarified the eastern and southern extent of LB and Iron Age habitation (Boling, 1988; Dornemann, 1983; Sauer, 1986). As in Syria, the sharp decline in the total number of recorded sites during the transition from MBII to LB continues into Iron I, but the distribution of populations changes. Surveys extending from north to south in Transjordan record 1037 MBII sites, 111 LB, 100 Iron I, and 27 with both LB and Iron I sherds (Boling, 1988: 16-35).

Against the suggested downward trends, the plateaus north of the Wadi Mujib show a slight increase in settlement density during the LB period and immediately south of the ravine the percentage of LB sites in ancient Moab is nearly double that of the total MB period. Moreover, LB density in Moab is twice that of northern Transjordan. Further south, LB occupation, except for Midianite remains, are poorly attested (Sauer, 1986: 8). The northern decline and southern increase and the movement from valley to plateau are probably related. People are moving southward and to the uplands in the LB Age.

In the far south on both sides of the Arabah, in the Negev (Timnah), and in the northern Hejaz region of Saudi Arabia (Tayma and Qurayya), concentrations of so-called Midianite pottery from the LB period are found. The limits of the Midianite finds confine the peoples' influence to southern, eastern, and southwestern zones of our model.

The distribution of Midianite wares in Arabia and contiguous areas suggests an association between the Midianite population and the demise of a northern LB Hittite empire, as well as two waves of LB/Iron I southerly migration (Boling, 1988: 26-28). If a Midianite "empire" flourished in Iron I, it was one more center of control that contributed to the swirl of movements. This one pulled from the desert side of the J-shaped Fertile Crescent and distinguished itself from groups north and west of the line.

The same pattern is not found in northern Transjordan wadis or on the eastern desert fringes. Few signs of MB and LB occupation are found there, but Iron I appears frequently. The patterns of continuity and discontinuity in Iron I vary greatly, however. In the north, for example, where few MB II sites yield LB sherds, a much higher percentage of LB sites are occupied in Iron I. The contrast between the MB/LB and LB/Iron transitions suggests more disruption and unrest between MB and LB than between LB and Iron I (N. Lapp, 1983).

LB sedentary occupation is now documented at a number of Transjordan sites including the Amman citadel, the Amman airport, Sahab, and in the Baq'ah valley. At all but the airport, Iron IA sedentary remains are also found. In fact, LB, IA, IB and Iron II pottery together with Mycenaean IIIB ceramics are contained in tombs in the Baq'ah valley suggesting not only a fully sedentary LB population in the area, but also that the region is already a trade route from the Jordan valley to Amman in the LB period (McGovern, 1980: 57-60). Araq el-Amir, a few kilometers west of Amman, also has a pure Iron IA level.

In the Yarmouk valley, Iron IB and IC predominate at Tell el-Ehdeb (Kerestes et al., 1978: 120) but further south in the Jordan valley, IA, IB, and IC are all abundant. Telul edh Dhahab, a double mound in the Zarqa valley, may be especially important because it lies near the Ajlun hills known to be a source of iron during later periods. On the west mound, Iron IC sherds, signs of a foundry, and iron slag are all found (Gordon and Villiers, 1983; Gordon, 1984). Whether they are contemporaneous will not be known until the site is excavated, but their presence offers a basis for exploring the origins of iron technology in the IC era.

Elsewhere Iron IC appears alone or above IB. Tenth century remains have been excavated at Deir 'Alla, as we have noted, and at Mazar (Sauer, 1986: 13). IC is documented at Tell Nimrin a few kilometers north of the Dead Sea and at Pella farther north in the valley. Tell er-Rumeith on the plateau east of Irbid has IC occupation but apparently not earlier than the late 10th century B.C.E. (P. Lapp, 1968; N. Lapp, 1975: 114). Similar ceramics are found on the plateaus in several tombs at Irbid and Madeba, at Khirbet el-Mekhayyat, and perhaps as far south as Buseira and Tell el-Kheleifeh (Sauer, 1986: 13-14).

Heshbon in the Madeba plain is not occupied earlier than Iron IA. Recent surveys connected with the site, with Tell Jalul, and with neighboring Tell el-Umeiri reveal a substantial increase in new foundations (more than 20% of the sites in two samples) during Iron I. This suggests the emergence of intensive agriculture during the period even though at Madeba itself, the only Iron IA remains are in tombs.

The picture in Edom farther south, while less clear, is notably different. Bennett claims there is no sign of Iron I at three prominent sites, Umm el-Biyarah, Tawilan, and Buseirah (Bennett, 1983: 16). Her conclusion is accepted with some skepticism, in part because the Wadi el-Hasa survey north of the cities records almost no LB sites but some LB/Iron I and Iron I sites, including both IA and IC ceramics (Boling, 1988: 24). However, among more than 1000 sites in the el-Hasa survey, only five in fact are Iron Age. Likewise, Dhiban, the capital of the Moabites, and Aroer, located on the north bank of the Wadi Mujib, each have Iron IA with no LB beneath.

With the exception of the Midianite finds mentioned above, little or no trace of LB occupation is found in the extreme southern Transjordan. For instance, in areas between Ma'an and Aqaba, territories traditionally allotted to the Edomites, no occupation between Chalcolitic times and Iron I is found while all phases of Iron I are possibly represented (W. Jobling, 1981: 109; 1982). The sample is small and therefore relatively uncertain, but five Iron Age sites in the Ma'an district seem to be settled complexes associated with a caravan route through the area.

Other Indications of Interdependence

Thus far, the analytical model of ancient actions portrays populations shifting dramatically several times between MB I and Iron IC, and contemporaries in each phase interacting constantly and symbiotically. In the last centuries, local initiatives, labor-intensive economies, and new syntheses of disrupted and continuing traditions combine to restore part of the region's previous status as a conduit for foreign trade, a role it never loses completely (Redford, 1985: 195).

The tension between local conditions that enable microscale subsistence on the one hand and regional factors that allow macroscale alliances on the other is evident. With incongruity, the latter are often credited to the arrival of exogenous peoples, while the former are explained by the absence of outside interference. Consequently, information about the area's own cultural and economic contributions and their influence on neighboring territories is seldom examined. However, Redford (1985: 197) insists that between the 13th and 8th centuries, Egypt's language and myths were influenced by West Asia, possibly by Israel and Hebrew directly. Still, in terms of today's scholarship, the Iron IC territories in David's world are cast predominantly as importers rather than exporters of goods, services, and ideas.

The northern "origin" of red, hand-burnished ceramics in the Amuq, the southern, Egyptian "source" for anthropoid clay coffins, and the western "approach" of Mycenaean and Philistine elements have already been cited. Together with the northern Syrian influence on architecture, they represent the directions from which currents swept into and through the Mediterranean basin during Iron I. Later we must consider whether a fifth eastern wind also blew, bringing "migrations" as is often claimed, but first the extent of the other pressures must be reviewed.

The collared-rim jar, once thought to be typically Israelite and now known as a widely dispersed, locally manufactured, Iron IA ceramic exhibiting slight regional or temporal variations, is a paradigm for the cultural processes during the period. In this and other instances, local artisans borrow heavily from before and beside them in their struggle to impose their own identifying stamp on their work. Rarely, however, do they succeed in totally suppressing the characteristics of their benefactors and predecessors.

Another example of such relationships is the Balu'a Stele from Transjordan, dating sometime between 1309 and 1151 B.C.E. It represents a local attempt to imitate an Egyptian art form and perhaps to copy the Egyptian language (Ward and Martin, 1964). The same influence continues and is reflected in 9th to 6th century stone statues found in the Amman area, but by then a cosmopolitan confluence of Egyptian, Syrian, and Phoenician traditions has become evident in locally reproduced objects (Horn, 1973; Dornemann, 1983: 154). Influences from inland Syria are by then one of the strongest (Dornemann, 1983: 162).

Similar northern Syrian and neo-Hittite archaeological associations are now recognized in the 10th century temple at Arad and indirectly in the Solomonic temple at Jerusalem (Shiloh, 1979a: 154-56). Their elongated tripartite form is similar to *bit-ḫilani* structures unearthed at Tell Ta'yinat in the Amuq, Tell Chuera near Taurus, Tell Ebla, and especially at the LB Tell Emar on the Euphrates (Haines, 1971; Crowther and Pichon, 1985: 132). Shiloh, however, argues that the similarities extend to form only and that Cisjordan building techniques derive from elsewhere. He accepts the northern Syrian background for the *bit-ḫilani* form but assigns building techniques to Phoenician influence. However, the 10th and 9th century Cisjordan ashlar masonry and proto-aeolic capitals, like the four-room house, he feels, are the products of local genius that may have influenced surrounding cultures (Shiloh, 1979b: 85, 88). Hence, LB and Iron I indigenous peoples not only merge their skills with plans derived from elsewhere, they also add to the fundamental architectural and artistic repertories.

Similar claims have been made on the basis of Iron I cultic installations and objects. Although some Cisjordan LB sacred structures and spaces continue to be used during Iron I, others are abandoned or greatly reduced in size. Stelae-*maṣṣēbôt* and cultic stands common in the LB Age also continue, but other objects such as the horned altar found both at northern and southern sites are Iron Age innovations (Shiloh, 1979a: 156).

Techno-economic Factors

Increased use of terraces, cisterns, and storage pits in the Cisjordan highlands during Iron I has already been cited. The strategies allow cultivation of cereals, vineyards, and orchards in ecological zones previously unexploited. Archaeological information now being collected in other areas suggests that identical risk-spreading tactics are employed in Transjordan and Lebanon (Hopkins, 1985: 256; Marfoe, 1979). Cultivation and transhumanent animal husbandry provide at least part of the economic base in most areas. Hence, Hopkins' examination of these factors as well as of land use and crop rotation, climate and rainfall, and labor specialization and utilization in Cisjordan apply to developments elsewhere. Transhumanent pastoralism is mixed with sedentary cultivation to provide consumable by-products from sheep- and goat-grazing while also utilizing youthful and elderly family members as labor. A combination of strategies is also designed to exploit intermittently fallow plots, orchards, and vineyards as well as harvested fields.

The amount of surplus from agriculture and nomadic pastoralism during Iron I is difficult to determine on the basis of today's Near Eastern archaeology. Nevertheless, production capacities and economic diversity known from the archaeology of earlier and later periods and inferred from archival sources such as tax records leave little doubt that the carrying capacity during Iron I is sufficient to sustain the population and generate limited surpluses if appropriate social, economic, and political mechanisms are in place. Peaceful conditions are needed in order to avoid waste and exploitation.

Similar uncertainty affects modern evaluations of metallurgy's role in the region's productivity. The transition from bronze to iron as the dominant substance for tools and weapons is gradual and correspondingly difficult to document. Worked, as opposed to meteoric, iron begins to appear in tombs, cultic spaces, and occasionally on occupational levels in Iran, Mesopotamia, Egypt, and Anatolia as early as the 5th and 4th millennia B.C.E. Use increases steadily into the LB Age when artifacts first appear in Syro-Palestine (cf. Waldbaum, 1978; 1980; McNutt, 1983: 117-134; Frick, 1985: 177-189; Stager, 1985: 10-11). From then until Iron IC, four trends are established.

First, the absolute number of iron objects from excavations increases steadily as does the ratio of iron to bronze finds. Second, the high ratio of iron jewelry over against tools and weapons reverses by the 10th century. The shift is clear even though weapons and armor continue amid grave goods, which indicates their enduring symbolic and prestige value. Third, the earlier predominance of iron among grave goods gives way to iron's greater frequency in occupational areas and on living surfaces. Fourth, the rapid increase in the use of iron is not restricted to a single "cultural" group. Attempts to credit the invention or introduction of iron technology in Syro-Palestine to either Philistine or non-Philistine peoples on the basis of locations of finds and associated ceramics are unsuccessful (cf. Waldbaum, 1978; 1980; Davis et al., 1985; Muhly, 1980).

The last trend prohibits attaching distribution patterns to specific originating cultural groups such as the Hittites, Philistines, Canaanites, or Israelites. The difficulty, coupled with the diverse developmental schemes outlined above, implies the futility of searches for an "ethnic" monopoly of iron technology. What can be known is that the metal is extremely valuable, indeed precious, before it becomes common and is sought for its usefulness (Muhly, 1980). Those who control or share its sources, products, or distribution mechanisms enjoy at first exceptional prestige and wealth and later power relative to the ore's availability and worth. In sum, throughout its LB/Iron I evolution, the ore is always a means of storing wealth and demonstrating privilege, and sometimes a way of satisfying practical needs.

Migration, Exchange, and Trade

By the end of Iron Age IC many of the exchange systems disrupted during the transition from LB II are re-established. Foreign goods reappear among archaeological finds. Together with signs of centralization, these demonstrate both contact with exogenous peoples and intraregional exchange.

Typically, historians associate Bronze Age collapse with interrupted trade. While no doubt true in part, the claim may leave a distorted impression. Redford's opinion has already been cited. Moreover, although the eastern Mediterranean basin is located at the margins of Eurasian and African land masses so that unrest in those centers and reduced exchange among them affects the territories between, diminution of outside support also forces local populations to develop new strategies of self-reliance through intra- and inter-regional exchange. Two elements in a suzerain's trade interest can be identified, i.e., geographic and production interests (Coote and Whitelam: 1987: 63-66). The LB/Iron I era is a time of oscillation between them. In alternating degrees, the region is valuable to outsiders, sometimes because of its strategic location as a conduit and bridge linking (or separating) competing powers, and sometimes because it is a source for commercial products and human services—primarily intensive labor and militia—who are employed locally or transported elsewhere.

The distinction is useful but it casts the region almost entirely in a pawn's role and ignores the mobility of products and personnel that characterizes life even when foreign trade slackens. Indeed the oscillation between international and intraregional exchange is a measure of the centralization-versus-egalitarian pressures in the area. When international domination or exogenous incursions prevail, foreign trade goods appear at local sites. When or where outside interests have less impact, local productions, sometimes reproductions, are found. This is obvious. What is less easily determined, however, is the extent of intraregional, interzonal exchange that thrives in spite of international fluctuations.

Marfoe's preliminary hypothesis regarding seasonal migrations in the Biqa that he tentatively applies to highland Cisjordan offers a heuristic tool for formulating an initial answer (1979). His extended argument rightly implies that migrations (movement of people) and exchanges (movement of goods) are two aspects of the same socioeconomic phenomenon. On the spectrum of strategies for spreading risks and opportunities, mobility of people and assets such as livestock stand at one end while specialized production, transporting, and marketing are at the other. But the continuum is unbroken. The interactions, although diverse, address real human needs and, like distinctions among African and Eurasian modes of production and reproduction (Goody, 1976), are symptoms and causes of other patterns of sociopolitical and religious behavior.

Summary of Preliminary Observations

Before leaving the analytical model, it will be helpful to summarize the archaeological information presented thus far.

First, excavations and surveys at a number of sites and regions scattered over the broad expanse of the eastern Mediterranean basin reveal a more diverse geographical and fluid social picture than static phasing allows. Compelling impressions of material "cultural" unity do not emerge, if at all, until the latter half of the 10th century. Even then peoples depend heavily on diverse traditions from near and far. However, some stabilization in an apparent fissioning process does occur during the first half of the century and is indicated by the incipient construction phases at several sites. But the preliminary developments also rest on diverse bases. In some instances, there is continuity with Iron IA occupation, in others local evolution—or devolution—from LB culture, and in some displacing or building upon Iron IB.

Second, when this assessment is considered together with the geographical spread of contemporary occupations throughout the seven zones mentioned above (and in Appendix I), certain patterns emerge. In the first place, in Cisjordan the areas that seem to experience the most continuous activity from Iron IA-IC lie between the two southernmost E-W geological depressions, i.e, the Jezreel and Beersheba corridors (Zone 3, the parallel portion of coastal Zone 5, and part of Zone 4), but the activity fans out in northernly and especially southernly directions in Transjordan (Zones 6 and 7). Secondly, in Iron I, populations shifted in directions and into areas that our geographical survey identified as offering only marginal subsistence. The movements are a swirl, but they certainly include movements from west toward east and from north toward south as well as into mountainous areas, wadi systems, and desert fringes. Finally, in spite of the pattern of concentration in certain regions and the apparent accompanying economic limitations, influences from beyond these zones play an important role in shaping artifacts, artistic and inscriptional materials, and architectural projects during Iron IC. By comparison with the periods immediately before, IC becomes increasingly cosmopolitan.

Third, the geographical extension of the LB, Cypriote, Mycenaean, Midianite, IA, and IB materials beneath IC is informative. Just as no single progenitor gives rise to IC, no single zone is its cradle. Although areas that are most clearly IC often exhibit only late 10th century (post-Davidic) finds, the unity achieved during this second IC phase often seems to rest on earlier IC movements toward unification.

Fourth, Iron IB is associated with various Sea Peoples who occupy the coastline from north to south, move overland along trade routes in Syria, and penetrate inland through the Jezreel corridor and into the Jordan and Yarmouk valleys. Their influence also extends through the southern W-E/SE corridor and across the northern Negev and may affect trade in the Transjordan Baq'ah valley. The distribution places the peoples not only in strategic trading zones and along trade routes but also in areas where they might serve as buffers and barriers between factions and against exogenous powers, especially Egypt, and in locations that mark the boundaries of ecological zones. They enjoy access both to the sea and to eastern and southern arid and semi-arid regions. Like others, they build on the cultures of those before them, but they also introduce influences from their trading partners and earlier contacts.

Fifth, because LB, IA, IB, and IC occupations are not entirely sequential, a complex matrix of material and social development must be envisaged. Such a hypothesis must await discussion of the systemic model where we ask how pockets of LB culture survive through times customarily represented by IA and IB occupation phases and how IA endures until IC at some sites while IB continues with IC at others. In short, we must explain how the Iron IC culture that eventually put its stamp on the region incorporates forms and traditions from all of its predecessors rather than building upon a single culture or society identified with Iron IA population. The difference between closed-society and open-society models is at stake.

C. *Preliminary Archaeological Systemic Model*

Drawing on modern ethnographical models, Marfoe (1979), as noted above, analyzes the extreme diversity in land use and social patterns in Lebanon during the Iron Age. Constricted, circumscribed microenvironments, domination by urban elites, perpetual political uncertainties, and economic crises in subsistence agriculture motivate inhabitants to protect themselves by spreading risks.

Agricultural risks are reduced by mixing cultivation and husbandry and by forming social networks that extend across production zones at various elevations on the plains and in the mountains. The arrangements grant access to a cross-section of ecologies including higher, more moist, or more remote environments that could save agriculturalists and pastoralists in times of drought or political devastation. The unpredictable and uncontrollable nature of affairs produce dynamic rather than static traditional societies whose basic socioeconomic instability and demographic fluidity are related to the ecology.

Because the hypothesis is inferred for Iron Age Cisjordan as well, three implications should be noted. First, in politically and economically unstable conditions, maintaining security proves more important than maximizing profit. The preoccupation results in a continuum of familial, communal, and regional relationships that are always conditioned by the physical, geographic, and economic environment. Rather than sharp contrasts between urban and rural, pastoral and cultivating, or sedentary and nomadic groups, a range of options and strategies develops across an uninterrupted spectrum. The polarities or dichotomies we often use to describe groups actually represent the extremes in symbiotic relationships. Individuals and groups either move back and forth among options or live continuously in more than one social world (Gellner, 1973: 2; Mohammed, 1973: 111). For example, sedentary agriculturalists may also engage in transhumanent or nomadic pastoralism, and nomads may have a permanent, albeit seasonal, home or may live in both tent and house.

Second, vacillations or oscillations among economic and residential patterns may represent simultaneous evolutions and devolutions in the dependence of groups on social structures and forms. When faced with forced or opportune change, groups on both sides of issues continue to seek homeostasis. As a result, when competing strategies gain or lose adherents, they do so at each other's expense: when one evolves, the other devolves. But individuals and groups on either side of the flux seek the equilibrium that will guarantee their personal survival, usually with the least amount of change, and this conservative tendency pushes people toward compromises that often prevent a system's total, catastrophic collapse. Social change (the transducer effect) and social continuity (the homeostasis) exist, therefore, in a symbiotic relationship.

Third, in order to cope with turmoils in high-risk, constantly changing environs, inhabitants distinguish among the various bonds and planes of classification in their relationships. By sorting economic, political, social, and religious domains, they are then able to manipulate these elements so as to achieve durable social safeguards. In other words, a life securely lived in the eastern Mediterranean basin is a life spent constantly juggling overlapping but discrete domains of existence such as residence patterns, economic subsistence strategies, social structures, and cultural identities. In this regard, the conduct is like that represented in genealogies which integrate personal with place names and reflect economic, political, social, or religious relationships or combinations of them. Each domain is separate but closely related to the others, and each must be evaluated when turmoil threatens. Thus, pastoralism is not synonymous with nomadism or tribalism, and sedentarism is not the constant companion of urbanism or agrarianism. They are strategies in differing domains that within the limits of an ecology can be mixed and matched as needed. Consequently, what appears to be stable, traditional, or secure in a society may really be only the calm surface above a pool of floating, fluctuating options and temporary arrangements. Beneath, the environment is constantly being manipulated in order to gain or maintain equilibrium and stability.

Shaping the Hypothesis

On the surface at least, the image described in this observers' hypothesis illumines the systemic processes in Iron Age society. Contemporary clusters of artifacts evolving in close proximity to others and at differing rates of development, cultural borrowing from contemporaries as well as predecessors, temporary and seasonal shrines and residences, and pressures to exploit marginally productive zones all suggest strategies for coping with freedom, turmoil, and uncertainty. Change occurs, but it seems to be accepted reluctantly. Adaptation, accommodation, and imitation are hallmarks of its material signs.

The diversity that has been noted in the constricted environment of the Lebanon Biqa is replicated in the eastern Mediterranean basin generally. Climate, geomorphology, geography, and other aspects of the ecology outlined above are conducive to diversified strategies. Although the shifting patterns of settlement placement, density, and form recovered in our archaeological summary suggest that Iron Age I is a time of increased self-reliance and exploitation of diverse ecologies, there are also signs that the changes are neither abrupt nor fundamental.

Modern ethnographies from the ecological zones in our analytical model help inform our observers' model, illumine the hypothesis stated above, and illustrate the complexity of social change in traditional societies. We must emphasize, however, that regardless of the striking similarities between the archaeological information and circumstances in the modern case studies, the ethnographic comparisons reside in today's observer's model, not in an ancient mind, and are only heuristic aids for understanding the ancient state of affairs.

a. *Risk Spreading in Traditional Societies*

Two complementary sets of studies pertain to our questions. The first examines the conservative tendencies among tribes whose members spread risks by seeking income away from tribal territories. In a sense, these focus on diachronic relationships between old and new ways. The second concentrates on adaptation among groups interacting across ecological zones. These tend to stress synchronic and symbiotic relationships although they also describe diachronic changes that groups undergo because of adaptations.

During the 1960s and 1970s, Sinai and Negev Bedouin tribal and regional bonds were threatened by modernity, urbanization, and imposed exogenous administrative control (Marx, 1967; 1984a; 1984b). However, in spite of general trends toward urban wage-labor employment that might have disrupted traditional life and values, the opposite occurred. As wage earners moved into labor markets, they formed tribal residential and employment enclaves in the towns. Homes and families were maintained in tribal territories in spite of the wage earners' long absences. Tribal corporate descent groups and territories were held intact with the absentees' rights preserved. Limited pastoralism and cultivation were continued in the territories even when they yielded economic losses that put a drain on the outside wages (Marx, 1984a: 1-2). In these cases, the Bedouin literally lived in two worlds that enabled them to enjoy the advantages of wage-labor without surrendering a "basic economy" among traditional tribal allies.

Tribal ties are maintained, Marx finds, in spite of potential havoc and expense caused by droughts, epidemics, floods, and raids because they provide assurances of agnation and kinship that guarantee access to communal natural resources needed when the laborers' wages are interrupted. Disruptions are in fact anticipated because of regional political turmoil and the laborers' fragile social standing. Therefore, although the town labor produces wealth, it is reinvested in means that ensure security among the tribes. Polygamous marriages that expand social networks and provide future supports, gold, other luxury items that retain their value across social boundaries, and movable assets such as cars and trucks that do not confine the laborer to a particular town are common investments that protect against political and economic uncertainties.

Risks are spread by retaining the security of tribal frameworks and simultaneously developing support networks in new environs (Kressel,

1984; Cole, 1973; 1975). For example, Kressel demonstrates surprisingly that the size of sheep, goat, and, to a lesser degree, camel herds grew among the tribes of a Bedouin group who moved from the Negev to Jawarish near Tel Aviv even though the number of people left behind to engage in pastoralism declined. The change in the ratio of herd owners to herd size resulted from a developing tribal stratification that was needed to cope with expanding urbanism and government bureaucracy. As land leases became increasingly difficult to negotiate, large-scale operations with their accompanying political and economic leverage became more important. Complementary changes occurred. On the one hand, some wealthy Bedouin, now elite commercial producers who bridged several social worlds (Ahmed, 1973: 77-78), were integrated into the larger economic world by taking Israeli partners. The Israelis provided contacts with the government and land owners while the Bedouin partners furnished the food producing flocks and cheap labor. On the other hand, however, tribal bonds and loyalties were reinforced because tribal territories and family members provided the additional and varied grazing areas as well as the workers needed to sustain the growing enterprise.

Adaptations and accommodations in the Sinai varied from those of the urban Negev Bedouin. Town laborers usually did not relocate families or give up the small herds and farms. Instead, they lived with kinfolk, in tents, or in their work places with no plans for building or resettling. When the expected release from the labor force came, small farms and orchards in the hinterlands were relied upon for subsistence. Then and at other times when laborers tired of the urban environment, the areas were idyllic retreats and safe havens of refuge (cf. Marx, 1984b: 182).

In contrast, the Al Murrah from the Empty Quarter of Saudi Arabia working in the oil fields sometimes did build small shacks and were accompanied by family, but wives and children returned to the desert during grazing seasons and went to their tribal territories in the summer. Consequently, the traditional settlements were often populated by old men, women, and children, but rather than indicating a deterioration in tribal life, the phenomenon represented "a large scale maintenance operation" (Marx, 1984a: 11). In other words, the unusual demography was the product of an attempt to achieve or retain social homeostasis.

Two aspects of the Al Murrah situation at the time of Cole's study pertain to our archaeological systemic model. First, the tribal territory located in the Empty Quarter had no permanently settled agricultural communities (Cole, 1973: 114). Four semi-settled date palm oases were occupied seasonally during the summer, but during the rest of the year, tribal members traveled widely, as much as 1000 km annually, in search of suitable grazing areas. Some houses were built near permanent wells as a result of the Ikhwan, i.e., Muslim Brotherhood, movement during the period of state formation (Cole, 1973: 117). Although the motivation of Ibn Saud, Saudi Arabia's founder-king and patron of the settlement scheme, was economic and military as we shall explain in Chapter 5, the Bedouins' inspiration was religious. Ibn Saud needed pacification, control over the moods of the warrior Bedouin, and the economic productivity of sedentary agriculture, and he legitimated his plans by appealing to the tribes' fundamentalistic Wahhabism. Religion, in this case, served two masters.

The second point is connected with the relatively new economic resources—oil—that developed Arabian infrastructures. The new wealth has produced more houses and settlers even in outlying areas. But the new dwellings are not homes for the wealthy. Instead, three or four emergent statuses are now found in the settlements. Tribal affiliation and an egalitarian ideology unite the first three: 1) the sheikhs or "big men"; 2) the average semi-settled tribal members who do not participate in the hospitality of the more fortunate lineage members; and 3) the nomads who camp at the wells but do not participate in oasis life at all. The fourth status is that of hired laborers who perform the tasks that the nomads shun (Cole, 1973: 119). Hence, one group, although not economically deprived, is cast as outsiders in spite of others' dependency on them. Interaction with urban centers and the military establishment has contributed to tribal leaders' preeminence and has resulted in the nomads treating many urban specialists, including members of the royal family, like tribal sheikhs (Cole, 1973: 123). The power of the tribal leaders, therefore, depends not so much on their mediator's role within their own group as on their ability to mediate symbiotic relationships between the nomads, who are self-sufficient with regard to food, and the urban specialists, who provide the nomads' other cultural, social, and physical necessities. Hence, Cole decries attempts to describe Arab Bedouin as if they were well-defined and clearly bounded social groups. Rather, they are intimately involved in the dynamics of the wider society (Cole, 1973: 127) and, it would seem, participants in an open society. In our case, we must ask whether the rapidly developing economy of Iron IC did not foster the need for similar mediators' roles, not merely within individual communities as has been argued (Flanagan, 1981), but also among disparate economic and social groups.

The final investigation in our first set of studies takes us back to the 19th century C.E. and into the border zone between desert and sown near Beersheba (Marx, 1967). Before the latter part of that century, the Bedouin rarely enjoyed peace or security. Tensions erupted among the Bedouin themselves and between them and peasants who converged from the north and west along the 200 mm annual rainfall line that ran from Rafah on the coast through Beersheba and east to Malheta before it turned sharply north into the Judean hills, the same demarcation cited in our description of the J-shaped geography. The ecological conditions in the Beersheba plain rather than population pressures seem to have been the principal cause for the turbulence (Marx, 1967: 8).

In peaceful times, military posts and trade from passing caravans attracted civilian populations to the area. They prospered, but peace also induced the Bedouin to spend more time farming and to pay less attention to tribal boundaries (Marx, 1967: 10). Seven confederations in the Negev at the time of the research comprised between three and 25 tribes ranging from 750 to 21,000 members. Not surprisingly, the larger tribes were in the plains and the smaller ones in the hills and mountains reaching toward Hebron. The two largest confederations formed smaller territorial combinations which Marx labels "groups of tribes" (Marx 1967: 11). They understood themselves to be descended from a common human ancestor. Coalitions followed changing territorial and political alignments and thus were very fluid. Member tribes made no formal arrangements for political cooperation, and the group had no paramount chief.

Except at the northeastern edge of the territory where the Hebron hills offered a natural division, no clear boundary separated the lands of settled populations from the Bedouin district. Thus, in the northwestern Negev, pastoral and farm lands merged without demarcations, but in the northeast the clear-cut geographical boundary accentuated the differences between peasant and Bedouin life-styles (Marx, 1967: 20). Unpredictable rainfall reinforced Bedouin interests in animal husbandry in spite of the risks of epidemics and extreme droughts. In fact, however, most inhabitants spread risks between farming and herding, considering the former their economic mainstay and the latter their economic reserve (Marx, 1967: 22). Hence, water, cisterns, wells, and springs were sources of contention and became boundaries between tribes.

The widest political associations were tribes headed by sheikhs elected from the most powerful of the smaller divisions, the subtribes. Three stocks made up tribes: Bedouin, peasants, and slaves. The last were descendants of Black Africans. All were welded into a single unit in subtribes. However, because the tribes did not hold land, their boundaries were not as well defined as those of confederations.

Each subtribe centered around a core of comparatively powerful Bedouin (Marx 1967: 65). External Bedouin groups, small related Bedouin groups, and isolated families affixed themselves to the core and claimed descent from the common ancestor. Negroid peoples and attached peasant groups also affiliated, but even though the peasants were legally juxtaposed as equals with the Bedouin, neither developed a common genealogy with the core. Hence, again, a two-tiered social classification.

As a result of pacification begun in the 1870s, peasants settled permanently in Bedouin areas where boundaries had been fixed and security increased, and they began to move slowly eastward in search of land (Marx 1967: 76). The peasants tended to migrate twice a year, once after the first winter rains when they moved into wadis for protection while they tilled their land on the plains, and again in late April or early May when they advanced closer to their land for the barley harvest. By contrast, the Bedouin remained in small groups living away from the center of their subtribe. Although they maintained a permanent camp mainly for older members, they migrated frequently from higher to lower elevations in their territory in search of pastures (Marx 1967: 84).

The processes outlined in these cases are but examples of strategies that individuals and groups employ when faced with ecological diversity and political turmoil. Their common denominator is adaptation to economic, social, and political realities. New roles emerge and old ones subside, but they do so gradually and in response to the tension caused by new realities confronting old values. Goal ranges and reference values interact. Risks are spread first by traditional means and in an effort to retain traditional ways until eventually the new forms that have evolved can hardly be recognized as devolved forms of old roles. Metamorphosis and homeostasis are partners in the process.

b. *Adaptation among Traditional Groups*

The second set of studies examine the symbiotic interactions among disparate social groups as they adapt to encounters with each other. Meeker's controversial study presents cameo sketches of three societies in order to illustrate how peoples whose traditions were shaped in nomadic and pastoral environments came to dominate urban centers in arid zones and to reconstruct those civilizations around their own ideals and values (Meeker, 1979: xi; cf. also 1980). Again the 19th century C.E. weighs heavily because of the importance of the writings of Alois Musil and Charles M. Doughty on the Rwala, but the Cyrenaican Bedouin who migrated to North Africa from Arabia in the 11th century C.E., and the so-called saints of Morocco are also considered.

Figure 20: Ecological Zones in Cyrenaica with corresponding Husbandry

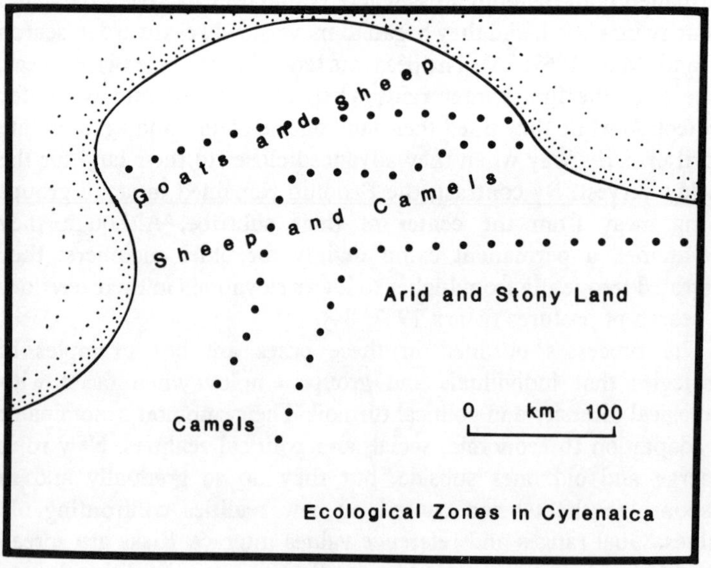

The pastoral zones and tribal groupings in Cyrenaica illustrate again how ecological matrices undergird human strategies [Figure 20]. Goat and cattle pastoralism dominate the coastal highlands where moisture is abundant, but as the terrain slopes downward toward the south and interior, rainfall declines progressively and the highland pattern gives way first to a zone where sheep and camel pastoralism prevail, then to full camel pastoralism, and finally to arid desert environs accessible only to the camel pastoralists. Demarcations of tribal territories, however, intersect the territorial bands so that tribes have access to narrow strips that cut perpendicularly across each of the zones [Figure 21]. The pattern allows tribal subdivisions

Figure 21: Distribution of the Hasa Tribes and Subtribes across Ecological Zones

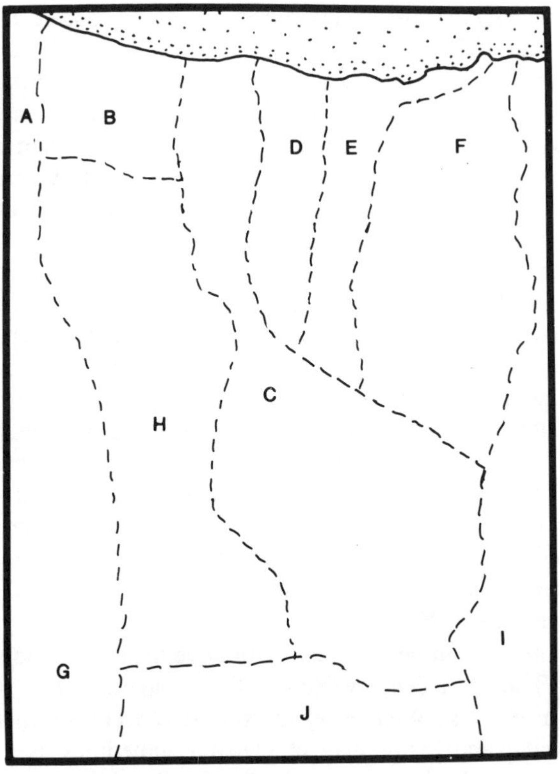

among groups like the Hasa to move back and forth from the shore to the interior and to have access to a cross-section of the ecologies in the entire region. The system demonstrates, for Meeker, that each "little group" strives to gain access to the scarce coastal agricultural land while preserving their ties to the pastures in the interior (Meeker, 1979: 204-205).

Geographically, the Rwala and Moroccan samples fall on either side of this pattern. The north Arabian territories stretch from the Nefud in Saudi Arabia northward to the area of Palmyra in Syria and eastward from the Transjordan plateaus along Jordan's present-day Desert Highway to the Euphrates valley. Morocco, on the other hand, enjoys a long coastline embracing both the Mediterranean and Atlantic, a coastal plain, the inland Atlas mountains and, farther to the south and east, the Pre-Sahara desert.

As expected, the contrasting environments have long been home to differing life styles and subsistence strategies. The Great Syrian desert harbors pastoral nomads almost exclusively. During earlier years these were primarily camel herders. On the other hand, a variety of pastoralists and agriculturalists, rural and urban dwellers, Bedouin, peasants, and specialists populate Morocco where settled and semi-settled Berbers live in proximity to nomadic and semi-nomadic Arabs.

The instability we have described elsewhere is found in both areas, but again with notable differences. Among pastoral nomads such as the Rwala, food gathering strategies result from passive adaptation to an ecology that on the one hand leaves them with limited economic self-regulation and on the other with constant needs for agricultural commodities, the handicraft and services of artisans, and manufactured products (Khazanov, 1981: 156). The dilemma poses two alternatives—settling or establishing contacts with sedentary peoples—neither wholly satisfactory. The first would transform life completely, and the second, although necessary, is made difficult by the mobility of the nomads which undercuts stable and systematic relationships with other groups (Meeker, 1979: 17).

Detachment from land creates distinctive life styles among camel nomads. The 19th century Rwala, for instance, were "polarized around the exercise of violence, an exercise conceived sometimes as an absorbing and joyful play of life and sometimes as a serious struggle against death" (Meeker, 1979: 19). The endemic violence of raiding and counterraiding affected domestic and alien relationships and was glorified in songs and stories. At the same time, verbal conflict was typical of camp life where the free time that pastoralism allowed was spent in idleness and ill-tempered combativeness (Meeker, 1979: 25). Physical labor was shunned and those who did it were looked down upon. The Sleyb, for instance, who were a class of desert tinkers, craftsmen, and laborers, were despised by the Bedouin in spite of their dependence on them for necessities as important as camel surgery and blacksmithing. The Sleyb went unrecognized to wander peacefully in small groups performing their services, but because they could not plunder or be plundered, the Bedouin viewed them as desolate and lacking "citizenship" (Meeker, 1979: 22).

In a sense, the Rwala created an economy of aggression that, like others, was profitable when it was expanding and costly when it was not. Because camels could be easily raided and were extremely mobile, roles of raider and victim were virtually and often suddenly interchangeable. The best protection for one's herd was to be raiding another's. This, and the fact that for practical reasons tribal groups tend to align with stronger and more successful groups, engendered delicate balances of power that in turn placed groups atop precarious structural faults. Peace, or minimally the avoidance of victimization, depended on a group's ability to inflict more violence than it received.

As we have seen, such tensions have led social scientists to speak of segmented societies and to describe their accompanying genealogies as political metaphors that represent social strategies for maintaining order. The advantages and disadvantages of strong leadership in segmented societies have been weighed less often. In theory, alliances are struck among individuals and groups in response to other threatening alliances, and the relationships among comrades are described in real or fictive kinship terms. As a result, at each level of size, all segments are equal and without division of labor between them. From the standpoint of the individual, each is at the center of a number of concentric circles with no conflict between one level and the next. Membership in the family, subtribe, tribe, or confederation merely represents the different levels of an individual's responsibilities, supports, and identities. Because there is no overarching political authority to impose order on the entire system or at levels within it, segmented societies depend on checks and balances of power between friends and foes to reduce or contain violence. In genealogies, the ancestors, saints, or other "progenitors" define social units and mark the various levels of their involvement so that communities and individuals know the extent of their obligations and can measure both their rights and the seriousness of their problems. The Arab saying, "I against my brother; I and my brother against our cousins; I, my brother, and our cousins against outsiders," illustrates both the strategy and the formative role of opposition in a segmented system.

Although he does not reject the concept of segmented society or deny that the Rwala should be portrayed as such, Meeker questions whether the model suits a fully nomadic, landless group such as the North Arabians.

> There are two contradictory motivations at work in the elementary form of a politically segmenting genealogy. There is a threat from abroad, which provokes an attempt to construct a political relationship as a source of protection from that threat. However, there is also an interest in preserving one's political freedom from such a relationship, which otherwise restricts an interest in political adventurism. This means that political relationships take a "segmentary form" at every level where the threat abroad (which brings men together) is indecisively balanced against a reluctance to relinquish an interest in political adventurism (which drives men apart) (Meeker, 1979: 188).

This means a qualitative difference between intertribal and intratribal political relationships. Rwala tribal members, according to Meeker, knew only the structure of low-level relationships, and in fact no precise intertribal structure existed except at times of conflict. Tribal chiefs and leaders, therefore, served as political architects who represented the confederation only at those times (Meeker, 1979: 192). Such alliances were temporary.

Without resolving the specific issue, we may liken the inter- vs. intratribal tension to the dilemma of macro- and microlevel associations in many societies (cf. Khalaf, 1987) or to societies' ambivalence about strong leadership which if benevolent is an asset but if tyrannical a terrible liability. Both cases illustrate people's reluctance to surrender local autonomy for the benefits of broader associations. Meeker, however, compares the differences to contrasts between the asymmetrical genealogies among the Cyrenaican Bedouin and the irregular segmentation at all levels in the genealogies of the landed Moroccans. Each reflects attempts to reconcile the dilemma of contradictory "political and domestic" interests (Meeker, 1979: 201, 218-219).

Tyranny from "strong men" with armed followers threaten constantly in Morocco. Because tyrants are close to home and frequently try to establish themselves permanently, all attempts to systematize political authority are feared. Consequently, political authority is popularly perceived as illegitimate, strong commitments are made to subgroupings portrayed in the genealogies, and consensus among an assembly of elders is the preferred means for reaching political decisions. Each tactic defends intragroup support against intergroup alliances.

In spite of the resistance, settled conditions often force tribal members to recognize a leader. Then, the Berbers and others devise *ad hoc* and temporary measures that provide for chiefs to serve one-year terms and for the office to rotate among tribal sections. The system of rotation and complementarity, similar to the *wesh* system among the Swat in northwest Pakistan, precludes the unit supplying the chief from participating in the election (Gellner, 1981: 118; Barth, 1959-60; Meeker, 1980: 686). The system operates at a number of levels of segmentation simultaneously but allows for variation among levels. At the top, for instance, a chief might be elected only when needed while at the bottom among a tiny group the entire population might vote. The flexibility respects the suspicious attitude toward organization while also preventing patronage from dominating.

A second strategy that protects against tyranny is the part played by saints in Morocco and elsewhere. Saints hold formidable mystical powers yet they own no land, belong to their own lineages rather than to those of the lay tribe members, and hold no political office. They live in settlements around shrines of founding ancestors to whom they and the people in the settlement are linked genealogically. No feuding is allowed at the shrine (Gellner, 1981: 120).

Again, Meeker interprets the ethnography differently from Evans-Pritchard, Gellner, and others. All agree, however, that it must be viewed against the background of the weak chieftaincy and lack of continuity within the political system (Gellner, 1981: 119). The fact that all chiefs are lame ducks elected by their rivals prevents permanence and tyranny, but it also denies them the means of maintaining order, save for their powers of persuasion and public pressure.

In this environment, the saints' role is to provide the continuity and stable framework lacking in the political structure. Because the shrines are located at the boundaries of lay tribal territories, Gellner interprets their role as that of mediators (Gellner, 1981: 120-121). Elections are held at the shrine (out of reach of feuds); the saints use moral persuasion and mediation to ensure unanimous elections; the saints are arbitrators, in effect the cornerstone of the legal system; and the shrines guarantee the boundary lines. Succession, although popularly attributed to the deity's choice, is determined by public confidence in the individual's generosity, pacifism, and prosperity, and the choice can fall to someone outside the saintly lineages. Nevertheless, the people know the choice is theirs, but the institution enables them to distinguish between divine and human factors in political life. The former are immutable, the latter changeable by consent.

Meeker's interpretation, based in part on Barth's studies on the Swat, emphasizes the continuity rather than the complementarity between chiefly and saintly functions. Recognizing that shrines are located where chiefs can not establish stable followings—in inferior geographic, economic, and cultural locales—Meeker argues for a transcendental dimension to political life. "Politics polarised around the exercise of force *leads to* religion polarised around peace" (emphasis his; Meeker, 1980: 696). In sum, among agrarian peoples the tension between resorting to force and coercion and engaging in diligent labor and peaceful cooperation gives rise to a continuous strategy for effecting both (Meeker, 1980: 697).

More will be said about adaptation and homeostasis in later chapters. This preliminary glance at comparative sociological information is sufficient to illustrate both the complexity and the manner that traditional societies confronting uncertainty in times of change use in resolving problems. Independence retained or gained is greatly prized, especially where tyranny has been a common experience. Needs for federation, unification, or other inter-unit alliances are met with caution and suspicion. The examples suggest that segmented systems and ideologies are a common response in Middle Eastern societies and that the values they reflect are protected in settled and agrarian areas as well as in the desert and among nomads. The relationship between these strategies and their environments as well as the dynamics of change that they mediate and reflect support an observers' hypothesis regarding the early Iron

Age. It is in effect a systemic archaeological model that describes the processes and relationships of the Iron Age in terms of a segmented model.

Segmented Model for Iron I Archaeology

The archaeological relationships of Iron Age I are synchronic and symbiotic as well as diachronic. The archaeological information in our analytical model interpreted in light of the complex processes that continue to shape Middle Eastern life demands something other than a unilineal, diachronic model of social change. This requires a move away from the emphasis on sequence dating and the biases for making so-called "Israelite" development normative for contemporary Iron Age cultures. These have led to oversimplified explanations that do not do justice to the complexity of early life. Then, as later, the ebb and flow of circumstances were reciprocal as well as sequential.

As has happened in other regions (cf. Shaffer and Lichtenstein, n.d.), "non-normative" information has been read through the lenses of later history and literature so that Iron Age groups have been understood as largely closed societies developing only within their own cultural contexts and in opposition to other groups. But geographical, ancient, and modern sources agree that interaction and variety characterize the region. Peoples throughout time have been affected by and have constantly monitored their ecological environs, retaining or adjusting their ways to suit the circumstances. Whether Iron Age people responded maladaptively or adaptively remains to be seen, but on the basis of material information alone, homeostasis bracketed by evolution and devolution was constantly met on the region's seaways, pathways, and plains.

Irregular typological changes have been examined. The developmental pattern in the material remains compares favorably to the processes seen in ethnographies of segmented societies. Dual but simultaneous processes of fissuring and fusing mark periods of unrest. In archaeology, the LB tradition, for example, terminated at some sites, continued uninterrupted at others, and absorbed new influences at still others. Or again, the spread of Iron IA artifacts into diverse ecological zones where local variations developed represents movement across geographical regions and symbiotic relationships among their inhabitants. And the appearance of IB materials with their Mycenaean influences, especially along trade routes and the margins of ecological zones, suggests both domestic and foreign

Figure 22: Initial Cultural / Ecosystem Interaction

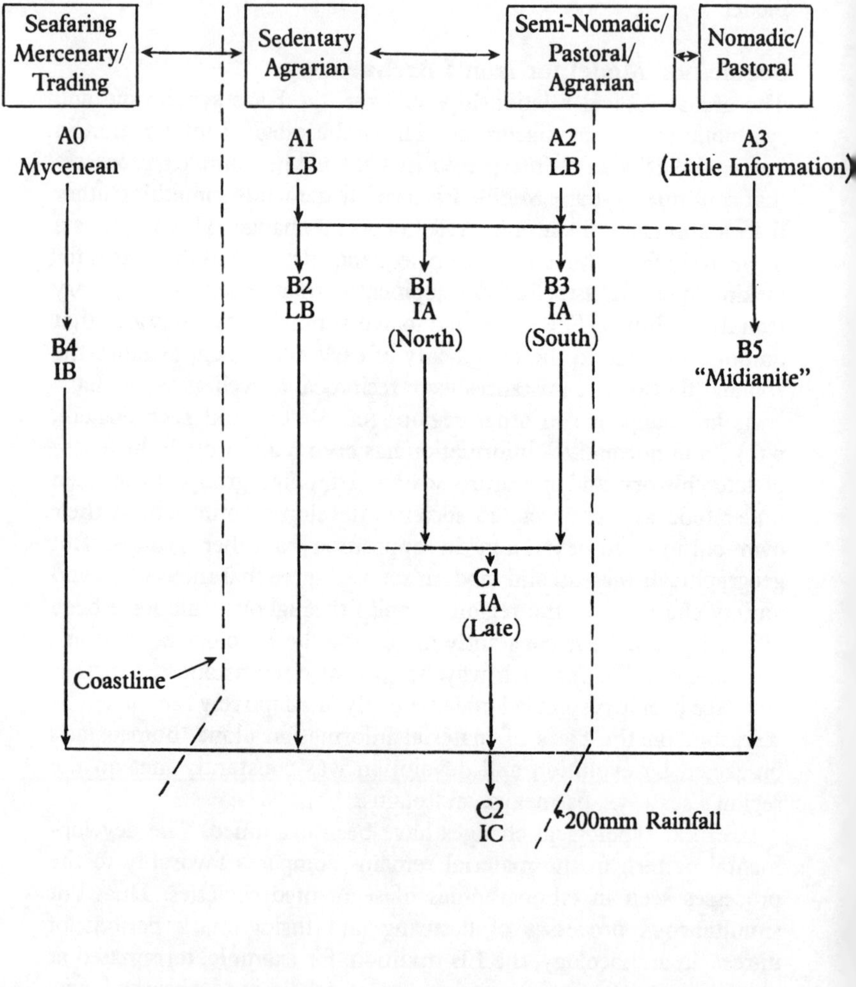

trading. Finally, IC—which draws on northern Syrian as well as Egyptian traditions and develops above LB, IA, and IB materials, again with their local variations— demonstrates a fusing of earlier fissioned groups.

The geographical spread of materials can be summarized according to four overlapping ecological zones [Figure 22]. Moving west to east from the Mediterranean toward the interior desert, these range from the sea to agricultural lands to steppelands to desert. They support contrasting but complementary residential and economic subsistence strategies: 1) seafaring mercenary traders; 2) sedentary agrarians; 3) semi-sedentary/semi-nomadic semi-agrarian/semi-pastoralism; and 4) nomadic pastoralism.

In the Iron Age, centrifugal and centripetal forces were at work in the wake of the end of the Late Bronze Age. These pushed and pulled peoples back and forth across the earth's surface primarily along trade routes, according to rainfall patterns, or along geographical corridors that allowed access to resources and subsistence living.

If drawn as a chart with archaeological cultural groups as the subjects, the processes resemble the genealogical tables used to represent segmented societies (compare Shaffer and Lichtenstein, n.d.). Cultures and regions, which are in effect personal and place names, are mixed as they are in ancestral genealogies. Likewise, tracing the fusions and fissions involve personal choices, like a genealogist's, about dominances, continuities, and discontinuities and about who is the chart's genealogical ego.

By setting the chart against a map of geographical, ecological, and archaeological zones, a limited number of explanations for historical development become possible. Here we will describe one, in preliminary fashion, that will be used below in the fuller holographic systemic model.

First, LB and Iron I cultures existed on both sides of the rift system and spread throughout much of Syro-Palestine. Although the LB culture continued to evolve with regional variations such as "Phoenician," "Aramean," and "Canaanite" characteristics, new forms evolved from endogenous and exogenous roots. The latter are most clearly evident in the remains of the "Sea Peoples." As mentioned above, they spread along trade routes, in connecting valleys (especially the Jezreel valley, the third E-W geographical corridor), and across an area that extends through the fourth, i.e.,

Beersheba, corridor and northward from it to the southern end of the northern highlands near Jerusalem.

The endogenous materials are frequently continuing or degenerate forms of LB traditions, locally produced without the technique of earlier artisans. The pattern is one of continuity and early evolution in the midst of devolving cultures. Devolution is indicated by reduced sizes and production quality and the emergence of artifacts that imitate earlier, more elegant forms.

The evolution of a new culture is indicated, however, by major shifts in population, the rapid development of earlier economic strategies, and the emergence of a new metal in the manufacture of utilitarian implements. The spread, as well as the concentrations, of IA occupation must also be noted. Not only are new, small, unfortified villages and hamlets founded in the Cisjordan highlands, but IA peoples also move into the wadis and onto the eastern and southern desert fringes of Transjordan and southward to arid and semi-arid regions of the Negev. These are agriculturally marginal zones that require labor-intensive cultivation—such as terrace farming and storage—or transhumanent or full pastoralism, or some combination of them.

It is difficult to determine the direction of the movement, and discrepancies between archaeological and literary information must be weighed eventually. Literary claims, however, typically credit such changes, whether Israelite, Aramean, Philistine, or otherwise, to hordes of invaders from the desert or sea. But as we have noted above, the presumed later dating, for example, of the collared-rimmed jar in Transjordan as suggested by Dornemann indicates movement from west to east and from north to south. The same has been inferred from sites such as Tel Masos. In the archaeological systemic model constructed in light of ethnographic materials, we must assume a symbiotic relationship among desert, sown, and sea with reciprocal exchanges and relocations occurring. The fundamental circumstances may have been quite similar to a combination of the ethnographies outlined above. In Iron I, peoples enjoyed access to both sea and desert across various E-W geographical, ecological zones similar to those seen in North Africa. Likewise, movements east and south of the J-shaped rainline, as with the 19th century Negev Bedouin, were unimpeded, and so on.

This does not mean that competition for resources was lacking. On the contrary, as with the tribal groups reviewed, security and insecurity, dominance and subservience, patron and client roles were quickly exchanged. And yet, an atmosphere of transformed peace prevailed where tyranny was reduced and diligence and skill rewarded. Iron was exploited by one or more groups; new lands were turned to production; population increased; and old traditions were clung to and transformed. Iron Age IC was a time of pacification, reduced fissioning, and centralization.

The demarcations between LB and IA on the one hand and between IA and IC on the other, in a sense, coalesced. This is not to deny the passage of time, but to point to sacred spaces used in the LB period and continued, albeit in reduced size, in IA and IC. Similarly, the presence of seasonally occupied shrines like Deir ʻAlla on the margins of the 200 mm rainfall line suggests an encounter between several worlds, as do transitions of earlier sites to IC. The passage to IC seems peaceful either because there are no signs of destruction or because a site is rebuilt after a hiatus in occupation. In effect, occupants were continuing or restoring their lives in traditional settings. Our inability to credit the introduction of iron technology to one or other group with certainty may be because of similar symbiotic relationships.

This description envisages synchronic interactions instead of conquest and displacement models. In other words, it explains tensions and transformations by making them part of the symbiotic relationships existing among disparate groups living as segmented tribes in extremely varied environments. Having said this, however, we must not ignore the differences within the Iron I complex. The new state that developed by its end included peoples who had lived in centralized polities as well as those for whom statehood, centralization, and non-tribal organizations were novelties. The monarchy of late IC was a secondary state, i.e., influenced by the state-forming processes of other polities (e.g. the temple form), but for many of its members, it was a pristine experience, their first taste of such centralization.

Leadership in such a setting was strained toward centralizing by the economic potential created by pacification and restrained from it by persons suspicious of potential tyranny and living with few surpluses. Economic and sociopolitical interests competed. Leaders' roles were those of homeostats and mediators who were called upon to satisfy those who saw society devolving, those who pressed it to evolve, and those who wanted it to remain the same.

The image is complex and multidimensional, but modern Middle Eastern ethnographies help illuminate the scene even though they cannot substitute for the real drama by becoming a pseudo-history of the Iron Age. A fuller illumination of the ancient scene must be gained by combining information from Israel's domain of notions, and to that we now turn.

Figure 23: Geological Fault Structures and Depressions

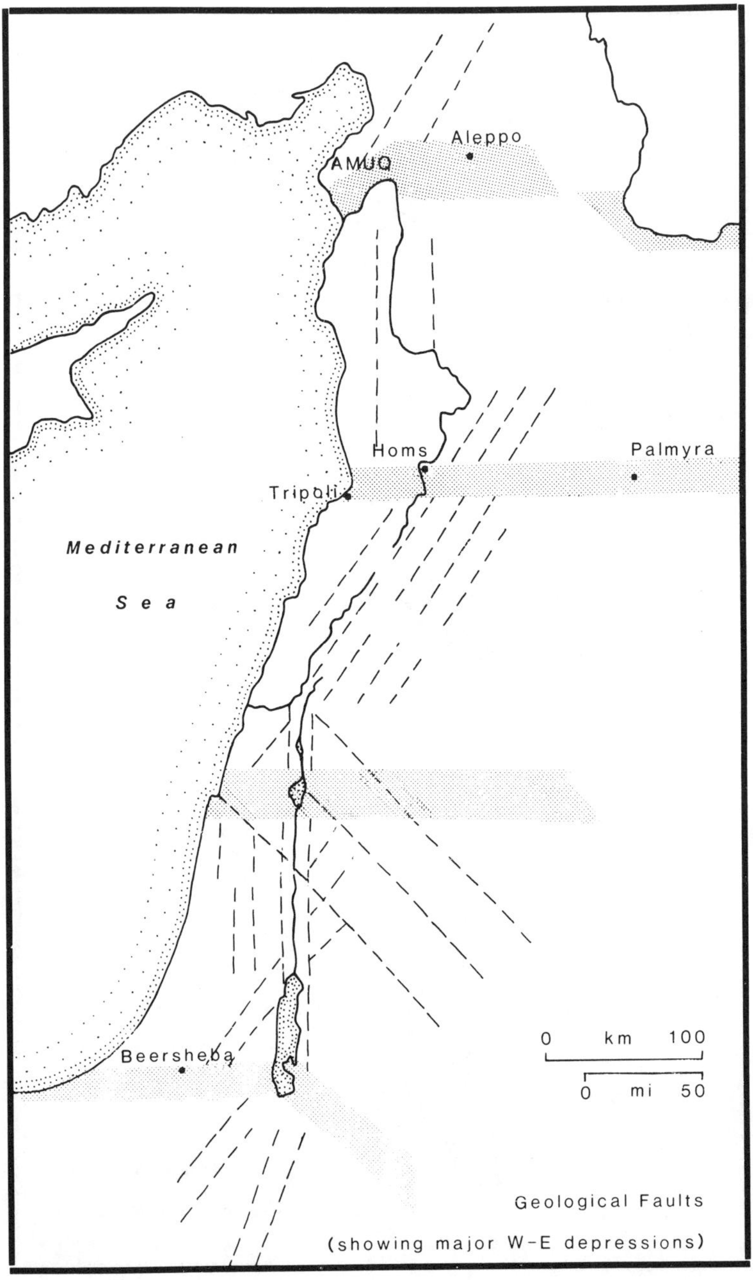

Figure 24: Geographical Zones in the Eastern Mediterranean Basin

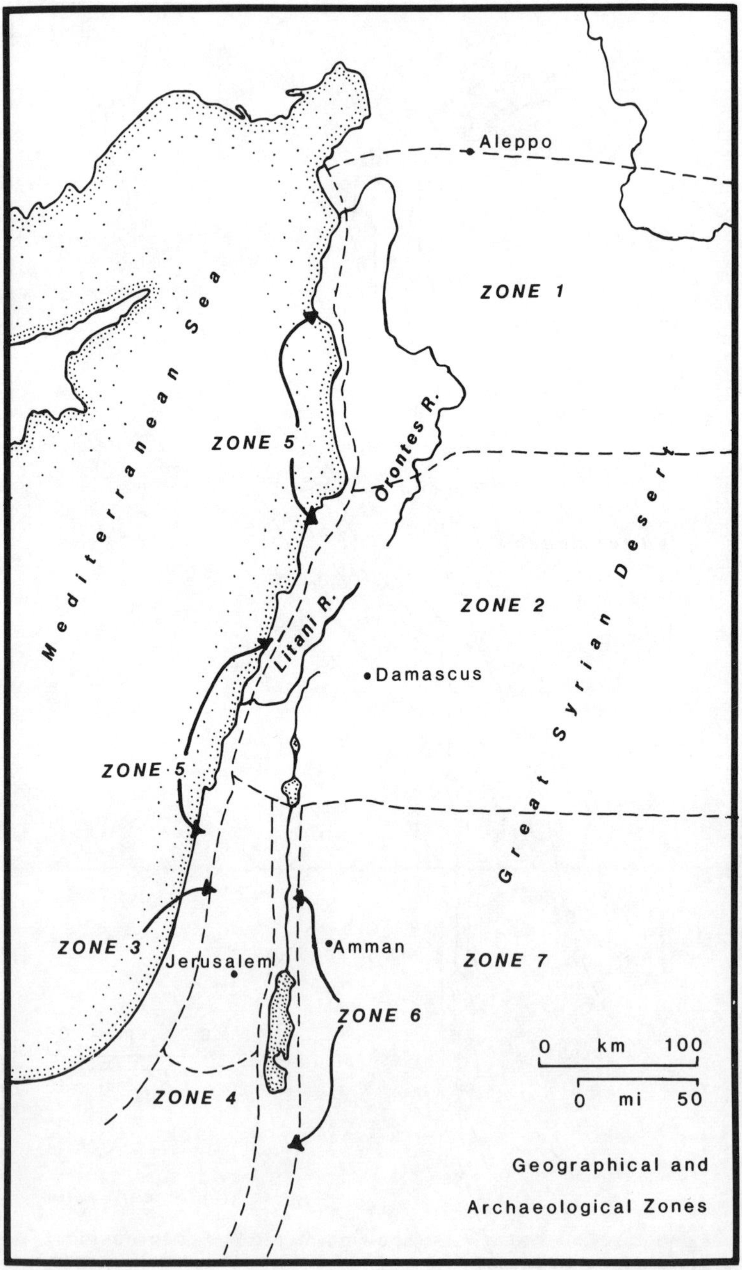

Figure 25: Types of Vegetation in the Eastern Mediterranean Basin

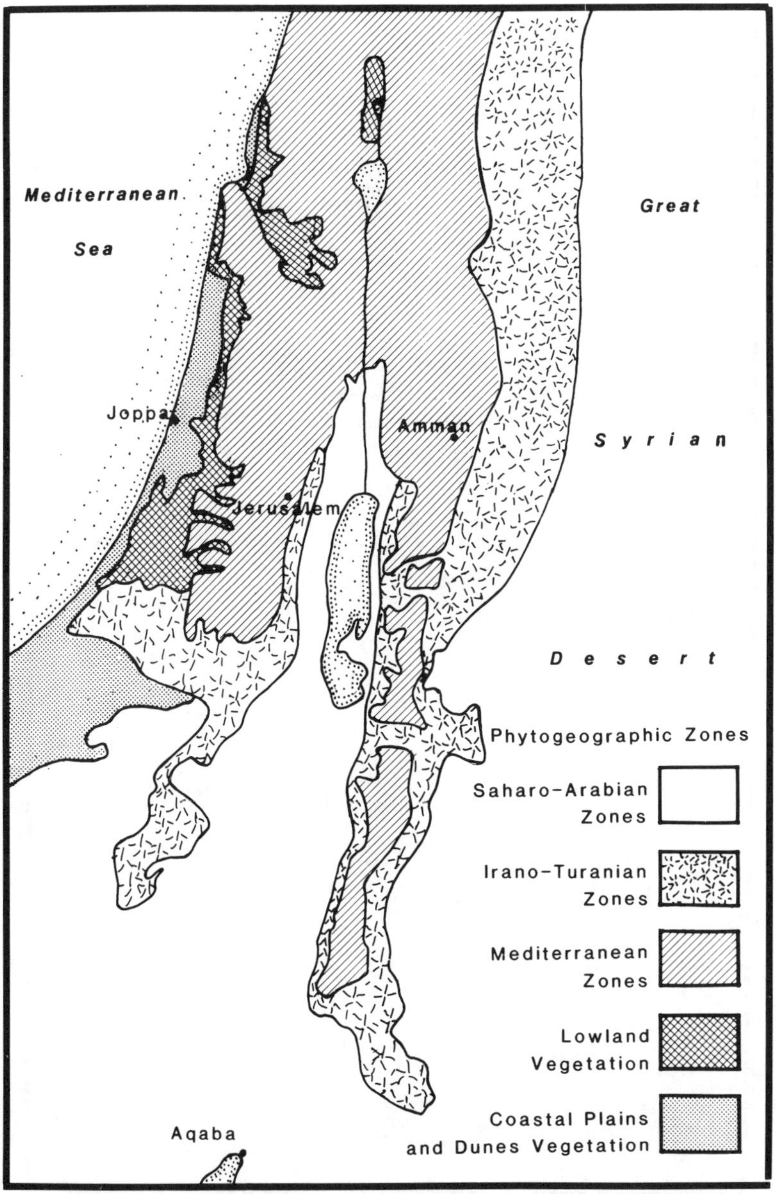

Figure 26: Location of Principal Archaeological Sites Mentioned in this Study

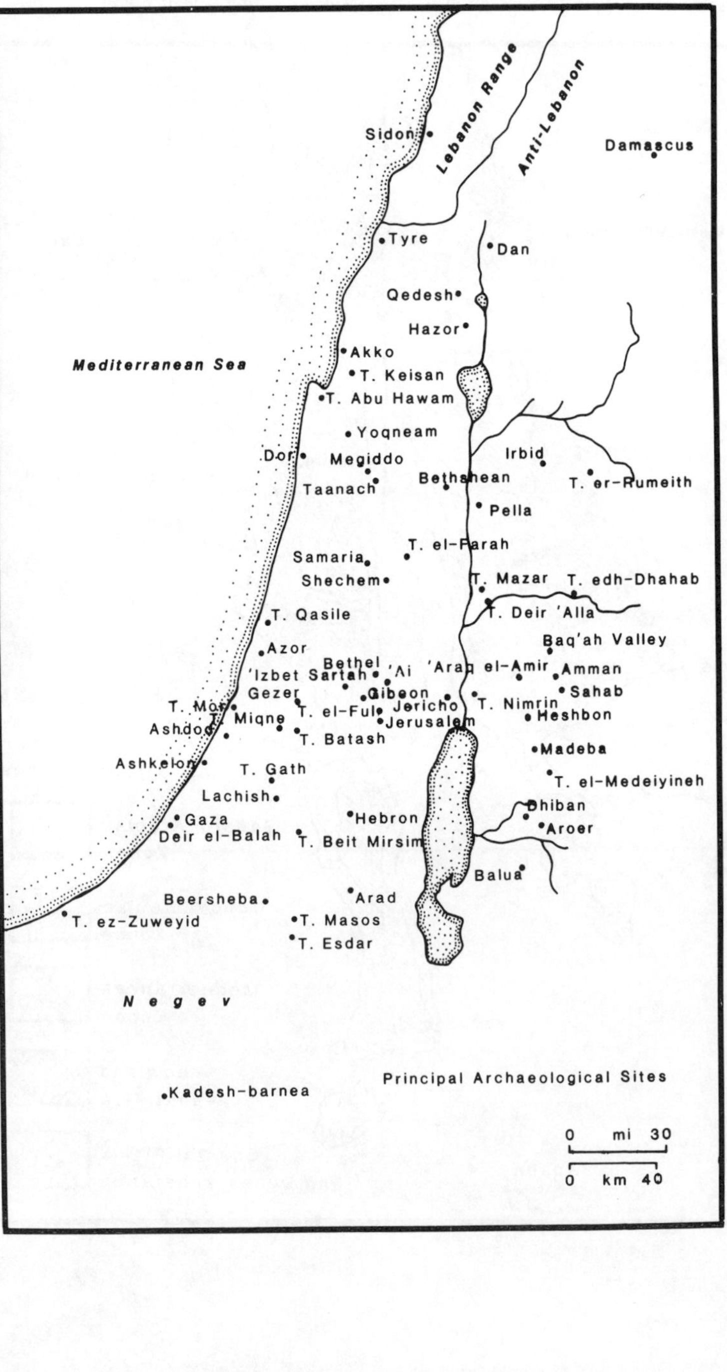

Chapter 4

DOMAIN OF NOTIONS: LITERARY IMAGES OF THE DAVID FIGURE

The Amarna Letters and Canaanite Society

The Amarna Letters portray the Late Bronze Age in Canaan as a time of chaos, dissension, and selfish competition among heads of city-states vying for their own survival and the economic resources of their closest neighbors (cf. Halpern, 1983: 65-80). Town is pitted against town, neighbor against neighbor. Tributes of agricultural products, trade taxes, women, and slave labor increase as vassal-suzerains seek to raise their personal standings with Egyptian overlords. The controlling centralized polity is decaying from its roots up.

Differences in language and content identify the Letters' origins by locale. Specific areas, in cases even individual cities, can be determined so that northern letters are generally classified apart from southern (Moran, 1975: 146-166). Several from Jerusalem's Abdi-Heba (*EA* 286, 287, 288; cf. *ANET*, 487-489) stand out because of their extraordinary northern Syrian scribal influences and because the leader credits his succession to the strong arm of the pharaoh (Moran, 1975: 155-156). Abdi-Heba's southern appointment is as a soldier heading a city-state. This contrasts with the usual process of gubernatorial succession within a "royal" family and, seen in the context of the northern literary affinities, situates Jerusalem betwixt and between Egyptian and Syrian cultural worlds. Jerusalem's intermediate location signals Canaan's perilous suffragan status. Abdi-Heba recalls his special relationship as shepherd of the pharaoh (EA 288) and appeals for protection against other vassal-suzerains and the tumultuous *'apiru*.

The peculiarities in the Jerusalem correspondence are textual and notional examples of the eclectic, exogenous, upward-looking leadership in the LB Age. It and other letters portray incessant competition within indeterminant pools of potential successors where, as in other fragile political systems (cf. Goody, 1966), eligibility is defined only by political favoritism and the cunning of contenders. The failure to define clear lines of succession contributes to political instability and leads to an economic dilemma: vassal-suzerains strengthen their own positions by deporting women and slaves at the very time they are trying to increase agricultural productivity in order to raise other tribute taxes. Simultaneously, they are appealing to their overlords for garrisons and reinforcements. Egypt is losing its grip on Canaan, which in turn is teetering toward transformation.

The scene portrays a fundamentally maladaptive system that depends on the stability and peace which it simultaneously disrupts. In peasant economies, increased productivity requires an increase in the numbers of producers. Lowering marriage ages increases sizes of family labor pools (Goody, 1976: 59). Marriage and reproduction are the very things made difficult or impossible by the tribute policies in Canaan. The demands for increased tribute in the economically restricted, territorially defined zones foster expansionist maneuvers that lead neighbor to prey on neighbor, cause internal dissent among classes, spawn unrest among contenders in the palace, foster rebellion, and yield gross inefficiency and low productivity (Lovejoy, 1983: 1-18, 269-273).

Slave societies are known for their inefficiency and inability to regenerate themselves. Due to shortened life spans and reduced reproduction rates, slave labor forces are constantly in need of replenishing from abroad (cf. Lovejoy, 1983: 7). In such circumstances, as Goody has shown for 18th, 19th, and early 20th century C.E. Northern Ghana (1977: 541-544), new resources are frequently captured in frontier zones. These are often stateless, less accessible hinterlands such as mountains and swamplands left unincorporated so that they may be raided by surrounding centralized polities.

In Egypt's and Canaan's case as depicted in the Amarna Letters and confirmed by the nations' mythologies, the system is religiously legitimated by beliefs in the divine right of power. Therefore, religion serves as a reference value that relates to the ecological and economic carrying capacities. In this context, those who constitute the slave pool naturally seek protection in rebellion and evasion. This puts pressure on the reference values. The slaves have little to lose where the indeterminate succession patterns and economic policies always favor the mutual arrogance of suzerains and vassal-suzerains at the expense of the populace. Halpern (1983: 77) argues in fact that the constant bickering reported in the Amarna Letters shows Egypt's lack of concern for local disputes as long as trade routes are guarded and a buffer against northern intruders maintained.

This assessment goes only part way toward explaining the advantages the Egyptians and other foreigners seek from the system. What many read as Egypt's inattention and neglect, particularly in the frequent mention of the classless, restive *'apiru* in the letters (cf. Mendenhall, 1973: 131-133), is actually a planned policy for exploiting the resources of a marginal zone.

As defense zones and labor pools, the Canaanite areas, like those studied by Goody (1977), are a patchwork of controlled and uncontrolled political districts. The former are taken by conquerors who leave behind their tales of conquest. The latter are populated by the threatened who support themselves in part by extracting protection payments from travelers passing through their district.

Although both areas share the same agricultural technology, greater military capability is found in the controlled areas. However, Goody shows that population density may, surprisingly, be greater in uncontrolled zones, even greater than in centralized states, because the would-be slaves form compact residential clusters in order to protect themselves against invaders. This equation stands in opposition to Ester Boserup's (1965) arguments that link rising centralization to increasing population density. It also reminds us of the variety of human options. Although Goody is careful to distinguish Sub-Saharan from Eurasian, including Middle Eastern, conditions, he finds that states are sometimes established only after raiding has depleted the population of an area (Goody, 1977: 542).

Whether these impressions exist only in the minds of ancient scribes and modern observers remains to be seen. In any case, biblical historians assume that some variation of this scenario was a backdrop for the emergence of Yahwism and the formation of endogenous monarchy in the land of Canaan. Even though the world reflected in the Amarna Letters antedates Iron Age IC by several centuries, the Settlement and Judges' periods are depicted as times of competition and unrest, and David's earliest followers are portrayed as economic, social, and political refugees who join one of their kind for protection and sustenance (Mendenhall, 1973: 135-136). Hence, our analytical model for the biblical domain of notions can begin in the midst of this literary scene. It starts after portrayals of the decline of Egypt, during the devolution of Canaanite society, and in the midst of the problems that both left behind. We recall that the analytical domain of actions ends with another rise of Egypt, thereby placing David's accession in the betwixt and between.

At the beginning, two factors must be recalled. First, as suggested in the discussion of Iron Age archaeology, social devolution is the other face of social evolution. Therefore, the stories of the rise of one group or set of groups are only half of the story. If other peoples' voices could be heard—and hearing them is one reason for developing a social world approach—stories of decline, loss, and letting go would be included in descriptions of evolution. The two parts of a story merge in the search for homeostasis, i.e., in attempts to stabilize and achieve equilibrium with as little change as possible.

Second, and again to repeat, the domain of notions attributed to Iron Age IC is available only in Yahwist religious texts that are in large part formed and transmitted within cultic settings and rituals. Therefore, the texts themselves are part of a ritual tradition.

Presuppositions regarding Biblical Images of David

The selection of biblical passages that comprise the analytical model is guided by the fundamental decision to assign literary studies primary custody over the ancient domain of notions. The choice forces questions about the relationship between literary and historical studies. In response, we have combined a literary critic's interest in the world created by a story with historical inquiry into the world of the story's characters. By asking what in the texts the ancients considered relevant for themselves and the lives of their successors, or again, why the texts bore meaning for the users' day, we have reopened the possibility of several kinds of worlds. The kinds that texts' producers and custodians sought to create, preserve, and hand on may, according to critics, elude our grasp. Some would say they did not and do not exist. The matter is not resolved here. Instead, historians are urged to be sensitive to the kinds of worlds in or around texts before conclusions are drawn about their historical accuracy. Our own view will become clear in the application of our hologram model.

Here, as the story-worlds of biblical texts are considered, readers are invited to distinguish the invariables in the David tradition from the variables, i.e., the qualities and actions that all the users attributed to David as contrasted with things writers felt free to change, omit, or add. Together the observations lead us to seek first David's religious significance and how that was applied throughout the tradition before reconstructing his world.

Taking leads offered by Gunn and Leach and cited in Chapter 1, our first step is to read the David reports simply as stories without determining their specific genres or original settings. They encode tensions, transformations, reversals, progressions, and dramas in poetic and narrative structures similar to those acted out in rites of passage (cf. Leach, 1983: 98-100). In David's case, as we shall see, several transitions and dramas remain constant as his role is repeatedly reassessed, recast, and shrouded in new details throughout the tradition. Thus, the invariables can be examined as a preliminary step toward historical understanding because they represent constants in the ancient domain of notions.

In order to proceed, integral portraits of David, i.e., whole notions, must be identified. Here we are again indebted to literary approaches for demonstrating that biblical images are holistic and multivalent and should not be modified initially by means of source-critical analyses. But the warning carries a dilemma. In seeking integral images within a changing tradition, some would urge us to be satisfied with the final image represented in the final form of the biblical canon. In practice, however, most critics work with smaller literary units. Moreover, important as final images are, social world critics are not convinced that they are the only images that can be isolated. The biblical tradition itself contains more than one image of David. Here, perhaps, the variables supersede the invariables because in the richness of the tradition, our character wears many different robes. Accordingly, principal corpora, with differing portrayals of David's specific role, within Hebrew literature can be defined. Hence, although tradition-history belongs to the systemic integrative stage of research, some means of identifying the major literary units that contain the traditional images is required at the analytical stage.

A practical middle ground is taken here. First, by isolating units that the tradition itself isolates, ancient actors' models are respected and not initially supplanted by modern observers' models. Units such as individual psalms, the books of Samuel, and the writings of the Chroniclers fall into this category. Second, a few other units are added because their acceptance in modern scholarship demands their review. These include the Deuteronomic History, the Court History, (and separately) the Succession Narrative, and several early poems now imbedded in narratives. For analytical purposes, units in both groups can be treated individually and without submitting them to extensive excavative scrutiny. Most literary critics will accept the judicious decision to treat the texts as static and as representing various actors' models for the purposes of the analytical model.

Our analytical model dictates no particular starting point for investigating the biblical domain of notions. Because of our emphasis on the ritual aspects of texts, it is appropriate to look at passages that are clearly ritualistic. This takes us first to the hymnic and priestly models found in Hebrew poetry and the writings of the Chroniclers.

A. *Psalmic, Chronicles', Deuteronomistic, and Samuel Images*

Models in Psalms

In the Hebrew Bible, David is mentioned in eighteen books plus the Psalter, while in the Septuagint he is mentioned in an additional four books of the Apocrypha. Although titles of nearly seventy hymns in the Psalter claim him as author, he is explicitly named within only five (Pss 78: 70; 89: 4, 36, 50; 122: 5; 132: 10; 144: 10). Together the references demonstrate that the representational model held by the Psalter's editors makes David central to the Yahwist cultic tradition.

Psalm 132

In its present form Psalm 132 commemorates Yahweh's election of Jerusalem and the Davidic dynasty. The psalmist portrays David as wanting a permanent dwelling place for Yahweh (vv. 1-5) and then recounts the transfer of the ark of the covenant to Jerusalem (vv. 6-10). Finally, the hymn recalls Yahweh's promise to establish a dynasty (vv. 11-13) and to dwell permanently in Zion (vv. 14-18).

Explanations of the psalm's setting and meaning vary widely. For our analytical model, we cannot assume that an early or late date, whichever is correct, would either prove or disprove the historical accuracy of the poem's allusions. The psalm simply stands in the Jerusalem hymnic tradition where it mythologizes events alleged to have happened in David's time, incorporates them into the liturgical repertory, and recalls them at crucial times when the mythic order maintained by kingship and cult is renewed. There, the psalm helps to fend off impinging chaos and confers meaning and order on the reciters' worlds.

The psalm offers initial information regarding David's role in the biblical tradition. It does not recount details of daily life like those that entertain readers of the Davidic narratives. There are no memories of a specific military, political, or social role for David such as warrior, compatriot of the Philistines, or husband of Saul's daughter. Instead, the psalmists go to the very heart of the Davidic tradition by preserving the two epoch-making transitions that secured Jerusalem for Yahweh and leadership for David's house.

Psalm 132 claims that the transfer of the ark to Jerusalem and the succession of David's sons resolves dangers similar to those faced in the composers' day. Yahweh's participation in David's affairs and blessing of Jerusalem guarantees the myth's effectiveness forever. Hence, establishing worship and dynasty in Jerusalem constitutes the foundations of eternal hope, and recalling and re-enacting the myth and ritual perpetuates the divinely sanctioned homeostasis.

In some respects, Psalm 132 parallels 2 Samuel 6 (=1 Chronicles 13; 15) where a portion of the so-called ark narrative now stands (McCarter, 1984). Although similarities are frequently cited, substantial differences exist. Not only does the psalm condense, omit, or otherwise fail to communicate the drama reported in Samuel, but it also telescopes events that Samuel and Chronicles depict as sequential, discrete, deliberate acts. Like the psalm, 2 Samuel 6 reports the finding and moving of the nomadic, portable ark-shrine to a permanent site, but it does not record the establishing of a ruling dynasty within David's lineage. For that one must turn to 2 Samuel 7 (= 1 Chronicles 17), where what the psalmists link as a single quasi-exchange of gifts unfolds only gradually in a narrative setting.

The differences are noteworthy. The psalmist seems to take David's own leadership for granted or to downplay it by failing to report its origins. The hero is already in charge, playing his chiaroscuro, behind-the-scenes, mediator role as the agent who gives Yahweh and Israel a permanent place of worship while receiving in return a promise for Israel that his ruling house will endure forever. His personal life is tucked away in the past, and he is remembered only for his contributions as transducer and homeostat. In the psalm, therefore, David stands in the betwixt and between, in sacred Jerusalem where ark and dynasty meet briefly in him while history moves along.

In contrast, 2 Samuel 6 concentrates on the transfer of the ark to Jerusalem and dwells on its relationship to David's personal elevation over Saul and Saul's house (v. 21). The Davidic dynasty goes unmentioned even though the termination of the Saulide dynasty is explained. The transferral of power from Saul to David is emphasized while post-Davidic succession is not addressed. Readers sense an attitude that might have prevailed before questions of dynasty arose or were decided. In any case, the final remark in 2 Samuel 6 only sets the stage for the second transition to dynasty: "And so Saul's daughter Michal [the potential queen-mother] was childless to the day of her death" (NAB v. 23). Readers are warned that no heirs will be forthcoming from Saul's line, but not until 2 Samuel 7 are they informed of Yahweh's plan for the future. There they are told that hope rests in David's house and not Saul's.

Psalm 132 telescopes the episodes spread through 2 Samuel 6 and 7. In our systemic model, we shall explore the reasons, but we may already suggest that the psalmists, interested in the outcome and relevance of the story for their own day rather than in repeating the story itself, were at liberty to combine episodes, making them two scenes in the same theological act. Transferring power to Jerusalem and perpetuating it manifest a single divine choice. Only the significant transitions accomplished by David are celebrated in the psalm because they remain relevant for later ages. In sum, where the psalm places Jerusalem in the spotlight, the narrative version emphasizes David.

Psalm 89

Psalm 89 combines reminiscences of the promised Davidic dynasty with mythical elements common in ancient Canaanite poems. The psalm's theme is announced in a prelude (vv. 2-5) that is followed by a hymn to the creator (vv. 6-19), a dynastic oracle (vv. 20-38), a description of a king's humiliation (vv. 39-46), and a plea by the king begging Yahweh to remember earlier divine promises (vv. 47-52). The psalm fuses a promise of divinely sanctioned dynasty with Yahweh's creative power. Accordingly, the deity, Israel's true king (v. 19) controls all creation while the adopted son, the earthly leader (v. 27), exercises sociopolitical control over a territory stretching from the sea to the river (v. 26).

But disaster strikes. Although assured that Yahweh would not withdraw his dynastic promise (vv. 37-38), the speaker (David?; cf. Mowinckel, 1962, I: 225) is dethroned (v. 45), taunted by neighbors (v. 42), stripped of youthfulness, and robbed of manhood by sterility

(v. 45; cf. Dahood, 1968: 319). Humiliated but confident, the speaker pleads for Yahweh to be faithful to promises made to David (v. 50).

Three aspects of the poem deserve special attention. First, according to Cross's (1973: 258-259) and Dahood's (1968: 309, 316) readings, verses 20-21 refer to a major transition in Israel's religiopolitical life:

> "I made a lad ruler in preference to a warrior, I exalted a youth above a hero.
> "I found David my servant, with my holy oil I anointed him."

The emphasis Psalm 132 places on the ark and its transfer to Jerusalem are missing here and in its stead is a rejection of a warrior (Saul?) and the anointing of a youthful David. For this poet, as for the writer of 2 Samuel 6, displacing David's predecessor is an epoch-making event marking the beginning of confidence in Yahweh's control.

The second notable factor is the speaker's fear of a reversal, a cancellation of Yahweh's election of David. The speaker, whether an individual or a group, experiences a rejection that, combined with sterility and old age, threatens the promised dynasty.

Finally, the sequence of real and potential catastrophes suggested by the psalm is similar to episodes described in the Deuteronomic History (2 Samuel 9-20; 1 Kings 1-2). We shall return to them later.

Read in a cultic context, Psalm 89 shows that the Yahwists' sociopolitical and religious homeostasis is delicately balanced. In order for David to displace Saul, Yahweh's favor must be withdrawn from the Benjaminite and bestowed on the son of Jesse. Such a change in divine plans is exceptional and could easily be undone by another change in divine disposition, either a coup or David's dying without an acceptable heir. If divine neglect persists, the psalm suggests, the elderly David's election will be negated and leadership will slip away through sterilities, death, or enemy aggression.

Thus, David's accomplishments teeter precariously between two acts of divine favor, one completed and the other anticipated. The first is Yahweh's decision to discontinue Saul's house; the second is the deity's promise of dynastic succession. Although the poem lacks the irony of a narrative, David seems poised between the fates which the prose version depicts by virtue of Michal's and Abishag's remaining childless, each for different reasons (2 Sam 6: 23; 1 Kgs 1: 4). In the narrative model, David's legitimacy as successor of Saul depends on his marriage to Michal, Saul's daughter, while succession hangs in the balance with David's potency. From David, offspring were refused to Michal and not possible for Abishag. Bathsheba as non-Saulide but non-concubine, wife-mother appears in the temporal and social breach that separates the other two women. In the narrative, questions about Saulide legitimacy persist, but the issue of whose house would inherit, Michal's or David's, is not squarely faced until the time when David's successor is chosen. Then, a son by Uriah's former wife is selected, and the second phase in the transition from house of Saul to house of David is accomplished. The psalmist's actor's model offers a similar but shorter version of the same two-act drama.

Figure 27: Stages and Transitions in the Yahwist Representational Model

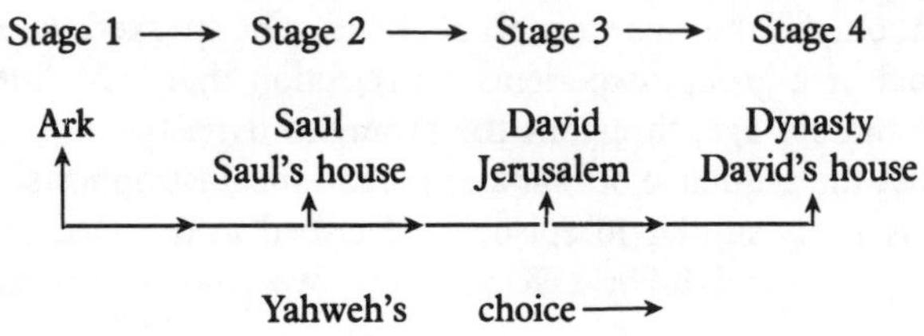

Four Stages in the Davidic Transition

Psalm 132, Psalm 89, 2 Samuel 6, and 2 Samuel 7 enumerate four stages contained in the Yahwists' representational model [Figure 27]. The Yahwists outlined the development from pre-Saulide, covenantal, pastoral nomadic tribalism to centralized, dynastic office.

Stage one is represented by the ark of the covenant which symbolizes a pre-monarchic and pre-Saulide ideology and value system. Stage two envisages the legitimacy of Saul and his house. Stage three is personified by David's personal legitimacy and is remembered as the time after Saul's theological demise but before dynasty and dynastic successors. (Here, David and Jerusalem share the spotlight, but on different planes of classification. In individual cases, one or the other or both are cited by the writers when referring to transitions involving this stage.) Stage four is dynasty, although in the texts reviewed no specific successor is named.

The four stages constitute the full sequence contained in this canonical, representational model of the biblical writers of Psalms 132 and 89 together with 2 Samuel 6 and 2 Samuel 7. But our description is a composite observers' model. Psalm 132 reports explicitly only two of the four stages (ark to dynasty), although David's and Jerusalem's legitimacies are implied; 2 Samuel 6 overlaps but has three stages (ark to Saul to David); Psalm 89 and 2 Samuel 7 mention three stages (Saul's house to David's legitimacy to dynasty).

Stages	(1)	(2)	(3)	(4)
2 Samuel 6:	1	2	3	
2 Samuel 7:		(2)	3	4
Psalm 89:		2	3	4
Psalm 132:	1		(3)	4

In 2 Samuel 6, the ark's transfer to Jerusalem is an occasion for David to affirm his divine election (stage three) and announce the demise of Saul's house (stage 2). Restoration of the ark and rejection of Saulide leadership (stages 1 and 2) merge as a single episode that contributes to David's ascendancy (stage 3). In 2 Samuel 7 and Psalm 89, David's personal legitimacy (stage 3) is reaffirmed, but dynasty (stage 4) is announced.

In Psalm 132, Davidic and Jerusalemite legitimacy (stage 3) form the central hope, almost in David's absence, and the transfer from the ark (stage 1) to dynasty and Zion (stage 4) are presented as its cause and effect. The psalmist relives the two creative acts as discrete parts of a single mythic moment [Figure 28]. Moving the ark represents a breaking away from the chaotic uncertainty caused by the absence of sacred place, and establishing a new ruling house guarantees against future uncertainty caused either by weak or non-existent leadership. Sanctifying a place is one thing and blessing a lineage another, but they are connected because as foundations of hope, Jerusalem and dynasty are inextricably bound in royal theology. Yahweh, David, and Jerusalem stand together as the bases on which the theology rests.

Figure 28: Myth Structure of the Yahwist Representation

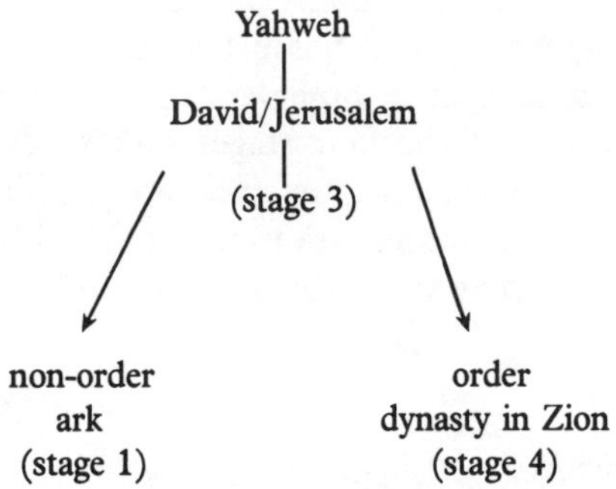

Preliminary Hypothesis

In the composite representation, the transition from stage one to stage four, from wilderness nomadic existence to Jerusalemite dynastic government, is an invariable, a map, that cradles the other nesting images. Later generations recall the transitions in myth and ritual. Which particular transition, i.e., which subset within the overall framework, receives attention at a given time depends on the needs and dispositions of the writer. But the canonical belief remains inviolate. Always David, Jerusalem, and Davidic dynasty are legitimate, and the transitions that brought each to prominence guarantees order in later worshiping communities.

Each transitional stage represents a reality that, according to the biblical writers, groups of ancient actors held to be legitimate and viable. The writers assert the transitions as representational models. The actors viewed the transitions as bases for stability and equilibrium to be recalled when order was threatened. Because of the ritual context of the hymns, the bases are actions and operational models, as well as representations. At threatening times of change, such as inaugurations of leaders or when the group is faced with enemies who held competing models, the Davidic transitions are recalled and re-enacted. Other important transformations may have occurred, such as the Philistines displacing Yahwist dominance or vice versa, but they are not encoded in ritual texts. The biblical tradition identifies the transitions within Yahwism as normative and legitimate. In them, the David character personifies and symbolizes Yahweh's choosing Jerusalem and dynasty.

Other Hymns within the Tradition

The transitions attributed to David and celebrated in Psalms 132 and 89 are recalled in many other ancient hymns. There the themes are preserved as part of Yahwist representational models confirming later institutions as normative and ideologically valid. We must remember, however, that the persons who first celebrate the poems do not necessarily form a single, Yahwist group. The operational definition of groups proposed by Holy and Stuchlik and others supports Leach's warning that we cannot be sure about the purposes or operations of the member-groups prior to the fusing of their traditions. The original hymnists may be worshipers, warriors, or others with diverse economic, political, or social goals, but their initial purpose and nature are concealed by the syncretistic tendencies of the biblical compilers. The editors, like modern interpreters, may either presume a cultural or historical association among the diverse factions or impose unity on the groups and poems to suit their own ends. But because the poems now stand within the biblical canon, continuity and similarity are implied where discontinuity and dissimilarity may have previously prevailed.

In the midst of what may be disparate actors' models, the psalmists continue to make a single, fundamental assertion: earthly stability depends on divine intervention. The divine balancing act attracts the hymnists' attention and becomes the subject of Yahwist cult. "Order" is paramount.

Many other poems related to David reflect this view. In the Song of Hannah, "a god who balances his actions" guards the king (1 Sam 2: 3, 10; McCarter, 1980: 68-71; see comparison with Psalm 113 in Freedman, 1980: 243-261). In David's lament for Saul and Jonathan taken from the Book of Jashar, the dominance of the Israelites over the Philistines is thrown into imbalance by the deaths (2 Sam 2: 19-27).

David's Last Words (2 Sam 23: 1-7) credit the eternal covenant (v. 5) for ensuring Davidic dynasty. Solar imagery (v. 4) is used to express confidence in perpetual order and stability. A promise is given that the loyal will flourish and the opposition wither (cf. McCarter, 1984: 481). Yahweh and El, Israel and Jacob are paired in the poem to make their dialectical relationships factors in maintaining the balance.

The doublet 2 Samuel 22 and Psalm 18 reports a cosmic struggle that pits the deity against the forces of chaos (2 Sam 22: 5-20; Ps 18: 5-20). In the second part of the psalm, human combat against adversaries and enemies matches activities in the social world with those in the divine realm (2 Sam 22: 32-46; Ps 18: 32-46). In the end, deity and king are linked in praise and guarantees of continued kindness (2 Sam 22: 47-51; Ps 18: 47-51).

In Psalm 78 in the Elohistic Psalter, after rejecting the north and the "tent" of Joseph, the deity is portrayed as choosing to dwell permanently in Judah and Zion and to elect David, the shepherd of Jacob. The transitions are parallel to the recollections in Psalm 132 where the nomadic ethos gives way to the settled urban environment (cf. Ps 78: 65-72).

Psalm 72, also in the Elohistic Psalter, was probably celebrated at the coronation for one of David's successors. Then just rule, glorious reign, universal dominion, protection of the poor, and prosperity of the kingdom are commemorated as the religious goals.

In Psalm 68, Elohim is mentioned twenty-four times. The psalm may have been sung as the ark is carried into battle. Then the Exodus and Conquest, the choice of Zion (vv. 16-19), Israel's victories, and the ark's procession (vv. 25-28) are recalled. The recollections introduce a statement of belief in the deity's spreading mighty rule (vv. 29-32) for which praise is given. This actors' model evokes memories of past events linked serially. As they stand, however, the events provide a basis for belief in the present and future.

Jerusalem is the center to which the tribes of Yahweh process and where the house of David rests in Psalm 122. Zion stands in the betwixt and between as the holy place where Yahweh dwells.

The final explicit reference to David in the texts of the Psalms is in the composite Psalm 144. The poem contains a supplication beseeching Yahweh's blessing, and it bases its confidence on David's survival.

The Psalms, Homeostasis, and Yahwism

Our holographic research strategy and analytical model prevent our saying with some that a pseudo-past has been created as a basis for belief, or with others that a cultic remembrance ensures that there were real historical occurrences at the base of the tradition. We can appeal neither to early dates as hints of historicity nor to late dates as evidence for the surviving power of real events.

Instead our approach accepts information in the psalms as notional, public, ideological, and assertive of representational models held by worshiping Yahwists during many periods in ancient history. By implication, however, the repeated concern about renewing social, political, and religious order suggests the presence of conflicting representational or operational models and affirms the worshipers' belief that divinely sanctioned space and persons offer the best sources of resistance.

The approach differs from earlier ones in a single, fundamental respect. It identifies the transitions in the texts as invariable "maps" in the Davidic poems. The major tensions and transitions believers face and resolve in their times, and the way they authenticate their responses, reveal that accomplishments attributed to David give worshipers guidance and confidence. They recognize his façe in their lives. Displacing Saul, moving the ark, and naming a non-Saulide son and dynasty impresses the cultic hymnists as being the acts of a strong, divinely-approved leader. The successes cast David as an archetypal mediator who leads the people through crises and transitions. As in other rites of passage, he and his texts stand at the juncture of several worlds, in the betwixt and between, where one representational model (Saulide) gives way to another (Davidic). The image and its record are transducers and homeostats.

Chronicles' Model

The writers and editors of the books of Chronicles adopt narratives from the Deuteronomic History where the books of Samuel and Kings are now preserved. The many conflicting details, variant names, and rearranged narrative units suggest an apparent disregard for consistency. These have invited continuing and detailed emendation by source critics who prefer to change the text according to their own perceptions of its diachronic development and of Israel's history. Certainly the text has its own history, but many of the variations in fact are important to the writers' model and are part of their story.

The Chroniclers' model places renewed emphasis on David's importance in the time attributed to him, in the writers' time, and for the future. The leader's decision to move the ark to Jerusalem and prepare for the construction of the temple (1 Chronicles 13-16; 21-27) marks a beginning and a turning point that sets Yahwism on a new and proper course. The actions stand as a precedent for later leaders to follow because, like David who brought the allegiances of the north home to Zion, his successors are judged on their efforts to restore a united people worshiping in Jerusalem.

Genealogies

The pre-monarchic period is summarized in an extended genealogy that reaches from Adam to Jerusalem geographically and to Saul's reign sociopolitically (1 Chronicles 1-9). It enables the narrators to move quickly toward David's and Yahweh's presence in the city, the topics of central concern. The technique also satisfies the need to explain the relationships among the disparate peoples who are envisaged as David's followers and who constitute the compilers' world.

The perspective of the genealogies is, as it were, from after and from above events. They look at the past and encode memories of continually fluctuating relationships. Earlier contacts among individuals and groups are alleged, but the intrigues, personalities, details, and stories that a narrator would include are forgotten or omitted. The fissions and fusions endemic to segmented societies are charted, but the causes are no longer remembered. Only the principal characters and overarching authorities who create unity and prevent further segmenting among places and peoples are included in the list.

Viewing the world from above the fray introduces the element of status. By beginning at creation and figuratively including the entire past, a particular kind of control or understanding is implied. Someone knows how and why things have turned out the way they have. The important thing is where events have led. The perspective is either that of a genealogical ego, for whom the relationships have been successful, or of an outside observer, who has a subsequent story to tell. It is not the report of a participant in the genealogical times, i.e., of someone on the ground for whom stories, details, and judgments would be important. The distinction will be useful later.

If depicted on a genealogical chart, the opening chapters in Chronicles would appear diamond-shaped rather than pyramidal. The structure points to Jerusalem and the temple. At the top is an individual, Adam, followed by branching (segmenting) as descent is traced to Israel. Then the chart branches out farther to enumerate the tribes and to include all the peoples in the ego's group. Finally, it narrows again as the course of affairs focuses on the dominant site and individual, Jerusalem and Saul, who connect the genealogies to the beginning of the narratives that follow.

Rapid movement from Adam through Noah and Abraham brings the reader immediately to Israel. Significantly, "Israel" is named here (2: 1-2) and consistently in Chronicles where other sources refer to "Jacob." Williamson correctly interprets the choice as a means of demonstrating that the primeval and ancestral stories reached their fulfillment in the twelve sons of Israel (Williamson, 1982: 45). Also, in light of claims made elsewhere in the corpus, the name reveals that Judah, Jerusalem, and the people who remained faithful to Jerusalemite cult comprise the true Israel.

Chapters 2-8 deal with the sons of Israel in a manner appropriate to David's world. The highly artificial, segmented list begins with Judah (2: 3–4: 23), places Levi at the center (6: 1-81), and ends with Benjamin (8: 1-40). This locates the end of the circuit in Jerusalem and makes the site a "successor" to Benjamin in the literature as well as geographically (Williamson, 1982: 46). In chapter 9, the scope narrows to record the principal functionaries in the post-Exilic city and then returns to Saul who was already cited in the Benjamin genealogy.

The arrangement is stamped with the Chroniclers' worldview. The constricted frame of reference that makes Judah Israel and Jerusalem its center is similar to the Jerusalemite psalm model. The sequence of the tribes, beginning and ending with territories that constitute post-Schism Judah, the importance of Levi and his position at the symbolic center of the tribal list (MT 5: 27-41; 6: 1-66), David's prominence within Judah (1 Chronicles 2-3), and the primacy of final place which puts Jerusalem at the list's culmination (9: 1-34) are clear signs that the genealogies are viewing the past from the heights of David's city. Their Israel is a large extended and segmented group who form a religious community centered in Zion.

Demise of Saul

By juxtaposing genealogical and narrative units, the perspective of the Chroniclers' model continues to link Israel's past to Jerusalemite leadership and worship. The transition to Davidic rule is accomplished by overlapping a unit that names Jerusalem's inhabitants with one of Saul's genealogies (1 Chronicles 9–10). The seam is rough and the sequence is at odds with other reconstructions (cf. 2 Samuel), but the meaning is clear: Saul is transitional, and the world he personifies ends with the rise of David.

The same willingness to arrange or rearrange materials exposes genealogical fluidity in the references to David within the tribe of Judah. In 1 Chron 2: 10-17, he is the seventh of Jesse's seven sons, and he has two sisters, Zeruiah and Abigail. The women are called sisters only here. Likewise, Elihu who does not appear on the Judah list is cited elsewhere as a brother. The name is either a variant of Eliab or indication of another brother, bringing the total to eight sons (cf. 1 Chron 27: 18).

A few verses later, Hebron's genealogy is listed in 1 Chron 2: 42-49. The section seems to contain a mixture of place- and personal names. A section referring to Caleb's descendants follows (2: 50-55), before the scene shifts abruptly back to David for the names of his sons born at Hebron (3: 1-4a) and at Jerusalem (3: 4b-9). The lineage continues through Solomon (3: 10-24) and is joined to another genealogy of Judah at the beginning of chapter 4.

The arrangement seems artificial and contrived. It selects some individuals while disregarding others named elsewhere in the same book. But adding, dropping, or changing names causes the genealogists no problem, and neither does assigning ancestral status to places as well as persons. This is because of the way genealogies function in societies and the way fluidity helps to achieve that goal (Wilson, 1975; 1977: *passim*; Malamat, 1968; 1973a). For the actors, discrepancies do not suggest artificiality. They signal the accuracy and continuing validity of genealogies whose purpose is to record the statuses and relationships within the various domains of the genealogists' contemporary society. Accordingly, in the Judahite genealogy, David is depicted as the youngest of Jesse's son, the least of the brethren, a position that serves to emphasize the distance he traveled during his rise to leadership. Sisterhood for Zeruiah and Abigail, mothers of Joab and Amasa respectively, is also important for the Chroniclers, but the genealogies alone do not tell us why. For that answer, we must look elsewhere.

Omissions are also important. No mention is made of David's marriage to Michal, daughter of Saul, here or elsewhere in the book although she is mentioned in the ark scene with no reference to her status (1 Chron 15:29). Instead, the sons born at the ancient Yahwistic Judahite center, Hebron, and at Jerusalem are listed. Hebron is the link that ties the section to what went before, and Jerusalem introduces a longer section about the city (1 Chron 9: 1-34) and connects David with the stories about him and Solomon in the remainder of the book (chs. 10ff.).

The particular relationships in the genealogies position David in the genealogists' and narrators' world. He is a Judahite, his rise is exceptional, he succeeds Saul, and he has heirs and potential successors born in a Yahwist center and at Jerusalem. His marital ties to Saul's house are not important. His status rests on other grounds.

We noted that the genealogies of Benjamin and Saul in chapters 8-10 weave Saul into the former history and make his death its termination. As if to remove all doubt, the Chroniclers end their report of Saul with an explicit theological assertion: "Therefore the Lord slew him, and transferred his kingdom to David, the son of Jesse" (1 Chron 10: 14). Yahweh kills the leader. It is Yahweh who transfers power to David. In step-like fashion by entwining the genealogies of David and Saul with the tribes of Israel, the writers declare that the former history has ended in failure, the old representational model esteemed among followers of non-Jerusalem leaders is no longer valid, and a new age can begin.

Legitimacy of David and Solomon

Similar doublets, whether they result from crude scissors-and-paste techniques or skillful use of foreshadowing and flashbacks, move the drama toward the temple. The repetitions as much as the narrative's literary unity lead some to suggest that the Chroniclers treat David and Solomon as a single episode in Israel's history (Williamson, 1982: 27). In one sense the claim is true because the temple dominates the writers' model, and according to it David and Solomon share responsibility for instituting temple worship. Therefore, their reigns are remembered as the ideal era when true Yahwists assembled in Jerusalem. On the other hand, David receives twice as much story space as Solomon. David's reign fills more than thirty-two pages (nineteen chapters) in the Massoretic Text (1 Chronicles 11-29), while Solomon's life consumes only fifteen (eight chapters: 2 Chronicles 1-9).

This attempt to give David major credit for worship in Jerusalem is reinforced by interweaving other themes. Again, commentators are tempted to correct the writings according to a modern historical model, especially where they feel history has been contracted and telescoped in order to enhance David's position. According to the Chroniclers, David is cast in the lead role not only when moving the ark to Jerusalem and voicing his hope for a temple, but also when purchasing the site (1 Chron 21: 15-26), building an altar (21: 26–22: 1), organizing materials and construction crews (22: 2-5), and charging Solomon—before he is designated successor—with specific orders and plans for building the edifice (22: 6-17; 28: 11-21). The leaders of all Israel, the Levites, priests, singers, gatekeepers, treasurers, magistrates, army commanders, tribal heads, and overseers are among the cultic and political personnel who are organized (chs. 22-27) and advised that David intends for Solomon to build the temple (22: 5-6; 28: 1-10). The Chroniclers insist that David formulated the detailed plans for the temple and that Solomon executed them exactly, principally because of his father's mandate (e.g., 2 Chron 6: 10-11). In their view, Solomon is also scrupulous about his father's precedents for managing the priests, Levites, and other court personnel, but he is not ultimately responsible (2 Chron 6: 14-16).

In the Chroniclers' model, the father proposes and the son disposes, but Solomon personally has to live up to the ideals established by David. For example, the building of the temple continues in the second book, but not before Solomon has led a procession to Gibeon for prayer and sacrifice at the tent of meeting carried by Moses (2 Chron 1: 1-6). Elohim (sic!) affirms Solomon's election and promises him riches (1: 7-12). Only then does Solomon return to Jerusalem, become "king of Israel" (1: 13), and give the order to commence the temple's construction (1: 18).

The terminology and action betray the strength of lingering loyalties for religious centers other than Jerusalem. An old representational model that favors a northern cultic center for the ark and prefers "Elohim" as a divine name has not been completely suppressed. Thus, although cautious to insist that the ark is already in Jerusalem (1: 4), in their new model the writers include a scene where Solomon repeats David's legitimating procession to Zion. By receiving a blessing in Gibeon and "carrying" it to Jerusalem, Solomon entwines the legitimacy of his enthronement with the city's legitimating act. Like the psalmists, the narrators remember the power of the transferral to Jerusalem and re-enact it in another rite of passage that legitimates Solomon.

Like David's reign, in this model Solomon's is largely devoted to temple matters. Even the census is for recruiting construction workers. The memory of David as the legitimating force for the project is pervasive (e.g., 2 Chron 2: 11, 13, 16; 3: 1; 5: 1). Nowhere is this more clear than in Solomon's dedication prayer (6: 12-42) and in the deity's promise to him (7: 12-22). The former begins and ends with a reminder of "Yahweh Elohim's" promise to David and of David's devotion. The divine epithet symbolizes the accommodation between north and south that Yahwism has endured in order to establish a united religiopolitical center. The expression of Elohim's promise to Solomon, therefore, is rooted in Yahweh's promise made to David, and not vice versa. For the Chroniclers, Solomon is a wholly pious, just, and faithful Yahwist who nurtures the religious roots planted by his father. Indeed, according to the model, the dynasty is evidence of Solomon's fidelity.

David in the Divided Monarchy

As expected, David plays a lesser role in the Chroniclers' descriptions of the Divided Monarchy but the writers' perspectives are still controlled by his image. For instance, in spite of Solomon's popularity, David remains the model and norm against whom subsequent monarchs are judged. Hence, the reformer Hezekiah is lauded because "He pleased the Lord just as his forefather David had done" (2 Chron 29: 2), and because he followed prescriptions of David (29: 25-30), re-established the classes of priest and Levites (31: 2), and instigated other types of religious reform (e.g., 31: 20-21). Likewise Josiah's reforms please Yahweh because they followed in the path of David and showed concern for cultic matters, priests and Levites, and law (2 Chron 34: 1-7).

Contrary to this suggestion, some analysts argue that the Chroniclers perceive Hezekiah as a second Solomon (Williamson, 1977: 119-124). For them, matters of temple concern, the Passover celebration, and the proclamation sent throughout all Israel from Beersheba to Dan (2 Chron 30: 1-27) witness to an admiration for Solomon that makes him the model instead of David.

Our interest in David's role within ancient Yahwistic representational models does not require us to prove him paramount in every ancient worldview. Nevertheless, on the same arguments as are put forward for the Solomonic silhouette behind Hezekiah's reform, an equally strong case can be made for the Chroniclers' appeal to David. Certainly, in the Chroniclers' age any attempt to depict Hezekiah as champion of a return to Jerusalemite temple worship would be expected to echo Solomon's activities. But, as we have noted, in the writers' model, Solomon is the builder who imitated and implemented his father's plans. Thus, the appraisal of his Passover celebration—"... for since the days of Solomon, son of David, king of Israel, there had not been the like in the city" (2 Chron 30: 26)—does not exhibit exclusive esteem for Solomon. It also refers explicitly to David, the basis of his authority. In the same manner, the four references to "land of Israel" in Chronicles are used not only for the nation during the reigns of Solomon (2 Chron 2: 16), Hezekiah (2 Chron 30: 25) and Josiah (2 Chron 34: 7), but also for David's reign (1 Chron 22: 2), which in fact is the first on the list (cf. Williamson, 1977: 123). The same can be said for the phrase "from Beersheba to Dan" in Hezekiah's proclamation (2 Chron 30: 5). The description has been interpreted as a Solomonic revival (and reversal), but the Chroniclers also apply it to David's reign (1 Chron 21: 2), and when they use it as a measure for Solomon's census, the editors explicitly cite its Davidic precedent (2 Chron 2: 16).

The same pro-Davidic bias is evident in the Chroniclers' selection of stories, additions, and emphases that show a preference for the south. There is no record of David's separate reign over Judah, no tension within his family, and very little mention of the schismatic northern kingdom. The north is usually referred to either negatively or in reports of attempts to win the errant Israelites back to Jerusalem. In texts where the north does figure prominently, the region is often treated unfavorably. Examples include the report of the Schism (2 Chronicles 10-12), the battle between north and south during Abijah's time that provides the setting for the king's stern lecture regarding David's perpetual covenant (ch. 13), Jehoshaphat's attempt to form an alliance with Israel (ch. 18), and numerous references to the northerners' apostasy.

Davidic Details

The writers' prevailing disposition is to accept details as found in earlier actors' models and set them alongside differing details and other models with little regard for apparent contradictions. Yet at times, details either in a source or the writers' own model are arranged to tell the story. As a result, names on a genealogical list must be judged in relation to others in the same unit before they are compared with remarks elsewhere in the corpus or in other sources. Names, places, relationships, and minutiae that at first glance seem unimportant or coincidental may prove significant when evaluated in their synchronic context.

a. *Genealogies of Rehoboam and Abijah*

One example of the technique is Rehoboam's genealogy included in the story of the Schism [Figure 29]. The report of Rehoboam's family (2 Chron 11: 16-23) credits him with two named wives among a total of eighteen spouses and sixty concubines. The wives are first Mahalath, daughter of Jerimoth, son of David and Abihail, daughter of Eliab, son of Jesse, and second, the favored wife, Maacah, daughter of Absalom, mother of Abijah whom Rehoboam intends to make king (v. 22). The relationships suggest a marrying-in strategy that sometimes characterizes royal families. Whether the Davidic house followed the practice remains to be seen, but the description illustrates the bias within the Chroniclers' model.

Figure 29: Abijah's Genealogy

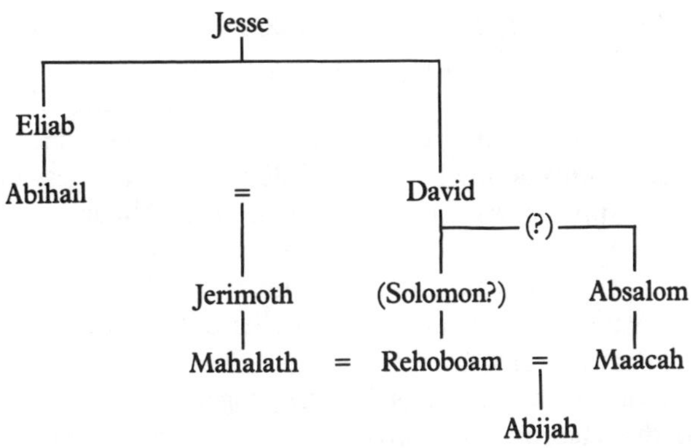

This genealogical chart includes several well-founded assumptions. If we assume that the writers understand Solomon to be David's son, and Rehoboam Solomon's son (cf. 1 Chron 9: 31), and that they equate the Absalom named here with David's ill-fated son mentioned elsewhere, the genealogy stresses the importance of the family of Jesse and descent from David. David is married to his brother's daughter, i.e., his father's granddaughter, and Rehoboam marries two of his father's brothers' daughters, i.e., granddaughters of his own grandfather, David. Such FBD marriages are preferred in many endogamous societies.

Comparison with other genealogies and lists in Chronicles demonstrates that the description of the relationships is intentional, i.e., it reflects statuses and relationships that some group in the society considered important. We cannot determine with certainty whether the relationships were dominant earlier and the Chroniclers merely appropriated them, or whether they were established in the Chroniclers' time. In either case, they now stand as part of the Chroniclers' model where they convey information about David's status in that model. This can be said even though, as we shall see, other details in the same model may seem contradictory.

In 2 Chron 13: 2, Maacah is called "Micaiah the daughter of Uriel of Gibeah" in contrast to "Maacah the daughter of Abishalom" in 1 Kgs 15: 2. Her relationship is confused in 1 Kgs 15: 10 where she may be Abijam's wife (Williamson, 1982: 245). In 1 Chronicles 3, when citing David's Hebron genealogy, a wife Maacah, mother of Absalom, is listed as the daughter of Talmai, king of Geshur (compare 2 Sam 3: 3). Interestingly, no Jerusalem wives/mothers are cited in Solomon's family list which follows in Chronicles, although Rehoboam appears as Solomon's son, and Abijah as son of Rehoboam (1 Chron 3: 10-16). Mothers are also generally absent from David's Jerusalemite lists (1 Chron 3: 1-9; 14: 3-6) where Bathshua, daughter of Ammiel and mother of four sons, is the only woman mentioned (1 Chron 3: 5).

The fluidity that surrounds Maacah, together with the contrast between the Hebron and Jerusalem practices regarding mothers' names confirms the compatibility of the Chroniclers' and our own investigators' models. In the description of David's reign, sons born at Hebron are ranked within his lineage according to their mothers' statuses. The practice is often followed in polygamous societies where competition among sons is determined by mothers' positions in the harem. However, when the Jerusalemite bureaucracy is firmly established, according to the model in Chronicles (and elsewhere: cf. 2 Samuel 3, 5), the importance of primogeniture for determining succession decreases, and mothers' names lose importance. The single exception is Solomon's mother, David's favored wife, who is remembered because of her son's success. But even her name becomes confused in the tradition (Bathsheba/Bathshua) (cf. Flanagan, 1981: 65).

Maacah/Micaiah is remembered for her status in the royal family even though her exact relationship to three generations of leaders is not clear. What we would describe as inconsistencies are ignored in favor of assigning her roles as daughter of Hebron-born Absalom, wife of Rehoboam, and mother of Abijah, and in Samuel possibly mother of Absalom. Accordingly in the genealogists' model, the Davidic dynasty survives the Schism, and challengers must reckon with the fact that Abijah is by every measure a descendant of the house of David and family of Jesse. While he reigns, the transition to Davidic dynasty remains inviolable.

The relationship of the genealogy to events on the ground that are inferred from the changes illustrates a number of points made earlier. The differences parallel the contrasts between culture and society, between domains of notions and domains of action, and between competing actors' models. Moreover, the example illustrates that the relation of theory to data discussed by scientists is at work in history writing as well. Believing in Abijah's Davidic lineage compels the writers to claim double descent within the family of Jesse. There is no way of knowing whether the cultural claim rests on biological "facts" or for that matter whether comparable social relationships functioned as described. We do know the cultural, notional reality, i.e., that Davidic ancestry is prized in the Chroniclers' world.

b. *Narrative Images of David*

The narrative description of David in 1 Chronicles 11-29 stands in sharp contrast to others elsewhere in the Bible. His reign is depicted as a smooth transition (1 Chron 10: 14) and continuing growth in power (11: 9) because of Yahweh's participation. But traces of another opinion are present. References to David's rule in Ziklag while banished from Saul's court (1 Chron 12: 1) and to his cooperation with the Philistines in their struggle against Saul reflect other views. However, the writers chose to present an Israel/Judah unity as if it were handed over from Saul to David who expands it (e.g., 14: 16) and adds other territories governed by non-Yahwist enemies of Israel (chs. 18-20). Interestingly, a guilty and penitent David is depicted in the story of the census, plague, and purchase of the temple site (1 Chronicles 21), but for the most part his image is that of a humble warrior-leader who establishes Jerusalem as a religious center, devotes his reign to consolidating and expanding Jerusalem's territorial dominance, and provides for the success of his son by organizing the government and laying plans for construction of the temple.

Toponomy and Symbolic Geography

The toponymy and symbolic geography in the Chroniclers' model also illustrate how their minds arranged concepts and terminology in order to strengthen Judahite claims on Davidic legitimacy. Although the technical meanings of "Israel," "all Israel," "Judah," and other terms used for territory and peoples have been studied extensively in recent years (cf. Williamson, 1977: *passim*), the relationship between the concepts and the Chroniclers' view of the transitions from tribal society to dynastic nation have been largely ignored.

At the descriptive level, the patterns compare with that noted in Rehoboam's genealogy. The Chroniclers integrate their sources' meanings with religious and political interpretations of their own. While an attempt to juggle terminology to suit the image of a "true" Israel is clear to a modern reader, the exact meaning of specific references within the ancient writers' representational model is not always certain. A survey of the usage demonstrates that the Chroniclers' model incorporates at least two primary meanings of "all Israel." At one level, the term signifies a religio-geopolitical expanse, and at another, a remnant of religious loyalists who reside in both the north and south.

"All Israel" (*kol yiśrā'ēl*) is a technical term when it appears in 1 Chron 9: 1. It stands as a summary and inclusio for the tribal lists that begin with a reference to the "sons of Israel" in 2: 1. It stands immediately before a reference to Judah (9: 1b) where the scene shifts to Jerusalem. This implies that the territory and city are the continuation of the former tribal group whose legitimacy passes to Zion.

All Israel appears next as a group that proclaims David's kingship at Hebron (11: 1-3). The terminology varies in this section. "All

Israel" assembles, but the text states that David had led "Israel" in battle during Saul's lifetime, that Yahweh Elohim had designated him shepherd of his "people (*'am*) Israel," and that "the elders of Israel" had come to anoint him. The implication is that all Israel is a unified body, composed of several former groups.

All Israel is one designation for the groups under Jerusalem's rule during the reigns of David and Solomon. All Israel joins the warriors in support of David (1 Chron 11: 10); the soldiers make David king over all Israel at Hebron (12: 39); David assembles all Israel from Egypt to Hamath—the most expansive claim—to bring the ark from Kiriath-jearim (13: 5, 6, 8). The Philistines hear that David is king of all Israel (14: 8); and all Israel assembles again in Jerusalem to transfer the ark to the city (15: 3, 28).

Yahweh refers to all Israel in the Dynastic Oracle (1 Chron 17: 6), and David's officers hold appointment in all Israel (18: 14). All Israel crosses the Jordan with David to do battle with the Arameans (19: 17). When David decides to take a census within Israel (21: 1), he dispatches Joab to traverse all Israel (21: 4). The report, however, lists Israel and Judah separately (21: 8). All Israel participates in Solomon's accession (29: 21, 23, 25), and at the time of his death, David's reign over all Israel is summarized (29: 26).

Solomon begins his reign by a pilgrimage to Gibeon in the company of all Israel (2 Chron 1: 2). All Israel participates at the dedication of the temple (7: 6, 8), and is mentioned in the summary of the king's reign (9: 30).

Until this point the pattern is largely consistent. The term does not appear in the tribal lists in chapters 1-8. The technical "all Israel" is used, however, in the summary statement that links the lists to Jerusalem and to David (9: 1). Saul leads Israel (10: 1) but no reference is made to all Israel during his reign. That is reserved for the time of David and Solomon when the term means the Yahwist territories under their control. It is important to note that while a few glimpses of a separate Israel and Judah survive as in the report of the census (18: 8), the Chroniclers' model really does not include a "United Monarchy." Instead, David and Solomon lead a single unified people known as all Israel.

Inconsistencies or competition between models claiming to represent the true Israel emerge in descriptions of the post-Solomonic era. When the symbiosis created by David and Solomon dissolves, Rehoboam goes to Shechem to be made king of all Israel

(2 Chron 10: 1), but Jeroboam and all Israel challenge him to lighten the burdens of his father (10: 3) and eventually break away leaving him with the "children (*bĕnē*) of Israel" who live in the cities of Judah (10: 16-17). Rehoboam flees to Jerusalem where "Israel has been in rebellion against the house of David to this day" (10: 19). He quickly gathers the house of Judah and Benjamin to fight against "Israel," but the prophet Shemaiah is ordered to direct Rehoboam and "all Israel in Judah and Benjamin" not to fight against their brethren (11: 1-3). Judah and Benjamin remain with Rehoboam (11: 12), and refugee priests and Levites from "all Israel" in the north join him (11: 13). He deals prudently with the people in Judah and Benjamin (11: 23), but eventually he and all Israel abandon the law (12: 1).

The distinction between the religious group all Israel and the geopolitical regions Judah, Israel, and Benjamin that the writers introduce at the time of the Schism continue during the remainder of their account. In a speech made during the battle with the north, Abijah addresses Jeroboam and political all Israel (2 Chron 13: 4) to remind them that the kingdom of Israel has been given to David and his sons (13: 5). Abijah and Judah go on to defeat Jeroboam and the political all Israel (13: 15). Later, during the alliance between Jehoshaphat and Ahab, the prophet Micaiah tells the northern king that all Israel, presumably his people, will be scattered like sheep without a shepherd (18: 16), but eventually Joash directs the priests and Levites to traverse Judah collecting temple funds from religious all Israel (24: 5). At the rededication of the temple, Hezekiah offers holocaust for all Israel (29: 24), but sends invitations to all Israel, Judah, Ephraim, and Manasseh to come to the Passover (30: 1). Later, however, a decree is proclaimed throughout all Israel from Beersheba to Dan, and the news traverses all Israel from Beersheba to Dan, and the news traverses all Israel and Judah (30: 5-6). Finally, during Josiah's Passover, the Levites are identified as responsible for instructing all Israel (35: 3).

The religio-geopolitical "all Israel" stretches from Beersheba to Dan (or from Egypt to Hamath [1 Chron 13: 5; 2 Chron 7: 6]) and includes the kingdoms of Israel and Judah that are aligned with Jerusalem during the reigns of David and Solomon. This covers the ideal religious group who worshiped Yahweh at the temple during Solomon's era is obliged to continue their allegiance, i.e., to remain members of all Israel.

When connoting the geopolitical entity, the term's referent is the portion of the Davidic-Solomonic jurisdiction where Yahwism thrives as the dominant religious system. On the level of their representational model, the Chroniclers understand the territory to be co-extensive with the Cisjordan and Transjordan regions traditionally claimed for the Yahwist tribes (1 Chron 9: 1) and later included in David's consolidation (1 Chron 28: 8). The tribal list includes the southern and outlying units such as Judah, Simeon, Reuben, Gad, Manasseh, and Jerusalem, beside those in northern Canaan.

Although this totality constitutes the basis for hope in a restored religious, geopolitical kingdom, we may ask whether the writers held an alternative operational model that was more realistic. A survey of the territories which various Judahite kings attempt to reclaim suggests that the Chroniclers also held more limited ambitions.

The script casts the Judahite kings in passive, opportunist roles. Some type of unification with the north—whether through marriage, alliance, or military conquest—always seems desirable. Rehoboam, Abijah, and Asa, for example, are credited with hopes and attempts to win back the seceded tribes. Advances on other fronts, however, depend on opportunities that open only occasionally. Jehoshaphat is given tribute by the Philistines (2 Chron 17: 11), strikes an alliance with Ahab against the Arameans (2 Chron 18: 34), and profits from an attack by the Ammonites, Moabites, and either Edom or (according to the Massoretic Text) Aram (ch. 20). Edom seems to break with Judah under Jehoram (2 Chron 21: 8-11) and it remains away until conquered by Amaziah who eventually loses a battle with Joash of Israel (ch. 25). Uzziah reclaims Elath, several Philistine cities, and the Meunites while the Ammonites pay him tribute (ch. 26). Jotham continues to dominate the Ammonites (ch. 27). Ahaz is defeated by the Arameans, the kings of Israel, the Edomites, and Philistines (ch. 28). Josiah purges Judah, Jerusalem, Manasseh, Ephraim, Simeon, and Naphtali of high places, and is slain at Megiddo in an attempt to reclaim the north (chs. 34-35).

The personal and military goals of these monarchs seem limited when compared with narrative accounts of David's campaigns. The ideal leader is credited with dominance over the Philistines, Moabites, Edomites, Ammonites, and Aram and with alliances with Tyre and Hamath (1 Chron 14: 8-17; 18; 19; 20). His successors seek only portions of the expanse. Hence, in the Chroniclers' model, strong foreign foes combine with internal disharmony among the

Yahwists to restrict opportunities for Jerusalemite leaders in the post-Solomonic era. According to the Chroniclers' parochial interests, religious legitimacy and continuity offer the only hope for restoration. The world in their model is religious, and David stands as its founder.

The way the two meanings of all Israel are used illustrates that the Chroniclers' apparent ambivalence toward the past is more consistent than it first seems. For them the time of David and Solomon is the summit of religious and political development when religious and geopolitical domains coexisted and were coterminous under a single leader. In that world, the temple stood for the unity of all Israel as a political, territorial entity and as a worshiping body who participated in Jerusalem's rituals.

David unified and moved the two-fold allegiances to the Jebusite center and provided for successors who would guarantee the continuity of the relationship. In this sense, those who claim that David and Solomon constitute a single epoch find agreement among the ancients who believed that the united, worshiping peoples of David's and Solomon's time represented the ideal historical reality. There, the two meanings of all Israel could be used without misunderstanding. Temple and territory were aligned.

Fluidity of Narrative Units

Earlier we mentioned fluidity in the way genealogical units and names are adapted in segmented societies to suit the purposes of leaders and to present a picture of the statuses and relationships in the genealogists' time. The process, we noted, brings together genealogical units that had previously functioned separately in social, political, economic, and religious domains.

Comparison with other materials in the Bible suggests that the genealogical tactics prevailed in the Chroniclers' world. In turn, the practice provides the basis for a hypothesis regarding the use of literary units. The hypothesis is that in order to present a synchronic image of Yahwist life and its dependency on David, the Chroniclers constructed a story comprising units that were previously independent or were parts of different structures and domains. The fusion of two all Israels is an example. So far nothing is new. We suggest in addition that the arrangement of materials corresponds to the same patterns and techniques as control genealogies. The narrative seams and breaks among literary units represent the unity and disunity, the continuities and discontinuities that genealogists depict by joining or separating genealogical units. In Chronicles the process creates an image that, although not necessarily "historical" in its detail and relation to referents, represents a dominant view of David during the time Chronicles is being written. It also illustrates the canonical and indexical claims that combine to support homeostasis at that time.

The hypothesis assumes that the ancient writers do not distinguish sharply between the functions of genealogical and narrative materials. The connection between 1 Chronicles 1-9 and the rest of the books supports the assumption. Where other writers might appeal to story-forms in order to organize their views of the past from creation down to the monarchy, the Chroniclers use genealogy. The function is the same, i.e., to account for a past that produced a Saul who lost his leadership role in favor of David. In the genealogies, relationships—as we saw in the Psalms—are charted, but the specific episodes, the events which make the genealogical elements important are neglected.

The same fluidity among narrative units is apparent. It is conspicuous in the absence of stories that might cast David in an unfavorable light. The tradition contains such accounts, and reports the discord and disunity, but the Chroniclers either choose to ignore them or they live in a parochial environment that suppresses them. In either case, it is the relationships among the surviving narratives that tell the story as much as the details within each isolated unit. Hence, terminology such as "all Israel" that by investigators' standards seem inconsistent probably revealed no contradictions to ancient audiences.

Investigators' Model

The structure of the representational model contained in the books of Chronicles confirms the transitions noted in Hebrew poetry. An inclusive story extends from First Parent to the writers' present, but the remote past is treated with dispatch. Exodus and Conquest are not known or are passed over. The story slows to a narrative's pace only when it reaches Saul, who is introduced fleetingly in death more than life. In the model, he stands as one pole, a representative and symbol of a position that the true Israel has moved beyond. He and the ark epitomize a former representational model shared in the north that stands in opposition to the authentic choice which Yahweh eventually made for David and Jerusalem.

Stage 1 Stage 2	→	Stage 3	→	Stage 4
Tribal Saul		David Solomon Temple Jerusalem		Dynasty

David stands at the center of the model where he plays the combined roles of divine agent, mediator, and founder (1 Chron 10: 14b). He unites all the peoples, Yahwist and non-Yahwist, and weaves them into a network extending from the Negev to Hamath and beyond. He formulates the plans and organizational arrangements for the temple; he designates his successor whose primary responsibility is to execute his plans; and he dies.

Building a temple, for the Chroniclers, is not simply a charge given to a son or a sign of David's religiosity. The edifice in the custody of Davidic successors bestows legitimacy on its custodians. As the keepers of the ark had ensured Yahweh's presence and movements, now the guardians of the sacred place are guaranteed the deity's abiding loyalty. For them, those who believe but stay away because of political, military, or religious restraints are denied the deity's presence. Restoring unity, opening access to Jerusalem, finding religiously and politically strong leadership—in effect finding a new David—run together in the hope of those who share the representational model. That individual would be committed to David's transitions, to drawing Yahwist worshipers back to Jerusalem, and to ensuring dynastic succession.

The symbolic geography of the writers has been sketched. In some ways, the Chroniclers' ideal Israel is less expansive than the one aspired to by the actors described in the model. Although David reportedly extended Jerusalem's control throughout the eastern Mediterranean basin, the non-Yahwist regions appear to be of little interest for the Chroniclers. Pagan aspects of the temple and pagan idols are suppressed in favor of the Yahwistic ideal. Acquiring or losing the non-Yahwist nations is mostly a measure of the Judahite monarchs' military strength and success in a geopolitical sphere. This is not the Chroniclers' first interest. For them, the representational model exhibits a religious ideology in which the transitions from Saul to David and David to dynasty offer foundations for faith and hope in the continuation of the deity's concern. Whether they could provide a basis for territorial reform is beyond their interest.

Because of this parochialism, the symbolic geography in the model focuses on the Cisjordan region. The audience for the model is the Yahwists, all Israel in Israel and Judah, whose boundaries are vague and blurred. Ritual celebrated in Jerusalem by the group is therefore a paradox, a celebration for a remnant and simultaneously a gathering of all the faithful. The remnant gathers to recall an ideal past and to pray for those who should join them.

The shift to a predominant interest in north/south unity and away from east/west relationships that our archaeological model suggests obtained on the ground during Iron Age I has a profound impact on biblical tradition. In this view, the river Jordan acts as a boundary and border more than as a center on a map of the tribal claims or of David's empire. The Chroniclers' record no ritual crossing of the Jordan as found elsewhere in the Bible even though movement to and from Transjordan is described (1 Chron 22: 15, 37; 19: 17). The true Israel, the one that interests the Chroniclers, lives in Judah and Israel, and it is their unity that the model idealizes.

Finally, Solomon and David are treated as a single epoch as Williamson suggests and for the reasons stated above. Fusing father and son in the model effectively places the successor in the founding phase of dynasty or, more precisely, postpones the dynastic debate until the Schism. The difference between this view and that of the deuteronomists will become clear as we proceed.

Deuteronomistic Model

For half a century, biblical historians have accepted the existence of a "Deuteronomic History" (and since, a revised "Deuteronomistic History") that extends from the beginning of the book of Deuteronomy to the end of the second book of Kings. Whether the Deuteronomic hypothesis will withstand further tests of time is uncertain, but the issue is beyond the scope of our investigation. Whatever the result, presently it will be useful to examine David's position within the cluster of elements that constitute a "Deuteronomic" or "Deuteronomistic" corpus.

The compilers' devotion to Moses and the covenant is explicit in the structure of their narrative. The story opens with a proclamation of the second law in the book of Deuteronomy and ends with an inclusio that reports a reform based on the discovery of a law book

(2 Kings 22). It begins with a divine promise of land to Moses and with a people on the verge of entering Canaan (Deuteronomy 1-4) and ends with an effort to reunite the territory under Josiah's leadership (2 Kings 23). Every major phase in the rise of Yahwist power is marked by concern for a covenant like the one mediated by Moses. The structure of the book of Deuteronomy is itself a covenant form, and scholars have detected covenant forms, covenantal language, or covenant imagery in the stories of Joshua (Joshua 24), Samuel (1 Samuel 12), and David (2 Samuel 7) (cf. McCarthy, 1965: 137 and *passim*).

Land, covenant, temple, kingship, and Jerusalem are among the themes that permeate and unify the Deuteronomic model. Two themes, Moses and Covenant, illustrate the writers' longing for kings who will return the nation to its Mosaic foundations. Moses sets the stage. By his speeches and mandates, he captures and encapsulates all previous experiences. He recites, summarizes, and hands them down as a commission for future generations.

The second hero in the Deuteronomic model is David (2 Kgs 22: 2). The point is debated, but von Rad identified him instead of Solomon as the writers' prototype (von Rad, 1953: 88; Flanagan, 1975). On the surface of the story, at least, David is the standard of comparison for Solomon (1 Kgs 3: 3), Asa (1 Kgs 15: 11), Amaziah (2 Kgs 14: 3), Ahaz (2 Kgs 16: 2), Hezekiah (2 Kgs 18: 3), and Josiah (2 Kgs 22: 2). Repeatedly, David's successors are condemned by failing to meet his standards (1 Kgs 9: 4; 11: 4, 6, 33, 38; 15: 3, 5), and he is given credit and lauded for his plans to build the temple (1 Kgs 5: 17; 8: 17; 2 Kgs 21: 7) even though Yahweh states opposition to the scheme (2 Samuel 7).

The effort to associate David and Solomon with the temple is similar but not identical to the way the Chroniclers treat their reigns as a single epoch. The models share temple worship as a criterion for true religiosity, but the Deuteronomists understand "failure to do what their forefather David had done" more broadly. Breaches include failing to live rightly and justly, violating the Lord's statutes and decrees and allowing Israel to be driven off its land. Thus, behind the ideal David stands a value system that Moses represents and that all leaders including David must obey. Unlike his image in Chronicles, David appears as the new Moses who combines loyalty to the covenant, unity of the land, and sensitivity to peoples' needs for centralized leadership in Jerusalem. Solomon, on the other hand, excels in so far as he brings his father's plans to fruition, as in Chronicles, by building the temple, but he fails by submitting to self-contradictory pagan, i.e., decentralizing, worship.

Unity of the Deuteronomic Model

As the books of Samuel and stories of David stand at the center of the Deuteronomic model, so the accounts of the transfer of the ark and of Yahweh's covenant with David stand at the heart of the books and stories of Samuel. There and in the Deuteronomic model, possession of Jerusalem and Yahwist legitimacy for its ruler are at the root of religious and political thought. The central message is nested, as it were, within the "concentric" Samuel and Deuteronomic models.

The legitimation of Zion in 2 Samuel 7 divides the Deuteronomic History. The stories that precede in Deuteronomy, Joshua, Judges, and 1 Samuel 1 to 2 Samuel 5 form a preface describing Yahweh's promise of land, the journey to its southern and eastern borders, a unified capture and settlement, and life in the land during the first generations of Yahwism. Against this background, the Philistine threat recorded in Judges and the first book of Samuel as well as Israel's decision to respond by centralizing are extensions of the land theme.

In the middle portion of the model from 2 Samuel 8 to 1 Kings 11, the Davidic and Solomonic eras are recognized as times of expansion and consolidation when Yahwist Judah and Israel become the core of a heterogeneous federation of peoples, tribes, and kingdoms governed from Jerusalem. In the post-Solomonic period of 1 Kings 12 to the end of 2 Kings the fragile unity quickly dissolves in part because of internal bickering among the Yahwists over legitimacy and succession rights, and in part because of the internationalizing of the empire. Reform movements under Hezekiah and finally Josiah loom as attempts to regain Yahweh's rightful land by restoring the deity to a lofty position in Jerusalem.

In order to tie the pre- and post-Davidic stories together and to stress the religious legitimacy of Judahite kings who retain Yahwistic values, the compilers skillfully employ several literary devices. Two are sufficient to demonstrate David's role in the model. The first is similar to one we've seen before. It places an idealized, universal "all Israel"—the term used otherwise by the Chroniclers—in the times of Moses and Joshua and makes it the model for Josiah's reform. The second entwines the themes of ark and house, i.e., dynasty and temple, again in order to legitimate Josiah's endeavors.

a. *Deuteronomic Meaning of All Israel*

The technical term, "all Israel" (*kol yiśrā'ēl*), appears nearly 90 times in the writings of the Deuteronomists (Flanagan, 1975). This compares with approximately 50 usages in Chronicles (including Ezra and Nehemiah) and only five occurrences elsewhere in the Massoretic Text. At least five meanings are detected in the Deuteronomic writings.

In Deuteronomy and Joshua the term signifies an idealized group to whom Yahweh gives the land. Moses addresses the assembly often, and Joshua leads it across the Jordan.

In Judges and the books of Samuel, the term means 1) the Israel unit that joins with Benjamin, 2) an Israel that includes Benjamin but not Judah, and 3) an Israel that shares its leader with Judah and Jerusalem. The meanings are fluid and change as the story moves from Samuel to Saul to David. Consistency is found in the group's separate identity over against Benjaminite and Judahite elements that come in contact with it and sometimes use its name to designate new federations. The idealized expanse of the largest all Israel is from Dan to Beersheba, boundaries attributed to David's time that become the basis for the religiopolitical usages in Deuteronomy and Joshua.

In the books of Kings, the Deuteronomists use all Israel only during the reigns of Solomon and the Divided Monarchs down to the fall of the northern kingdom. In Solomonic stories, the ambivalence between all Israel signifying Israel plus Judah and representing Israel alone continues. In references to the divided kingdoms, unlike the Chroniclers, the Deuteronomists alway mean the schismatic northern kingdom that excludes Benjamin and Judah.

In Deuteronomy, Joshua, and in one instance Judges, the phrase represents a unified Israel, i.e., the people who share a common life in the settlement period and who are called to reunite under Josiah. The meaning is similar to the "true" Israel of the Chroniclers in the sense that both are theological categories, but here and elsewhere the Deuteronomic term always implies a geopolitical residential group, and it never refers to Judah or the Judahite kingdom (i.e., Judah plus Benjamin) alone.

The restricted northern meaning appears in the opening chapters of 1 Samuel, but by the time of the Deuteronomists, the most expansive territorial limits—"from Dan to Beersheba"—had been imposed on earlier scenes (cf. Judg 20; 1 Sam 3: 20). The expression appears again in the Abner negotiations (2 Sam 3: 10) and in Hushai's remarks (2 Sam 17: 11) and probably during the census (2 Sam 24: 2, 15). The inclusive meaning is retained during Solomon's reign (MT 1 Kgs 5: 5), although on the occasion of the dedication, all Israel reaches from Hamath to the Wadi of Egypt (1 Kgs 8: 65).

This discrepancy regarding all Israel's extent as well as the differences between all Israel as Israel minus Judah and as Israel minus Benjamin indicate that the Deuteronomists use the term in several ways even when reporting David's and Solomon's times. The term means the entire expanse governed by them, either from Dan to Beersheba or from Syria to Egypt. Following the Schism, however, the term means only the divided northern kingdom, and after the fall of the north it is not used again in the Deuteronomic model. It is not applied to Judah alone as in Chronicles.

In spite of these variations, the all Israel proper to the representational model of the Deuteronomists is clear. It associates land and conquest themes in order to create or exaggerate impressions of a unified territorial conquest and its fulfillment in the Davidic era. The Davidic precedent is held up as a standard and model for Josiah's reform and for other post-Davidic leaders. David is the "center" of the Deuteronomic corpus.

b. *Ark and House Themes*

The second theme is a combination of two related motifs. Again, they link pre- and post-Davidic stories and focus attention on David and Jerusalem. By connecting ark to house, the transitions from Saul and ark to David and Jerusalem and from David to dynasty noted in the Psalms and Chronicles are fused in a single continuous story.

Reportedly, Moses builds the ark and entrusts it to the tribe of Levi (Deut 10: 1-9). He places the law within it, arranges for the law's reading, and prepares for his successor Joshua to escort the sacred chest into the Promised Land (Deut 31: 9-13, 25-26). Joshua is joined by all Israel during the crossing of the Jordan and afterward (Joshua 3-8). Each stage in the ark's progress toward its destination on Mt. Ebal is marked by an elaborate ritual.

The Jordan plays a dialectical boundary/center role in the Deuteronomic model. As the story stands, the entry of the ark into Canaan is the first paradox. The entire procession from Transjordan to highland Cisjordan has the characteristics of a rite of passage that celebrates the entry and founding of a new homeland. Accordingly, the river stands as a threshold and boundary, the betwixt and between to be crossed when wilderness is left behind and the community reassembles in the land of Canaan. In this reading, Moses represents the old order, the wilderness, or more exactly, the unsettled, homeless, landless life. Joshua at Ebal and later David in Jerusalem epitomize the new order that is both a continuation of the Mosaic ideal and the end of the wandering years. Not surprisingly, for the Deuteronomists the ark's first home in Canaan is in the heartland of the northern kingdom from whence it travels circuitously to Jerusalem.

The ark is mentioned only once in Judges (20: 27) , when the Israelites do battle against the Benjaminites. It is not mentioned again until the Philistines capture it, move it to Ashdod, and subsequently return it to Yahwist control (2 Sam 4: 1–7: 1). The Massoretic Text reports that Saul is accompanied by the ark in his battle against the Philistines at Michmash (1 Sam 14: 18), but the versions refer to an ephod instead. In any case, the next important episode for the ark is in 2 Samuel 6 when it is transferred to Jerusalem in another rite of passage (Flanagan, 1983b).

After the move to Jerusalem, references to the ark become less frequent but, because of their relation to the house theme which gains importance as the ark's diminishes, they are no less significant. In the dialogue between David and Uriah where the soldier exhibits a lingering attachment to the ark, "house" is used seven times (2 Sam 11: 6-15). "House" is stressed again when Nathan rebukes and David repents (2 Sam 12: 7-20).

During Absalom's rebellion, Zadok and the Levites begin to carry the ark from the city only to be sent back by David. Again the procession is ritualistic and contrasts with David's return when he meets many of the same individuals and groups that he had encountered during his exit.

In the Deuteronomic model, the procession is more than a retreat before an aggressor. It is also the undoing of the first entry into Canaan. The leader is dethroned, choas reigns, and although custodian of the ark, he is driven beyond the border in a ritualized retreat to the wilderness.

The importance of the ark is made explicit by David's words. "If I find favor with the Lord, he will bring me back and permit me to see it and its lodging. But if he should say, 'I am not pleased with you,' I am ready; let him do to me as he sees fit" (NAB 2 Sam 15: 25-29). Within the Deuteronomic model, the statement places the rebellion and exile in the larger context of divine control over David's destiny (cf. von Rad, 1965: 201). It marks the line between competing representational models that support and oppose David's legitimacy and are acted out in the social drama. In the scene, David tests divine will by sending the ark back to Jerusalem. Would the ark's presence in the city protect an illegitimate rebel usurper, or would David continue in Yahweh's favor?

The need to choose between ark and David is kept before readers by frequent references to the house theme. During the passage from Jerusalem, Ziba, the servant of Saul's son Meribaal, quotes his master's claim that the house of Israel had returned the kingdom of his father (2 Sam 16: 3), implying that David had stolen it away. The concubines he leaves in his house (2 Sam 15: 16) to be taken over by Absalom (2 Sam 16: 21), are returned after the exile (2 Sam 19: 2). House is mentioned in each of the references and three additional times in a single verse, but without mentioning the ark or its habitation (2 Sam 20: 3).

By leaving the ark behind but returning to the house, David performs another rite of passage and new entry similar to the ark's first entry. This one involves crossing the river Jordan twice. The route takes him from Jerusalem to wilderness to Jerusalem, from aggregation to liminality to reaggregation. Like the ark's journey from Transjordan to Gilgal and eventually to Jerusalem, David returns across the river, first to Gilgal and then to Jerusalem. He leaves the land without the ark in order to test Yahweh. He re-enters, regains Jerusalem, and replaces the ark and the lingering allegiance to it. The ark and the representational model it stands for are displaced. The cycle from Moses to David is complete. The days of wilderness and wandering are ended. David is now the symbol of Yahweh's presence in Jerusalem. He is the new Moses, the new Joshua, and the new ark, the permanent representative of Yahweh among the people.

The next two references to the ark are in the Solomonic succession scene (1 Kgs 2: 26; 3: 15). In the second, after offering sacrifice at Gibeon, Solomon returns to Jerusalem to stand before the ark and offer sacrifices (1 Kgs 3: 15). Thus, in spite of the Deuteronomic demand for centralized worship, the king circulates as the ark had done before.

The final appearances of the ark in the Deuteronomic History are during the construction and dedication of the temple (1 Kgs 6: 19; 8: 3, 5, 7, 9). Again the theme is permeated with references to houses. "House" is used frequently to refer to both the temple, the house of Yahweh (e.g., 1 Kgs 6: 1-10; 14-18), and the palace, the house of the king (1 Kgs 7: 1). The ark is placed in the temple, a dedication prayer is offered linking the temple to the promise made to David, and the ark, now displaced by the temple and house of David, is not mentioned again in the Deuteronomic corpus.

To summarize: in this representational model, the prominence of the ark diminishes while the importance of the houses of the deity and monarch increases. The transitions are made quickly in 2 Samuel 6 and 7 when David displaces Saul and dynasty is promised, but according to the model, carrying out the plan takes longer than announcing it. Allegiance to the ark endures among those who are not engaged in temple-building, but building the edifice and placing the ark in it ensure the dynastic claims of its builders. Hence, competing representational models.

A paradox emerges. In one sense, the temple stands as a continuation and extension of the hopes symbolized by the ark. The building in fact is a house for Yahweh primarily because it shelters the ark. But in another sense, the temple displaces the ark by making Jerusalem Yahweh's permanent home and its leader the permanent representative. The change is so great in fact that the Deuteronomists remember no mention of the sacred chest after it is situated in the temple sanctuary.

Observer's Model

The ark/house theme and the idealized geopolitical entity, all Israel, demonstrate that the transitions to Jerusalem and dynasty stand at the center of the Deuteronomic model. The stages are presented serially. First is the period of the ark, second the time of Saul, third the reign of David, and finally the reign of Solomon. Solomon appears as part of the dynastic issue, not as part of the founding phase preceding the Schism as in Chronicles. Competition for succession begins earlier in the Deuteronomic model.

David is linked to Moses and to the covenant by stories and themes rather than genealogies. Partial and previously separate images of pre-Davidic Israel are unified and universalized. The fullest rendition is the military skirmishes that are welded into a unified conquest and settlement in Joshua that ritually brings an exogenous ethnic people from across the Jordan in the company of the ark.

As in Chronicles, several symbolic geographies coexist. One portrays the early settlement of the Yahwists and David's subsequent conquests as extending east of the Jordan, north as far as Hamath and south to the Negev and Edom. The other, the dominant Deuteronomic image, portrays Moses, Joshua, and David as away from home and outside their land when in Transjordan. The two images partially obscure each other but not sufficiently to bury what the writers consider to be the rightful home for the followers of Moses and Joshua, for the people of the tribal period, and for the leaders of centralized Israel and Judah. Their center is in the land of Canaan and eventually in a Jebusite city that is the personal property of David, paradoxically a zone within the confines of no other state. Another paradox is implied when Saul's successor, Ishbaal, continues to lead Israel but is portrayed as so weak that he must rule from outside, i.e., beyond the borders in Transjordan.

The tension between wilderness and settled representations is resolved by the Deuteronomic interpretation of legitimating movements. Land, conquest, covenant, ark, and house themes coalesce to explain the passing of Yahweh's favor from one model to the other. Wilderness, wandering, and Transjordan are depicted as former life (cf. Jobling, 1986: 107-119). Settlement, Cisjordan, and Jerusalem are the current legitimate consequences of the divine plan. On one level, diachronic evolutionary progress moves from wilderness to settled life, while on another, movement is cyclical and oscillating so that relationships between the two sides of the Jordan are reciprocal and revolving. Hence, the wilderness beyond the Jordan is both a place of exile and refuge and a place of nostalgia and recuperation where leaders seek Yahweh's protection, the support of loyal allies, and the time to recover from life's rejections. On both levels, its edge is marked by the Jordan, a place of turning, and a betwixt and between. On the other side divine favor is either evoked (Moses), bestowed (Joshua), transferred (Ishbaal) or reaffirmed (David).

The Deuteronomic model, unlike the Chroniclers', retains the Samuel writers' views of David's blemishes and vices as well as his charms and virtues. He rises from humble and unlikely origins, from a shepherd's pasture to the palace of a large federation. He serves Saul, marries his daughter, and befriends his son, but still is not acceptable in that court. He aligns with Israel's principal enemy, the Philistines, and serves as their vassal at Ashdod, Ziklag, and probably Hebron. He leads his house in war against the house of Saul and benefits from the treason of Abner, Saul's uncle, and the murder of Saul's son. He commits adultery and arranges the death of the victim's husband. He begets sons who commit incestuous rape, fratricide, and open revolt against his own authority. He is slow to quell unrest in Benjamin, and he allows his sons to vie in struggles for premortem succession before finally allowing a favorite wife, Bathsheba, to dictate his successor.

In contrast to the Chroniclers', the Deuteronomists' model is a view from the ground, from below Olympus, from amongst the participants. The same Jerusalemite centralizing biases are evident, and the early periods of Moses and Joshua are mythologized, but observers feel like witnesses to real-life situations and characters. The feelings are especially strong in the Samuel material, but also to a certain extent with Solomon in the book of Kings. They differ from impressions of Moses and Joshua on the one hand and of monarchs of the Divided Monarchy on the other.

The differences between Samuel and other portions of the narrative, as well as between this image of David and that in Chronicles, explains in part the function of the narrative units. According to our hypothesis, like genealogies they have been strung together serially in a pseudo-chronological sequence according to relationships perceived at the time of Deuteronomic writing. The Samuel corpus is the largest of these single literary units to be lifted more or less intact by the Deuteronomists. Thus, the extended Deuteronomic account reflects an interest not simply in the outcome of early Israel's activities, but in explaining to contemporaries how and why various fortunes rise and fall. Placing the David story at the pinnacle of the account where it fulfills the promises to Moses helps compilers and readers to sort the permanent and lasting from the transitory and dispensable. The alleged transitions to Jerusalem and temple in David's era are the maps for later generations, the invariables, and the episodes that guarantee stability.

In the Deuteronomic model, Moses and David, Yahweh's covenants in the wilderness and in Jerusalem, and temple and dynasty are explicate manifestations of the implicate divine plan guiding life as well as all virtuous people and kings. David is writ large on the map because he is responsible for maintaining and fulfilling the Mosaic covenantal tradition and for employing it as the basis for unifying Yahwists in Jerusalem. Furthermore, he provides for the covenant's continuance by establishing a dynasty whose principal responsibilities include constructing a permanent resting place for the ark in the house of Yahweh in Jerusalem.

The transitions in the model are slightly different from those in Chronicles. By linking 2 Samuel 6 and 7 and placing them ahead of the problems within David's palace, the Deuteronomists hurriedly shift the focus from Saul's fate to Solomon's succession [Figure 30]. Although David plays a leading role, in a sense, he hovers between them as a transducer and stabilizer who mediates the transition. With the oracle in 2 Samuel 7 following Michal/David dialogue in 2 Samuel 6, dynasty becomes the issue immediately. The childlessness of Michal, the daughter of the northern leader, is announced at the end of 2 Samuel 6, and Davidic dynasty, presumably non-Saulide, is proclaimed in 2 Samuel 7. Hence, Solomon appears as the outcome of the dynastic promise rather than a participant in the founding phase of Jerusalemite life. On one level, dynasty is not yet established and events have to be allowed to unfold during the remainder of David's reign. On another, the fact of dynasty has been declared by 2 Samuel 7, and the remainder of the story is exciting but of passing interest. As a result, where the Chroniclers connect the dynastic question to the post-Solomonic Schism, the Deuteronomic model links Davidic dynasty and Solomonic succession closely to David's personal legitimacy (2 Samuel 7). This allows David's and Solomon's stories to unfold in unison as Davidic succession is threatened by elder sons who are eliminated one by one. Like the waning and waxing of the ark and house themes, David's personal legitimacy and that of his dynasty overlap.

Figure 30: The Deuteronomists' Representational Model

Stage 0	→ Stages 1-2	→ Stage 3	→ Stage 4	→ Stage 5
Moses	Saul	David	Solomon	Josiah
Ark	Ark	Jerusalem Dynasty Temple plan	Jerusalem Dynasty Temple	Jerusalem Dynasty Temple
Wilderness /Land	Land	United land	United land	Reunited land

Samuel Model

Although the Samuel materials are part of the Deuteronomic corpus, differences between them and other portions of the Deuteronomic model are clear. The ark and house themes are closely entwined in Samuel; "all Israel" before and after the books have a consistency in usage that is lacking in Samuel; the narrative is less formalized than the speeches and laws in Deuteronomy and the brief summaries of monarchs' reigns in Kings. The canonical division sets the books apart. These factors justify our reviewing Samuel for separate notional representations within our analytical model.

Samuel and the Deuteronomic Model

Much of what was said about the books in the Deuteronomic model applies equally when they are treated separately. Because the Deuteronomists incorporate the Samuel model in their own, previous discussions about all Israel, ark and house, and much of the overall structure of the narrative that now extends from 1 Samuel 1 through 2 Samuel 24 is relevant but need not be repeated.

In Samuel, the story moves in two directions at once. On one level, it traces religiopolitical change from the birth of Samuel and rise of the Philistine threat in the land of Canaan down to the mature years of David's reign. On another, it portrays reversals, encounters, and cycles whereby individuals, events, and attitudes move around and on and off the writers' stage during narrative time. Many concerns introduced at the beginning return, albeit transformed, in or at the end of the narrative. Diachronic changes and synchronic relations are skillfully interwoven as fates unravel to tell the story.

Jerusalem stands at the center of both movements. Diachronically, it divides the books into two parts. In the first part, the city's capture and legitimation mark the end of Saulide leadership, extra-Jerusalemite rule, and a Philistine military threat to Israel's existence. Jerusalem signals the opening of a new phase in Yahwist life. Then David, not Saul or a member of his house, serves as the divinely authorized leader. Leadership which previously belonged exclusively to northerners and Israelites enters the south and Judah. From there, the pendulum's swing comes to rest in the center, Zion, where the central questions in the story change. Should the city remain the legitimate center for political Israel and Judah? Who should be its and their legitimate ruler?

Not only do David and Jerusalem stand as poles opposite the resisting Saulides and hostile Philistines, but relocating in Jerusalem also marks the beginning of the books' second part where instability within David's family is depicted. This second set of difficulties is not resolved until the end of 2 Samuel. Then the opening scenes and problems of 1 Samuel are also reversed and resolved. A solution for David is a solution for Israel. The unifying threads are the tension between David (personally) and Saul and his house, the fluctuating fortunes of the ark, and the guiding hand and voice of Yahweh during David's exile.

In the first part of the story, the ark is lost to Philistine control and crosses the frontier into Philistine territory. Efforts to give it a home among Philistine deities fail. It returns to the borders of Judah and Israel, but not to prominence until it is reclaimed by David. Similarly, David is "lost" by Saul and exits from Israel into Philistine embrace. According to the Samuel model, he becomes their warrior and uneasy client. His relationships to Saul and the Philistines are at times congenial but never completely trustworthy. Thus, David, like the ark, moves from camp to camp and from pole to pole within a world of constantly shifting allegiances. Sacred chest and leader are both abandoned by Saul, taken into custody by the Philistines, and united in Jerusalem.

In light of these parallels, those who label the Court History in 2 Samuel 9-20 "irony," "entertainment," and "wisdom" might expand their claims. If the terms describe that unit, they apply equally to David's entire story. The portrayal of him is filled with paradoxes, contradictions, reversals, and unexpected events that offer the ancients enjoyment and excitement while reinforcing the tellers' claims.

The Philistines' role in this drama must be recognized. Their prominence begins in the book of Judges and continues in Samuel, where it becomes entwined with ark, land, conquest, and Jerusalem themes. The Philistines appear as enemies of Israel, allies of David, enemies of David, and so on. Their fate and that of the Yahwists may not be a love/hate relationship, but the associations are certainly ambivalent and at times even fruitful. David both needs and rejects the Philistines.

In his lifetime, David is evicted twice from centers of power, first from Saul's entourage and then, as we have seen, from Jerusalem. On both occasions, he seeks refuge in the wilderness that is figuratively beyond Israel's borders. It is important that his first protection comes from the Philistines. His initiation into Saul's company is at the Philistines' expense. But in spite of his fraternizing with Israel's enemy, readers know, because of the anointing scene, that he has been chosen to lead Israel. As the story unfolds, however, his "refuge" among the Philistines balances with that in Transjordan during Absalom's coup. He begins as a client of Yahweh's enemies who captured the ark but could not control it, and he finally subjugates the Philistines and displaces the ark as the sign of Yahweh's presence. Only David survives.

Understanding these entwined roles is essential in order to appreciate the representations and operations in the Samuel model. Complex, ambivalent neither/nor, both/and roles are assigned to David as he migrates between friend and foe. However, once it is clear that Yahweh prefers David to Saul (2 Sam 6: 22), the scene shifts but the tensions remain, now because of rebellions led by Absalom and Sheba.

The basis for the tensions in the story is Israel's lack of enthusiasm for the Jerusalemite leadership. Sheba's animosity suggests as much (2 Samuel 20). And the argument between the Israelites and Judahites for the privilege of escorting David from Transjordan also reveals competing northern and southern actors' models (2 Samuel 19: 45). In the Deuteronomists' model, an all Israel Israelite group reportedly accompanies the ark during its initial entry into the land of Canaan, but in the Samuel model, thanks to David's affinity, the Judahites enjoy the privilege of escorting David, its replacement. At this point, we resist ascertaining whether either crossing is historical, whether one story is modeled on the other, or if so which version is the model and which the replica. Clearly, however, the synchronic relationships within the Samuel model demonstrate that the centers of power and legitimacy are shifting from Israel to Judah and Jerusalem.

For the writers, Absalom's and Sheba's rebellions represent the old allegiances struggling to survive (2 Samuel 15-20). The competition between old and new loyalties is their story. The house of Saul wages an unsuccessful war against David after Saul's death (2 Sam 3: 1); David displaces Saul's house (2 Samuel 6); and the Judahites are favored over the Israelites (2 Sam 19: 45). Still, resistance to David endures and enables Sheba to organize a Benjaminite rebellion. Interestingly, this group remains Judah's ally in the Deuteronomic model of the Divided Monarchy, but here it supports the northern Saulide resistance directed against David personally. Who supports Absalom is not as clear. Albrecht Alt (1959, 2: 120) suggested years ago that Absalom's power base is exclusively northern in spite of his decision to launch his revolt from Hebron, the ancient southern Yahwistic center. However, it may be important that some biblical traditions remember Hebron as being settled by an early independent Yahwist group that does not share the conquest traditions which the Deuteronomists use as part of their unified model (cf. Flanagan, 1976). Resistance to David in the story seems to be more pervasive than territorial groupings can explain. From the observers' standpoint, when Absalom's and Sheba's rebellions are considered together, the opposition in the notional model appears to be religiously motivated. Some peoples perceive David as a usurper and illegitimate pretender who can never legitimately lead Israel (as opposed to Judah). According to them, that right belongs to Saul's family and tribe. Although a son of David, but one born in Hebron, Absalom plays on those sympathies. Hence, in the model, he returns to the place where the Yahwist groups first organized around David. He must, in a sense, retrace David's steps from Yahwist Hebron and retake Jerusalem. Sheba tries the same, but from a different starting point. Both attempts fail.

The overarching structure of the books of Samuel, especially the stories set in Jerusalem with their reversals and contradictions, demonstrates how David overcomes threats from the Philistines and house of Saul. Although he struggles to achieve paramountcy in his own city, neither his power nor its location and independence guarantee his survival. Not only must he withstand an attempted coup in order to return to his house and suppress a second rebellion (2 Samuel 20), he must also allow the slaying of Saul's survivors (2 Samuel 21), do final battle with the Philistines (2 Samuel 21), offer a song of thanksgiving (2 Samuel 22), and utter his final words (2 Samuel 23). To consolidate his power, he finally orders an ill-begotten census for which he must do penance (2 Samuel 24). Because Yahweh incites David to take the census, readers are perplexed by the outcome. Suggestions that enrolling in a census requires ritual purity hold a plausible explanation (McCarter, 1984: 512-514). Violations would lead to a plague. Therefore, the census exposes the religious as well as military, economic, and political character of Jerusalemite centralization. The plague caused by impurity betrays a hidden condition that must be removed if David's leadership is to survive. His sovereignty and its relationship to Yahweh are not resolved until he repents, buys a worship site as a final resting place for the ark, and makes offerings.

The pattern parallels and balances the beginning of Samuel. There an elderly couple give birth to the prophet who chooses David and serves the ark at a northern shrine. By the end, the Judahite arranges a permanent home for the ark in Jerusalem, but he and not it is Yahweh's representative.

Succession in the Books of Samuel?

Succession is not a major theme in the books of Samuel. The model's structure confirms that the primary tension is pro-Saul (and anti-David) interests versus pro-David (and anti-Saul) hopes. David and the house of David stand in opposition to Saul and the house of Saul. The question is which group legitimately represents Yahweh, not which individual in David's line can be his successor. That issue is not faced squarely and raised explicitly until 1 Kings 1-2 which the biblical canon places outside the Samuel model.

This claim stands as an observer's hypothesis to be tested against information in the actors' model. Arguments in favor of the hypothesis are cumulative. First is the double meaning of "house" in the stories. Here, the writers play with the two meanings in several ways. David's house is preferred to Saul's and, in contrast to other ancient Near Eastern societies and to other Yahwist models such as the Chroniclers', David's house rules without the legitimation of a temple, a house for the deity. Strong resistance to centralization and monarchy are evident throughout.

Second, Solomon's role as part of the founding era in David's legacy, as portrayed by Chronicles, has been contrasted with his portrayal as "preassigned" dynastic successor, the view of the Deuteronomists. He plays neither role in the Samuel model: David and Davidic dynasty are chosen, but no successor is named. This difference signifies a distinction between David's and his successors' legitimacy that is absent in the other models. The same contrast was observed in our comparisons of Psalm 132 with Psalm 89 and with 2 Samuel 6 and 7. We shall return to this point below.

Third, the structure and themes of the books of Samuel demonstrate their compilers' interest in resolving questions raised in the opening chapters. These are satisfied by their descriptions of David's life that reach their culmination in 2 Samuel 24.

Fourth, David's survival rather than succession is the burning issue. The intense and recurring struggle between David and either Saul or Saul's followers occupies much of the narrative even after Saul's death. For example, during the war over Benjamin's allegiance, the house of David grows stronger while the house of Saul grows weaker (2 Sam 3: 1). The language can mean several things, but the context leaves the impression of a battle between Saul's dynastic supporters and David personally, i.e., over David's legitimacy. In segmented societies, when leadership passes from one segment or moiety to another, horizontal and vertical competition are apt to erupt simultaneously. Competition between the displacer and other outside groups (e.g., the Philistines) continue while members of the displacer's own segment begin jostling and jousting for power during the unstable transition period. The two processes become one in cases like Absalom's where a contender seeks support for premortem, primogeniture succession within the successor's family by aligning with discontented losers in the other segment. Paramount leaders, especially when only marginally eligible, must continually safeguard against contenders from without, within, above, and below. David in the Samuel model exemplifies the need for such circumspection.

Finally, impressions derived from the Samuel model suggest that rules of succession are not clearly defined in the writers' model. The transition periods following Saul's death, during David's later years, and even after Solomon's reign according to other models are all marked by discord and rebellion. One must wonder whether a pre-Darwinian survival-of-the-fittest mentality did not undergird national policy. Such should be expected in segmented tribal models. Whether or not this is so, the model's view is that successful leaders are leaders who are successful, i.e., who survive. Capable leaders are those who outwit and dominate opponents even though they suffer temporary setbacks.

Whether such impressions are too pessimistic to represent the dominant Yahwist thought remains to be seen, but they offer reasonable bases for suggesting that the writers of Samuel are concerned with Davidic and not Solomonic legitimacy. They also lay the groundwork for questions about succession and individual successors in comparative studies. There, we shall see, questions about dynasty and succession are rhetorical until a leader is established against outside contenders. Not until the person demonstrates ability to sustain power and reaches a point where regularized succession is possible can minds turn to questions of dynastic continuity.

Davidic Genealogies

Our observers' impressions can be measured against the actors' model in the Samuel texts according to two types of information: genealogical information encoded in the books and the house theme we have been discussing.

Although neither the Deuteronomists nor the compilers of Samuel share the Chroniclers' enthusiasm for genealogies as a literary device for advancing a storyline, references to family members and court lists serve important functions in their models. Occasional references to lineages, wives, sons, and family as well as to court officials punctuate the books of Samuel and confirm the writers' respect for statuses and relationships in the rapidly changing world depicted as David's time.

I have examined the genealogical information in Samuel and compared it with the Chroniclers' in several earlier studies (Flanagan, 1981; 1983a). These serve as the basis for our abbreviated review.

Saul's era is remembered as a period of national trauma and personal uncertainty. He interprets the bond of loyalty that his eldest son, Jonathan, strikes with David as an affront to his own dynasty and a reason to put David under house arrest (1 Sam 18: 1-4). He tries to assassinate David (1 Samuel 20) and pursues him relentlessly in the Judean wilderness (1 Samuel 21-26). Rebellions against David, as we have seen, continue to be raised in Saul's name.

The model's portrait of David contrasts sharply with that of Saul. David defeats the giant who threatens Saul's soldiers (1 Samuel 17), he labors for the hand of Saul's daughter, Michal (1 Samuel 18), he spares Saul's life (1 Samuel 24; 26), he mourns Saul's death (2 Samuel 1), he cares for Meribaal, Saul's grandson, and saves him from death at the hand of the Gibeonites (2 Sam 9; 21: 7).

Michal's place in the model's social drama is crucial. Not only is she married to David (1 Samuel 18), but she also devises plans to save him from Saul (1 Samuel 19). Eventually, however, she is taken from David and given to Palti as wife (1 Sam 25: 45), perhaps as a ploy for weakening the son-in-law's claim within the northern house (McCarter, 1980: 400). Her return is a condition for David's negotiations with Abner for Ishbaal's crown (2 Sam 3: 12-16), but she shortly falls into disfavor and is confined to a childless life in the Jerusalem harem (2 Samuel 6). In the writers' world, the move leaves her empty-handed in the bartering for dynastic power by wives and concubines.

These relationships offer a background for the silhouette that the genealogical references to Saul's and David's families give to the books of Samuel [cf. Appendix III].

When the treachery visible in the narratives is compared with the genealogical materials, David's rise from amid the ruins of Saul's house can be traced. By the end of the books of Samuel, every known male in direct and collateral lines of descent from Saul except two or three ineligible successors is dead. Only Saul's grandson, Meribaal, and his great-grandson, Mica, seem to have survived. The slaughter of the last seven sons by the Gibeonites is, according to the present arrangement, the final nail in Saulide coffins filled with potential successors of the former leader (2 Samuel 21).

Two conclusions can be drawn. First, David's legitimacy as leader of Israel, according to the Samuel model, depends in large part on his marriage into Saul's family. And second, his role as leader in Judah does not depend on his affinity to Saul.

a. *David's Succession in Israel*

The rise of a leader often includes marriage into another tribe, even that of the incumbent chief. A group satisfied with the generosity and abilities of their leader expects the same benevolence to continue through the family. In the absence of male heirs, whether in direct or collateral descent lines, rights sometimes pass through daughters to their husbands who reign on behalf of the wife's father's line for a generation or until succession returns to the central line through the daughter's children or by devolving to a grandchild by another mother. Michal's childlessness, the house arrest of Meribaal and Mica, and the death of all other sons and grandsons in the direct line, and perhaps even Abner in the collateral line, curtails succession among the Saulides. The survival of Mica keeps the hope alive but unfulfilled (2 Sam 9: 12; cf. 1 Chronicles 8; 9).

David uses Michal to gain optative affiliation with Saul's family. The practice allows married couples to choose affiliation with either parental group, and they usually elect residence among the one that bestows the higher status. The practice is a form of adoption that enables the husband to stand in for his wife and to inherit from and succeed her father (Service, 1962: 162).

The scene is set during the negotiations with Abner when a weak direct-line descendant rules from exile (Ishbaal) and a strong independent leader with estranged ties to the predecessor's house is in power in a neighboring territory (David). The external candidate has support in the north, but his marriage bond must be re-established. When the direct line son and a collateral line traitor (Abner) are eliminated, the way is open for David to succeed Saul legitimately as leader of Israel. The second issue, namely, whether the line will continue from David or return to Saul's house, is raised by Michal's childlessness but is resolved only later by the Dynastic Oracle.

b. *David's Leadership in Judah*

The only genealogical units in the books of Samuel that pertain to David's family are the remarks about his "sister" Zeruiah who is the daughter of Nahash of the Ammonites (2 Sam 17: 24-26), the lineage of Bathsheba and Solomon (2 Sam 11; 12: 24-25), and lists of sons born at Hebron and Jerusalem (2 Sam 3: 2-5; 5: 13-16). In the Hebron lists, mothers' names are included, but they are lacking in the Jerusalem list. The lists offer only a few clues regarding David's rights, but they can be combined with information in the narratives in order to determine their place in the writers' representational model.

First, David marries outside his kin group, taking wives among Yahwists and non-Yahwists alike. The tactic is that of a pastoralist seeking to expand the network of relationships that will help him economically, socially, and politically. One wife is from Jezreel (northern or southern?), another the wife of a wealthy pastoralist, a third the daughter of the king of Geshur, and many others whose lineages are unknown (2 Sam 3: 2-5). The reference to Zeruiah's lineage as daughter of Nahash suggests that David also marries into the Ammonite royal house.

Secondly, migration offers contenders a convenient means of escaping problems by withdrawing to a remote area away from an incumbent's authority. Saul's conviction that Jonathan should protect his succession rights against David (1 Sam 20: 31) demonstrates that David's loss in competition for paramountcy motivates him to flee to an outlying district. There, he is free to demonstrate and develop his skills while creating a powerbase of his own outside the incumbent's house. Studies show that unsuccessful candidates form independent chieftaincies, move to peripheral areas, and in many instances enjoy a temporary lull in competition before making another attempt at the high office (Robertson, 1976; Barth, 1961: 84-85; Service, 1962: 155).

But the model also shows David to be anything but neutral. His network includes first the Philistines, Saul's principal enemy in the model. Depicted as traders, smiths, and warriors, the group sponsors him at Ashdod, Ziklag, and probably Hebron as he expands his alliances among the Judahites.

Whatever the details in the model, such maneuvers in outlying regions typically affect descent lineages and genealogies that are re-adjusted to reflect actual social relationships. Structurally, the new leadership gives rise to newly developed genealogical patterns such as conical clans and related *ramage* descent groups. The limited genealogical information about David contains genealogies kept orally at Hebron for his *ramage* with him at the head and his sons listed according to their mothers' positions (cf. Flanagan, 1983a). No connection with the house of Saul is suggested. The implication, confirmed by narrative reports of David's service to the Philistines and his redistributor role in the south, is that he holds office in Judah by a separate claim independent of his association with Saul or his marriage to Michal. He, like the Philistines, is not incorporated into Saul's lineage. He wins the Judahite office from a Philistine base by organizing and maintaining support among individuals and groups who seek a strong personal allegiance to him. He is their "big man" and protector, their provider, their redistributor of booty and bounty. His successes invite followers to join him for the benefits that allegiance offers.

When David's relationship to Judah is set beside his expansionist campaigns in other non-Yahwist regions, an important distinction between representations and operations becomes apparent. According to the representational model, in the marriage chambers and on the battlefield, the leader wins the allegiances of a disparate lot modern scholars call the "Davidic Empire." On the operational level, therefore, Israel and Judah were but two of many jewels in David's crown. At the level of the Samuel Yahwist representations, however, Israel, its leadership, and Judah's relationship to both are the central concerns. The writers ask, could a Judahite son of Jesse in Jerusalem be Yahweh's representative? They answer in the affirmative, but they do not suppress the resistance visible on the level of operations.

Framework of Genealogical and Officer Information

The way in which the genealogical information, together with bureaucratic lists, is used to organize the narrative sheds important light on the structure of the Samuel model.

No attempt is made to include David in Saul's genealogies even retrospectively. The absence may say something about the degree and speed with which power is transferred to David or, as is more likely, that Saul's position is never consolidated sufficiently to merit attaching it to the successful Davidic line. We can only conjecture why the Benjaminite and Judahite components of later times did not explain their connections genealogically. Saul is remembered, and hopes for his line endure, but only as a northern, regional alternative to Davidic rule, not as its continuation.

Instead, the Samuel model charts the progressive development of centralization by an adroit use of genealogical and administrative lists. The materials outline a patronage network that is gradually, but not completely, replacing segmentary tribal structures.

In the books of Samuel, genealogical units and administrative lists stand at the centers of thematic units rather than at their beginnings and ends. They serve as maps and mnemonic devices for tracking the course of the story. We refer here to stories and themes more than to literary blocks or segments. Sections between the lists advance plots and foreshadow sections that follow. When the lists are read alone, however, the main storyline's development toward stable Davidic Jerusalemite rule under Yahweh is evident in both the content and geographical settings of the lists. This is the "official" view of genealogists and administrators that subsumes and obscures much of the diversity we have been noting. The polyvalent evolution is on one plane from familial, village, and tribal leadership toward urbanized patronage and administrative bureaucracy, and on another from David's image as northern outcast and fugitive to southern warrior-chieftain and finally centrist Jerusalemite paramount leader.

The lists begin with Saul who, although he exhibits grave failings, is apparently at the pinnacle of his strength (1 Sam 14: 49-51). His family list is juxtaposed between the statement of his ill-fated cursing of the would-be successor Jonathan and the start of the ultimate slide that motivates Samuel's search for alternative leadership.

A. 1 Sam 14:49-51	at Gibeah?	: : 1 wife (named)
(Saul)		: : 3 sons (named)
		: : 2 daughters (named)
		: : father's brother's son = commander (named)
B. 2 Sam 2:2-3	Ziklag to Hebron	: : 2 wives (named)
(David)		: : [no sons]
		: : his men and their families
C. 2 Sam 3:2-5	at Hebron	: : 6 wives (named)
		: : 6 sons (named)
D. 2 Sam 5:13-16	Hebron to Jerusalem	: : "more" concubines and wives (unnamed)
		: : "more" sons and daughters (11 sons named)
E. 2 Sam 8:15-18	at Jerusalem	: : [no wives mentioned]
		: : [sons priests?] (unnamed)
		: : 6[+?] officers
		: : 5[6?] officers
F. 2 Sam 20:23-26	return to Jerusalem	: : [no wives mentioned]
		: : 8 officers
		: : 7 officers

The "story" is clear. Interests turn increasingly from the politics of marriage, reflected in the patronymics identifying wives, to concern for succession and administration, shown in remarks about filiation and office-holding. The place of the lists within the stories indicates the compilers' proximity to narrators and oral culture where genealogists assess shifting statuses, roles, and relationships and where stories are crafted around genealogists' recollections (cf. Goody, 1977: 74-111). Again we see signs that the same fluidity as is found in genealogies applies to the narrative units. The compilers rearrange both to tell their story and reflect changing circumstances.

When the narratives of Samuel are read independently without regard for the genealogical units, the same progression can be seen in spite of the reversals and balances that give the books their symmetry. Stages in David's rise paralleling those in the lists can be discerned. The first is personified by Samuel; the second by Saul; the third by David at Hebron; the fourth by David at Jerusalem before his exile; and the fifth by David upon his return to Jerusalem.

Meaning of the House Theme

Behind the Samuel narratives, and running through them, are

several themes, most importantly the ark, sacred space, and house. Although the same themes were investigated with the Deuteronomic History, they deserve separate consideration here. The way the themes are entwined raises questions about the place and meaning of the succession theme in the books of Samuel. Commentators since Rost usually find the theme in the dynastic oracle in 2 Samuel 7, the Bathsheba affair and birth of Solomon in 2 Samuel 11-12, the deaths of Amnon and Absalom in 2 Samuel 13-19, and Adonijah's and Solomon's successions in 1 Kings 1-2.

Excavative methods and systemic analyses are not needed in order to note the difference between accession and succession in these episodes and the fact that they extend beyond the corpus of the books of Samuel. Not only does the succession scene fall outside the Samuel model, but the homicides in Samuel also relate to the competition between Saul's and David's houses rather than to Davidic succession. Saul's and David's households both suffer devastation. Furthermore, the succession units such as 2 Samuel 11-12 are all connected thematically with 1 Kings 1-2. Admittedly, this is used by some to argue for the integrity of the succession theme within the Samuel narrative as Rost proposed, but it actually indicates that the two themes, dynasty and succession, can be easily separated according to Davidic or Solomonic models. For example, Nathan appears only in 2 Samuel 7, 2 Samuel 11-12, and 1 Kings 1-2. Bathsheba and Solomon appear only in the last two. One must wonder whether the episodes do not pertain to a succession crisis and belong to Solomon's story rather than David's.

On its surface, our interpretation may seem like standard source criticism, but that is not really the case. Of course our information is derived from literary sources, but we are concerned with the models encoded therein. For our hypothesis, to be developed later, whether portions of the text existed separately is not as important as the social world(s) reflected in the narratives.

If dynasty and succession are considered separately, we can see that representations favoring David and Solomon are telescoped in the existing Samuel model (as they no doubt were in the world of some ancient actors). Whether the unity is owing to the Deuteronomists or some post-Davidic, pre-Deuteronomic model cannot be determined with certainty. But together the representations featuring the father and son confirm what has only been hinted before. In the myth structure of the Yahwists, David's and Solomon's accessions are related but separate themes.

Here the canon adds information. It respects the tendency of societies to delay decisions (and discussions) regarding succession until a leader has evoked the loyalties that in turn call for dynasty. More will be said on this subject later, but now we may sketch the transitions envisaged by the Samuel model. The transition to dynasty is included, but it is merged with David's and Jerusalem's legitimacy in 2 Samuel 6 and 7 rather than standing as stage 4 as in Psalms 89 and 132.

Stages 1 & 2	→Stage 3	→Stage 4
Saul	David	(not in Samuel)
Ark	Jerusalem	
Saul's house	David's house	

We may conclude by returning to 2 Samuel 6 and 7 where David's legitimacy and Davidic dynasty are treated separately. The literary bond joining the chapters is universally recognized as weak and artificial. Now we may suggest that the distinction between David's accession over the house of Saul (2 Samuel 6) and the promise for dynasty within his house (2 Samuel 7) is known to the creators of the Samuel model. The distinction is blurred in the present structure of the story. How it appeared in other models must be examined below.

Summary: Ancient Holograms

This synchronic analysis of ancient Yahwist representational models of David considers Psalm 132, Psalm 89, the books of Chronicles, the Deuteronomic corpus, and the books of Samuel with little regard for specific historical events that may or may not have influenced the writers. The analysis isolates transitions and stages in David's story, and proposes that they are the invariables, the maps in ancient claims about David. As occurs in ritual, the literary figure is recalled, set in new surroundings, and clothed in new robes when the Yahwists undergo transformations or when they struggle against impending foes. Because transitional eras are potentially formless and threatening, the representations offer security and meaning by blending canonical, i.e., traditional, images with indexical realities in order to mediate changes and sustain or regain homeostasis in the community.

In the sense described in an earlier chapter, the models are ancient holograms portraying ancient life. In each case, their creators look across a contemporary landscape and back in time, drawing impressions from both. The former is pockmarked by ruins and tells and inhabited by friends and foes. The latter is filled with genealogies, stories, and songs about the places and peoples that shape and populate their worlds. Informed by the attitudes, customs, and ideologies of their own days, they use what they know to illuminate information about the past in order to give meaning to the present. They illuminate the David image with their own hopes, expectations, and beliefs that comprise their contemporary religious culture.

The memories translate into actions in Yahwist rituals. In the cult, confidence in Yahweh's protection offers structure and meaning amid the world's uncertainties. There, in the betwixt and between, the David figure becomes real because of their confidence in his ability to mediate differences and lead diverse peoples. The rituals keep his qualities alive so people can participate in them and in the deity's power that is manifest through them.

The accounts are also holograms because of the relationship between the variables and invariables that are spread across the surface of the texts. If the texts were torn into parts and the pieces distributed, David's "whole" image would still be visible in each part. Perspectives would be lost, but each model, like those in the units considered here, would illumine the same fundamental transitions. In each, there would be the change from ark to Jerusalem, and in some, from ark to dynasty. In every case, despite its beginning and end points, the image of David as mediator would stand at the center.

B. *Systemic Model of the David Images in the Bible*

In order to establish a reasonable understanding of the metamorphosis within Israel's appreciation of the David figure, broad diachronic stages in the Davidic tradition can be identified. It is here that so-called excavative methods of biblical scholarship can be put to best use. Unlike earlier applications of the methods, however, our goal is not to discover an original, pristine form of a text that might have pre-existed editorial changes. Likewise, we neither need nor expect to detect every textual mutation along the path to final form.

Instead, we search for and examine major transformations and tensions in the mental representational and operational models held by the ancient Yahwists. The grounds for these have been laid in our analytical model. They will now be recast as a hypothesis in a systemic model to be tested further in an integrative model in the next chapter.

The relationships among the various literary analytical models suggest the metamorphoses in the domain of notions. Several stages in the Yahwist centralization theme have been identified, and others implied. Stages beyond those discussed become evident when extra-biblical materials (especially the epistolary Canaanite Amarna information, Merneptah Stele, and pre-Yahwist poetry), early Yahwist poems, biblical narratives, and the "all Israel" traditions are examined together for signs of social, literary, and cultural continuities and discontinuities leading up to and beyond the David stories.

Self-Perception in Non-Yahwist Israel

Stages in the meaning of "all Israel" are outlined above. A further look illumines a stage that was mentioned only in passing. The stories contain notions of a pre- or non-Yahwist entity known as "Israel." The name itself appears to be a verb compounded with *'el*, a reference to the deity of El worshiping communities (Freedman, 1980: 84).

Biblical passages that distinguish between Benjamin and Israel in all Israel (2 Sam 3: 12, 17, 19, 21; 20: 1; 1 Kgs 12: 16) recall notions of a non-Yahwist, indigenous northern coalition known as Israel that merges with a Yahwist Benjaminite group as depicted in the accounts of Saul (Flanagan, 1975: 165). Gottwald and Lemche accept this Isra-El as a non-national, retribalized league (Gottwald, 1979: 493-497; Lemche, 1985: 430). Ahlström proposes that the Israel mentioned in the Merneptah Stele dating to ca. 1208 B.C.E. refers to a portion of the Cisjordan highlands east of Shechem (Ahlström, 1986: 40; Ahlström and Edelman, 1985). On the basis of the stele, Freedman proposes:

> The name "Israel" is pre-Mosaic, non-Yahwistic; it is patriarchal in origin and was applied to a tribal league which was already in existence in Palestine for some time before the Exodus or the emergence of Mosaic Yahwism (Freedman, 1980: 143, n. 38).

Accordingly, the Song of Deborah (Judges 5) depicts the same non-

Yahwist Israel constituted as a ten-tribe confederation (Freedman, 1980: 153).

Thus, earliest Israel in the domain of Egyptian and Canaanite LB notions is a sociopolitical or geosocial grouping that exists independently of the emergence of Yahwism in Cisjordan. Seemingly, the Yahwists eventually assume the name, associate it with their deity, and expand (and contract) its territorial and religious meanings as circumstances dictate.

Such references and the growing scholarly consensus regarding the origins of Yahwism in the land of Canaan recommend that the early Yahwists in Cisjordan remember the emergence of *'apiru* from Canaanite society where they held little standing. Their plight shines through the Amarna Letters. Yahwist models eventually appropriate the name and identity of the Canaanite El-worshipers and associate both with themselves. Whether the change is perceived by the actors as a devolution of non-Yahwist city-state society or an evolution of Yahwist non-state society would be a matter of perspective. For observers, the change is simultaneously a disintegration of an older sociopolitical form and the emergence of a new one. Some participants precipitate and welcome the changes; others resist (e.g., Amarna Letters); still others are probably torn and wavering (e.g., the Samuel stories discussed below), being dragged along by the flow of events initially with little direction and control over their own feelings.

Convergence of Traditions

Scholarly consensus today indicates that the earliest Hebrew poetry is based on non-Yahwist prototypes and becomes Yahwist probably during or after the 12th century B.C.E. Although similar agreement has not been reached regarding the dates and sequence of the early poems, Freedman has modified Albrights attempt to establish such a listing (Freedman, 1980). According to his hypothesis, the 12th century's three poems, Exodus 15, Psalm 29, and Judges 5, are characterized by a "militant Mosaic Yahwism" manifested in the predominant use of the divine name "Yahweh." The poems stand closest to Canaanite prototypes, and at least one—Judges 5, because it lists members of the ten-member pre-Yahwist confederation—reflects both non-Yahwist and Yahwist levels in the tradition. Freedman insists that "El" is an attribution of that divine name to Yahweh and not a merging or blending of El and Yahweh traditions (Freedman, 1980: 84). The distinction is extremely subtle considering the limited sample of information. It may reflect modern presumptions that are based on biblical claims. In any case, the interpretation is an observer's hypothesis and is open to further testing and modification.

During the second phase, i.e., roughly the 11th century, ancestral revivals reintroduce divine epithets associated with the Abrahamic deity. The movement further equates Yahweh with El, the deity of the ancestors. Poems from this phase include Genesis 49, Numbers 23-24, and Deuteronomy 33. Accordingly, the El/Yahweh symbiosis antedates centralized Jerusalem rule and does not depend on the post-Solomonic Schism.

In the third phase, beginning in the 10th century, a plethora of titles and epithets appear, signaling the syncretistic tendencies of Jerusalem and its leaders.

Here we must stress again the tenuous bases for the chronology and the fact that multiplying sources of notional representations ensures neither the holders' intention to report history nor the historicity of the poems themselves. The literature suggests only that within the domain of Yahwist notions, claims are made that the El and Yahweh federations are in some way continuous and related, that membership is fluid (cf. tribal names), and that all the divine epithets are envisaged by the biblical tradition as eventually finding their way into a common alliance with Yahweh. Moreover, to identify a source as limited as a poem and assign it a date within a century or so leaves a great deal of room for speculation. The information sources could contain regional representations rather than universally shared Yahwist beliefs, or the seriation may be confused, and so on. Hence, conclusions must be correspondingly general and hypothetical.

Nevertheless, relating the poems to each other suggests synchronic and diachronic relationships among the different models they contain. The models, some of them seemingly contemporaneous, are held by assorted groups who sing the songs and celebrate the rituals within regionally diverse Yahwist constituencies.

The importance of this is clear. First, the groups represented by the poems comprise temporally and regionally assorted memberships that change as the poems are used. For instance, LB "Song of Deborah" becomes Yahwist. At every stage, the poems assign meaning to their users' lives, but the groups' self-understandings also interpret the poems. Therefore, according to an operational description of groups, their reciters' original purposes or operations can be recovered only with difficulty if at all. Some who used the poems may have been worshipers, others warriors, others groups with different economic, political, or social goals, sometimes with more, sometimes with fewer members.

Second, the metamorphoses throughout non-Yahwist and Yahwist levels indicate that the poets, mythmakers, and biblical compilers presume cultural and historical divisions (and connections) or impose them on the poems and groups. Because the poems are now collected in the biblical canon, impressions of continuity and similarity are created where discontinuity and dissimilarity may have prevailed. Conversely, a radical discontinuity between "Canaanite" and "Israelite" usages may have been artificially imposed at a later stage of development.

The transitions from one phase to another in the poetic tradition, therefore, represent simultaneous diachronic and synchronic developments in Yahwist actors' models. They are diachronic because the beliefs of the constituencies change over time; they are synchronic because the changes either incorporate or disenfranchise beliefs that tolerate divine epithets other than "Yahweh." Oscillation and periodic homeostasis rather than either evolution or devolution are seen in the pattern. Individually, the poems stand for beliefs shared by a particular group at a given time.

In light of this, the dates of the early poems do not necessarily mean that the entire eastern Mediterranean region experience the same metamorphoses simultaneously. During the transition from pre-Yahwist to Yahwist phases (as suggested by the reuse of Canaanite material), at least two representational models coexist and claim legitimacy. The biblical tradition represents the success of one and looks disparagingly on the other, although the tradition also links itself to the other.

Moreover, during the transition from the first Yahwist phase to the second, roughly from the 12th to 11th century if Freedman is correct in his tracing of Yahwist usages, the Yahwist actors' model in the poems changes by combining models held by both Yahweh- and El groups. The pattern is the same as that in the all Israel tradition. As noted, this predates the Schism by several centuries and raises doubts about the original spread of the El beliefs into Judah in the manner proposed by Cross and Freedman (Cross, 1973: 192-213; Freedman, 1980: 131-166, 167-178). The long tradition of El materials in the Bible suggests instead a northern, i.e., central

Cisjordan, setting. In any case, a third change appears to follow when the composite El/Yahweh model is further modified to include models containing additional divine titles and epithets. Whether the additions represent an incorporating of non-Yahwist models into Yahwism, or a conscious expanding of religious complexity and richness from within the Yahwist model would be a matter of ancient opinion that is difficult to determine without extra-biblical sources. What is clear is the presence of poems that continue in the El/Yahweh tradition and are celebrated on major occasions as the Yahwist constituency changes during Iron Age IC and later.

The metamorphoses do not alter the fundamental religious assertion of the hymnists, however. In the poems credited to the 10th century, it is still the deity, known by whatever name, who, although now in concert with an earthly ruler, maintains the balance, equilibrium, and homeostasis required for social, political, and religious survival.

Samuel's Role

The same "Canaanite"/"Israelite" and El/Yahweh symbioses and dialectics appear again at the beginning of the books of Samuel. In 1 Samuel 1, for example, the story of David begins as if in mythical time by recalling the birth of Samuel (="His-name-is-El") who is dedicated (=*šāʾûl*) to Yahweh (cf. McCarter 1980: 62). Although commentators repeatedly try to unravel the chapter's literary traditions on the basis of the wordplays on Samuel's and Saul's names, they have little success. One reason is their willingness to follow the biblical example in dismissing or modifying indicators of Canaanite religious influence.

Besides confusing El elements with Yahwistic references, the tradition contains other apparent complications that may represent the merging of several early myths into a single model. The route of Elkanah and Hannah is an example. Elkanah (= "El has produced"), Samuel's father, is portrayed as leaving his home in Ramathaim (1 Sam 1: 1) on the western slopes of Ephraim east of Tel Aviv to go to Shiloh in the eastern hills ca. 33 km north of Jerusalem (v. 3). Apparently he does this repeatedly in order to worship Yahweh Sabaoth. Here and elsewhere Shiloh is presented as Samuel's childhood home, the residence of Eli's priesthood, and the last resting place for the ark before its loss to the Philistines. From there Elkanah goes home to Ramah (not Ramathaim) within the territory of Benjamin where Samuel is conceived and born (vv. 19-20). The location, which in effect makes Samuel a Benjaminite, is important later as a place of refuge and prophecy during David's escape from Saul's persecution (1 Samuel 19). Elkanah finally returns to Shiloh to dedicate the son to Yahweh (1: 28).

Changing "El" to "Yahweh" again connects El and Yahwist themes that echo through the next chapters. They are recalled in accounts of failure within Eli's house (ch. 2) and Samuel's call in the temple at Shiloh (ch. 3) where he serves before the ark of Elohim (1 Sam 3: 3). Recollections are also provoked by the fate of the ark, now the ark of Yahweh (4: 5), in the hand of the Philistines (1 Samuel 4-6). Eli dies upon receiving news about the ark, again the ark of Elohim (5 times in 4: 12-22). The literary tension continues at Philistine Ashdod where the ark is attributed to both Yahweh (5: 3-4) and Elohim (5: 1, 8, 10, 11) until its return when it becomes the ark of the God (*'elōhē*) of Israel or of Yahweh (ch. 6). The Samuel story continues, however, during the debates about centralizing (chs. 7-8) and reports that Saul, a Benjaminite, encounters him in Zuph near Ramathaim and is then sent back to Benjamin, Gilgal, and Gibeah (chs. 8-10). The ambiguities in the model could hardly be missed by the ancients.

The allegorical aspects of the accounts are abundantly clear (cf. Rosenberg, 1986: 1-46). Samuel in the service of the ark of Elohim ministering to Yahweh at the temple (*hêkāl*) in Shiloh is called by Yahweh to displace Eli's family. Three times the deity calls "His-name-is-El" until finally Eli and Samuel recognize the source and respond. No attempt is made to impose a logic on this and the other stories because that would drain them of their richness and meaning. The person Samu-el, a pre-Yahwist shrine, and allegiances that cluster around earlier rituals are all taken over by Yahweh. Benjaminite and non-Benjaminite, El and Yahweh are united. A single voice for Yahwism is confirmed.

Saul and David Materials

The journey from Ramathaim in Zuph to Shiloh and Ramah and back to Shiloh entwine stories about Samuel with those of the ark and Saul. Ancient perceptions of continuity and evolution toward centralization are easily demonstrated. On one level, the storyline in the books of Samuel moves progressively toward centralization, as we have outlined. As the allegory is now constructed, dynasty is introduced in 2 Samuel 7 after David relocates his capital in Jerusalem. Another mythical view, i.e., a level in the story pertinent to the books of Samuel alone, has been suggested and will be examined below.

The all Israel references follow the first storyline as outlined above. But the pattern in the actors' model also conforms to that indicated by the poetry cited above. The first Israel is not Yahwistic. The second is an all Israel federation of the old Israel and Benjamin. Next is an all Israel that includes the old federation, Benjamin, and Judah. In the Deuteronomic model, Benjamin stays with Judah and separates from all Israel. Finally, in the Chroniclers' model, the name all Israel is appropriated for Judah and Jerusalem.

Unscrambling the Omelet: Stages in the Composite Myth?

Actors' models from four types of sources have been discussed: poems; narratives; all Israel references; genealogical materials and administrative lists. Initially, the metamorphoses indicated in the various literary genres can be arranged serially in an observer's model, but because the outline is an observer's, the arrangement is artificial and hypothetical. In other words, it is not necessarily a sequence that always controlled the ancients' storytelling.

One reason for uncertainty is conveyed in Leach's warning about unscrambling an omelet (1983a: 23). As suggested by the archaeological information and the competing representations and operations suggested by the literature, all groups in the eastern Mediterranean basin do not go through the same changes simultaneously, and not everyone accepts new representations. The merging of Isra-el with Yahwism and then Israel separating from Yahwist Benjamin and Judah in the Schism indicates the depth of convictions, the endurance of sharply opposing representations, and length of memories.

For our purposes, nine broad spatial/temporal divisions may be indicated initially. Others implied in biblical sources we did not consider can also be cited afterward. After listing the divisions, we may hypothesize regarding the way they relate to each other. The tentative dates in the list below pertain to representational models and do not refer to dates when texts were composed.

Stage A1. Pre-Yahwist: a model that recognizes the deity El (e.g., proto-Judges 5, Samu-el, ark of Elohim, pre-Yahwist Isra-el)
Stage A2. Early Yahwism: (ca. 12th c.?) a model that refers only to Yahweh and does not mention Israel (e.g., Exodus 15)
Stage B1. Symbiotic Yahwism: (ca. 11th c.?) a model that uses 'Yahweh' and 'El' (e.g., the ark of Yahweh and ark of Elohim, stories of Saul, an all Israel that comprises Israel plus Benjamin)
Stages C1. Syncretistic Yahwism: (ca. early 10th c.?) a model that exhibits some variety in divine epithets and knows an all Israel that comprises Israel plus Benjamin and Judah (e.g., stories of David in the books of Samuel, lists of David's family at Hebron)
Stage C2. Syncretistic Yahwism: (ca. mid-10th c.?) a model that admits many divine epithets and knows an all Israel that comprises Israel plus Benjamin and Judah (e.g., 2 Samuel 23, 2 Samuel 21-24, lists of David's family in Jerusalem, lists of court officers in 2 Samuel 8 and 20; Psalms 89 and 132)
Stage C3. Eclectic Yahwism: (ca. late 10th c. or later?) a model that uses many epithets and knows of Solomon's succession (e.g., succession stories, Solomon's list of court officers, an all Israel that comprises Israel plus Benjamin and Judah [the repositioning of the Dynastic Oracle in 2 Samuel 7, cf. below])
Stage D1. Divided Yahwism: (Schism) a model that knows an all Israel that is Israel minus Benjamin and Judah (e.g., post-Schism stories in the Deuteronomic History, the El Psalter)
Stage E1. Theologically United Yahwism: (Deuteronomic) a model that aspires to a united Israel and envisages a united past to support it (e.g., stories in Deuteronomy, conquest in Joshua)
Stage F1. Priestly Yahwism: (Chronicles) a model that knows Judah alone as all Israel (e.g., genealogies and lists and all Israel references in Chronicles)

We should not be deceived by evolutionary presuppositions and melioristic biases that might lead us to view the stages as entirely sequential. With painstaking care and an elaborate system of cross-references and footnotes, the information summarized on this list could be divided further and drawn as a hypothetical segmented chart. The development of ideas and models would look like a genealogy of ancient notions and in many ways would be similar to developments noted in archaeological information. A brief sketch illustrates the congruences [Figure 31]. It includes several models

Figure 31: A Genealogy of Ancient Notions

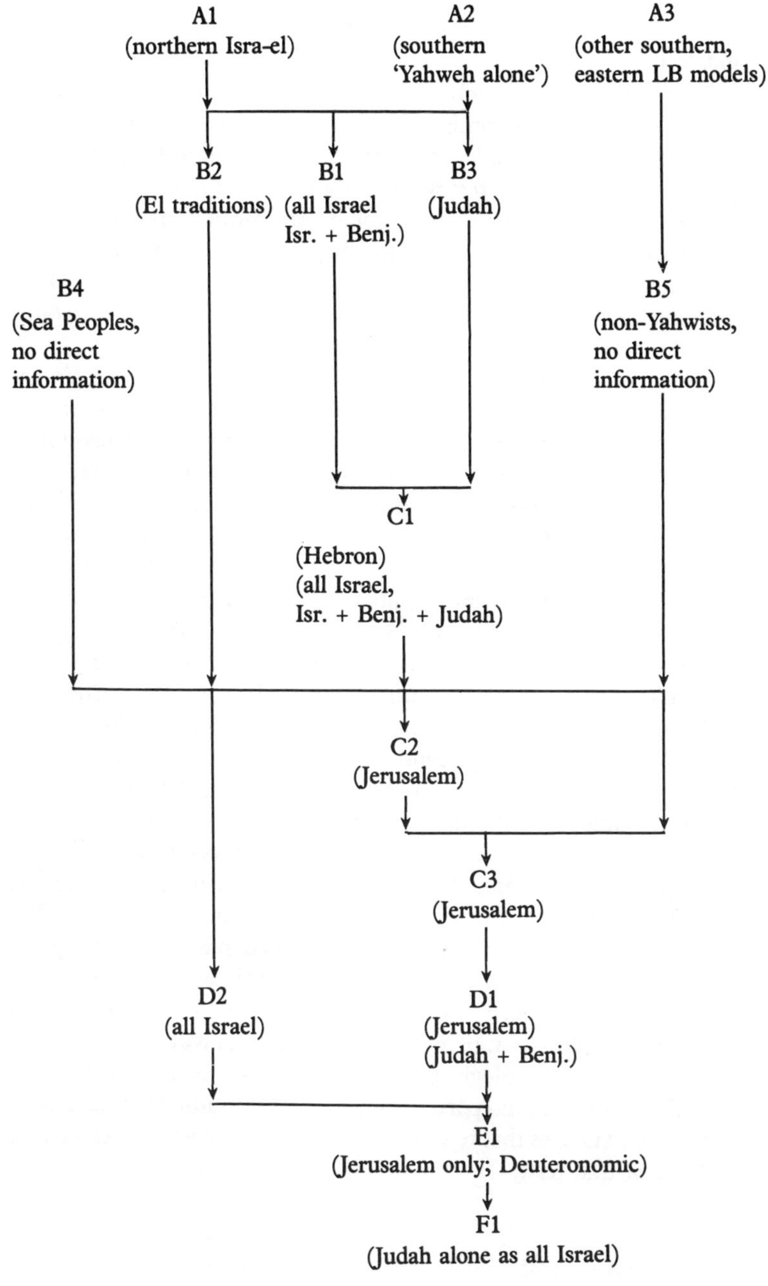

that we can reasonally assume existed although we know them only indirectly.

The outline and sketch illustrate the complexity and balanced opposition in models coming together around the figure David and Jerusalem. For example, separate El and Yahweh models are combining, Samu-el stories are being reinterpreted as Yahwist accounts, and all Israel is undergoing transformations that balance all Israel with Benjamin, then with Judah, etc. The metamorphoses move the segmented, symbiotic units toward Yahwism and increasing centralization before it begins fissioning and eventually becomes isolated.

Some models seem to change more quickly than others. In the stories, David and Solomon facilitate the process by incorporating non-Yahwist peoples (and presumably their disparate models) under their aegis and by mediating transitions as such expansion requires. Other models no doubt continue, but we lack direct information regarding them. Our sketch distinguishes northern and southern Yahwistic traditions, the latter probably reflected in the spy stories and Caleb traditions in the Numbers 13-14, Judges 1, and Joshua 14 (cf. Flanagan, 1976: 177-180). Hence, the path of Yahwist religious metamorphosis leads from both north and south, while the path of endogenous sociopolitical centralization leads from the North.

The transitions from ark, confederation, and Saul to David, then to dynasty all fall within Judahite and Jerusalem settings, i.e., from C1 forward. Several subphases suggested by 2 Samuel 6, 2 Samuel 7, and other materials discussed earlier occur within Stage C2. The ritual functions that concern the David model probably applied in those phases. The Samuel models separate David's legitimacy and dynastic legitimacy from each other and from succession. The Deuteronomic model telescopes Davidic and dynastic legitimacy and links Solomonic succession and Joshian legitimacy very closely to them. The Chronicles model coalesces Davidic, dynastic, and Solomonic legitimation in a single epoch. In this way, Jerusalem is a multiple exposure holographic plate. The city brings together the partially congruent and partially incongruent traditions of the past in multilayered images that reflect changes in the Yahwists' understanding and use of that past.

Displacement and Dynasty

If the developments through these stages are read as progress, questions are raised about David's apparent lack of assertiveness in the models. Do the writers depict him as directing events or as reacting passively to them?

At first glance, the models present David as reluctant and having *laissez-faire* attitudes toward difficulties and crises in his world. Examples include sparing Saul's life while Saul threatens and pursues him (1 Samuel 18; 20; 24; 26); shunning the opportunity to seize leadership over Israel after Saul's death (2 Samuel 1); allowing Amnon's crime against Tamar to go unpunished (2 Samuel 13); and withdrawing from the capital city without resistance when Absalom rebels (2 Samuel 15-20). The pattern is so common that commentators have proposed reasons for David's "weakness."

Others, however, interpret David's apathy as a strength. His portrait, it is suggested, is either a way of showing that the deity controls human events or of indicating the compilers' prophetic view in which pronouncements are fulfilled by the passage of time and turning of events.

These are not incorrect understandings of the actors' model, but they do not go far enough in exposing the complex socioreligious components in the David stories.

First, a distinction can be drawn in instances when David does not act as aggressively as modern observers believe he should. David's attitude toward Israel and Yahwists can be distinguished from his treatment of non-Yahwists and foreigners. With the latter, as indicated by the stories of Goliath, Nabal, the Ammonites, the Philistines, and others, he is depicted as a fearless and cunning individual, aware of his advantages, and shrewd in choosing the most effective, quickest reaction. He stands ready to deploy any tactical strategy regardless of its ruthlessness and devastation.

When dealing with Yahwists, however, David seems to rely on other equally astute but less authoritarian and less immediate maneuvers. In many cases he acts vicariously. He fails to respond assertively when to do so would mean repaying hostility, aggression, or tyranny in kind. For example, David remains an ally of the Philistines and does not seize the initiative with Israel after Saul is killed (1 Samuel 29-31), he does battle against Israel and Saul's followers only after Saul's death (2 Sam 3: 1), and he does not prevent the deaths of Abner, Ishbaal, his own sons, and Saul's descendants (2 Samuel 3-4; 13-19; 21). But according to the actors' model, he does not involve himself personally in any of the conflicts and is portrayed as being physically removed from all the difficulties.

The same distinction is found elsewhere. In the opening scene in 2 Samuel 1, an Amalekite youth brings news of Saul's and Jonathan's deaths and offers their official regalia to David. Hoping that his allegiance will engender patronage and protection following David's raid on his people, the messenger meets immediate death instead. By ordering the youth's assassination, David eliminates someone who suspects his intentions and simultaneously demonstrates non-complicity. He affirms his own innocence by avenging Saul's and Jonathan's deaths, and he fulfills his filial duty to his former protector and his wife's kin.

A second aspect of David's apparent reluctance to intervene is suggested in the first. When hostilities erupt, as between Saul's and David's houses, he attempts to contain them at the lowest possible levels of the segmented system (cf. 2 Sam 1: 12-3: 1). This strategy should not be mistaken for passivity. It is calculated deliberateness that uses effectively one of the check and balance mechanisms that segmented systems employ for resolving conflicts and maintaining order. For example, in the tension between the houses during Ishbaal's reign, the attempt to contain violence begins with a ritual duel between selected representatives of David and Ishbaal (2 Sam 2: 12-16). Neither the Israelites nor all Israel are involved. This form of trial-by-ordeal is common in segmented societies but proves unsuccessful here. The conflict widens to include David's followers and the men of Israel (vv. 17-23). Still unresolved, a negotiated settlement to the conflict is attempted (vv. 24-32). Only after this fails does war engulf the two houses (3: 1).

The circumstances and accompanying dialogue, told from David's perspective, illustrates Ishbaal's ineffectiveness in containing conflict and retaining allegiances. The structure of the account makes an additional point. Both David and Ishbaal are conspicuously absent, the conflict erupts immediately after reports of their respective accessions in Judah and Israel, and the initial struggle is for the allegiance of Benjamin. The same issue arises again with Sheba's rebellion in 2 Samuel 20 and is not finally resolved until the post-Solomonic Schism. In David's case, the tensions spread upward and outward through the moieties' segments. But David makes no attempt to seize Ishbaal's authority directly as he might given Abner's disloyalty and the proximity of Ishbaal's capital to David's ally, Nahash of the Ammonites. Instead, as an astute leader seeking to expand his network of allegiances and dependencies, he waits.

When Abner approaches to offer all Israel's allegiance, David still appears to procrastinate by attaching conditions that protect his innocence (2 Sam 3: 6-69). Demanding the prior return of his wife Michal affords him legitimacy as Saul's successor. The concern is especially timely because of Ishbaal's incompetence and precarious situation. Restoring the marriage bond also serves as a sign of the current peace treaty, undoes the insult Saul perpetrated by giving Michal to Palti without compensation to David (1 Sam 25: 44), and grants David a role in determining the destiny of Saul's lineage (cf. 2 Sam 6: 16-23).

The calculated deliberateness contrasts with David's immediate reaction against Ishbaal's assassins shortly afterward (2 Sam 4: 1-12). Both are parts of a well-planned strategy that reaches fruition when David accepts the treaty of Israel elders (2 Sam 5: 1-5). Thus, in the representational model, David rejects illegitimate opportunities presented by deceitful and self-serving opportunists but stands ready to work according to society's norms and to accept responsibilities when called by the people or their legitimate representatives. He is ready, in effect, to answer the call of his deity.

The portrayal satisfies the storytellers' interests by presenting a David who respects the deity's suzerainty and the peoples' religiosity as well as the norms of society. Because Yahweh is the supreme overlord in the Yahwist segmented social structure, all affairs are ultimately under the deity's control, and matters that escalate finally reach Yahweh's council. Human leaders are intermediaries and agents, not lords in their own right, and their offices are not to be bartered for outside the religiously legitimate segmented system. Religious legitimacy alone, without popular support (or popular support without legitimacy—as with Absalom?), is the practice of foreigners and usurpers not of faithful Yahwists. David understands the need for both and works effectively, according to the model, in securing them.

A second perplexing aspect of the David stories is the reversals and displacements that control the content and structure of the narrative. Although constraints of narrative style cause episodes to be arranged serially, the model "nests" inversion scenes within each other and organizes them chiastically as the narrative unfolds. The structure also allows the reversals to be built up from a number of smaller, similarly structured incidents and episodes.

Obvious pivotal shifts are David's displacement of Samuel, Saul, the Philistines, and Absalom. In the main storyline, however, his succeeding Saul, a Jerusalem center replacing northern and southern holy places like Shiloh and Hebron, and overcoming Philistine dominance by Jerusalemite subjugation are central. These are the macro-metamorphoses that the story is about. But the principal storylines are replicated on smaller scales in story units such as David's elegy for Saul and Jonathan (2 Sam 1:17-21), Meribaal's protection and house arrest (2 Sam 9: 1-13), the parable of the wise woman from Tekoa (2 Sam 14: 1-33; cf. Bellefontaine, 1987), and Sheba's revolt (2 Sam 20: 1-25). Each encodes and encapsulates the norms and relationships that are at stake throughout the entire model.

One problem in describing the artistry within the Samuel materials derives from the narrators' ability to portray progression and reversal simultaneously [Figure 32]. Any description drains the account of its vibrance and richness.

After the relocation in Jerusalem, the storyline moves from point to point ending in a second "capture" of Jerusalem with definite stages of development marking the way. But the story also reaches back constantly to undo and redo things said before so that fulfillment themes—actually metamorphoses—reappear constantly. The interactions of the dual processes are like conflicting centrifugal and centripetal forces that struggle to push the story forward while constantly refocusing it on a single constricted meaningful vortex. These are literary versions of the horizontal and vertical axes found in rituals that Rappaport describes as canonical and indexical. In the story, a central message endures but its telling is reshaped repeatedly (indexed) from scene to scene. The fundamental metamorphosis is mapped and recalled as the story enfolds and unfolds.

Figure 32: The Dynamics and Metamorphoses in the David Story

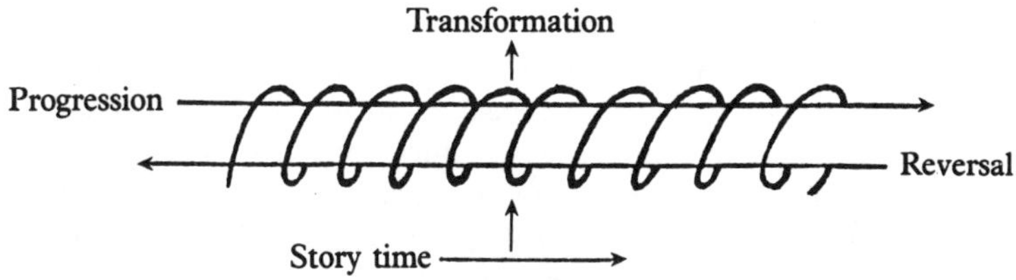

The troublesome, so-called appendix in 2 Samuel 21-24 should be read in light of the reversal, displacement, fulfillment themes. The unit plays an important part in the actors' model. David's rise dominates 1 Samuel and 2 Samuel 1-5. The principal rite of passage is set in 2 Samuel 6, and a series of threats to his sovereignty are described in 2 Samuel 8-20. We may omit, for reasons argued elsewhere, the David and Bathsheba materials in 2 Samuel 11-12 (Flanagan, 1972), and terminate the model at the end of 2 Samuel 24 before the Solomonic succession scene in 1 Kings 1-2 as is done by the canon. These portions (2 Sam 11-12; 1 Kings 1-2) we have already described as belonging to a Solomonic actors' model that is part of the updating process, i.e., the indexing, at work in the Davidic myth.

We have demonstrated how episodes at the beginning of the Samuel stories are reversed and fulfilled at the end. But, the model asks, will David be custodian of the ark—and hence of Yahweh's presence—or Yahweh custodian of David? In other words, will Yahweh's presence continue to be manifested through the ark controlled by David, or will David mediate the presence directly by displacing the ark? We have given the answer above, but now we suggest that the difference between Yahwist and non-Yahwist ideologies and political systems is at stake. Shall there be an overlord besides Yahweh or not?

The answer is in the negative. It is given in the appendix (chs. 21-24) where the role of spirit-mediator moves finally from ark to David, and David is positioned between Yahweh and the people rather than between Yahweh and the ark. With a census and a plague as their instruments, David and Yahweh enter into a ritualistic and cosmic duel. In a section laced with cultic imagery, the struggle is cast as the ultimate contest that makes David a vassal and mediator in his own right rather than as custodian of the ark.

In ordering the census David acts like a tyrannical monarch capable of taxing production and conscripting soldiers and forced labor, the very factors that caused the decay described in the Amarna Letters. Therefore, to order a census is an intolerable assertion of political power within the Yahwist actors' model. If completed, the plan would have drained economic resources, replicated foreign polities, and violated religious egalitarian values. Yahweh's response is unequivocal, appropriate, and clear. By sending a plague, the very population base and sensibilities David's plans depended on and would have exploited are attacked. Yahweh makes David's plan maladaptive even though David is said to have been ordered by the deity to take the census (2 Sam 24: 1). The divine response reduces David's economic surpluses and increases resistance to taxation and conscription. As cause and effect, human acts and divinely controlled natural disasters are inextricably linked in the actors' model. Yahweh's sovereignty is finally demonstrated in socioeconomic realities.

So David submits, the attempt to monopolize force is thwarted, a threshing floor is purchased, an altar erected, and offerings made (2 Sam 24: 18-25). The redistributive economy of the chieftaincy is maintained, the bureaucracy of monarchy forestalled, and the limits of legitimate centralization set within the model. Likewise, the legitimacy rooted in the ark, Samuel, and Saul and handed down with the ark, comes to rest in David's offerings on Aruanah's threshing floor.

The threshing floor in Jerusalem is foreshadowed by the threshing floor at Ramah, the place of Samuel's birth (1 Sam 1: 19). Other scenes in the appendix also reverse or balance earlier ones in the Samuel narratives. The slaughter of the house of Saul (2 Sam 21: 1-14) and the symbolic suppression of the Philistines (2 Sam 21: 15-22) are but two examples. The message is that just as the old guard of Samuel, Saul, and Saul's house lived under Yahweh's judgment, David must also accept and express his dependency. Proper order is established.

Proposal for the Dynastic Oracle

But did the actors' model end this way prior to its becoming a Solomonic model? Although any answer will be helped by examining the arrangement of literary information and therefore brings excavative biblical methods to the fore, the question is not necessarily or exclusively literary. Our concern again is with the representations and norms that imbue the literature rather than with the history of the literature.

The literature portrays and creates a social drama. David's social drama like others is an aharmonic processual unit "... which, seen retrospectively by an observer, can be shown to have structure" (V. Turner, 1974: 35). The breach is the loss of the ark, the crisis is the Philistines, and the redressive action is the paramountcy of Saul and his son. Yet those responses fail miserably, and then the crisis escalates. David's paramountcy becomes the effective redressive action in terms of the social drama. On the one hand, it reintegrates the Yahwist community that has been sundered by the blunderings of Saul and Ishbaal, and on the other, it affirms the loss of hope in effective leadership coming from Saul or his house. Viewed in this way with the central rite of passage in 2 Samuel 6, there is a question about the drama's ending. Does it end immediately in 2 Samuel 7, and if so, why the rest of the story about David's house? An affirmative answer would confirm Rost's Succession Narrative. This is the course many commentators have taken. But we have argued to the contrary. In explaining further, we must remember that at this level, we are asking how the story is told in David's social world, i.e., how the model envisages the process, not what happens on the ground or how the story is retold after its outcome is known. We are searching for a plausible hypothesis and not for one-for-one, text-event relationships.

As the model now stands as text, the contents of 2 Samuel 6 and 2 Samuel 7 are fused. The process of telescoping David's and Solomon's images is already begun. Chapter 7, however, is commonly designated an anti-temple, pro-David, Dynastic Oracle that terminates Saulide legitimacy and opens the way for Davidic successors (cf. Noth, 1967). But no specific successor is cited and even monarchy itself is not clearly implied.

Our analytical model has shown that the actors' model in the books of Samuel pertains solely to David and his leadership and does not include reference to Solomon or perhaps even to succession. David's dialogue with Michal in fact emphasizes that Yahweh has chosen him over Saul and Saul's house, but there is no reference to David's house (cf. 2 Sam 6: 20-23). The exception is 2 Samuel 7.

Elsewhere, "house" emerges as a replacement for "ark" such as in 2 Sam 20: 3.

The appendix in 2 Samuel 21-24 fits into this dialectical development/reversal theme because it completes and connects the narrative's plots and subplots and balances the structure that pivots on the relocation of the ark and displacement of Saul in 2 Samuel 6. But something is out of place. From 2 Samuel 6 forward, the "house" theme is developed in a way that suggests the issue of a ruling house is not resolved in the story at the time of the relocation of the ark. Our question now is, are the steps toward dynasty telescoped this way in the notional model of Samuel, or is the arrangement part of the fusing of David's and Solomon's reigns in a single epoch?

Comparative studies confirm a separation. Dynasty, which is the passing down (devolution) of office within a circumscribed pool of eligibles, is not to be confused with monarchy, which is a form of government. Many modes of each are possible. Because of the ceaseless rivalries and competition for paramountcy in acephalous and segmented social systems, personal and dynastic legitimacy are not demonstrated by mere accession to office. Rules for succession develop over time so that succession within a kin group is not automatically presumed on the basis of a single, successful paramountcy (cf. Goody, 1966: 13, 39-46). We have summarized the process of indeterminent succession among the Yahwists. At stake are social stability and access to limited resources, i.e., office and power. With the Yahwists, as in other segmented models, being chosen leader is only a step toward legitimation, and that but one step on the way to dynasty. True leadership has to be demonstrated repeatedly and sustained in order to retain legitimacy. And dynastic privilege does not follow immediately.

From the viewpoint of the model, centralizing in Jerusalem under David is one thing (1 Samuel 1 to 2 Samuel 20), submitting the new administration to Yahweh's control another (2 Samuel 21-24), determining whose dynasty will legitimately prevail another (2 Samuel 7), and deciding who will be David's legitimate successor still another (1 Kings 1-2). But the last is not at issue until David's abilities wane. Then the model is updated and succession by appointment within David's kin group is incorporated (1 Kings 1-2). Hence, Goody's comment on succession is relevant:

> Raising men from the dust means an increase in appointive as against hereditary succession as well as an increased use of clients,

> retainers and of other similar roles where ties of subordination are personal rather than hereditary in kind. And many writers have linked appointive office and the institution of clientship to the development of more centralized systems of government (Goody, 1966: 40).

Therefore, monarchy, dynasty, and kinship are not always partners.

This is a long preface to a question about the role and position of the dynastic oracle within the actors' model. In an observers' model, it stands logically between David and Solomon where it is properly part of the dynasty theme rather than the theme of David's personal legitimacy.

Most critics believe that the oracle is redacted, emended, and adjusted several times—like genealogies—in order to keep it current and meaningful as events transform its importance for understanding the past. In the artificial and fluid arrangement of a narrative, its place could easily be changed or otherwise assigned as well. Our investigators' model suggests that in the representational model of the Yahwists, the dynastic oracle belongs after the cosmic duel, the purchase of the threshing floor, and David's submission to Yahweh portrayed in 2 Samuel 24. The census (a thrust toward fuller centralization) has been thwarted. Would David's full submission require him to build a temple? Other Near Eastern societies would answer in the affirmative. But here the ambivalence toward monarchy that is in the model from the time of Samuel forward appears again. Nathan first answers, yes, and then says, no. He speaks for the uncertainty among the Yahwists and for competing models. His final response is Yahweh's final assertion in the model against centralization. The Yahwists cannot have a temple—or a king—but they can have a chiefly Davidic dynasty. That is legitimated in the oracle which completes and concludes the Samuel model.

Mythically 2 Samuel 7 summarizes and completes themes that extend through the books of Samuel down to 2 Samuel 24. In our observers' model, the redressive action of raising David over Saul's house ritually enacted in 2 Samuel 6 reaches stage four in the social drama at the end of 2 Samuel. In this case, the myth affirms both reintegration and irreparable schism. The legitimacy of David's house is separated from its base within Saul's family and Israel, and a divided Yahwist community torn by the urge to solve its problems by becoming like other nations is promised divine protection without a temple. The values of the age of the ark are preserved by a non-kingly, "non-templed" dynasty.

The oracle's anti-temple thrust conforms to the overall structure of the books as well as the particular issue of Davidic authority in the final chapters. The progression and balancing of the story requires something like the Dynastic Oracle after 2 Samuel 24 to complete and counterbalance the complex, interconnected Samuel, Ramah, Shiloh, Saul themes introduced in the opening chapters of 1 Samuel. These opening and closing thematic assertions then balance on the pivotal 2 Samuel 6, where Jerusalemite and Davidic rule are first legitimated. The oracle scene, laced with cultic inferences, completes the rite of passage initiated at Shiloh and Ramah and advanced by the relocation of the ark in Jerusalem. The world that was, the one centered around the ark, is fulfilled and displaced by another world centering on David and his house now firmly established under Yahweh in Jerusalem.

To summarize: we hypothesize that the Yahwists' actors' model in early Iron Age IC includes only Davidic interests. These are David's personal legitimacy and the legitimacy of his house. The biblical writers draw on that model and set it at the base of the enduring David tradition.

Stated this way the claim sounds like a truism. Solomon is not an issue until Solomon is the issue! However, the claim's importance for the Yahwist tradition is that the Samuel model, while explaining developments and metamorphoses, also proposes sociopolitical restraint. Religiously and ideologically, the initial model opposes full centralization in favor of a chieftaincy model. In other words, David's leadership is seen not simply as a step along the path to fuller centralization but as an alternative path. Yahweh obstructs the first path. Yahwist leadership cannot include the same monopolizing of force as other centralized groups, and it has no need for legitimacy derived from temples and temple-building. The Dynastic Oracle, therefore, forbids the centralization implied by temples. David's house is affirmed, but it is his house without full centralization. Hence, at this stage in the actors' model, Davidic leadership and dynasty are the normative representations. Later, his chiefliness is quickly buried beneath Solomonic regalia, but his mediator's role survives in other guises. It becomes the map to guide later Yahwists.

A final observation is in order. Because of lack of knowledge about emerging and incipient statehood, biblical commentators make uncritical assumptions about the cultural evolutionary sequence among the Yahwists. Typically, tribalism, monarchy, dynasty and succession are listed, in that order. In the Samuel model, chiefly dynasty and succession intervene between tribalism and monarchy. In the Yahwist models, therefore, the sequence: 1) tribalism, 2) dynasty, 3) succession, and 4) monarchy. In Samuel, dynasty is already accepted in Saul's house with the accession of Ishbaal, and it is being established in David's. The sequence explains how the later tradition could cling to Davidic dynastic legitimacy in the absence of monarchy and enable institutions other than monarchy to appropriate its legitimacy for themselves. Full statehood and monarchy are not included in the actors' model of Davidic legitimacy. Some form of dynasty is.

Conclusion

Throughout the actors' models examined here from the earliest expression as recalled in the books of Samuel through its reuse by the Chroniclers and its celebration in the hymnic tradition of the Second Temple, David stands as a mediator always remembered for being in the betwixt and between. As if he lives a cultic life at the crossroads of diachronic and synchronic axes, he is portrayed as standing between north and south, between the Judahites and all Israel, between the Benjaminites and Judahites, between Saul's and his own dynasties, between egalitarianism and monopolized force and, like the ark, between human and divine realms. Over time, the cult places him between ark and temple and between Yahweh and a host of earthly and cosmic foes. Those roles are remembered, mapped, and made the norm for orthodox Yahwist notional models.

In the broader sweep of the biblical story, the David figure stands as an ego in an ancient segmented model of sociopolitical and religious relationships. The Yahwists describe themselves and their relationships to their contemporaries in segmented imagery and terminology. The phenomenon goes beyond the material studied here to include the Priestly corpus which, like the Chroniclers' model, depicts humanity in genealogical, segmented categories.

Opposing and non-Yahwist models are remembered in the biblical tradition. In fact, the latter are what constitute the "other" in David's social drama. But the mediating, centralizing/uncentralizing

David and his city, Jerusalem, dominate and control the course of affairs in the story. The perspective of this hologram is Yahwist, and David is portrayed as the founder of the religion's tradition in Jerusalem. Successors must measure their legitimacy against his model.

III

A HOLOGRAM OF THE EARLY IRON AGE

Chapter 5

THE SOCIAL WORLD OF DAVID'S DRAMA

Anthropologist Claude Lévi-Strauss (1955) likens myth analysis to the writing of music. Harmony (synchronic dimensions) and melody (diachronic dimensions) must both be attended to. Processual studies on rites of passage and social dramas treat these phenomena as intra-stage and intra-status transformations, in other words, as horizontal and vertical adaptations in society (cf. T. Turner, 1977: 68). Rappaport analyzes the same realities first as canonical and indexical aspects of ritual and then by connecting religious intentionality to environmental settings as reference values acting on the goal ranges of an ecology.

In a sense, these efforts to analyze simultaneously the diachronic and synchronic relationships of populations are motivated by a desire to escape arbitrary Western concepts of space and time. Since Frankfort and Albright at least, biblical historians have struggled to measure at once the relationships of contemporary peoples who spread across a geographical plane and the relationships that bind such groups to those before and after (cf. Gellner, 1985). The studies have been hampered by presuppositions regarding a Cartesian space-time grid (cf. Flanagan, 1987).

Discussion of the philosophical foundations and the changes in these concepts must await another study. Here, our analogies and metaphors are directed toward a specific instance without examining its full ramifications. Our interest is in Iron Age processual axes and intersections as they are played out in David's social drama. But because our interest is in past social worlds and because we look back from the present, our gaze is inward toward the intersections and vortexes in the tradition rather than outward from the past at worlds unfolding. With Bohm we seek the implicate order within many explicate manifestations. The latter, in a sense, stand before us in the ancient sources that have been looked at in discipline-based analytical and systemic models. There, we gathered explicate remains strewn through texts and tells by the forces of ancient social worlds. Now we seek to look inward and beyond for a coherent multidimensional image—and for the processes that shape it—by integrating the separate analytical and systemic images from archaeology and literature and by illuminating their intersections with relationships from better known and observable societies. Then the social world behind the sources will be seen, and its meanings understood, but only from an observer's perspective.

We make no attempt to "synchronize" the details in the sources or our interpretations of them. A lock-step reconstruction is impossible. The ancient past, the precise congruence of "this statement" with "that action," and the details of daily life cannot be reclaimed with such accuracy. Instead, information from the ancient domains of actions and notions are allowed to interfere and are illumined in a way that enables multidimensional images, i.e., hypotheses, to be proposed. The images will be holograms of the early Iron Age.

Holographic and ritualistic models and metaphors are mixed as outlined in Chapter 2. Holography and holograms, like Lévi-Strauss' harmony, expose synchronic and symbiotic relations; rituals follow the melody of social change. On another level, the level of comparison, the axes are illumined by two types of studies. Synchronic comparative studies expose relationships between and among contemporary groups from different ecological niches as they interact with each other; diachronic studies outline developments as the societies are evolving or devolving toward or away from centralization. The former stress adaptation and ingathering (or diversifying) that lead to evolution (and devolution); the latter concentrate on the evolution (and devolution) that ingathers (or scatters) disparate groups. Like a musical score and its performance, each "record" and each form of analysis is a dimension of the other.

A. *Beyond Space-Time Systemics*

Analysts continue to debate whether segmented social organizations, systems, and ideologies existed in ancient Israel and whether the metaphor is an appropriate heuristic tool (cf. Rogerson, 1985; Gottwald, 1979: 322-333; Crüsemann, 1978: 201-215; Frick, 1985:

51-70; Lemche, 1985: 202-230). We have stated our strong belief that they are appropriate, and we have used such metaphors to describe the ancient world in models of domains of actions and notions. Applied here, the debates raise important issues: did the Yahwists' representations depict Iron Age society according to segmentary principles as we have claimed, and if so were their actions organized accordingly? In other words, did the Yahwists envisage themselves as members of segmented systems, and did their notions and actions in the Iron Age correspond positively? Was there a radical dissonance between self-perceptions and social structures?

The questions are raised again in order to call attention to the scholarly tendency to treat Israel as a closed society, or a series of closed societies, and to accept models that equate it with a single unified socioecological environment or ethnic group. For example, peasant revolt models assume sedentary, agrarian ecologies but are less appropriate for desert, nomadic zones; conquest hypotheses as applied to Israel are more appropriate to nomadism than to other residential strategies; and infiltration models are most compatible with semi-nomadism/semi-sedentarism. By itself, each is too limited for the complex, diverse world in our analytical models. Each hypothesis fails to treat adequately some aspect of the diversity and complexity represented in the other two. Hypotheses based on segmented models, on the other hand, not only account for greater diversity, they are also more congenial to the ancient uncentralized but centralizing, transitional world.

At stake are the nature of relationships among the Yahwist, the character, function, and religiosity of centralized Yahwist leadership, and the validity of Yahwist religious values. The distinctions between notions and actions and actors' and observers' models expose the issues. If Yahwist religious ideology and social reality differed radically, the social behavior and social systems attributed to David and accepted by tradition as normative within Yahwism are fictitious, unrealistic, or meaningless (cf. Gellner, 1985: 154-155). In that case, the real social networks and values that connected Iron Age beliefs to contemporary practices are either unknowable or irrelevant, except perhaps as unattained and unattainable maladaptive or apocalyptic ideals. The religion would be appropriate to only one environment, Yahwism would be defined more narrowly than our study of the sources implies, and the Davidic paradigm for later action would be fraudulent.

The archaeological and literary information collected separately in this volume suggests that relationships similar to those in segmented ideologies and systems informed the folk and structural models embedded in both domains of the Yahwist world. The Yahwists' notions and actions both contain signs of segmentation. Moreover, the sources portray the Yahwists as an expansionist group that adopted the model from their predecessors, shared it with new members, and used it as a basis for forming alliances with their neighbors. In sum, representations and operations attributed to the Iron Age both appear to have been structured and to have functioned segmentally.

As is clear, the issue directly affects modern explanations of religious, economic, social and political change. For instance, if observers' models based on conquests, Oriental Despotism, or Asiatic Modes of Production can account for the origins and centralizing tendencies of ancient Yahwist society, by implication similar processes functioned exclusively or predominantly among the Yahwists (cf. Gellner, 1984: xii-xiii). If so, then the positive symbiotic relationships between leaders and peoples or among groups of peoples found in the sources either did not exist or our impressions of them are gravely biased. Such bonds would be mere figments of ancient and modern segmenting minds. Because the segmentation would be only notional, the ecological and economic continuities it presumes would be fictions. The religious transformations detectable in the sources would again be reduced to unattained ideals, and Yahwism would be inextricably wedded to revolutionary, reactionary, anti-centrist, or nomadic social forms. The long story of Yahwism and its elasticity would be lost.

Segmented Character of Societies

The partners in the symbiotic relationships of Iron Age I cited in our models are nomads, semi-sedentarists, sedentarized peasants, village residents, and urban populations. Segmentation is not intrinsically alien to any of them, and the essential claims for a segmentary model are met by all. The concept of segmentary systems in modern social science is rooted in Durkheim's *The Division of Labor in Society*, but recent descriptions of classic segmented systems often include a variety of features. Sahlins, for example, lists six essential characteristics (Sahlins, 1961: 330; cf. Khazanov, 1984: 144-148). Gellner, however, correctly reduces the essentials to two, both met by the early Iron

Age and early Yahwism. First, the main agency for maintaining order at every level of segmentation is always opposition between groups. And second, the criterion by which groups are defined is "coextensive with the kin and territorial definitions which operate within the society itself" (Gellner, 1973: 4). We may accept Gellner's criteria and look for balanced opposition and signs of co-extensive phenomena in our models.

Figure 33: A Classic Form of a Segmenting Genealogy

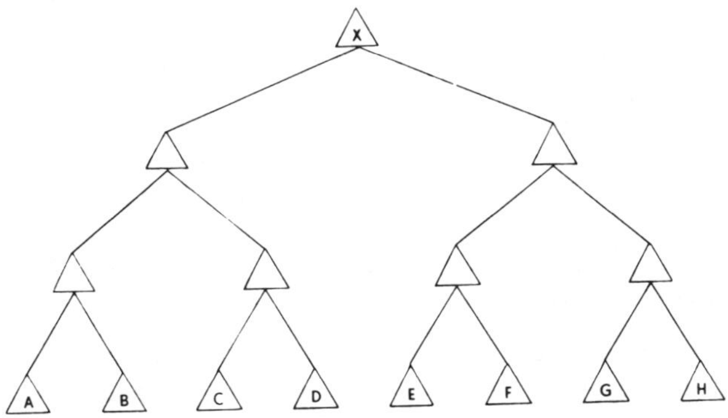

A simple sketch of the classic segmented system includes an ancestor who represents political unity with two or more descendants [Figure 33]. The latter can signify either unity or opposition depending on the circumstances and whether the model functions publicly, i.e., politically, or domestically. The individuals may stand against each other, or they may be allies against outsiders, as we noted in the Arab proverb cited earlier (Chapter 3). For this reason, some analysts argue that the model exemplifies lateral and vertical tensions simultaneously and therefore represents disintegrating cohesiveness rather than unity. This interpretation contains a hint of social devolution. In either case, the role of the ancestor figure is maintenance of order so that, should a descendant be attacked from outside, the ancestor represents the limits of the group called to respond. Everyone below the ancestor is a member of the offended segment and responsible for protecting it.

Individuals can be members of more than one segmented system at one time. People's economic, social, political, and religious domains do not always coincide, and their regional and supraregional identities derive from different allegiances. Hence, individuals can, for example, be members of one segmented system for economic purposes and another for religious reasons. Earlier remarks about operational groups with overlapping membership apply here as do the ethnographic examples of persons working in urban environs while maintaining family relationships in remote areas. Lebanese sociologist Samir Khalaf points toward the phenomenon in his description of his country's dilemma:

> Lebanon is gripped by a nagging predicament: the very forces that enable the Lebanese at the micro and communal level and from which they derive much of their social and psychic supports, disable them at the macro and national level by eroding their civic consciousness and symbols of national identity. The formation and deformation of Lebanon . . . are rooted in the same forces. The recurrence of violence is . . . one indication that the Lebanese have not as yet developed the appropriate political formula that allows them to live in both worlds . . by retaining and reconciling both forms of loyalties (Khalaf, 1987: ix.)

In segmented metaphors, segments sharing responsibilities are nested genealogically. As hostilities escalate to higher levels, they spread among descendants, and as they spread, they escalate. The contest between the Judahites and Israelites at Gibeon has been cited as an example (2 Samuel 2). This is why efforts are made to contain hostilities at the lowest possible level and among the smallest groups. The balanced structure, therefore, helps to contain violence by maintaining equality. Inequality and imbalance therefore spell defeat for the smaller or weaker group.

In the absence of centralized power, segmentation is crucial for peace and social stability.

> There is moreover a very specific point at which the notion of segmentation is invaluable. Segmentation is intimately connected with a certain kind of equality, specifically the equality of power and of the ability to impose sanctions on others. In segmentary societies power is evenly diffused, to a very unusual degree, over the whole social structure. This is sometimes denied but, in my view, erroneously. . . . The theory of the mechanics of segmentary society hinges on the fact that there is no center at which the means of cohesion are concentrated and which can impose its will on other groups. Everybody has to combine, in the approved segmentary

> manner, for purposes of self-defense and the deterrence of aggression. Such equality is of course only an approximation, but segmentary societies come much closer to equality of power than do most others (Gellner, 1973: 4).

The last remarks are important. Balance and equality are prized, but the egalitarianism of a segmented system is not absolute. Idealized sketches of such systems are usually drawn symmetrically, but actual genealogies that are metaphors for the systems are less regular. Their balance is understood only by the participants who know the relative "weight" of individuals and groups in the segments. As a system, Gellner's dictum ("stability without government") applies, but ranking within segments, fluidity among segmental allegiances, overlapping but discrete spheres of influence and planes of classification, and shifting resources and values prevent stability from becoming ossified. But they are also the factors that allow equilibrium to be maintained in times of change. Fissioning and fusing can be incessant, and real centralization can occur only when the processes are slowed or halted. Strong leadership is one means of maintaining strength because it attracts and sustains loyalties.

> By ideologically defining any political action as an affair of segments in balanced opposition, and not as an affair of particular individuals, the notion of segmentary lineage structure allows for the emergence of men entrusted with considerable authority and wielding great political power. As long as political leadership remains personal and does not become institutionalized into an office, it can be accounted for within the given ideology, and the ideological dictum of egalitarianism can be upheld in spite of considerable political inequality on the ground (Holy and Stuchlik, 1983: 103).

Development Within the Iron Age Segmented System

Figures 22 (p. 184) and 31 (p. 259) illustrate the development of archaeological and biblical categories from disparate economic and residential bases. They summarize and integrate many of the points discussed here and in earlier chapters. The relationships among the segments (and boxes) at points of fission and fusion are suggestive of the segmented models inferred from literary and archaeological sources. The junctures in both sources form the interference pattern encoded on our hypothetical holographic plate. How the stages and transitions in the model drawn from one domain compare with those from the other is important. Those comparisons (relationships) are what we illuminate by comparative sociology. Claims of stability and change and material signs of the same are correlated and illuminated.

The models identified in earlier chapters can be summarized in order to integrate them holographically. The geography and ecology at the eastern end of the Mediterranean basin that set the goal ranges for biblical stories comprise exceptional variety and complexity. These are populated by densely compacted and highly diverse social patterns. They comprise the residential and economic strategies relating to the primary ecological zones outlined in Chapter 3. Understanding their synchronic and symbiotic relationships illuminates many of the diachronic changes represented by boxes and branches below them in Figures 22 and 31.

In the archaeological model, four types of ecological-residential strategies were cited: 1) nomadic and pastoral, 2) semi-nomadic (or semi-sedentary) pastoralist and agrarian, 3) sedentary and agrarian, and 4) seafaring, mercenary, and trading. The categories themselves are composites that could be separated either according to dominant modes of residence or modes of economic production. The two are not the same. Hence, when met on the ground and in practice, the groups symbolized by the composite types would be less easily categorized than is suggested by the diagram.

Because of the environment in the eastern Mediterranean basin, the categories tend to fall into a J-shaped striated pattern following rainfall and vegetation differences in the Fertile Crescent and its neighboring desert zones. The pattern could be comfortably superimposed, generally at least, on a map that shows the area's physical, geomorphological, and meteorlogical features. On a stylized map that locates the Mediterranean coastline and the ca. 200 mm rainfall line separating cultivating from non-cultivating zones, the four boxes could "slide" southward until their axis turned approximately 90 degrees in the Negev and Sinai zones. The same relations would apply throughout, but the direction of their orientation would rotate along the geographical lines seen earlier.

As noted, the socioeconomic groups represented by the four cultural/ecological categories tend to sort themselves along axes that extend from the Mediterranean toward the interreaches of either the

Great Syrian or Sinai deserts. Similar to (and because of) the rainfall patterns, the orientations are predominantly E-W and only in the south do they become NE-SW and N-S. There the axes run obliquely from the coast, through central Cisjordan, across the 200 mm rainfall line and either southeastward toward southern Transjordan or southward into the Negev. Because of these orientations, the interactions, tensions, and adaptations among ecologically based residential and economic groupings tend to orient themselves similarly. Several, in fact, are the paths of interaction examined in Emmanuel Marx's ethnographic studies summarized above.

In the same way, and on a macroscale, the geography envisaged in David's stories of contacts and interactions can be situated according to these orientations. He moves outside the 200 mm line during much of his early life, but penetrates the innerland on both his entry and re-entry into Jerusalem. Jerusalem, however, stands close to the border and joins Damascus and Amman in respect to its position between desert and agrarian zones. The stories portray David's first incursion as that of a giant-killer on his way to fame and acceptance by Saul. He travels inside on other occasions when in the company of his suzerains, the Philistines. He moves inside again, this time to the boundary when he relocates in and later retakes Jerusalem.

Because of the unusual geomorphology in the region, the ecologies and corresponding social strategies exist in exceptionally close proximity and variety. Moreover, as we have suggested, the zones central to David's drama are mainly bounded by two of the major E-W geological corridor-depressions and the N-S Jordan valley. One of the former is the depression extending from Haifa through the Jezreel valley, across the Jordan, into the Yarmouk river and onto the plains beyond. The second cuts from the southern coast eastward to the Beersheba basin where it turns slightly southeastwardly toward the base of the Dead Sea and into the Wadi el-Hasa of southern Transjordan.

David does marry outside these boundaries, perhaps into the royal houses of Ammon and Geshur. The coincidence suggests two things. First, the marriages to Michal daughter of Saul, to Maacah daughter of the king of Geshur, possibly to Zeruiah (his sister?) daughter of Nahash, to Abigail the wife of a wealthy pastoralist, and to others suggest that David is marrying upward into chiefly and royal houses and outward among many segments of society. In terms of geography and social class, David spreads his risks. Second, many of the Iron IB remains that are beyond the Mediterranean coast are scattered along and within short distances of the corridors and valley. The distribution cross-cuts several zones from which David reportedly took wives.

One wonders whether the two phenomena are related. Another wife, Ahinoam (2 Sam 3: 3), happens to be from Jezreel, a place with the same name as the site of Saul's last battle (1 Samuel 29). David is excluded from the battle, according to the story, because of fears about his loyalty. Commentators typically locate the wife in a southern Jezreel and the battle at a site in the northern corridor, but the coincidence of names hints that the writers may assume that the two places are the same. We cannot know, but the loyalty issue would be crucial if a warrior were asked to fight against his wife's people. In the heat of battle, David would have several self-serving options open to him. He would be protected regardless of the outcome. In any case, a strategy in David's marriage pattern begins to emerge. He does not avoid "pressure points" in the sociopolitical system. He embraces them by marrying inside and beyond them laterally and vertically in the segmented system. He thereby builds an increasingly secure network of alliances.

Because of rainfall and vegetation patterns, pastoral migrations tend to follow the axes indicated by the boxes, but perennial rainfall variations force other specific risk-avoiding maneuvers. Locally, no hard and fast rules obtain, but the general pattern is still visible today in spite of modern political boundaries. The clearest examples, perhaps, survive further to the north in Syria where nomadic pastoralists move annually from the desert to positions as far west as the Orontes valley and coastal regions. The pressures on seasonal movements are, therefore, both bidirectional and multidirectional. During Iron Age I, as Marfoe argues on a microscale for the Biqa in Lebanon, they are similar. In fact, as we noted, the distribution of the distinctive Iron IA indicator, the collared-rim jar, stretching in Cisjordan throughout the area between Galilee and Beersheba but extending eastward to Sahab and south in Transjordan to the very fringes of southern Edom, probably corresponds to migration patterns. We also accept Dornemann's suggestion that the slight differences that distinguish Cisjordan from Transjordan typologies are diachronic and do not depend completely on regional or ethnic diversity. Hence, the general, long-term pattern of movements were eastward along the geographical paths and from sedentary/agrarian to nomadic/pastoral zones, but seasonal needs took peoples in the other direction as well. In effect, relations were symbiotic and not unidirectional as conquest and infiltration models suppose.

Many reasons have already been cited for the swirl of centripetal and centrifugal movements in Iron I. Comparative ethnographies suggest ideological, economic, religious, and political reasons for occupying marginal zones (cf. Kelly, 1985; Meeker, 1979; Goody, 1977). When closed societies such as LB kingdoms and city states give way to open societies that allow new mixes of values and worldviews like those identified in the biblical models, our explanatory options increase proportionally. We have suggested that movement into hinterland regions means low economic productivity and few surpluses, additional need for spreading risks, and— especially for agrarians—shifts to alternative strategies for exploiting the environment. Increased pastoralism and labor-intensive terracing, irrigation, and storage systems beome common. The latter, of course, require long-term commitments of capital and labor that further reduce the potential for surpluses. Not surprisingly societies caught in such circumstances typically resist pressures for costly forms of governance and worship.

A second feature of life in Iron Age I is beginning to emerge from archaeological information now that the period is no longer interpreted exclusively in "Israelite" terms. The devolution of structures that correspond to the evolution of new ones is apparent. The processes are two facets of a single phenomenon and not unrelated occurrences. Furthermore, social devolution like its counterpart typically moves in stages rather than from full life to sudden collapse. Forced decentralization finds peoples struggling to retain old ways in face of new realities and, in turn, finds them sliding "downward" only as far as the stage of development immediately below the last one achieved. Hence, as statehood is thought to be a stage of centralization that follows chieftaincy, in devolution, chieftaincy is apt to follow statehood. The importance for the emergence of Yahwist communities out of LB cultures is that we should expect Yahwist and non-Yahwist factions to share at least one aspiration, namely, a desire for equilibrium and stability. Therefore, leadership that is successful in achieving it for one segment would be recognized and envied by the other. In fact both might accept and describe such an individual as their own. This must be kept in mind when recalling the complex relationships among David, the Israelites,

Judahites, Philistines, and others. We know the Yahwist tradition's view of the outcome, but we have no direct information about how others saw him.

Our outline of Iron Age archaeology conforms with today's trend toward recognizing the coexistence of LB, Iron IA, IB, and even IC materials. Irregular and overlapping typological metamorphoses suggest that change is gradual and peoples differ in their responses to it. Some cling to the old; some embrace the new. Some, like the David figure, probably move back and forth between communities that embrace one or other religious model. Not surprisingly, the chart of archaeological processes of change given above also compares favorably to the multibranched iconic, segmented models used to demonstrate the development of semitic languages and to the general description of movements within the biblical stories. This may be stressing the obvious, but archaeologically speaking, Iron Age I is a segmented society rather than a succession of centralized, closed systems. Interactions, symbioses, and compromises are suggested by the typologies and for the societies they represent.

Parallel biblical information can also be summarized briefly. We have identified stages in the actors' models and associated them with development of centralization in Jerusalem. Thus far our attention has focused on metamorphoses evident in the development of representations, in effect, on changes in the way different stages in the biblical tradition look upon the emergence of centralized monarchy in Jerusalem. According to the cumulative composite myth, 1) a pre- or non-Yahwist Isra-el, in which Samu-el plays a role, merges with Yahwists in Benjamin to form "all Israel" under Saul. 2) After a while, David rises to leadership among the Philistines, and 3) eventually he is accepted by a council of elders as simultaneous leader of a Judah federation and the Philistines. 4) Later he assumes leadership over the northern group and simultaneously leads the two moieties, Judah and Israel. Then he turns against the Philistines. 5) His own legitimacy is continually threatened until, in the myth, first he, and then his house, is legitimated. This is not the succession theme associated with Solomon, but a Davidic theme whereby he displaces first Saul, then Saul's house, then the Philistines, and finally the ark of the covenant. Only afterward, in a final combat with Yahweh where census-taking and plagues are the duelists' weapons, does David finally submit himself and his model of leadership completely to the deity. Chieftaincy over the two large segmented moieties, Israel and Judah, and other sociopolitical units is thereby legitimated. The symbioses continue under Solomon.

We have noted several important points that reappear in this brief paraphrase of the biblical tradition. In the first place, the representational model that dominates the books of Samuel legitimates not only the central paramountcy of Davidic chieftaincy, but also legitimates resistance to fuller centralization in the form of statehood and monarchy. In a word, as we have noted, the idealized David is the uncentralized centralizer and the centralizing decentralizer. He is acceptable to all the contemporary ideologies, and his leadership is economically and sociopolitically viable.

Secondly, for Jerusalem to centralize further or to explain monarchy's failure requires a reworking of the myth in order to anchor later developments in the idealized Davidic model. It is dynasty, not monarchy, that stands at the base of the tradition. In the retellings, the relationships in the David figure remain paradigmatic and foundational. Each new development is likened to changes he mediated. His image, in a sense, contains implicate orders that become explicate in later, sometimes contrasting, forms. The dynasty unfolds in tumultuous and unexpected ways.

Thirdly, although isolated pieces of information in narratives continue within the tradition, the biblical writers freely ignore the diachronic sequence imposed by their precedessors. In a sense, each telling creates its own sequence, but underlying transitions are kept intact while being nested like levels in a segmented genealogy. For example, the Deuteronomists or someone earlier changes the setting of the Dynastic Oracle, and the Chroniclers ignore the role of Samuel in the story of David's rise. But the dynastic decision becomes simply another version of Yahweh's choosing David, Solomon's legitimation is portrayed as another level in the transition from Saul, and Josiah's reform is presented as a restoration of David's legitimating role. Like ripples emanating in concentric circles from a stone thrown into a pond, the Yahwists' memories or models of David have their own identities, but they rest on the crucial, ritualized transition to David's house that is encoded at the base of the tradition. The so-called "historical" materials that link the models are subject to change as image of the "ego" of the story changes.

Interference Pattern

If we follow the biblical precedent and read the information sources together but without the restraints of the narrative sequence and rigid archaeological space-time systemics, the archaeological and literary models suggest simultaneous processes of devolution and evolution similar to the symbioses among sedentary, semi-nomadic, and nomadic peoples documented in comparative sociology. In Iron IA, Cisjordan peoples begin to move away from their sedentary agrarian environments into remote highland areas and eastward into Transjordan wadis, plateaus, and desert fringes. Some towns and villages are established, especially in the highlands, and transhumanent residential and economic patterns are embraced. Population in outlying zones rises, in some areas, steeply. Simultaneously, semi-nomadic and nomadic peoples interact with these outsiders. Stories of Judah and Transjordan, seasonal shrines, and settlements along trade routes are indicators.

The centrifugal and centripetal movements are intersected by Mediterranean IB traders and mercenaries who take economic advantage of the turmoils by supplying new goods, mediating trade between other groups, and serving as mercenaries. In the representation, they are looked down upon and feared by the other peoples, even those who depend on them. Their attempts at establishing sociopolitical dominance are extremely threatening but meet with only limited success. Iron is one of the luxury items prized and traded, and it soon appears among grave goods in the status burials of both IA and IB peoples. The biblical model assigns the mercenaries the role of smiths and hence the disparaging glances. This is but one indication that the relationship of the IB outsiders to their trading partners is anything but harmonious. Pillaging, combative skirmishes, and military threats abound, and in the model, the Philistines are blamed for many of them.

The remnants of the non-Philistine LB peoples who coalesce in segmented non-Yahwist Isra-el probably support a diminished role for centralized polities. They manifest their preference by adopting a system of unstable leadership that combines rotations similar to *wesh* system and temporary offices like those among settling nomads. The duration of the system is unclear, perhaps because it evolves into a Yahwist federation. But it predates and overlaps temporally the seeming rise in the popularity of Yahwism in Cisjordan. According to the model, the unity or some portion of it encounters a group in the highlands of Benjamin whose traditions include nomadic sociopolitical models.

The image interferes constructively with impressions based on archaeological information. Symbiotic adaptations follow. According to the biblical writers' model, Benjaminite traditions subsume those of the LB sedentary peoples, and leadership emerges from within the Yahwists. There is indication that El-based leadership either embraces the new religion or temporarily shares responsibilities with a Yahwist (Samuel). Thus, the extent of the merging is unclear. But indications are that an agrarian economy continues to expand in the highlands and across the rift into northern Transjordan where the economic and sociopolitical strategies of additional nomads and semi-nomads are encountered. The biblical tradition, however, depicts the religion as moving in the opposite direction. The difference may be explained by the dominance of conquest mythology that accompanies the Deuteronomic quest for unity or by two earlier planes of centripetal and centrifugal swirlings that cause economic forces to press outward and sociopolitical ideals to press inward across the rainfall line. The processes may also explain differences in the terminology, *nāgîd* and *melek*, applied to the system's leaders. Whether the former should be translated as "prince"—suggesting the devolutions within Canaanite sociopolitical leadership—or "chief"—in order to stress the evolving paramountcy of a nomadic state—remains an open question. The actors' model remembers that some people prefer to emphasize that the leader is not a king, while others stress the cosmopolitan aspects of the entity by appropriating *melek*, a title with considerable semantic range.

Both terms expose the reality of two groups jointly and simultaneously seeking homeostasis by embracing either the same leader (Saul and later David) or several leaders working in unison (Samuel and Saul). The terms' richness and ambiguity are appropriate for the complexity of the metamorphoses. Therefore, to go beyond an earlier proposal that *nāgîd* implies chieftaincy (Flanagan, 1981), we may hypothesize that in addition to social evolution, the terms *nāgîd* and *melek* also suggest both devolution and the synchronic and symbiotic merging of disparate ecologies and notions. The leadership of the saintly Samuel and chiefly Saul represent at once phases and amalgamations in the metamorphoses of Iron Age governance. However, not all LB peoples join the merger or the segmented system, and they and the IB peoples continue their separate, troublemaking lives as the outsiders.

Separately, IA nomads and semi-nomads in the southern Cisjordan and Transjordan form a moiety with sedentaries and seek to encapsulate, suppress, or otherwise relate to the IB peoples in the area. The last seems to be the early pattern. Apparently, towns of the two groups coexist with minimal harmony, and the biblical model implies that administrative skills used among the IB groups could be appropriated by the IA peoples. In effect, the leader of the trading/agrarian/mercenaries in Ziklag, namely David, becomes the head of a religiously mixed moiety centered in Hebron. If the transition is smooth, the reactions apparently are not. The leader, facing the usual dilemma of allegiances and loyalties, chooses—according to the model—to align more closely with the IA pastoral nomads rather than continue accommodating the IB peoples.

The pressure to decide is contained until the northern IA moiety on both sides of the Jordan seeks alliance with the Hebron leader. Then the risk of losing IA Yahwist support is too great to postpone a decision. The suzerain-vassal, patron-client relations with the IB peoples are reversed. Leadership relocated in Jerusalem. The IA moieties in alliance with IB peoples, other separate IA polities in Transjordan, and disparate northern coastal and inland groups with whom parity relationships are struck all affiliate with the new leadership in Jerusalem. Several adaptation patterns are employed simultaneously. Jerusalem, sociopolitically a rather artificial center, is the personal holding of the ruling family. The relationships with different peoples depend in large part on the historical and ecological circumstances of each group. For a while at least, the dual terminology known in the northern moiety continues. The complexity of political arrangements, which is no doubt greater than described here, requires adroit leadership. The biblical view is that of the Israel/Judah moieties interpreted by the Jerusalemite leaders, but other models are surely operating among the non-Yahwists. Even so, the Israel/Judah model does not hide the tensions between nomads and agrarians, etc., described above. According to our interpretation, economic and sociopolitical interests, ruling and laboring strata, geographical zones, and historical development all militate against harmony and permanent centralization. But paradoxically, they are contributing causes to unification as well, because leadership is emerging from within.

The stages indicated by the passing of leadership expose the juggling act that is required to stop fissioning in the complex segmentary system that is evolving. Interestingly, the model that is idealized—certainly not the only one remembered—portrays a pastoral nomad who rises to leadership among the Philistines, but successfully adapts to Benjaminite, Israelite, Judahite, Transjordanian, ruling class and peasant expectations and needs as well. Ideologically, however, his ideal role is that of a Yahwist pastoral nomadic chieftain and a former *'apiru* who adapts to the needs and aspirations of all segments within the system. The early representation legitimates the presence of shared leadership and the absence of the symbols of a monopoly of force. David's successor, on the other hand, moves further away from a nomadic and pastoral base and, although he apparently survives for a full lifetime, the former nomadic state soon disintegrates. Iron Age IC ends.

B. *A Hologram of the Early Iron Age*

Comparative studies cited in earlier chapters have been used to illuminate information in one or other ancient domain. Those comparisons apply equally in understanding the integrated hologram, but they need not be repeated. Additional studies that illumine synchronic interactions first and diachronic developments second occupy our attention here.

The tension between a readiness to resort to force and an involvement in diligent labor and peaceful cooperation is described as a dilemma between controlling wealth and producing it (Meeker, 1980: 697). The same differences separate those who control the balance of power from those who concentrate on the flow of goods (Gellner, 1973: 6; 1984: xii), which is another way of noting that sociopolitical interests are sometimes at odds with economic goals (Khazanov, 1984: *passim*).

In Near Eastern societies, a third, intermediate role can be identified. It includes those who concentrate on the institutions of mediation between nomads and non-nomads (Gellner, 1973: 7) or who enjoy special status as a ruling segment in a differentiated segmentary system (Khazanov, 1984: 146). Traders who act as go-betweens and vagabond artisans who are identified with no social group but who ply their needed skills among many are two categories of this kind. We have examined saints who adjudicate conflicts and chieftaincies with their redistributive economies whereby leaders allocate resources they neither produce nor own. Each fills this breach. All the types in some sense have "priestly" roles. Some in fact are patently religious, a quality that should be expected in civilizations that are "notoriously religious" in spite of the oft-presumed irreligiosity among Near Eastern nomads (Gellner, 1973: 8).

To place sociopolitical and cultural phenomena on one side of a divide and economic and ecological on the other and to note that individuals and structures mediate, integrate, and otherwise regulate relationships between them is to call attention again to separate domains of information and the need to look between, at points of intersection, in social world analysis. Transhumanence, semi-nomadism, chieftaincy, and other similar classifications are not mere blends of alternatives that are meant to resolve tensions. They are socio-economic strategies and social structures in their own right.

Many ethnographies expose the complexity of intermediaries' roles. A review of specific strategies, beyond that in the archaeological systemic model in Chapter 3, is not possible. We are aided, however, by generalizations in Anatoli Khazanov's *Nomads and the Outside World* (1984). The study is especially important because of its Russian origins. For Marxists, nomadism represents an anomoly in the socioeconomic system. Like others, however, Khazanov argues that nomads rarely exist in isolation and instead always define themselves over against the outside world. Nomadism and segmentary systems are especially compatible. "Pure" nomadism seldom occurs because nomadic groups depend on outsiders for technology, goods, and services that they need in order to continue their migratory, low-labor-intensity ways. As Gellner notes when summarizing Khazanov's earlier studies,

> . . . there was urban-tribal economic interdependence, combined with political and cultural tension: political development was cyclical; and social stratification and political centralisation was weak amongst the nomads except at times when they turned themselves into a dominant, conquering stratum of a wider society (Gellner, 1984: xxv).

Sedentary and Nomadic Strategies for Pacification and Change

Based on ecological and economic criteria, Near Eastern nomadism stands as a distinct type having at least four subtypes: Arabian, North African, Saharan, and Northeast African. Each in turn exhibits great diversity, including the nomads of the Sahara and Arabia and the semi-nomads engaged in herding husbandry in North Africa, Syria, Iraq, and regions of Cisjordan (cf. Khazanov, 1984: 53-59). Migrations are determined in large part by water and grazing resources. Consequently, personal and social ties also depend on wells, oases, and pasturages. In the Fertile Crescent where livestock is pastured in fields after crops are harvested, social-ecological symbioses lead to extensive sedentary-nomadic interaction. The varied and erratic rainfall patterns, however, make migrations routes somewhat unstable and lead to patchwork patterns of social alliances.

In Syro-Palestine as elsewhere, all forms of pastoralism are methods of economic adaptation to environmental settings. This means that boundaries are decided by ecology and technological development, factors that also affect patterns of social development, the interaction among nomads, artisans, and cultivators, and the appeal to segmented systems. Against evolutionary expectations, nomadism and pastoralism often emerge out of agrarian societies as ways of spreading the latters' food-producing economies into semi-arid and hinterland areas (cf. Khazanov, 1984: 69). Although the strategy increases overall efficiency by raising productivity and decreasing labor needs thereby improving the macroeconomy, as we noted, the improvements include a downside and paradox. While fuller exploitation of the environment means overall economic improvement, the pastoral nomadic sectors suffer. As dependency on sedentaries increases, the pastoralists may be reduced to subsistence-level existences.

This profit-loss ratio is linked to technology. Because nomads lack the internal capacity for progressive technological change, they are forced to adopt outsiders' innovations acquired through trade with sedentaries or roaming artisans. The latters' industry in producing and repairing tools and weapons, in acting as veterinarians, and in supplying market goods is essential, yet the groups are despised. They are considered homeless even though materially they enjoy better nutrition and living accommodation than the nomads who support them (Meeker, 1979: 22-23). Hence, the combination of low productivity, low population density, and dependence on non-nomads creates anomalies among the nomads.

First, dependency means that even though grazing is the basis of nomadic existence, nomadism cannot be fully identified with pastoralism. Second, although nomads are inseparably linked to and define themselves over against sedentaries, the symbioses also allow them to dominate certain ecological zones. Outsiders have difficulty in penetrating the zones, and so the nomads maintain extensive political control that is often disproportionate to their numbers and economic contribution.

In such worlds, ecological, economic, and political balances are extremely fragile and frequently volatile. Meeker (1979) stresses the importance of violence in Near Eastern life. He argues that attempts to achieve peace through violence so dominate nomadic existence that violence becomes a way of life, almost an ideology, affecting all levels of personal and social relationships. To Western proponents of centralization, the practice seems logically flawed because it prevents the very results it intends to achieve. Peace sustained through violence—first-strike capability—is, for observers, a contradiction and absurdity. To citizens of segmentary worlds, however, it is part of the check and balance system that brings acceptable security to daily life. It is a means of protecting the mobile resources of peoples who have no permanent dwelling. It is also at times sporting and much less violent than outsiders believe.

Regardless of the advantages and disadvantages, the notion of peace through violence affects both sedentaries and agrarians, although in different ways. Among sedentaries where economic resources cannot be moved and leaving one's property is unreasonable, residents cope with conflict by investing confidence in saints, sacral zones of refuge, and mediator's roles of various kinds. Along with segmentation, social stratification, and differentiated planes of classification, the strategies allow tensions in social, political, economic, and residential spheres to be separated and handled one at a time and to be passed out of the community where they can be resolved. The mediators also help to regulate relationships among the sedentaries and between them and the outsiders.

The contrasts between nomads and outsiders reach to the highest levels of organization. Among nomads, organizations arise in accordance with political necessity and disappear when the need passes (Khazanov, 1984: 148). In many instances, the need for political integration and concentration of power depends almost entirely on the nomads' relations to other societies, whether sedentary or nomadic (Khazanov, 1984: 151).

Chieftaincy is one example of limited centralization. Although attainable among pure nomads, the office there is not exactly the same as in other societies. Of eight chiefly traits commonly cited by modern scholars, Khazanov finds nomadic chiefdoms at variance with four (Khazanov, 1984: 165-169). Both groups have hereditary social differentiation, inequality, and an aristocratic status or ethos; both limit paramounts' functions and link them primarily to legal procedures, cermonial roles, and external relations; both lack the coercive power to impose decisions; and both lack ways of preventing fission. But nomadic chieftaincies are generally weaker, not theocratic, and not peaceful. Additionally, nomads are less apt to replicate the functions of a central chief in lower levels of the segmented structure. In other words, power is more diffuse among nomads.

Adaptation of Insiders and Outsiders

The two planes of adaptation—economic and sociopolitical—are more easily discriminated in theory than in practice. Because neither sedentaries nor nomads are passive participants in their social enterprises and social dramas, feed backs and oscillations cause the varying economic needs and sociopolitical aspirations of individual strata and groups to merge and blend so completely that they can be separated only analytically. Four basic types can be cited (Khazanov, 1984: 198-224).

1) The most radical adaptation for nomads is economic accommodation to sedentarization, increased agricultural production, and development of handicrafts by the nomads themselves. However, the changes meet with cognitive, social, and ecological obstacles that tie the nomads to their former existence. Cognitively, traditional ways of life must be broken down and eliminated from their ideology. Reinforced by their tribal aristocracies, nomads perceive sedentarization as a loss of freedom accompanied by demeaning manual labor and disruption of traditional values.

As we have seen, ecological resistance is greatest because of the intimate connection among nomadic economy, geography, and residence patterns. Each is usually unsuited for sedentary life. Consequently, full sedentarization is usually ecologically possible only when accompanied by migration to new ecological zones. This presents an argument against nomadic migratory models as the sole explanation for Iron Age I Syro-Palestine because mass movements or infiltrations of this type are seldom fully self-conscious. Instead, they usually result from more gradual interactions between the nomads and sedentaries according to circumstances in a given time and place. Then, the change resolves the economic differences by making the two groups one.

2) Adaptation can be accomplished, without the total transformation of either group, through trade. The exchanges are either between the groups directly or through mediators who are often nomads brokering economic interests indirectly. In the latter instance, the trading partners may both be sedentaries who depend on a long-distance caravan trade provided by the nomads, or they may be sedentaries and nomads who utilize each others' resources.

Again there are obstacles and paradoxes. The first is the difficulty that nomadic economies have in generating the surpluses needed for trading. If necessities are offered for trade, essentials such as diet suffer. Trade sometimes works to the detriment of tribal redistributive systems by exchanging items needed in the nomadic society. Conversely, however, exchanges between nomadic aristocracy and wealthy sedentaries provide goods needed to strengthen and stabilize nomadic social and economic positions. In these instances, the partners' wealth and motivations dispose them to trade luxury goods in order to make higher level contacts, but the economic benefits of such exchanges more than likely do not reach the ordinary people. In sum, specialization and instability among nomads dictate their interest in trading, but the same factors prevent surpluses that can be sold regularly and for the benefit of all.

3) Nomadic societies are sometimes encapsulated within sedentary states where they merely align their forces with those of the ruling polity according to the latter's policy toward them. In return they serve as mercenaries, and a blind eye is turned that allows them to pillage on their own. Hence, the relationship imposes controls on them at the state level but affords them considerable freedom locally.

Entry into such systems is easier when sedentaries control expansive territory and engage in policies of conquest. Then the nomads' political submission is economically advantageous for both groups because it legitimates the pillaging of other nomads and distracts them from pillaging sedentaries. The sedentaries often allow nomadic organizations to remain intact and deal with the people indirectly through the sheikhs who serve as mediators. Hence, the nomadic leaders enjoy renewed authority with considerable autonomy.

4) At times nomads subjugate sedentary societies. Because of their mobility and military superiority, both periodic raids and long-term agreements for protection and dependence can be forced on the sedentaries. The economic advantage of this kind of sociopolitical superiority is obvious: the nomads seize products and animals without having to give anything in exchange.

Because raiding is too unreliable to support a long-term relationship, nomads prefer regular payments of tribute, taxes, or rents in return for guarantees of protection against other nomads. The tactic appears in the story of David and Nabal (1 Samuel 25). As there, tribute relations are usually initiated at a local level between small groups and as a result of specific circumstances. Therefore, regions with either no sedentary polity or a weak one are usually not subjected to massive unified conquests. Skirmishes are the rule unless raiders encounter strong resistance from a real force which then precipitates a conquest. A series of skirmishes and local raids, however, does not preclude later attempts at conquest.

Finally, nomads can make sedentaries subjective by incorporating agricultural and artisan economies into their own societies. These diversify their economy and make them less dependent on the outside world.

Tendencies toward Statehood

These alternatives provide a base for considering processes of state formation among adapting societies. The emergence of nomadic states is linked to external expansion, usually at the expense of sedentaries, and does not necessarily require conquest. Military aggression is only one of many processes of state formation. Likewise, not every subjugation of peoples by nomads leads to statehood. Sufficient stability, scale, and a degree of social differentiation must already be found among the conquerors and the conquered for states to develop. In many cases the nomads merely adopt or build on the stratification they find.

Social differentiation along sedentary and nomadic lines divides the states into several strata of rulers and dependents. These normally form two sub-systems joined only by political ties. Full integration is difficult and rare. The greater changes typically occur in the nomadic sub-system which for the first time becomes a class society when the aristocracy sets itself apart. However, neither this nor vassalage in the societies should be interpreted as signs of feudalism, which is a more holistic phenomenon than the one discussed here.

As with adaptation, the process of state formation is potentially self-defeating for the nomads. Social and economic expansion can cause their society to lose the characteristics that made it successful in the first place and thereby leave it vulnerable to other nomadic groups with similar intentions. Responses to this dilemma fall into three types (Khazanov, 1984: 228-302). In reality, the typologies are often mixed and can be identified only according to the predominance of one set of features or another.

1) The first type results in vassal-tribute and other forms of collective dependence and exploitation. Social relations depend on the relationship of the nomads as a whole to the subjugated people or state, the relationship between the nomadic aristocracy and the sedentary population or state, and the relationship between the nomadic aristocracy and ordinary nomads. Dominance over external forms is most important. Sometimes the sedentaries preserve their own state and are joined to the nomads only politically. Integration is limited; social groups live side by side but not together. Nomads, agriculturalists, and townspeople are incorporated under the stimulation of the nomads. The nomadic aristocracy needs the towns, which appear to be artificial, as centers of political power, handicrafts, and trade.

If external expansion continues, and it frequently does, fewer opportunities for exploiting the sedentaries occur, and one of three modes of future change ensues. a) The nomadic state can disintegrate. Towns decline, sedentary territories break away, and structures devolve. b) Or the nomadic society ceases to be distinctive and absorbs the characteristics of the sedentaries in all but its structure. c) Or a third variation actually leads to the second typology below.

2) In the second type of state, nomads, agriculturalists, and townspeople form two sub-societies socially but not politically or geographically. Politically they integrate fully but economically only partially. Relations are determined primarily by the relationship of ruling classes to peasants as an exploitable class, by relationships

between the ruling classes of the two groups, and by the relationship of the ruling classes to the nomads. Here ordinary nomads are not the basic class and rarely form a separate class by themselves. In most cases, the nomads move into agrarian territories and share the same ecological zones with cultivators. As a result, the symbiotic relations lead more quickly to a synthesis of the two ways of life than in the first type of state. The more this is achieved, the more the nomads are stratified according to privilege determined by ties to the dynasty, tribal status, etc.

As integration proceeds, the ruling dynasty faces a choice and dilemma: whether to foster integration by moving their interests toward those of the sedentaries and the polity as a whole or to preserve their position within the nomadic society. Usually, clear choices are avoided and conflict erupts between factions. Tensions divide the aristocracy from the original nomadic dynasty, the dynasty from ordinary nomads, and sedentaries from the nomads, and so forth.

3) In the third type of state, a single unified sociopolitical and economic system emerges in conjunction with the development of a division of labor between the nomadic and sedentary groups. Both processes often occur separately, but they seldom develop in unison, so that there are few states of this type.

A final peculiarity of Near Eastern nomadism deserves comment before leaving our discussion of state formation models. As noted, dynasties have to choose between remaining nomadic and consolidating power around sedentaries which means risking nomads' support. Avoiding the choice is a fine art in the Near East. The stories of David and Jerusalem come to mind. Gradually distancing oneself from nomadic groups and identifying with the sedentary aristocracy is one strategy. Ambiguous policies toward the nomads is another. Wearing the clothes of tribes, spending several months in their midst, and allowing sedentaries and nomads to use differing titles are more specific examples of attempts to retain allegiances across these social frontiers in times of change.

In many cases the contradictions are caused by the need for the dynasty and government to centralize and regulate state life which runs counter to the interests of individual groups. The tensions are similar to those that enable unity locally while disabling it above the local level. Among nomads, inner circle, middle circle, and outer circle tribes—the sheep, sheepdogs, and wolves, as they are called—

are divided according to whether they receive, pay, or do not pay taxes (Gellner, 1969: 3-4; 1981: 30). This and similar circumstances illustrate the difficulties and the possibility that one and the same ruler or ruling class may exhibit several degrees of political devolution/evolution simultaneously. By living in several worlds, such leaders may be a ruling class to the sedentary agrarians and at the same time a dynasty to the nomads. If the chasm is too deep, nomadic support is lost and schism occurs.

Applying Synchronic Comparisons

The separation of the domains within actors' and observers' models parallels the comparative sociologists' distinction between economic and sociopolitical adaptations. Archaeological information indicates that economic factors in Iron Age I were pushing peoples eastward and southward into previously unexploited ecological zones. Literary models suggest that sociopolitical (and religious) innovations were penetrating settled areas by moving in the opposite directions. Representations such as those in Exodus 15, the Moses models, and countless stories about the wilderness place the origin of Yahwism in the desert regions somewhere in a southern or southeasterly zone, the area of the LB Midianite ceramics. Thus, centrifugal and centripetal forces were moving not only in different directions, but also were traveling primarily on separate planes of classification.

At the same time as the LB Age centralized sociopolitical and economic systems were devolving and struggling for homeostasis, a new Yahwist identity devoid of such structures was also evolving and seeking homeostasis. The former had sustained order among agrarians and sedentaries while concurrently the latter had emerged first among pastoralists and nomads and then among semi-agrarians and agrarians. Historical circumstances at the epicenters of international power beyond Syro-Palestine contributed to the changes. But the metamorphoses also depended on ecological adaptations that were dictated by the geography of the eastern Mediterranean basin. On the social level, processes of fissioning and fusing typical of segmented societies regulated and adjusted the highly fluid alignments as they shifted.

Other forms of mediation were also required. Discrepancies between sociopolitical and economic domains had to be resolved; residential and economic strategies had to be adjusted; geographical and sociopolitical changes had to be assimilated; and distributions of surpluses, access to power, and cognitive self-understandings had to be monitored. From the mix, the stories of David and his leadership in Jerusalem emerged. Harmony and melody were brought together in a single score.

In order to identify the metamorphoses, we may return to the discussion at the beginning of the chapter and to the preliminary reconstruction described above. A series of checks and balances stand behind the developments represented there. By illustrating them, somewhat artificially, as poles of dialectical relationships, synchronic relationships and the contrasts dividing the two sides of the segmented system in the biblical model become clearer [Figure 34]:

Figure 34: Oppositions in David's Story

	200 mm rainfall line	
	↓	
	⟵	Sociopolitical movement
	: :	(Primarily literary
	: :	information)
Economic development	⟶	
(Primarily archeo-	: :	
logical information)	: :	
	: :	
Semi-agrarian; Agrarian	: :	Pastoral; Semi-pastoral
Political devolution	:	Political evolution
Saints	: :	Chiefs
Israel	: :	Judah
Samuel	: :	xxx
Samuel–Saul	: :	xxx
David the ally of Saul	: :	David the refugee
Philistine opposition	:→	
→ (Philistine)		David →
	→:	Philistine alliance
Ishbaal	: :	(Judahite) David
House of Saul	vs	House of David
	(Jerusalemite) David	
Ark	: :	David
	Jerusalemite Dynasty	

The outline exposes a number of characteristics in our hologram of Iron Age I.

1. The partial coherence and partial incoherence of images encoded in archaeological and literary sources correspond to the comparing/contrasting economic and sociopolitical spheres exposed in adaptation processes. Separating the domains of information, then allowing synchronic and symbiotic relationships in them to interfere constructively, and finally illuminating the interference pattern with information from comparative adaptation studies exposes a multidimensional image, i.e., a hologram of Iron Age I. The image has depth as one of its dimensions.
2. Gellner's two criteria for segmented systems are met. Balanced opposition at every stage of development and on every plane of classification is exposed, and segments correspond to territorial and kin groupings. The lists and genealogies that structure the Samuel model, introduce the Chroniclers' story, and control the Priestly view of the past demonstrate that the tradition continued to treat early Yahwist society as a series of nested segmented systems.
3. The archaeological image of the Iron IB peoples and the literary image of the Philistines' relationship to Israel, David, and Jerusalem cohere and expose mediator roles.

The last point deserves elaboration in light of adaptation studies. The vision of David's rise in the wake of Saul's demise mythologizes the shepherd youth passing from Judah into Benjamin and the house of Saul, into exile and the embrace of the Philistines, back to Judah as an ally of the Philistines, and finally to Jerusalem (twice) as chosen leader of Judah and Israel and a host of non-Yahwist groups. Samu-el exercises his saintly role among the devolving Isra-el federation by embracing the ideology and sociopolitical structures of the chiefly Saul and the tribe of Benjamin. A type 2 Iron IA organization evolves as "all Israel." The entity tends toward type 3 integration, but does not achieve it. Politically the Samuel and Saul elements (Isra-el and Benjamin) are unified, but economically they are partially separate, and socially they continue as sub-societies. Continuing LB archaeological forms alongside those of Iron I witness to the subgroups. The resistance to fuller integration here and at later stages is visible in the divisions that occur at the time of the post-Solomonic Schism.

The federation attracts allies and opponents. The prevailing myth is that marginal exogenous IB peoples, the traders, mercenaries, and artisans on whom the IA peoples depend, attack the federation militarily and symbolically by capturing their symbol of non-centralized unity, the ark. Material information confirms some unrest but cannot provide information about the fate of the religious symbol. Comparative sociology documents depreciating attitudes toward such marginal groups. However, the mercenaries customarily perform mediating roles and sometimes provide leadership for those who lord themselves over them. The presence of iron artifacts, smelters, and seasonal shrines at sites such as Deir 'Alla in conjunction with IB wares, may—as suggested above—explain the utilitarian economic base from the IB peoples and account for the Yahwists' dependency and the Philistines' threatening ascendancy. The Yahwists needed the Philistines, but they despised them.

David's initial association with Yahwism and Saul is documented not so much by the myths of origin that situate the youthful giant-killer, musician, and warrior in Saul's employ as by the stories of the transfer of the ark. There, marriage to Michal is alleged. Jerusalem's first connection to the religion, of course, depends on the stories of David.

Ethnographic comparisons explain how a role such as David's can be connected with both the ruling house of a federation and the coalition's principal opponent. We have cited studies on competition for paramountcy wherein a losing contender withdraws to an outlying zone to begin building a separate power base. The genealogies from Hebron and archaeological information from sites such as Tel Masos lend credibility to a similar process in Judah. Adaptation studies also demonstrate that affiliation with mediators facilitates a rise to leadership. The details are very sketchy in the sources, but a figure like David could exercise simultaneous but discrete leadership roles among the Philistines, Judahites, and northern all Israel alliance.

The centralization processes in Judah differ from those in the north. Ecology offers a partial explanation. IA pastoralists raiding, IB mercenaries trading, and David marauding eventually give rise to a nomadic state in which a mediator becomes head of a city-state and then is chosen by the ruling Yahwist council of Judah. John L. McKenzie's observations are correct (J. McKenzie, 1983: 30). The relationships between David and the Philistines are peculiar and close, and the association contributes to his rise. In the hologram, his rise to power begins with the Iron IB Philistines.

A type 1 form of nomadic state develops. Its duration cannot be determined. The northern chieftaincy apparently devolves further until the ruling council attempts homeostasis by seeking leadership within the southern federation. Again, association with the Philistines serves David well. Israel like Judah turns to one who has already demonstrated the compatibility of Yahwism, strong leadership, and accommodation with the mercenary mediators. There is little constructive interference from archaeology to support the specifics in this image, but the pattern of notional information and lack of it in records of action illumined by comparative examples make the biblical story plausible. The Yahwists remember choosing a Yahwist, and the Philistines, wisely, leave no record of their fatal mistake in allowing David to expand, except archaeological information suggesting that their expansion is henceforth contained or controlled. From the choice comes Jerusalem, an artificial administrative center for the nomadic state.

Relationships of constituent units to Jerusalem follow the adaptation models outlined above and vary according to ideology, ecology, and local precedent. A form approximating type 2 adaptation with separate social sub-societies, partial economic unity, and full political integration connects the two IA moieties to each other and to Jerusalem. Nomads, agriculturalists, and townspeople in Israel and Judah form the sub-societies as moieties in the same overarching segmentary system. The balanced opposition as well as competition for paramountcy continues. Not surprisingly, but ironically, the conservative northerners opt for a "chief" while in the south, where David rose with Philistine support, and in Jerusalem, he reigns as "king" (cf. Flanagan, 1981: 68). The second form of adaptation applies to units other than Israel and Judah. Relationships with non-Yahwist constituents are governed either by type 1 vassal-tribute models between the subjugated polities and the ruling house in Jerusalem or by parity treaties. The differences depend on the degree of integration. Again, type 3 adaptation is never achieved with any of the groups.

Diachronic Analogue to the Rise of Davidic/Iron Age Centralization (cf. Appendix II)

As studies on adaptation in ecologically diverse societies illumine the synchronic relationships in Iron Age I, so processual studies on state formation illumine its centralization. They are the melody that accompanies adaptive harmony. In an earlier study on leadership in Israel, I used Elman Service's evolutionary stages to elucidate biblical information regarding David. There, I identified Saul's reign and the early years of David as chieftaincies (1981). Frank Frick was making similar arguments simultaneously and has since presented them in a monograph (1985).

The decriptions here modify and expand those earlier impressions, but they do not radically alter them. Since the 1981 article was written, I have benefitted from a biography of King Ibn Saud, the founder-king of Saudi Arabia, and from extensive conversations with its author, Sheikh Mohammed Almana, the King's English translator and interpreter during the crucial years of state formation. A summary and analysis of those sources illuminates many important elements and processes in Iron Age sources. The book (Almana, 1980) is itself an interesting analogue for the story of the Davidic court (2 Samuel 9-20), and the stories told by Almana (1981) during the interviews are fascinating. In order to respect their integrity and that of the Saudis' experience, I give my account separately in Appendix II. There, the intriguing life of Ibn Saud, and the stories about the remarkable leader, have an existence of their own. They are worthy of study apart from any comparisons I or others might draw between them and characterizations of the early Iron Age. In this chapter, like the ancient psalmists, I include only brief summaries of salient points and leave the details for the longer narrative in Appendix II.

1. At the turn of the 20th century, Abdul Aziz Ibn Saud began a long career that led to the formation of the modern Kingdom of Saudi Arabia and to his own long years as the nation's first monarch. The trek started in exile in Arabia's east coast sheikhdoms where the conquering Rashids had forced Ibn Saud's father and family to flee from the central Nejd [Figures 37 and 38, pp. 328-329].
2. The return to power was remarkable. The story includes accounts of Ibn Saud's cunning and daring as well as reports of his prowess as a skilled warrior, magnanimous victor, benevolent redistributor of booty, and authoritarian leader. His loyal followers, British travelers, and President Franklin

Roosevelt all lavished praise on him as a skillful, wise, and forceful leader.

3. Besides the force of arms, Ibn Saud employed other tactics in unifying the disparate and hostile Arabian tribes. He drove out the Hashemite King of the Hejaz and conquered many groups by battle, but he also married into many tribes in order to gain their support and allegiance, and he won others by making it more profitable for them to be his ally than his enemy. He held a daily *majlis*, an "open house," to which every person in the Kingdom had access. He lived for several months at a time in areas outside the capital, Riyadh, in order to ensure such contacts. The tactics enabled the King to retain close relations with his people and to keep his finger on the pulse of the nation.
4. Religion played a very important role, however. Not only was the Wahhabi movement used as a basis for unity among his tribes, but strategies also involved forming the Ikhwan, the Brotherhood, a conservative if not fanatical Moslem element that tolerated no compromise with policies of modernization. The Wahhabi's belief in the absolute and exclusive sovereignty of their deity, Allah, and their shunning of all symbols that might distract from that belief served Ibn Saud both well and ill. The religious view enabled him to find a common ideology among his people, but it made them suspicious of moves toward centralization and its symbols. On religious grounds, Ibn Saud himself shunned the use of the title, "King," and was called by his given name even though he headed a nation that was becoming a fully centralized economic power in the Middle East.
5. One of Ibn Saud's strategies for settling the restless and warring Bedouin was to found villages around desert wells and to appoint religious leaders to instruct the habitants of Allah's will: Allah's wars were only those called by Ibn Saud. The plan failed, the Ikhwan rebelled, and Ibn Saud was forced to suppress the movement in a massacre of his own people.
6. Political stability finally came in the form of wealth generated by a new important economic resource. The discovery and concession of oil, a commodity needed in order to fuel the industrialized West and its great war,

brought large infusions of capital to the Saudi economy in time for Ibn Saud to continue his chiefly, redistributor's role. Hence, as he had done earlier by pacifying his followers with booty from the next victims of his raiding (who would quickly become followers and recipients in subsequent raids), the chiefly monarch continued to use largess and generosity as a means of pacifying and consolidating his people. For them, but never for himself, the new lavishness brought pressure on the conservative, spartan Wahhabi religious values.

Davidic Likeness

The stories of David are easily likened to the portrait of Ibn Saud. They are so similar in fact that it would be repetitious to cite the comparisons in their entirety. Many are merely strategies that are either common among tribal groups undergoing centralization or tactics that have been mentioned above. Three, however, deserve special attention.

First is the dual designation of David as *nāgîd*, and *melek* discussed above. Second, is the frequent reference to David's popular base and his immediate contact with it. Time and again, his success is attributed to his knowledge of local conditions and ability to form coalitions and win followers. In fact, Absalom reportedly assisted his revolt by exploiting fears that David was removing himself from his people. Third, like Ibn Saud, the pressures toward centralization displayed in the David stories are balanced by those against, and both are linked to the Yahwist iconoclasm. This has been exposed in discussions of the Dynastic Oracle in the Samuel model.

The comparisons are sufficient to make the biblical model realistic and plausible. The memories encoded in it and passed on to listeners and readers are of an astute and clever leader who used all the mechanisms of a segmented society to weave for himself a web of alliances that drew the people toward fuller centralization. Religion served the cause and frustrated it simultaneously. David, like Ibn Saud, appears more flexible in adjusting beliefs and economies than did some of his followers.

Religion, Leadership, and Stories of Centralization

The processes and stages along the path toward centralization in Jerusalem and Riyadh are similar. The stories as told by loyalist scribes impress readers who appreciate the subtle maneuvers and clever devices even though they might not share the religious views of the centralizing heros. Ibn Saud, we are told, embellished accounts of his own success, especially his taking of Riyadh, so often that the details of the event are no longer known. But they are not the story. The story is the event and its meaning for life in the Middle East.

Sheikh Almana, my informant, insists that he has not been forced to select among the stories and episodes that might be included in a biography of the King. Seemingly, in his mind and for his audience who were the outsiders, every episode and all of them together are the story of Ibn Saud. One more episode or less would not change the real story. The source of an account is not important. The story is his, Almana's, and it is Ibn Saud's, and the two are the same.

The same is true of the biblical story of David. In this case, because the David figure is a classic within a religious tradition, the issues are even more complex. Among the Yahwists, adjustments suggested by the story are mediated by rituals. And, as we shall see, the rituals not only regulate the metamorphoses, they also produce myths, poems, and narratives. How do societies like the Iron Age Yahwists adjust competing sociopolitical aspirations and economic needs? Which domain, if either, is home to religion? How do social worlds find their way into myths and stories? The answers are found in societies' responses to turbulence and change.

In earlier chapters, the systemic ecology of Roy A. Rappaport and the processualism of Victor Turner were introduced as analytical tools. Both anthropologists direct attention to similar socio- and cultural-religious questions and both find ritual central to the understanding of human thought and action. Their approaches, although different, are complementary.

As we have seen, Rappaport divides religion into three interrelated categories (religious experience, ultimate sacred propositions, and ritual) and relates them to social and ecological processes [Figure 35]. Religion is encoded with the tensions in those processes, and it regulates the processual domains.

His analysis of adaptive and maladaptive systems divides societies according to the integrity of their religion and its appropriateness for a particular ecological and social environment. Adaptive, we recall, means consonance between goal ranges (ecology) and reference values (ideology); maladaptive means dissonance. Hence, maladaptation of the sociopolitical to the ecological domain such as threatened Ibn

Figure 35: A Systemic Ecological Model of Religion

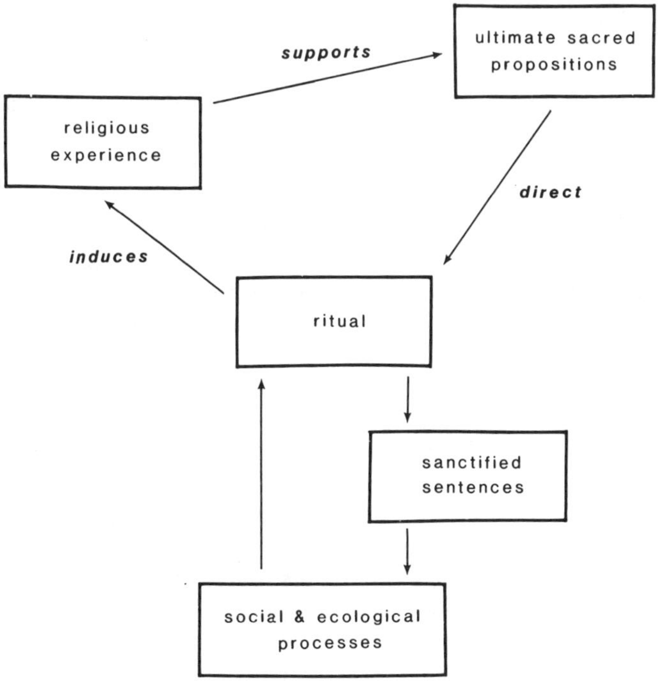

Model of Religion
(after Drennan)

Saud (cf. Appendix II) sometimes occurs during the adaptation of agrarian and pastoral ecologies. Then religion obstructs the adjustments needed to accommodate the sociopolitical aspirations to the new ecological realities. The David stories that show resistance to a temple and census illustrate the point. Stating the matter this way shows that "sociopolitical" is not identified with "religious," just as religion cannot be identified exclusively with an ecological-economic domain. Religion somehow is in both, in neither exclusively, and in the betwixt and between. Hence, even though economic explanations may illumine the emergence of new administrative structures in this and other cases, they fail to account for the retention of old folk models or the emergence of new ones that enable the new system to operate. Similarly, because synchronic, diachronic, and symbiotic relationships affect religion continually, we may assume that they are all at work in ritual and implied when rituals are discussed.

The transducer and homeostatic functions of religion and ritual serve adaptations by mediating, symbolizing, and enacting systemic adjustments. Thus, social cohesion is aided in a number of ways. Rituals strengthen the bonds that unite members in a single local social group. Rituals adjust unpredictable inequities by facilitating redistribution of resources. And they sanctify important messages and conventions by imparting to them affiliation with ultimate sacred postulates.

In different categories, these processes would describe the formation and transmission of a tradition. The circumstances explain how a seemingly insignificant outsiders' ideology gains a place for itself in the social dramas of the world. It captures a set of experiences in a powerful symbol and offers them and it as a root paradigm that infuses meaning in the lives of others.

Social values, norms, and representations are among the propositions to be sanctified ritually. Persons and institutions associated with the propositions, such as leaders and their offices, also achieve sanctity through rituals. So do the messages emanating from them. Rappaport shows a correlation between the level of the control mechanism or official making a proclamation and the degree of abstraction in the message. Lower level authorities speak concretely and in response to details. Higher messages are correspondingly more general, abstract, and vague. Systems depend on the differences as a way of freeing upper administrative levels from involvement in local matters and allowing their attention to be devoted to wider realms of importance. In this model, the ultimate pronouncements of the highest administrative office are so abstract as to be unverifiable and unfalsifiable, i.e., they are ultimate sacred propositions.

The postulates cannot be verified or falsified because they have no material referents (Rappaport, 1979: 228). The absence allows the postulates to remain flexible, capable of sanctifying numerous situations. Oversanctification, i.e., "overspecifying," leads to inflexibility and maladaptation. The postulates' acceptance in new situations is a function of their sanctification (Rappaport, 1979: 229). Messages and conventions from those in charge are credited with truthfulness which makes the pronouncements acceptable in society and, in turn, makes the response of the social group predictable.

The gradual escalating of biblical models in the cult where they lose details but retain the fundamental Davidic map suits this description. We have described the David myth in terms similar to

Rappaport's ultimate sacred postulates. As such, it is unverifiable and unfalsifiable, has a quality of unquestionableness, and is flexible enough to sanctify numerous situations. Only when the Davidic role in the model becomes oversanctified, and therefore inflexible and incapable of sanctifying change, is that particular application of the story rejected. Several times the biblical writers recast the story in order to revive its sanctity and remove its inflexible attachment to particular socioeconomic forms, institutions, or structures.

Applied to the transition toward sedentary, agrarian life witnessed during Iron Age I, Rappaport's model interprets the transitions and attempts to maintain group unity and harmony as ritual enactments. With sedentarization, migratory groups lose their flexibility for resolving conflicts by fissioning or fleeing. Surpluses are few. Competition for access to resources intensifies. And conflict either threatens or arises. The communities' response is to transfer the turbulence outside the community or onto another level through ritual where it is resolved religiously. For example, the strategy of dual, religiously legitimated paramountcy for a single leader enables distinctive economic and social systems to remain intact while integrating Israel, Judah, and others politically. The tactic preserves the procurement and distribution systems needed for subsistence but allows for adjustments and adaptations dictated by political and cultural realignments during Iron Age I. Thus, ultimate sacred propositions and rituals resolve or forestall conflict, either directly or by sanctifying the decisions of individuals or groups charged with ensuring order (cf. Drennan, 1976: 350).

Expansionist Example

Rappaport's model was first tested within a closed society where cultural representations and norms, geographical expanse, group identities, and social and economic needs remained relatively constant (Rappaport, 1968). Variables such as population density, dominance, climate, etc., affected his subjects' activities, and indeed were the object of his study, but by and large the subjects' world was self-contained. Whether the model would be useful in understanding open and expanding societies remained for Raymond C. Kelly's study of the Nuer and Dinka to demonstrate (Kelly, 1985).

The Nuer conquest of their neighbors, the Dinka, is an example of a maladaptive expansionist society. The maladapting, however, is rooted in unrealistic cultural norms and goals (reference values) rather than in the economy and ecological goal ranges of the regions. The latter play an important role, but in Kelly's judgment are not the crucial reasons for Nuer failure.

The ethnographic details need only be summarized. Among the Nuer, brideprices are paid in cattle. The price is religiously legitimated. Kelly finds that the minimal allowable price frequently exceeds the capacity of the Nuer's grazing lands. As a result, payment levels are maintained by raiding the Dinka. Cattle are seized and land taken, but a high percentage of the peoples living in the conquered areas are also assimilated into Nuer society. Because tribal holdings are distributed equally even among the captives, and because the acceptable brideprice increases in times of surplus, the temporary cattle surpluses only escalate the price and further deplete holdings. The addition of fertile, marriage-age females is also unbalancing because it further increases the demand for brideprice cattle. Marriages are either postponed or more raiding occurs. Both disrupt society. The spiral of maladaptation escalates.

The Dinka, on the other hand, customarily adjust their brideprice to conform to cattle supply. As a result, systemic adaptation is undisturbed and internal life remains wholesome and peaceful. Marriages are held on schedule and raiding is unnecessary.

The case illustrates the relationship between culturally defined reference values and biologically and ecologically defined goal ranges. It is not drought, overpopulation, mismanagement of herds, or conquest by a better-equipped people that upsets equilibrium among the Nuer, but self-contradictory cultural values. Kelly likens the situation to a thermostat controlling a furnace set to turn on at 65 degrees and off at 68 degrees while in the same room an air conditioner is set to drive temperatures down to 65 degrees. The systems are locked in maladaptive competition and one mechanism will eventually overrun the other or both will fail.

Rituals in Iron Age I

Our own description has gone beyond the scope of closed societies into the expansionist symbiotic worlds of agrarians and pastoralists. Like Kelly's investigation, the Yahwist case offers an opportunity both to apply Rappaport's model and to identify differences between his explanation of the Maring and our understanding of another society.

In light of the analyses given above, we may hypothesize that Yahwist rituals served to maintain equilibrium in Iron Age society (cf. Figure 35 above). Raiding and other forms of redistributing surely occurred as they do among the Nuer and Dinka, but opposing groups were also integrated ritually and came to accept shared sacred postulates.

Information in archaeological and literary analytical models testifies to the prominence of rituals in Iron Age I. Seasonal ritual centers such as Deir 'Alla, the appearance of iron in the manufacture of luxury (exotic) items and grave goods (including ritual implements and weapons), small cultic installations above the ruins of LB temples and shrines, and frequent references to the ark with its nomad/sedentary symbolism at a shrine attended by Eli and Samuel all reveal the value placed on ritual. One of the most illuminating examples, of course, is the relocation of the ark in Jerusalem and eventual construction of the temple.

The list includes items that are innately mysterious either by origin, process of production, or cultic entailment. For example, meteoric iron, the earliest known, comes from the heavens, is used in rituals, and finds its way into tombs. Later, when new technologies are developed for forging, the transformation and the forging process take on mysterious qualities of their own. Then they become symbols of the metamorphoses produced by the new substance's use in daily life (cf. McNutt, 1983). Hence, social, economic, and political adaptations associated with iron during Iron Age I become symbolically linked to the forging process and accordingly increase the need for sanctification and ritual. In the same way, and as part of the same transformations, new institutions and personalities require legitimation.

In this way, in the systemic ecology model, the ultimate sacred propositions of one group's religious system are borrowed, sometimes as marks of status, elevated to a new status within the integrated communities, modified accordingly, and invested anew with ultimate sanctity. The process is clear in Iron Age I when Yahwists adapt LB prototypes, merge northern and southern myths, combine sedentary and nomadic stories, pass around the symbolism of the ark, and so forth. As in other societies, the process explains the rapid diffusion of the religion and its propositions among highly disparate peoples. The process can be illustrated by an iconic model [Figure 36].

Figure 36: A Systemic Ecological Model of the Integrative Function of Religion

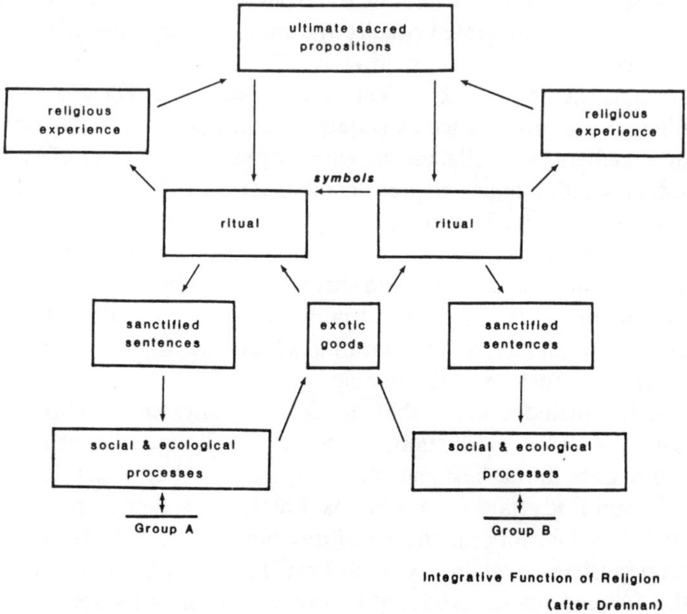

The integrative functions of the model explain religion's role in the social world behind the Samuel and Saul stories as well as in David's pacification and unification program. We have shown that resistance to centralization shaped the stories of dynasty and temple. Sedentary rituals are expensive. Goods and labor are consumed, prestige items must be acquired and often destroyed, specialists must be trained and supported. And a ritual system to support ultimate sacred propositions must be maintained. In light of this, it is hardly surprising that nomadic peoples do not develop independent, visible, permanent forms of ritual, or at least it is understandable why observers have failed to detect them.

But sedentaries in the devolving societies of the LB/Iron I transition also have no goods to spare. Temples and shrines, so-called stressors on the system, meet with resistance. Hence, the prohibition against building a temple in the David stories accurately reflects the socioeconomic setting of the period as well as segmented groups' predisposition against centralizaton. Reference values are coordinated with goal ranges.

A possibly fatal downward economic spiral is prevented by the prohibition against cultic and political overcentralization. Increased productivity such as is witnessed in Iron Age I—like the temporary surpluses caused by Nuer raids—raises social expectations and transforms the values encoded in ultimate sacred postulates. These could give rise to increased ritual specialization that in turn requires greater increases in productivity. And so on. Innovation and technological advances offer few opportunities to keep pace with the demands economically. But during Iron Age I these are already fully exploited by the new agrarian settlements' storage facilities and terraces. Iron, although potentially of great practical value, is still a luxury item and is less economical than bronze for utilitarian objects. Technological innovations are unavailable among nomadic elements except through trade with the outside, in this case, the sedentaries. Hence, the rejection of the legitimacy of the pressure toward an upward escalating spiral of products and expectations is accomplished by denying religiously and ritually the validity of the spiral itself. The solution is an extremely practical option, and perhaps the only one that would allow endogenous leadership and beliefs to survive without exogenous support.

Stated in other words, a sacred message prohibiting temple and establishing non-monarchic Davidic dynasty is linked to an ultimate sacred egalitarian proposition. The ritual and statements legitimate the absence of monarchy and temple. It raises the "void"—as it must have been viewed in the ancient Near Eastern world—to the level of sanctity. In an exceptional way, this is a case of an anti-cultic, ritualistic sacred postulate! It may, in part, explain why no other contemporary ancient civilization mentions David. Centralized polities have difficulty in understanding and relating to uncentralized groups. Then as today, the former consider the latter irrelevant. In any case, the model is adjusted later in order to allow temple building and to substitute the imposition of force as a means of maintaining order. But the change can only be introduced by retelling, restructuring, and rewriting the myth. The change must also be based on the root paradigm, the David figure. Shortly, however, political ends exceed economic means and the ends are protected in spite of their excess. The system becomes maladaptive. The means themselves collapse. The ends become the bases for argument and unachievable hopes pushed further and further into the future. The controlling hierarchy, which depends on sanctification, renders itself incapable of regulating the very processes that gave rise to it. Cognitive dissonance and systemic maladaptation combine to force a schism and a partial return to former alliances.

Kelly's concern is the Nuer who, in spite of their expansionist values, represent a single cultural group moving against another single group. The Near East during Iron Age I is much more complex. Several sets of reference values—themselves the products of diverse ecologies—that initially regulate areas with extremely varied goal ranges are brought into competition for dominance and, in the case of Israel and Judah, for extra-territorial acceptance. Equilibrium requires not only accommodation to one or two sets of goal ranges but to many and to long-standing cultural reference values as well. Realistic cultural norms are required, but historical models for centralization in the region include externally imposed order funded by taxes and conscriptions siphoned from the region's economy.

The complexity and the usual responses to it in the ancient Near East are important because they mean that a loss of equilibrium has different consequences in each of the two Yahwist moieties. To examine the differences would take us well beyond the Davidic era and into the post-Solomonic schismatic period. However, the anti-centralist political base in the wilderness traditions set the pastoralist Yahwists against monarchy. On that basis, we may note the irony in the acceptance of the ideology in the agrarian north where long-term experience of oppressive centralization affects all Israel in ways that are not experienced in Judah. As a result, in the latter, David's rise is more straightforward, while in the former, uncertainty and doubt restrain the process every step of the way. Like the Dinka, Iron I Yahwists sought realistic cultural norms, but in this case, within diverse ecological settings that made strategies complex and acceptance fragile.

Lack of information prevents observers from knowing how the non-Yahwists felt about Jerusalem's handling of the sociopolitical and economic balances. The slide of El worship into Yahwism in the north, however, suggests that all peoples were adapting and ritualizing the adaptations as they progressed.

Social Dramas

We have examined the structure of social dramas in an earlier chapter. There, we saw that the four-phase dramas often arise from political competition for limited resources such as land, wealth, power, or prestige (V. Turner, 1980: 152). Opposing factions are customarily led by individuals whose influence and powers of persuasion equip them to muster support for their cause. Many actually use the dramas to legitimate their own roles and views.

The description suits Iron Age I and puts in other words some of the issues analyzed according to the systemic ecology model. The approaches also share a concern for religion in society, an interest that leads Turner to apply this metaphor and that of rites of passage widely in his attempts to expose social discontinuities and continuities. The crises in the dramas, while disruptive and unsettling, expose stable social structures (continuities) as well as patterns of conflict (discontinuities). The former stand beneath the conflicts and remain basic and durable although they gradually change (V. Turner, 1980: 151). Changes, in fact, that must and do occur in times of adaptation are the causes of social dramas that are mediated by rites of passage. Because every social drama alters the structure of social fields such as the relationships among segments in a society (cf. V. Turner, 1985: 198), the image of David's Yahwist drama affects the transitions and metamorphoses outlined in this volume.

Social dramas allow us to examine the relationship between occurrences in a society and the society's myths. Turner boldly claims that social dramas, as he describes them, are universal (V. Turner, 1980: 152). They emerge in every society, where rituals, as in the dramatic structure, are one of the redressive actions societies choose in coping with crises. The realignments experienced during the liminal stage of the paradigm passage, illumine the tensions in the present society. The structures of the former that have been encoded in poems and stories associated with the ritual, now assign meaning to the present circumstances. Literary (or oral) expressions, therefore, arise from dramatic ritual settings and become interpreters of subsequent times and occurrences. The dramas produce stories of the dramas.

Thus, in the dramas, the relationship between past dramas and later similar processes is reciprocal. The dramas are recalled in stories that become models for subsequent actions. Like holograms, the past becomes present and the present is seen in the past. The paradigms provide structure and meaning for understanding new processes in later lives. Newly understood, the experiences turn back on the original story and drama to add meaning to them. Symbol and meaning are reciprocal; their texts are polyvalent. "In the redressive phase, the meaning of the social life informs the apprehension of itself, while the object to be apprehended enters into and reshapes the apprehending subject" (V. Turner, 1980: 156).

In the social drama paradigm, the third or redressive phase becomes a model for later redressive actions. In David's case, the relations of mediator encoded in his figure as well as his mediator's role among other persons, events, and institutions are paradigms for post-Davidic Yahwists. Hence, the place of the David figure in the poems and stories of the Bible! It is the symbol that accumulates patina while it becomes a classic.

A Davidic Hologram

The biblical images encode and transmit Yahwist responses to crises in Iron Age I and thereafter. These are holograms of life partially in phase and partially out of phase (i.e., social dramas) that are remembered and illumined by later turbulences and responses. The whole of subsequent human uncertainties is "seen" in the "records" of the past. Later Yahwists view the past, like one sees a hologram, as both real and intangible, but especially as complex, full of meaning, and meaningful. The meanings it has are retained in partial testimonies to be illumined by the viewers' comparable experiences.

Drama is also visible in the tells and surveys of Iron Age archaeology. Its richness and polyvalence come to light in the congruence and incongruence of the archaeology and stories, the myths that celebrate the role of Yahwism. The transitions seen in both domains are paradigms for lives lived in companionship with constant change. Like holograms and holomovements, the images are of many crossings. They encode and mediate the abandonments and discoveries, the promises and fulfillments, the betwixts and betweens that fill lives. On historical ground and mythical terrain, David's image is a representation filled with meaning and illumined by reality. David's figure is a classic. David's story is a social drama. David is a hologram of the early Iron Age.

But. . .

Appendix I

GEOGRAPHICAL AND ARCHAEOLOGICAL SURVEY

Seven geographical and archaeological zones within our analytical model are indicated in Chapter 3 (cf. Fig. 24, p. 190). They comprise extremely varied ecologies that support equally diverse socioeconomic strategies. Both types of information are important for social world studies, as is the need to move back and forth between inductive and deductive approaches. Because of this, a general view of regional diversity is presented in the analytical model in Chapter 3, and additional information is made available here. Again, in the second instance we merely 'scratch the surface' of the beautifully varied terrain in the eastern Mediterranean basin.

Zone 1: Northern Syria

Near the Syrian/Turkish coast in the mountainous Jebel Ansarieh, Jebel Akra, and Gavour Dagh regions, peaks up to +1600 m rise between the Mediterranean Sea and the floors of the Ghab and Amuq plains where the Orontes river winds northward. The river's basin is a lowland fault structure, part of the great rift system, approximately 80 km long and 16 km wide, lying approximately +200 m above sea level.

The area is an example of two important hydrology types in the Middle East. First, it is one of the few zones with a perennial river. Although the Tigris, Euphrates, and Nile systems with their tributaries affect extensive areas, the Orontes, Jordan, and Litani are the only continuously flowing rivers in the area central to our interest. Elsewhere, seasonal flow has left numerous wadi systems. The deep ravines are often flooded during rainy seasons when their impermeable soils are severely eroded. During dry seasons, however, many wadis are sufficiently well supplied from springs and basins that subsistence agriculture is supported.

Secondly, Orontes hydrology is endoreic, i.e., a closed or inland drainage system. In this case, however, the structure has broken through to the sea. The characteristics of the structure are especially prominent in the area of the Dead Sea. Low annual rainfall combines with physical features to form interior basins closed off from the sea by surrounding ranges. The basins are often guarded by outwashed alluvial fans caused by gravels and silts scattering down from slopes above, sometimes ending in marshes or saline bodies of water. In antiquity the Orontes valley was filled with such marshlands and swamps that remained until the mid-twentieth century C.E. when the river was channelized, the valley drained, and the lands claimed for agriculture.

West of the mountains, a number of wave-cut limestone terraces protrude toward the Mediterranean. They offer limited opportunity for cultivation between the range and the sea. To the east, the Ghab and Amuq rise from the Orontes floor to Jebels Zawiyeh and Akrad respectively. There elevations reach +600 m. Still further east, open plateaus of *terra rossa* soils and steep-sided hills stretch toward the Aleppo basin. From there, they give way to the Euphrates valley and the arid plains of the eastern desert. On the south, the Ansarieh range ends in the depression lowlands of the Tripoli-Palmyra gap that has filled with the rich alluvial deposits that make cultivation possible.

The two northernmost major E-W depressions described in Chapter 3 form partial borders from Zone 1. The area between them, i.e. north of the Tripoli-Homs-Palmyra corridor, contains many of the soil types found in other zones of the Mediterranean basin. These include ergesol surfaces in the limited beach areas along the Mediterranean and bench soils in the hills and mountains, but the most prominent are the brown and yellow-brown stoney soils and the fertile *terra rossa* soils in the plains and western plateaus.

Zone 2: Lebanon Range, Anti-Lebanon, Hauran, Jebl Druze, and Leja

South of the Tripoli-Homs-Palmyra corridor, a single anticline has formed the NW-SE Lebanon range. Although a variety of sandstones, marls, limestones, and lignites make its slopes fertile but generally impermeable, moisture is available because of the altitude. Elevations reach as high as +3083 m ESE of Tripoli so that heavy precipitation there and springs at +1000-1500 m combine to make modern irrigation possible.

East of the range, a fault-line marks the edge of the Biqa valley floor that rises +1000-1300 m at its highpoint near Baalbek. From there, it slopes gently to the north and south. Surface soils are thinnest at the divide which is the watershed for the Orontes and Litani rivers. Although the Biqa and its Litani river are often described as extensions of the Jordan rift, some geologists and geographers argue that they are one of a series of rifts that is intersected by others and divided into Arabah, Jordan, Biqa, and Orontes segments (Fisher, 1978: 404). In any case, folding and upheaving has caused elongated domes on either side of the system that helped to form highly individualized and varied geographical zones.

Three subregions lie east of the Biqa. The closest is an anticline divided into the northern Anti-Lebanon and southern Hermon ranges. The surface of the former is predominantly limestone and has fewer sources than the Lebanon range. Consequently, its slopes are better suited for grazing than for cultivation. Structurally, the latter is a continuation of the Anti-Lebanon, but in places it is nearly +600 m higher. Precipitation is correspondingly high. Snow covers its peaks for much of the year. Drainage flows westward to the Jordan and Litani rivers and eastward toward the Damascus oasis.

Next are the extensive Hauran lava flows east of Hermon and south of Damascus. Here, elevations reach +1000 m, winter rains are abundant, and surfaces rolling. Seasonal cultivation is possible. In fact, the region has been a granary of the Middle East in several historical periods.

Finally, further south and east is the El Leja region with its many caves and the basalt cone of the Jebel Druze that reaches to +1800 m. Where environmental conditions and human occupation have not modified the rugged surface, passage is difficult and possibilities for cultivation limited. Nevertheless, the basalt serves as an accessible building material, and occupants have devised strategies for surviving in the desolate area.

Zone 3: Uplands of Palestine

The slope and altitude of the Lebanon range diminish into a dissected massif south of Tyre where the Litani empties into the sea. Structurally, the anticline that comprises the range and the northern highlands of Cisjordan is broken into a number of detached blocks containing limestone, chalk, and small deposits of iron ore. Separate Upper (northern) and Lower (southern) Galilee regions can be isolated according to rainfall, vegetation, and settlement patterns. The Lower area ends abruptly at the edge of the third major corridor identified in Chapter 3. The cross-cutting fault that stretches from the Mediterranean to the Jordan rift and beyond forms the Esdraelon plain. The plain varies in width from about 30 km across at the sea to 2-4 km further inland. Near the Jordan, it widens again to 8-15 km. Its flat floor contains deep, black fertile soils composed of weathered limestone and basalt. Nearby springs make it highly suitable for agriculture.

The northern dome continues south of the valley where it gradually becomes more strongly anticlinal in the highlands, toward Jerusalem, and in Judah. Two synclines, one forming the region near Nablus, the other cutting a corridor between the Carmel and Iron hills, now divide the northern section into three distinct fold structures. The Carmel ridge extends inland SE of Haifa, the Iron hills form a small range further south, and a hilly area forms the edge of the Jordan valley. As a result the terrain is extremely varied, but the deep folds, striking warps, and low basins filled with *terra rossa* soils have been exploited by labor-intensive agriculture since antiquity.

In the central highlands to the south, the dome rises both north and south of Jerusalem, positioning the city in a topographical saddle. Erosion has moved the watershed of the entire dome eastwards and has caused the formation of three distinct zones extending along a N-S axis. The western foothills, the Shephelah, slope toward the sea; the main ridge and crest of the highlands rise in the center; and the eastern section, a desert zone, pitches sharply downward to the Jordan trough.

The Shephelah's broad terraces and low hills are covered by rendzina and alluvial soils and, because of diminished rainfall, erosion has been less there than in other regions. On the eastern side of the highlands, however, chalk and marl protrude on the surface. The area falls within the rain shadow, and the terrain is susceptible to vast erosion. As a result, the limited precipitation has caused a number of narrow, deep gorges running mostly in W-E directions.

Zone 4: Negev

The Negev forms a transitional geological zone between the highlands and Shephelah on the north and the Sinai on the south. Bounded on the east by the Wadi Arabah, the surface rises to a dome near Beersheba and declines in the west where a narrow coastland strip borders the Mediterranean. Although the Negev is primarily covered by thin layers of water-deposited sediments, the unit was formed from the southern tectonic lobe so that much of it is underlaid with the same geological complex as North Africa and Arabia. Therefore, its axes are not N-S as the Mediterranean and Arabah boundaries might suggest. Instead, the zone's geology is oriented along semi-circular lines fanning out toward the south where the Negev plateaus lead to the Sinai.

The Beersheba basin in the northern part of the Negev is filled with loess deposits exceeding depths of 30 m in some places. Alternating rains and droughts form surface crusts and produce flashfloods. Irrigation is possible, however, and agriculture can be extremely productive.

Zone 5: Coastal Plain

The narrow coastal plain that was seen in northern Syria widens and becomes increasingly open and continuous as it moves southward. While west of the Jebel Ansarieh it is little more than a series of small enclaves interrupted by mountain spurs reaching to the sea, south of Haifa silts from the Nile and Sinai have formed the expansive plain of Sharon and the Gaza strip stretching along the coast and inland toward the plains. Coastal areas overlaid with alluvial soils from the Judean hills formed swamps that have been converted to agriculture. Some of the only truly dynamic and semi-static ergosol surfaces in the eastern Mediterranean are found along the southern shore.

Zone 6: Jordan Trough

The Jordan depression marks the eastern boundaries of the Cisjordan highlands and Negev. Its lowest point, at the floor of the northern part of the Dead Sea, is -800 m lower than the surface of the Mediterranean. The shoreline of the enclosed body, however, is ca. -400 m. In the Wadi Arabah, sea level is reached approximately 130 km from the Dead Sea, North of the sea, the valley varies in width from 32 km near Jericho to 10 km near Lake Tiberias. The borders are almost entirely fault edges on the east and massifs on the west. Small streams have carved deep wadis at right-angles to the valley and some, such as the Wadi Mujib, are so precipitous that they prevent N-S passage along the trough. Northern depressions left by downwarping formed Lake Tiberias and the now drained Lake Huleh.

Zone 7: Eastern Plateaus

Above and east of the Jordan valley, upland areas caused by high faulting give way to vast plateaus stretching toward the Great Syrian Desert and the Wadi Sirhan. The terrain flattens and becomes a floor of desert flint and sand gofs watched over by the buttes and ridges left by the receding Tethys Lake. The surface varies from hilly and jagged badlands to open, gently rolling expanses, but a few kilometers east of today's Desert Highway, the climate and geomorphology make the area unsuitable for anything but seasonal pastoralism. Some of the highest elevations are on the plateaus of ancient Edom.

Appendix II

THE RISE OF IBN SAUD

In the summer of 1981, Sheikh Mohammed Almana was an elderly gentleman living in Al Khobar in Saudi Arabia's Eastern Province where he is Chairman of the Board of the Almana Hospital. I was his guest for five days. He invited me to visit with him for long hours, to accompany him as he kept his busy schedule of meetings with staff, visitors, and family, and to visit freely with his staff and family about himself and his hero, the King, who by every measure was a remarkable individual and a person of destiny. Sheikh Almana enjoys great stature in his community and among his employees. With humility, he credits his successes and blessings entirely to his deity, Allah. Among them he lists long years, good health, worthwhile work, a large family educated in America, and a share of earthly goods. His book is a portrait of the King, as the subtitle suggests. I am grateful for the glimpse it offers and for the kindnesses and hospitality shown me by the Sheikh and his staff in Al Khobar.[3]

Born in Zubair on the trade route between Iraq and the Nejd, the central region of Arabia, Almana was taken to Bombay at the age of ten by his father. The father and his brothers were horse traders who supplied the British and Indian military and civilians. Almana spent the next twelve years in India where he was educated in Jesuit schools in Bombay and Punjab. He became fluent in English and Urdu as well as his native Arabic and was seemingly destined for the medical profession, a career encouraged by his father and by the Arab community in Bombay.

But he was fascinated by stories about Abdul Aziz ben Abdul Rahman bin Feisal al Saud and was determined to enter his and his peoples' service. The young and idealistic Almana worked his way back to Arabia through Iraq as a journalist until on May 26, 1926, he began his service to Ibn Saud, eventually becoming the chief interpreter and translator for English and Urdu, a position he held until 1935 when he left Saudi Arabia to return to his father's business in Bombay. After a few more years in India, he returned to his native land, this time to the Eastern Province where he worked first as a translator for Caltex, since Aramco, and eventually formed a construction firm and subsequently built the hospital, a project that satisfied his early ambition to be associated with the medical profession.

Almana's years at court were years of nation building and he was, in a sense, a court scribe. The Hejaz had just been conquered and there were no further territorial frontiers to challenge Ibn Saud. This meant that the leader had to devise ways of settling the volatile tribal warriors in order to ensure their loyalty. This period and the years of the king's rise starting in 1902 form the major part of Almana's book and our conversations.

Ibn Saud's Roots

But Ibn Saud's story and Almana's tales begin much earlier. The former can be traced to Saud Ibn Mohammed Ibn Mugrin Ibn Markhan Ibn Ibrahim Ibn Musa Ibn Rabia Ibn Mana Ibn Assad Ibn Rabia Ibn Nizar Ibn Maad Ibn Adnan, an ancestor from a section of the Aneyza tribe who was invited in 1446 C.E. to settle in the region of Dariya (Almana, 1980: 257). The proximate history begins much later, however, and can be conveniently divided into three major periods. The first extends from 1745 to 1818 when Mohammed Ibn Saud finally joined the religious revival of Mohammed Ibn Abd al-Wahhab and agreed to be the movement's political arm. The second spans 1818 to 1902, a period first of relative independence for the House of Saud, but finally a time of submission to the rival Al-Rashid house in Ha'il (1865-1902). The last stretches from 1902 until the present, i.e., from Ibn Saud's capture of Riyadh to his death in 1953. For our purposes, the last period is the most important, although we must recall that the roots of Ibn Saud's success reach back to the origins of the Wahhabi religious movement and that the Saud family has for years headed an elaborate tribal organization upon which centralized monarchy could be readily built (Almana, 1981).

Wahhabism—Unitarianism to its adherents—is a transcendental movement within Islam that stands as an alternative to immanent wings such as the Sufi brotherhoods. Derived from the legal school of Ahmad Ibn Hanbal, it shares Hanbalism's insistence on the absolute incomparability of Allah. Puritanical in their application of this doctrine, the Wahhabis reject as polytheism all structures, persons, and beliefs that obscure the oneness of the deity. Saints are banned, ornate graves shunned, sacred stones discarded, domes on mosques removed, and even formal observances of the Prophet's birthday forbidden. Tobacco, music, silk, precious stones, ornate minarets, and prayer beads all fall under the same strictures.

Obedience to the pristine law found in the Koran, the Sunna, and the first three centuries of the *ijma* is fundamental for the Wahhabis. They profess strict egalitarianism that admits no exception. The *jihad* is invoked as a means of expanding the community but is not limited to armed conflict. Their leader, the *imam*, may declare a *jihad* in order to justify policies especially against those whom the Wahhabis consider polytheists (Winder, 1980: 8-15).

The political potential for leaders embracing the movement is clear. The House of Saud aligned with Wahhabi leaders and used the movement's iconoclastic fervor to overcome tribal and regional differences by harnessing religious passion for equality and purity to aspirations for strong, central leadership.

By the time Abdul Aziz Ibn Saud was born, probably in November 1880, the Sauds had lost power and were living in abject poverty. Dariya had been reduced to ruins, and two hundred years of struggle between the Rashids and Sauds for control of central Arabia had given the former the upper hand. Even Riyadh, which the Sauds held, was continuously threatened.

Abdul Aziz Ibn Saud's Rise

The Saud family fled from Riyadh in 1890. They traveled first to Bahrain, then Qatar, and then Kuwait where they lived a restless life under the protection of the coastal sheikhs who were also originally from the Aneyza tribe [Figures 37 and 38]. During their sojourn, occasional raids were made against the Rashids, but none was successful. By the time young Abdul Aziz reached his twentieth year, boredom with life, longing for the excitement of battle, and pride spurred him to urge Sheikh Mubarak of Kuwait to equip him for a long trek back to his family's city. He knew that he had no power base while under another's protection, and a recent loss in battle with the Rashids had cost Mubarak greatly, so the Sauds' welcome was wearing thin.

The story is of a talented young leader who rises from exile to form and become head of a wealthy nation. Ibn Saud was given forty of the least desirable camels, a few companions, and sent on his way. He hoped to win supplies, warriors, and tribal allegiances by raiding as he went, but he met only limited success. He gained perhaps 200 followers, not enough to satisfy him (Philby, 1952: 11). Here, biographers' reports begin to vary, probably because Ibn Saud recounted his adventure frequently (hundreds of times according to Almana), each time with the elaborations typical of Arabian folklore (Howarth, 1980: 17; Lacey, 1981: 46-47).

The young leader realized that success depended on daring action, a heroic deed that would win the admiration and allegiance of large numbers of followers instantly. He determined to capture Riyadh. The journey took him from Kuwait through the desolate Rub al-Khali, traveling by night and camping by day for safety's sake and in order to keep the Ramadan fast. After

Figure 37: A Tribal Map (Partial) of the Arabian Peninsula

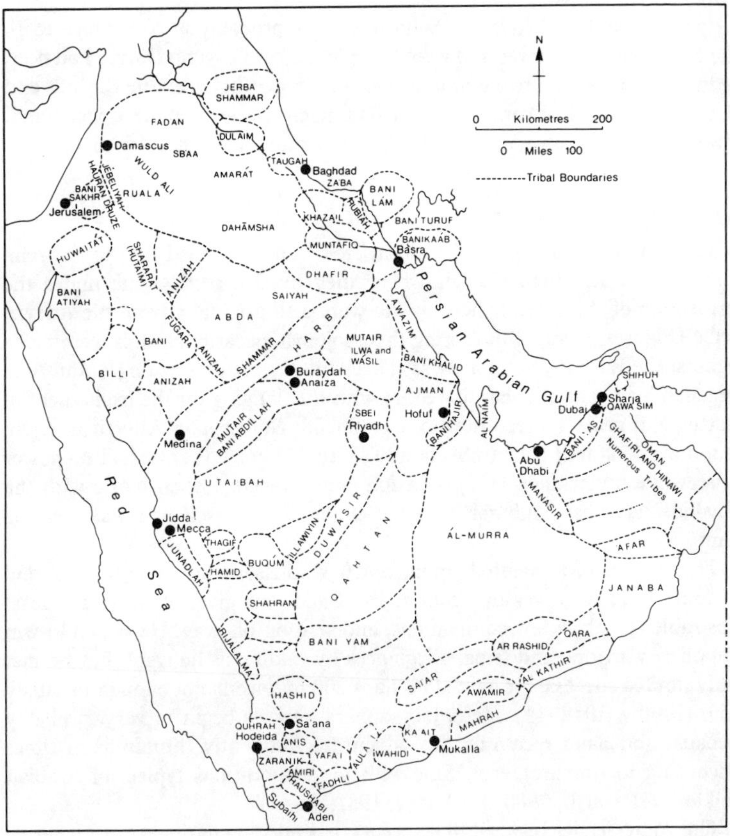

Figure 38: Unification and Formation of Saudi Arabia after Ibn Saud's Capture of Riyadh

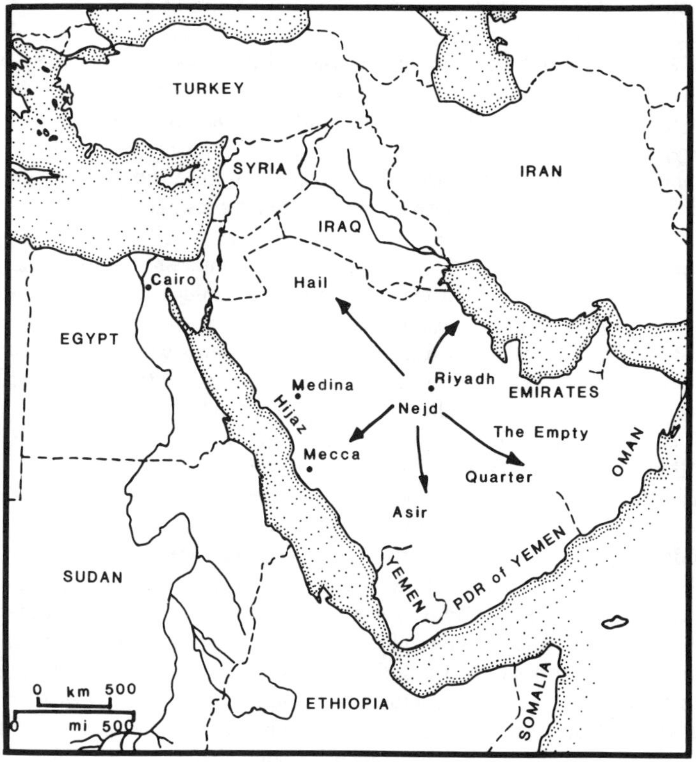

ten days he reached the vicinity of Riyadh where he announced his plans to his followers. So hopeless was the task that only a handful—some say six, others ten—chose to accompany him into the city. The rest were told to stay in camp, await the leader's return, and if he did not appear by the break of dawn, to flee for their lives.

Ibn Saud scaled the city wall, landing on the terrace of a person he knew to be a former servant of the Saud family. The individual's wife had wet-nursed Saud when he was young, and so the intruder was quickly at home and learned all that the couple knew about the movements of Ajlan, the Rashid Amir of the city.

The governor routinely slept in a well-guarded fortress but after morning prayers crossed the street to the house of one of his wives. Abdul Aziz and his supporters advanced to the house to await their victim. According to the story, Ajlan's wife had also been wet-nursed by the same woman. The bond established a quasi brother-sister relationship with Ibn Saud that prevented her from forewarning her husband of Ibn Saud's presence (Almana, 1980: 36).

Ajlan emerged on schedule. Abdul Aziz, beside himself with excitement, sprang into the street. Ajlan managed to retreat through the fortress gate, and according to Almana, into the sanctuary of the mosque. Saud's cousin, Abdullah Ibn Jelawi, pursued him and cut him down with a sword. The surprise attack and killing threw the garrison into turmoil. Rumors spread at once that a huge force had fallen on the city. Ibn Saud marched to the center of the courtyard, proclaimed himself victor, and the garrison surrendered.

All biographers record two consequences of the capture. First, the tactic was successful in winning the immediate alliance of many followers. The Rashids had been oppressive, and the Sauds were a welcome relief. But the sudden shift in loyalties must also be seen as evidence of the fragile and volatile relationships that bind tribal peoples. Impressions and perceptions of power are nearly as important as power itself. Both strengthen the leader's hand. A strong leader is followed because it pays to do so. Bounty from raids moves through tribes with almost the same effects as currency in centralized economies. Therefore, the capture of Riyadh was important because it launched Ibn Saud on an upward economic spiral that enabled him to satisfy the needs and whims of his followers and therefore to gain more allegiances.

A second consequence was the display of wisdom that accompanied the Sauds' return to the city. Abdul Aziz did not claim the sheikhdom for himself, but turned leadership over to his father, even kissing the father's feet and offering his back as a step when his father dismounted from his camel. Such deference is cited as a valuable quality in the young leader, and it was a quality he retained throughout life. The father accepted the son's humility and abdicated at once, appointing the conqueror effective head of state and commander of the forces (Philby, 1955: 240).

Other Personal Qualities of Ibn Saud

Every commentator on Ibn Saud's success cites the same factors in his rise. Foremost were his personal qualities and his intimate knowledge of inter-and intratribal politics. Both equipped him exceedingly well for the personal legitimacy every successful Arab leader must possess (Hudson, 1977: 18-20).

The similarities to reports of David are striking. When listing Ibn Saud's advantages, David Howarth writes:

> Next, he had his own physical distinction, and that was worth more. Most of the Bedouin were small, but he was six feet three and lean and muscular, and he could out-run or out-ride or out-shoot almost anyone else in the desert. He towered above his companions; nobody could ever neglect his presence. He was not merely handsome, his dark stern eyes and strongly-jutting nose, and his black hair and sparse beard and full lips with their suggestion, contradicting the eyes of amorous sensuality, made him the very type of Arab masculinity; and he was certainly aware of this quality and used it (Howarth, 1980: 27).

Elsewhere Howarth and Holden and Johns are content to repeat the description that Gertrude Bell forwarded to the Arab Bureau after her first meeting with the leader:

> Ibn Saud is now barely forty, though he looks some years older. He is a man of splendid physique, standing well over six feet, and carrying himself with the air of one accustomed to command. Though he is more massively built than the typical nomad sheik, he has the characteristics of the well-bred Arab, the strongly marked aquiline profile, full-fleshed nostrils, prominent lips and long, narrow chin, accentuated by a pointed beard. His hands are fine, with slender fingers, a trait almost universal among the tribes of pure Arab blood, and, in spite of his great height and breadth of shoulder, he conveys the impression, common enough in the desert, of an indefinable lassitude, not individual but racial, the secular weariness of ancient and self-contained people, which has made heavy drafts on its vital forces, and borrowed little from beyond its own forbidding frontiers. His deliberate movements, his slow, sweet smile, and the contemplative glance of his heavy-lidded eyes, though they add to his dignity and charm, do not accord with the western conception of a vigorous personality. Nevertheless, report credits him with powers of physical endurance rare even in hard-bitten Arabia. Among men bred in the camel saddle, he is said to have few rivals as a tireless rider. As a leader of irregular forces he is proved daring, and he combines with his qualities as a soldier that grasp of statecraft which is yet more highly prized by the tribesmen (Holden and Johns, 1981: 64).

Almana, still fiercely loyal, adds a religious note by claiming that Ibn Saud grew to adulthood "... gifted by God not only with all the talents and bravery of his ancestors, but also with a uniquely inspired hand of leadership capable of forging a permanent kingdom in the desert where others had failed" (Almana, 1980: 26). His fuller, more explicit portrait expands Howarth's description:

> By the time Prince Abdul Aziz Ibn Saud had reached his twentieth year it was already plain that God had marked him out for great things. In sheer physical size he towered above his companions, being fully six feet two inches tall, a most unusual and impressive height for a desert Arab. Everything else about his appearance was on the grand scale, from his strong, jutting nose to his full lips and fine beard. He had a natural kingly bearing and was dignified and graceful in his movements; as a horseman and warrior, he was beyond compare. From an early age he had about him a charm and magnetism which those who experience it found impossible to describe in mere words. In short, he was a born leader, and had already built for himself in Kuwait a substantial personal following (Almana, 1980: 30).

Although a skeptic might dismiss a portion of these descriptions as hero-worship, hyperbole, or mere repetition, it is hard to deny impressions so consistent and widespread. Philby was awestruck by the man. British officer and Arabist William Shakespear claimed to have formed a warm friendship on his first meeting and never abandoned his affection and support (Holden and Johns, 1981: 41). Shakespear was so respectful that he accompanied Ibn Saud into battle against the Rashid forces and stayed to die when others fled ahead of the enemy sword. Even Franklin Roosevelt, himself two months away from death, was so impressed when they met that he remarked that he had learned more about Palestine in five minutes with Ibn Saud than from all the memoranda he had read on the subject (Holden and Johns [quoting Colonel Eddy], 1981: 137).

Ibn Saud's Resources

When Ibn Saud turned to conquering, pacifying, unifying, and settling the warring tribes, he did not rely on charm alone. His familiarity with tribal intrigues served him well. A villager by birth and residence, he learned the Bedouin ways thoroughly especially during his sojourn among the Al Murrah in the Rub al-Khali. An expert rider and warrior, Ibn Saud is reported to have been so adept at following tracks as he had been taught by the Al Murrah that he could tell the sex, color, origin, and destination of a camel from its footprints! Such stories probably tell us more about the society that passes them on than about the individual featured in them, but they do indicate that the villager Ibn Saud was respected for knowing his way around the nomadic world.

Less suspicious are reports of his marital prowess. Because the leader observed Arab norms regarding scrupulous privacy about his family life, no exact count of wives, concubines, and slaves can be made. Estimates of wives range from twenty to three hundred. Forty-five sons were reportedly born of wives. No tally of daughters is available, but this does not signal an unimportant role for women in Ibn Saud's world.

Though Ibn Saud maintained the Islamic limit of four wives at one time, he had favorites to whom he remained married for decades. Nevertheless, he used marriage as an effective political and military tool. He frequently divorced one wife (legally an easy matter in Islam) before embarking on a campaign in order to be able legally to take another if circumstances dictated. A hostile tribe could be easily subdued, enemy territory crossed, or useful information gotten in return for the honor of the leader marrying a tribe member.

Militarily, Ibn Saud's campaigns can be divided into three groups. First was the series of tedious raids and battles that won the allegiance of the sundry tribes in the central and eastern provinces. Almana insists that many were *ghazzu*, i.e., raids made for sport with little bloodshed and with outsmarting an opponent the primary objective (Almana, 1981). Circuitous routes and cat-and-mouse tactics characterized them, but the stakes were high. Such victories finally won Ibn Saud control of much of Arabia and the title of Sultan of the Nejd.

The second group comprised campaigns against the Hashemite Sherifs in the Hejaz, the western zone. There, the Turkish and British roles glamorized by T. E. Lawrence were important. The Hashemites had become intolerable to the Sauds. Once they were subdued, Ibn Saud's domain not only stretched from coast to coast, but he also enjoyed control of the lucrative pilgrimage routes and the commerce that accompanied the Hajj to Mecca.

When the Sherifs of Mecca were expelled, Almana states, the Hejaz bureaucracy was kept intact except for the highest echelons which were filled by Saud family members (Almana, 1981). Also, with the Hejaz, Ibn Saud gained the title "King of the Hejaz" which he bore together with "Sultan of the Nejd" (Almana, 1980: 75).

With no territories left for expansion, the emerging bureaucracy and the King-Sultan's generosity at the daily *majlis* created a serious strain on economic resources. Almana and others report the hardships (Almana, 1981). Foreign aid was becoming available but it was primarily from Western countries trying to control policies against other Westerners. In order to stabilize his central government, Ibn Saud developed a plan for settling the Bedouin and turning them into peaceful, controllable, productive agriculturalists. The plan called for establishing settlements around tribal wells and appointing religious *ulemas* to instruct the settlers in the truths of Wahhabism. Religion was reasserted and the Ikhwan, i.e., the Brotherhood, was created to carry out the mission. Almana insists that the settlement policy was one of the most important events in Saudi Arabian history but is overlooked by Westerners (Almana, 1980: 81).

The Ikhwan were to bring political stability while helping economically and militarily. New agricultural production was expected to fuel the redistributive generosity of the leader while settled conditions were to provide warriors whose whereabouts would be known and whose loyalties could be trusted in times of conflict.

The transition was neither easy nor total. Bedouin resisted sedentarism and recalled that the pleasure had gone out of Bedouin life when Faisal Ad-Dawish (Chief of the Mutair) built the first mud hut (Almana, 1980: 81). The Bedouin soon became restless and bored which, coupled with their religious intolerance, made them eager for battle.

The Ikhwan especially became increasingly troublesome. Uncalled and unwarranted ruthless raids into neutral territory or into Iraq threatened the stability of the national alliance and invited British intervention. The problems eventually led Ibn Saud into his third type of campaign, those directed against his own followers.

Ikhwan leader Faisal Ad-Dawish, who had once been subdued but later pardoned for health reasons, recovered to plague Ibn Saud. The leader was angered by such ingratitude and marched against the Ikhwan, finally suppressing them in a blood bath at Sibillah in 1929. The zealots had overstepped their limits and, unlike Ibn Saud, could not adjust their beliefs to make room for change and modern life.

For our comparison, suppression of this rebellion and its consequences after 1932 are important. The adjustment of sociopolitical (religious) aspirations to conform to economic realities was an issue. Ibn Saud resolved it in favor of change and accommodation. A few years later, after Sibillah, the Kingdom of Saudi Arabia was formed and "His Majesty King of the Hejaz and Sultan of the Nejd" became the "King of Saudi Arabia." Almana claims that when unification was being discussed he proposed "Arabia" as the country's name (Almana, 1981). He believed the name allowed for further expansion and for the formation of a united Arab kingdom, a view the King seemed either not to understand or desire. But Philby had gotten the king's ear and convinced him that "Saud" should be in the title. I asked whether the king shared Almana's "vision" and was told no. Perhaps Almana's estimation was colored by his negative feelings toward Philby.

More importantly, Almana asserts that Ibn Saud resisted the title "king" on religious grounds. "Only Allah is King," I was told (Almana, 1981). The title was first adopted from the Hejaz because the office was there. Ibn Saud accepted the title but refused to use it himself. "King" was not used in Riyadh even after the formation of the kingdom, and the king preferred that it not be used in his presence anywhere (Almana, 1981). Ibn Saud had achieved regal splendor and power, but he thought of himself as tribal sheikh.

The new monarchy and its trappings did not obscure the chiefly traits of the founder-king. Principal among them was Ibn Saud's continuing use of the *majlis* as a means of keeping in touch with his people and for redistributing goods that he owned or had been given. Later in his reign when he heard that staff members were shielding him from individuals seeking advice and assistance, he ordered every sheikh and amir to announce that every citizen had access to him and that he would personally attend to their problems. In this way, the redistributive economy of the chiefdom continued. Abdul Aziz Zanil Jawasir, Almana's cousin who had been attached to the Political Committee and eventually became translator for Prince Faisal in the Hejaz, volunteered to me that the king never had money. "What he received he would redistribute immediately." Employees were penniless but were cared for simply by presenting a request to the king. However, the largess flowed in two directions. Visitors to the *majlis* brought all kinds of gifts depending on rank and means (Almana, 1980: 178). Prestige, generosity, and wealth, all highly prized virtues in Bedouin life, were communicated and were more valuable than the gifts themselves.

Almana personally characterized life in the court as "semi-Bedouin" and contrasted it with the cultural riches of Bombay (Almana, 1981). The king was shrewd and wise, according to Almana, but illiterate except for the Koran. (This claim does not accord with impressions given by others, but I recall no one who explicitly contradicts Almana.) As a sage, his conduct, especially his treatment of enemies, sometimes appeared contradictory or paradoxical. Winning Arabia, Almana insists, was easier than keeping it.

Against this background, the paradoxes take on meaning. Al Rashid challenged Ibn Saud to a duel by sending a letter citing the futility of the bloodshed and perpetual hostility between them. He suggested a winner-take-all contest between them personally. Ibn Saud's size, agility, and experience seemed to dictate acceptance, but he declined. With his usual tact, he replied, commending Al Rashid for his courage and noting the opponent's willingness to die. He went on to state that he preferred to live and remarked that "a man who wanted to live left the path of wisdom if he fought a man who wanted to die" (Almana, 1980: 45). Besides, he insisted, such matters were Allah's business and the deity would decide the final outcome.

When Ibn Saud's forces finally killed Al Rashid, it was by warriors' stealth. Like the ancients, the forces entered Al Rashid's camp, took him by surprise, and hurried back to their leader bearing the victim's signet ring as proof of their success. Ibn Saud refused to believe until he saw the head of the deceased. The warriors willingly fetched the gruesome trophy (Almana, 1980: 48).

Displaying the head of a victim was not a totally exceptional show of Ibn Saud's strength. Such manifestations offered irrefutable proof of victory, impressed the ordinary citizens, and ensured their allegiance. But the procedure was not usual. Ibn Saud was widely known for his magnanimity in victory and courage in defeat. His treatment of the Rashidi princes following the killing of Al Rashid is an example. Many of them, including the troublesome Mohammed Ibn Talal, were taken as honored guests into Riyadh where they eventually became members of the court (Almana, 1980: 59). As with Meribaal in the David stories, the hospitality served a dual purpose by making the princes guests while putting them under guard. On one occasion, Ibn Talal tried to escape dressed in woman's clothing, an act that failed and caused him embarrassment for the rest of his life. Following the attempt, he was kept under tighter guard but was also allowed to accompany the king into battle, although under close surveillance.

The practice of co-opting allies from among enemies through forgiveness and generosity is not peculiar to Saudi Arabia. It ensures the victor that the vanquished will not rise again, and it leaves the opposition leaderless and aimless. When integrated into loyal service, the vanquished have in a sense also achieved their victory because they gain access to the limited resources they previously sought through force. The victor in turn has secured the talents of a proven organizer who is capable of mobilizing large followings.

Importance of Ibn Saud's Biographer

Almana's position cast him in a role where his views represent Saudi and courtly domains of notions. In speaking of court life, he offered an insider's view of events and personalities. Reviewers have noted that his book has warmth, knowledge, affection, and a liveliness that other biographers, even Philby, lack (Little, 1980; Legg, 1980; Mostyn, 1980). His own assessment explains why:

> We were the king's brains, his arms, his legs, everything. We knew everything that was going on. We traveled with him and had access to his *majlis* anywhere. He got his information from us and we carried out his wishes. We would hear about where he had gone and what he had said even when we were not present. The court talked among themselves (Almana, 1981).

He went on to describe how the court traveled with the king because it was his "personality." "Without us he would not be who he was." Almana's brother, who had also been a translator in the court, and his cousin from Bahrain, the translator from the Hejaz, agreed.

In Almana's view the correspondence of the book to events is very close. Speaking of his desire to write, he recalled that he was Jesuit-trained and had thought about writing a book like Yeats, Shelley, or Austen. But he realized he should be in Arabia and should write about Ibn Saud. He had been fascinated by the king for years and in 1915 had begun to collect stories about him to be written later. In three different contexts, each time approaching the question from a different direction, I asked how he selected the episodes finally included in the book. From all the available stories, memories, anecdotes, documents, and records, how did he choose? Always I was given the same reply. Almana denied that he had made a selection! He insisted that the book is a portrait, as stated in the subtitle, not a selection of materials. It is the king! Almana was so adamant that I received the impression that my question lacked sensitivity for Ibn Saud's personal integrity and the unity of the biography that makes him known. Neither were mosaics, and every episode captured something of the whole person.

When asked for whom Almana wrote, he replied, "The World." The book was for outsiders because "the Nejdi [Arabs in Central Arabia] already know these stories better than I." Regardless of whether friends and staff directly influenced the writing of the text, as has been hinted, Almana certainly considers the book his own and feels that it is the whole story of Ibn Saud. Like a hologram, the whole image is in every part.

Similarities between Ibn Saud and David

Almana's book and conversations demonstrate that the views expressed are his own. But comparing episodes with those in the David stories proves neither the latter's historicity nor the motives of the storytellers. Even an overall pattern of similarity does not confirm Davidic history. It is the relationships and tensions in Ibn Saud's and David's stories, and how the former illumines the coherence and interference in ancient sources, that is important. The changes and tensions fall into three groups. Each is found in Almana's stories and the Bible, each nests cumulatively in the other, and each illustrates the simultaneous pressure for and against change.

a. *Personal Metamorphoses*

First are the personal changes in the leader. Ibn Saud, a sedentary villager, became acceptable in the nomadic world and at the center of an emerging bureaucracy. He put his stamp on each. He adopted the various lifestyles of his people and found no reason to choose among them. But on another level there was progress from the hinterlands of Dariyah and coastal exile to a nation's capital. Although Riyadh in his day was hardly an urban center, it grew in importance and complexity as Ibn Saud gained authority.

But traditional restraints caused the court to move seasonally in order for Ibn Saud to hold his daily *majlis* in the Hejaz and Eastern Province some months each year. This prevented centralization from developing too rapidly and from coming between him and his people. It also allowed him to continue to receive first-hand knowledge of the tribes.

The same ability to live in several worlds is noted in comments about Ibn Saud's regal physique. Descriptions note his size, appearance, bearing, and glance, but witnesses admit that he defied their expectations. He embodied and personified a betwixt and between quality by being both a sheikh in a king's role and a king with a sheikh's qualities.

Ibn Saud's self-perception seems to have matched his image. In Riyadh, he continued to live in the large but simple fortress that had been his home since its capture. Ambivalence about monarchical titles did not prevent him from willingly and actively gaining personal control over most of the peoples of Arabia. And yet as his power increased, his reliance on tribal tactics continued. He used marriage effectively in building the nation and reportedly relied heavily on the advice of Nura, his sister, and Hassah, a favorite wife from the Sudari family. So close was he to Hassah that her sons, known as the "Sudari Seven," have shared many of the country's most powerful positions. Her position in the harem at the time continues to win them offices such King, Minister of Defense and Aviation, Minister of Interior, Deputy Minister of Defense, Governor of the Riyadh Region, and Deputy Minister of the Interior thirty years after the founder's death. Moreover, all the kings to date have been sons of Ibn Saud. The patterns demonstrate that in spite of the extraordinarily rapid move toward modernity, the country and its royalty have retained the traditional values Ibn Saud embodied.

b. *Systemic Change*

But systemic change, the second kind of metamorphosis on our list, came slowly in spite of the vibrance and early economic power of the new nation. Ibn Saud's continuing reliance upon the *majlis* has been cited. Likewise, the continuing tribal values allowed Ibn Saud and his first successors to retain control over the country's wealth and to redistribute it as if they were sheikhs and sole owners. Inadequate infrastructures and accounting systems eventually caused great problems and embarrassment for the royal family. Although the stories of lavish excess popularized in the media did not begin until after the oil concessions, the collection, payment, and distribution systems were already causing dissension shortly after the capture of the Hejaz (Almana, 1980: 174-175; 196-198). Only gradually did circumstances force tribal custom and family preference to make way for governmental ministries with budgets and accountability.

A final example illustrates both of the first two paradoxes and the way Ibn Saud's self-perceptions affected his administration and those dealing with him. Following the Crimea Conference in 1945, President Franklin D. Roosevelt arranged to meet the king in the Great Bitter Lakes in Egypt. The president quartered on the U.S.S. Quincy and provided the U.S.S. Murphy for Ibn Saud. The president's log of the trip that was "restricted" until the end of World War II tells the story.

Wednesday, February 14:

At anchor, Great Bitter Lake, Egypt.

. . .

1120: The MURPHY came alongside and moored port side to the QUINCY. As she came alongside she presented to those of us in the QUINCY a most unusual and strange sight. The destroyer's decks, usually stripped, were covered with Oriental carpets and gold-gilded chairs were scattered about the decks. King Ibn Saud sat with great natural dignity and charm in one of the gilded chairs on the forward part of the destroyer's superstructure deck. The various other members of his party, dressed in their flowing robes and accessories, were standing about the decks. The King's guard, with rifles, scimitars and long swords very much in evidence, were lined up—single file—along the starboard side of the destroyer's forecastle, facing us in the QUINCY. They were, no doubt, every bit as much amazed as we were at what was transpiring.

. . .

Although a cabin was assigned the King while aboard the MURPHY, he preferred to live outdoors. Awnings were rigged in tent like style on the destroyer's forecastle and King Ibn Saud lived there at night, just as if he were making a pilgrimage to somewhere in the vast desert regions of his own homeland. The "tents" were heated by charcoal bucket fires (The White House, 1945: 44-45).

. . . [summary entries after 2330:] . . .

The sovereign of Saudi Arabia is generally known abroad as King Ibn Saud. His full name is 'Abdul 'Aziz ibn Abdul Rahman al-Faisal Al Saud. He is known to his subjects as "The King" or as "'Abdul 'Aziz".

. . .

The King is first a Moslem and secondarily an Arab. As the leader of the Wahhabis, guardian of the Holy Places of Mecca and Medina, and as an independent Moslem sovereign, he considers himself the world's foremost Moslem and assumes the defense of Moslem rights. Hence his opposition to Zionism. The Wahhabis regard themselves not as a sect, but as the only true Moslems, while non-Wahhabi Moslems are considered to have lost the purity of their faith.

The King's party brought along their own foodstuffs in the MURPHY, mainly native fruits and live sheep. The King had wanted to bring along some 50 or 60 sheep for this purpose (and to assist in feeding the MURPHY's personnel) but was dissuaded from doing so because of space limitations. The MURPHY left Jidda with seven live sheep and a deck load of fruits and other miscellaneous luggage. The sheep were quartered on the ship's fantail and daily slaughterings were done there.

The King also brought large jugs of water for his personal use. He drinks water from two holy wells, one near Mecca and one near Riyadh.

Enroute from Jidda to Great Bitter Lake, everyday just prior to prayer

> time one of the higher officials of the party would contact the ship's navigator and request a bearing on Mecca. The chaplain would then lead the congregation in prayer, facing in that direction.
>
> A direct radio circuit was set up from the MURPHY to the Prime Minister at Mecca, each half hour the radio operator (who was the Saudi Arabian Director of Communications) would call Mecca and, using Arabic language but international procedure, ask "O.K.?". Mecca would reply "O.K." and sign off. The King also had in his party an official whose sole duty it was to monitor all the radio news broadcasts and report their substance to him (The White House, 1945: 48-49).

The scene portrays poignantly two societies struggling to understand each other and one society caught between the ecologies of sparsely populated desert regions and economies of a Western militarized world. The Arabian leader was forced by choice and circumstance to function in both. Judging from the impression he made on Roosevelt, he met the challenge admirably. His simplicity and reverence on one level did not hinder his dealing shrewdly, insightfully, and self-interestedly on another.

c. *Religion and Change*

Finally, and most importantly, Almana' s stories demonstrate how Ibn Saud used religion to negotiate the shoals betwixt and between his several worlds. Wahhabism inspired his rise, inflamed his followers, solidified his settlement scheme, influenced his self-understanding, and, as Roosevelt recognized, continued to dominate his daily life. But its conservative tenets also caused severe problems. Uncontrollably zealous Ikhwan threatened his national security until he was forced to suppress them violently. General religiously based resistance to modernization slowed the move toward Western 20th century ways, but Ibn Saud himself adjusted his ideology. For example, radios were an especially important educational and propaganda instrument among the desert nomads. Religious resistance to them was overcome only by convincing the people of radio's usefulness in spreading Allah's message, and to do so Ibn Saud personally broadcast recitations from the Koran several times a day. In subsequent administrations, the same religious sensibilities continued to dictate policies toward family, women, tourism, trade, development, and many other national interests.

Roosevelt's perception of Ibn Saud as a religiopolitical leader was correct. The monarch functioned simultaneously on several planes of endeavor and juggled competing representations that floated in the minds of observers and his people. Politically, centralized and uncentralized, i.e., national and tribal, aspirations competed as did Riyadh's and the provinces' interests. Religiously, faith in the absolute sovereignty and universality of the deity divided believers' feelings about monarchy. On the one hand, with Ibn Saud, Allah spoke with one voice—and that was good. But on the other, Wahhabis resisted a monarchy that might upset the proper relationship between the deity and the political leader, threaten traditional values, and inaugurate customs not literally sanctioned by the Koran.

The iconoclasm of Wahhabism made the tension all the more acute. In fact, when I asked Almana several times about the rituals of kingship, the king's inaugurations in the Hejaz and later in Riyadh, how battle victories were submitted to Allah, and what ceremonies accompanied the king's official functions, he denied all ritual implications. He overlooked even the *majlis*. Yet his book mentions episodes of tribal leaders processing before the king to offer obeisance one by one following their defeat. It describes in detail "the symbolic acceptance of defeat by a vanquished chief" whereby the women of the Ad-Dawish were formally, properly, and for three days put under the protection of the Sauds (Almana, 1980: 109-110). Likewise, following the capture of Mecca, "He [Ibn Saud] entered the Holy City, not as a conquering monarch, but with bared head and dressed in the simple robes of a pilgrim" (Almana, 1980: 72). Apparently, the king's religious and political roles were so closely entwined that Almana failed to accept the distinction my questions implied.

The integration of domains did not create a theocracy but it did merge the symbols of religious, social, political, and economic realms and bestowed them on the person of the king. The political and religious wings that initially brought the Wahhabis and Sauds together were both dominated by Ibn Saud. Whether this would have happened if Wahhabism had developed its own religious symbols is a moot point. But tying religious and political fates together and investing their outcome in a single leader, Ibn Saud's fortunes were certainly and inextricably linked to his ability to control Wahhabi feelings. Paradoxically, he was legitimated religiously, but he also became a sign and bestower of religious legitimacy.

Appendix III

SAULIDE AND DAVIDIC GENEALOGICAL CHARTS AND LISTS

Symbols used in the charts are: Δ signifies males; O signifies females; = signifies marriage or concubinage.

1 Sam 14:49–51

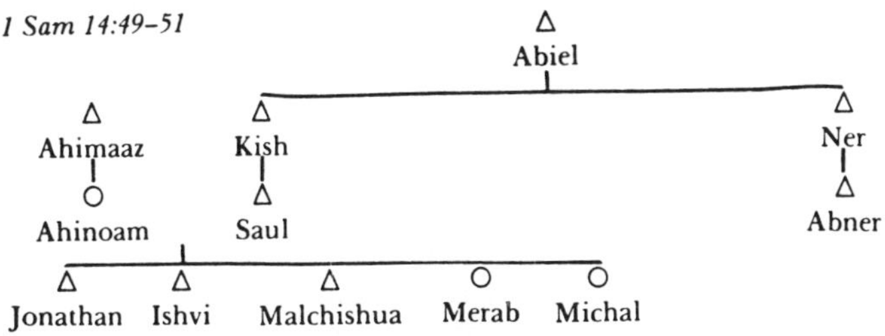

1 Sam 31:2 = 1 Chr 10:2

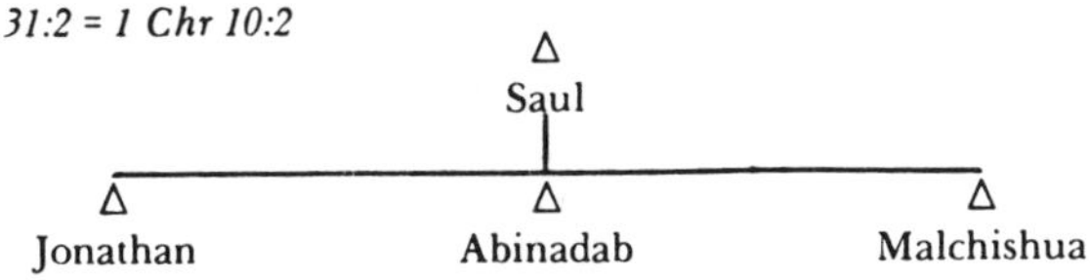

2 Samuel 11; 12:24–25

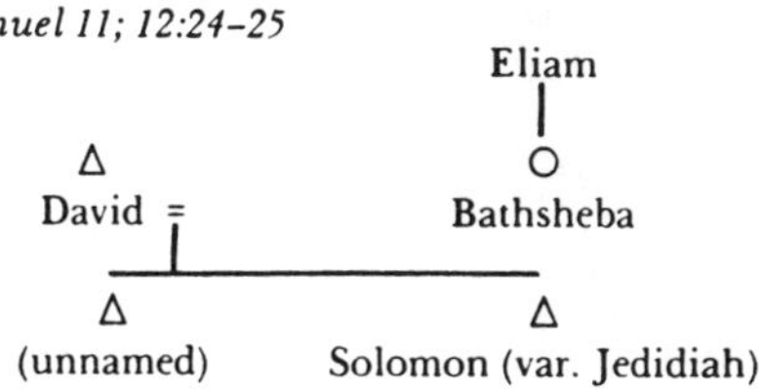

2 Sam 17:24

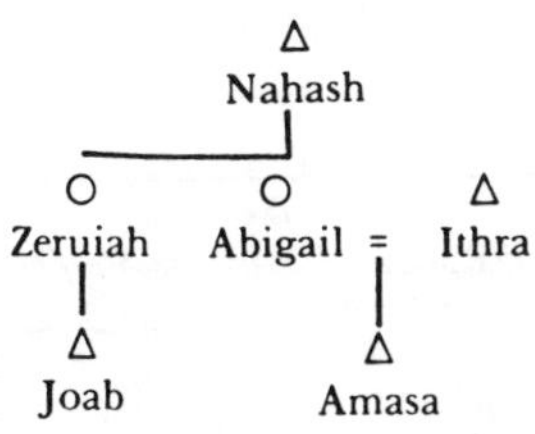

2 Sam 21:7–8

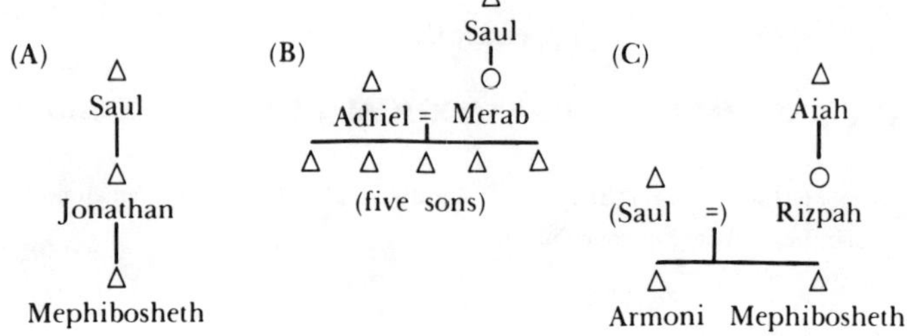

I Chr 2:9–17

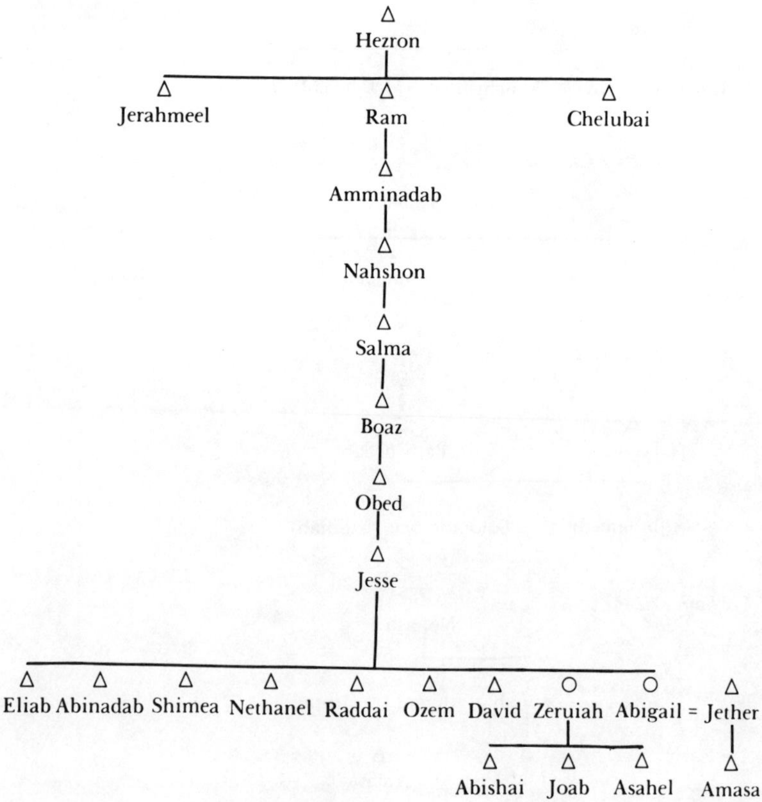

I Chr 8:33–40

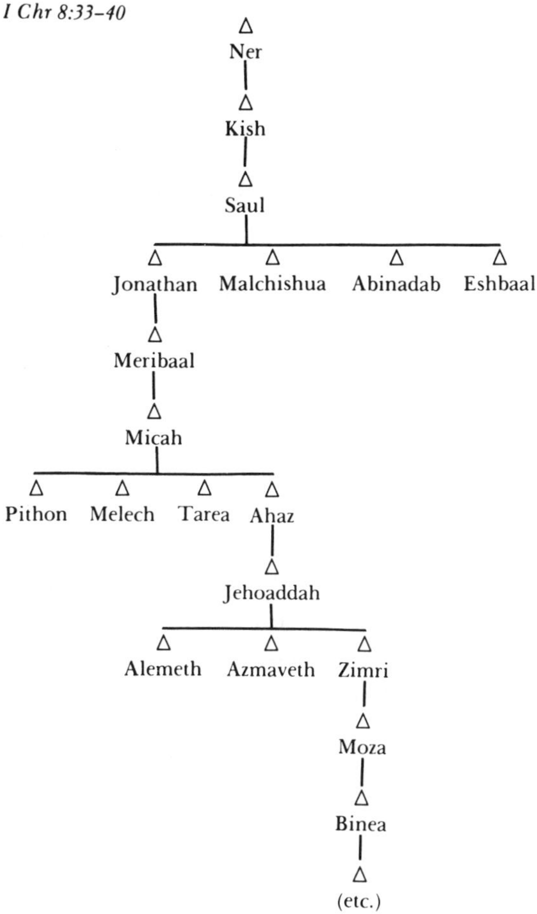
Ner
Kish
Saul
Jonathan
Malchishua
Abinadab
Eshbaal
Meribaal
Micah
Pithon
Melech
Tarea
Ahaz
Jehoaddah
Alemeth
Azmaveth
Zimri
Moza
Binea
(etc.)

I Chr 9:39–43

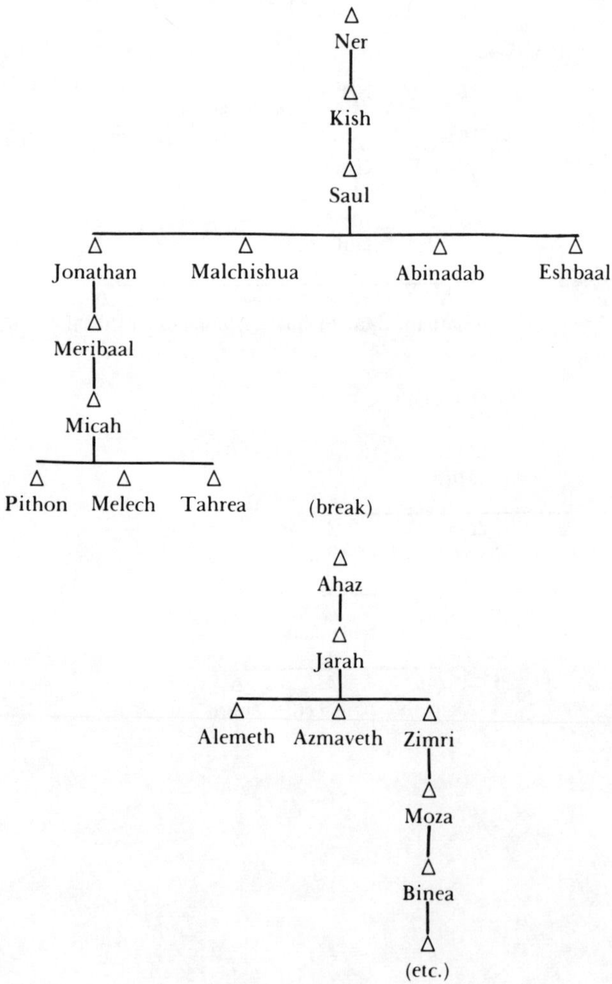
Ner
Kish
Saul
Jonathan
Malchishua
Abinadab
Eshbaal
Meribaal
Micah
Pithon
Melech
Tahrea
(break)
Ahaz
Jarah
Alemeth
Azmaveth
Zimri
Moza
Binea
(etc.)

Ruth 4:18–22

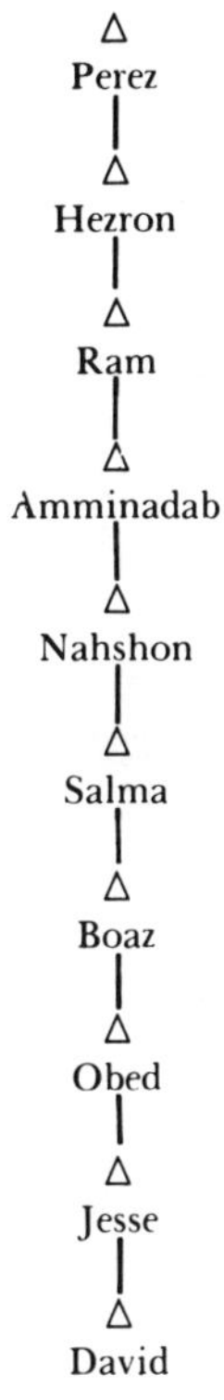
Perez
Hezron
Ram
Amminadab
Nahshon
Salma
Boaz
Obed
Jesse
David

(Lists of sons with mothers' names born to David at Hebron and Jerusalem)

2 Sam 3:2–5	*1 Chr 3:1–9*	*1 Chr 14:3–7*
(Hebron)	(Hebron)	
Amnon (Ahinoam)	Amnon (Ahinoam)	
Chileab (Abigail)	Daniel (Abigail)	
Absalom (Maacah)	Absalom (Maacah)	
Adonijah (Haggith)	Adonijah (Haggith)	
Shephatiah (Abital)	Shephatiah (Abital)	
Ithream (Eglah)	Ithream (Eglah)	
2 Sam 5:13–16		
(Jerusalem)	(Jerusalem)	(Jerusalem)
Shammua	Shimea	Shammua
Shobab	Shobab	Shobab
Nathan	Nathan	Nathan
Solomon	Solomon ("four by Bathshua")	Solomon
Ibhar	Ibhar	Ibhar
Elishua	Elishama	Elishua
	Eliphelet	Elpelet
	Nogah	Nogah
Nepheg	Nepheg	Nepheg
Japhia	Japhia	Japhia
Elishama	Elishama	Elishama
Eliada	Eliada	Beelida
Eliphelet	Eliphelet	Eliphelet

NOTES

1. Wilson's description is as follows:

> I begin with questions of interpretation of problems raised by the biblical text, although these questions may be very general (e.g., the phenomenon of prophecy in Israelite society). After defining the problem, I look for comparative data that speaks to the problem. At this point both ancient (mainly Near Eastern) and modern (mostly raw anthropological) data are collected and analyzed to see if I can find any patterns, no matter how complex. If I think that such patterns exist, then I formulate a hypothesis that similar sorts of patterns might have existed in Israelite literature and society. I then test the hypothesis against the biblical text. This testing involves two things: (1) a search for evidence to support or challenge the hypothesis and (2) an application of the hypothesis to apparently unrelated or obscure material to see if I can make more sense out of it than previous interpreters have. At this point the text remains the controlling factor in the process. Any adequate hypothesis must adequately explain what is in the text. The hypothesis may say more than the text says, but it cannot say less. Successful hypotheses can then become tools for new interpretations (Wilson, private communication, May 4, 1984).

2. There are more than fifty kinds of holograms, each with its specific technology. The description here generally suits transmission holograms and reflecting holograms made on glass panes. Embossed holograms, such as those stamped on the substrata of credit cards or affixed to journal covers, employ the same fundamental technology, but with variations in the processes. The surface is silver, the images have a limited depth of field, and a spectrum of colors is visible. The characteristics needed for our use, however, are present in all holograms.

3. Sheikh Mohammed Almana died June 9, 1987. Word was received after this manuscript was completed.

BIBLIOGRAPHY

Abel, F.M. 1935-1938. *Géographie de la Palestine*. 2 Vols. Paris: J. Gabala.

Abramson, Nils. 1981. *The Making and Evaluation of Holograms*. New York: Academic.

Ackroyd, Peter R. 1981. "The Succession Narrative (so-called)." *Interpretation* 35: 383-396.

Aharoni, Yohanan. 1979. *The Land of the Bible*. Philadelphia: Westminster.

—1982. *The Archaeology of the Land of Israel*. Trans. Anson F. Rainey, London: SCM. Originally published, Jerusalem: "Shikmona" Publishing, 1978.

Aharoni, Yohanan and M. Avi-Yonah. 1977. *The Macmillan Bible Atlas*. New York: Macmillan.

Aharoni, Yohanan, Volkmar Fritz and Aharon Kempinski. 1974. "Excavations at Tel Masos (Khirbet el-Meshash): Preliminary Report on the First Season, 1972." *Tel Aviv* 1: 64-74.

—1975. "Excavations at Tel Masos (Khirbet el-Meshash): Preliminary Report on the Second Season, 1974." *Tel Aviv* 2: 97-124.

Ahlström, Gösta W. 1986. *Who Were the Israelites?* Winona Lake, IN: Eisenbrauns.

Ahlström, Gösta W. and Diana Edelman. 1985. "Merneptah's Israel." *Journal of Near Eastern Studies*. 44: 59-61.

Ahmed, Abdel Ghaffa M. 1973. "Tribal and Sedentary Elites. A Bridge Between Two Communities." Pp. 75-79 in Cynthia Nelson (ed.). *The Desert and the Sown*. Berkeley, CA: University of California Institute of International Studies.

Albright, William F. 1932. *The Excavation of Tell Beit Mirsim. Vol I. The Pottery of the First Three Campaigns*. Cambridge, MA: American Schools of Oriental Research.

—1938. *The Excavation of Tell Beit Mirsim. Vol. II. The Bronze Age*. Cambridge, MA: American Schools of Oriental Research.

—1943. *The Excavation of Tell Beit Mirsim. Vol. III. The Iron Age*. Cambridge, MA: American Schools of Oriental Research.

—1945. 'The Chronology of the Divided Monarchy of Israel." *Bulletin of the American Schools of Oriental Research* 100: 16-22.

—1957. *From the Stone Age to Christianity*. 2nd ed. Garden City, NY: Doubleday. First edition, Baltimore: Johns Hopkins, 1940.

—1964. *History, Archaeology and Christian Humanism*. New York: McGraw-Hill.

—1966. *Archaeology, Historical Analogy, and Early Biblical Tradition*. Baton Rouge: Louisiana State University.

—1969. *Archaeology and the Religion of Israel*. 5th ed. Garden City: Doubleday.

Almana, Mohammed. 1980. *Arabia Unified. A Portrait of Ibn Saud*. London: Hutchinson Benham.

—1981. Personal Interviews. Al Khobar, Saudi Arabia.

Alter, Robert. 1981. *The Art of Biblical Narrative*. New York: Basic Books.

Atlas of Israel. 1970. *Atlas of Israel*. 2nd edition. Jerusalem: Survey of Israel, Department of Labour.

Augé, Marc. 1982. *The Anthropological Circle*. Cambridge: Cambridge University.

Ball, Edward. 1982, "Introduction." Pp. xv-1 in Leonhard Rost, *The Succession to the Throne of David*. Trans. Michael D. Rutter and David M. Gunn. Sheffield: Almond.

Baly, Denis. 1974. *Geography of the Bible*. Revised edition. New York: Harper and Row.

—1984. "The Geography of Palestine and the Levant in Relation to its History." Pp. 1-24 in W.D. Davies and Israel Finkelstein (eds.). *The Cambridge History of Judaism*. Vol I. Cambridge: Cambridge University.

—1987. *Basic Biblical Geography*. Philadelphia: Fortress.

Barton, John. 1984a. *Reading the Old Testament*. London: Darton, Longman and Todd.

—1984b. "Classifying Biblical Criticism." *Journal for the Study of the Old Testament* 29: 19-35.

Barth, Fredrik. 1959-60. "The Land Use Pattern of Migratory Tribes in South Persia." *Norsk Geografisk Tidsskrift*. Bind XVII: 1-11.

—1961. *Nomads of South Persia*. Boston: Little Brown.

Beaumont, Peter, Gerald H. Blake, and J. Malcolm Wagstaff. 1988. *The Middle East: A Geographical Study*. 2nd edition. London: David Fulton.

Beidelman, Thomas O. 1974. *W. Robertson Smith and the Sociological Study of Religion*. Chicago: University of Chicago.

Bellefontaine, Elizabeth. 1987. "Customary Law and Chieftainship: Judicial Aspects of 2 Samuel 14.4-21." *Journal for the Study of the Old Testament* 38: 47-72.

Bennett, Crystal -M. 1983. "Excavations of Buseirah (Biblical Bozrah)." Pp. 9-17 in J.F.A. Sawyer and David J.A. Clines (eds.). *Midian, Moab, and Edom*. Sheffield: JSOT.

Binford, Lewis R. 1962. "Archaeology as Anthropology." *American Antiquity* 28: 217-225.

—1968. 'Some Comments on Historical versus Processual Archaeology." *Southwestern Journal of Anthropology* 24: 267-275.

—1972. *An Archaeological Perspective*. New York: Seminar.

—1977. *For Theory Building*. New York: Academic.

—1983. *In Pursuit of the Past*. London: Thames and Hudson.

Black, John Sutherland and George Chrystal. 1912. *The Life of William Robertson Smith*. London: A. and C. Black.

Black-Michaud, Jacob. 1986. *Sheep and Land*. Cambridge: Cambridge University.

Blenkinsopp, Joseph. 1966. "Theme and Motif in the Succession History (2 Sam. xi 2ff.) and the Yahwist Corpus." *Supplements to Vetus Testamentum* 15: 44-57.

—1969. "Kiriath-Jearim and the Ark." *Journal of Biblical Literature* 88: 143-156.

Bohm, David. 1965. *The Special Theory of Relativity*. New York: W.A. Benjamin.

—1980. *Wholeness and the Implicate Order*. London: Routledge & Kegan Paul.

Boling, Robert G. 1988. *The Early Biblical Community in Transjordan*. Sheffield: Almond.

Boserup, Ester. 1965. *The Conditions of Agricultural Growth*. Chicago: Aldine.

Bounni, A., E. & J. Lagarce, N. Saliby. 1979a. "Novelles archéologiques Ibn Hani." *Syria* LVI: 416-417.

—1979b. "Rapport préliminare sur la deuxième campagne de fouilles (1976) à Ibn Hani (Syrie)." *Syria LV*: 233-301.

Braemer, Frank. 1984. "Prospections archaeologiques dans le Hawran (Syrie)." *Syria* LXI: 219-250.

Braidwood, Robert J. and Linda S. Braidwood. 1960. *Excavations in the Plain of Antioch*. Chicago: University of Chicago.
Briggs, John P. and F. David Peat. 1984. *Looking Glass Universe*. New York: Cornerstone Library.
Bright, John. 1956. *Early Israel in Recent History Writing*. Studies in Biblical Theology, 19. London: SCM.
—1976. "The Organization and Administration of the Israelite Empire." Pp. 198-208 in Frank M. Cross et al. (eds.), *Magnalia Dei*. Garden City: Doubleday.
—1981. *A History of Israel*. 3rd ed. Philadelphia: Westminster.
Broshi, Magen and Ram Gophna. 1986. "Middle Bronze Age Palestine: Its Settlement and Population." *Bulletin of the American Schools of Oriental Research* 261: 73-90.
Brueggemann, Walter. 1968. "David and His Theologian." *Catholic Biblical Quarterly* 30: 156-181.
—1971. "Kingship and Chaos (A Study in Tenth Century Theology)." *Catholic Biblical Quarterly* 33: 317-332.
—1972. "On Trust and Freedom. A Study of Faith in the Succession Narrative." *Interpretation* 26: 3-19.
—1985. *David's Truth*. Philadelphia: Fortress.
Bunge, Mario A. 1964. "Phenomenological Theories." Pp. 234-254 in Mario A. Bunge (ed.). *The Critical Approach to Science and Philosophy*. New York/London: Free Press/Collier-Macmillan.
—1973. *Method, Model and Matter*. Boston: D. Reidel Publishing.
Campbell, Edward F. 1968. "The Shechem Area Survey." *Bulletin of the American Schools of Oriental Research* 190: 19-41.
Carlson, R.A. 1964. *David, the Chosen King. A Traditio-Historical Approach to the Second Book of Samuel*. Stockholm: Almqvist and Wiksell.
Carneiro, Robert L. 1981. "The Chiefdom: Precursor of the State." Pp. 37-79 in Grant D. Jones and Robert R. Krautz (eds.). *The Transition to Statehood in the New World*. Cambridge: Cambridge University.
Childs, Brevard S. 1970. *Biblical Theology in Crisis*. Philadelphia: Westminster.
Claessen, Henry J.M. and Peter Skalnik (eds.). 1978. *The Early State*. The Hague: Mouton.
—1980. *The Study of the State*. The Hague: Mouton.
Clarke, David L. 1973. "Archaeology: the Loss of Innocence." *Antiquity* 47: 6-18.
—1978. *Analytical Archaeology*. 2nd edition revised by Bob Chapman. London: Methuen. First edition 1968.
Clements, Ronald E. 1976. *One Hundred Years of Old Testament Interpretation*. Philadelphia: Westminster.
—1984. Review of Edmund Leach, *Structuralist Interpretation of Biblical Myth* in *Theology* 87: 306-308.
Coats, George W. 1981. "Parable, Fable, and Anecdote. Storytelling in the Succession Narrative." *Interpretation* 35: 368-382.
Cohen, Ronald and Elman R. Service (eds.). 1978. *Origins of the State*. Philadelphia: Institute for the Study of Human Issues.
Cole, Donald P. 1973. "The Enmeshment of Nomads in Sa'udi Arabian Society: The Case of the Al Murrah." Pp. 113-128 in Cynthia Nelson (ed.). *The Desert and the Sown*. Berkeley, CA: University of California Institute of International Studies.
—1975. *Nomads of the Nomads: The Al Murrah Bedouin of the Empty Quarter*. Chicago: Aldine.

Collingwood, R.G. 1961. *The Idea of History*. Oxford: Oxford University. Originally published 1946.

Conrad, Geoffrey W. and Arthur A. Demarest. 1984. *Religion and Empire. The dynamics of Aztec and Inca expansionism*. Cambridge: Cambridge University.

Conroy, Charles. 1978. *Absalom Absalom! Narrative and Language in 2 Sam. 13–20*. Analecta Biblica 81. Rome: Biblical Institute.

Coote, Robert B. and Keith W. Whitelam. 1987. *The Emergence of Early Israel in Historical Perspective*. Sheffield: Almond.

Cross, Frank Moore. 1973. *Canaanite Myth and Hebrew Epic*. Cambridge, MA: Harvard.

—1979. "Early Alphabetic Scripts." Pp. 97-123 in Frank Moore Cross (ed.). *Symposia*. Cambridge, MA: American Schools of Oriental Research.

—1983 [1973]. "W.F. Albright's View of Biblical Archaeology and its Methodology." Pp. 1-4 in E.F. Campbell and D.N. Freedman (eds.). *The Biblical Archaeologist Reader IV*. Sheffield: Almond.

Crowther, Margaret and Elizabeth Pichon (eds.). 1985. *The World Atlas of Archaeology*. London: Mitchell Beazley.

Crüsemann, Frank. 1978. *Der Widerstand gegen das Königtum*. Neukirchen-Vluyn: Neukirkener Verlag.

Culley, Robert C. 1979. "Introduction." *Semeia* 15:1-4.

—1985. "Exploring New Directions." Pp. 167-200 in Douglas A. Knight and Gene M. Tucker (eds.). *The Hebrew Bible and its Modern Interpreters*. Chico, CA: Scholars.

Curd, Martin. 1981. Review of David Bohm, *Wholeness and the Implicate Order* in *Physics Today* 34: 58-59.

Dahood, Mitchell. 1965. *Psalms I*. Anchor Bible 16. Garden City, NY: Doubleday.

—1968. *Psalms II*. Anchor Bible 17. Garden City, NY: Doubleday.

—1970. *Psalms III*. Anchor Bible 17A. Garden City, NY: Doubleday.

Davis, D. et al. 1985. "A Steel Pick from Mt. Adir in Palestine." *Journal of Near Eastern Studies* 44: 41-51.

Dever, William G. 1977. "Palestine in the Second Millenium BCE: the Archaeological Picture." Pp. 70-120 in John H. Hayes and J. Maxwell Miller (eds.). *Israelite and Judaean History*. Philadelphia: Westminster.

—1982a. "Monumental Architecture in Ancient Israel in the Period of the United Monarchy." Pp. 269-306 in Tomoo Ishida (ed.). *Studies in the Period of David and Solomon and other Essays*. Winona Lake, IN: Eisenbrauns.

—1982b. "Retrospects and Prospects in Biblical and Syro-Palestinian Archaeology." *Biblical Archaeologist* 45: 103-107.

—1985. "Palestinian Archaeology, 1945-1979. Portrait of an Emerging Discipline." Pp. 31-74 in D.A. Knight and G. Tucker (eds.). *The Hebrew Bible and its Modern Interpreters*. Chico, CA: Scholars.

Dornemann, Rudolph H. 1983. *The Archaeology of Transjordan*. Milwaukee: Milwaukee Public Museum.

Dothan, Trude. 1979. *Excavations at the Cemetery of Deir el-Balah*. Qedem 10. Jerusalem: Hebrew University Institute of Archaeology.

—1982. *The Philistines and their Material Culture*. New Haven: Yale.

—1985. "The Philistines Reconsidered." Pp. 165-176 in Janet Amitai (ed.). *Biblical Archaeology Today*. Jerusalem: Israel Exploration Society.

Drennan, Robert D. 1976. "Religion and Social Evolution in Formative Mesoamerica." Pp. 345-368 in Kent V. Flannery. *The Early Mesoamerican Village*. New York: Academic.

Drysdale, Alasdair and Gerald H. Blake. 1985. *The Middle East and North Africa*. New York: Oxford.

Dunnell, Robert C. 1982. "Science, Social Science and Common Sense: The Agonizing Dilemma of Modern Archaeology." *Journal of Anthropological Research* 38: 1-25.

Eisenstadt, Samuel N. 1963. *The Political Systems of Empires*. New York: Free Press.

—1973. *Tradition, Change, and Modernity*. New York: John Wiley & Sons.

Ellen, Roy. 1982. *Environment, Subsistence and System*. Cambridge: Cambridge University.

Fabian, Johannes. 1982. "On Rappaport's *Ecology, Meaning, and Religion*." *Current Anthropology* 23: 205-211.

Fisher, William B. 1978. *The Middle East*. 7th ed. London: Methuen.

Flanagan, James W. 1972. "Court History or Succession Document? A Study of 2 Samuel 9–20 and 1 Kings 1–2." *Journal of Biblical Literature* 91: 172-181.

—1975. "Judah in All Israel." Pp. 101-116 in James W. Flanagan and Anita W. Robinson (eds.). *No Famine in the Land*. Missoula, MT: Scholars.

—1976. "History, Religion, and Ideology: The Caleb Tradition." *Horizons* 3: 175-185.

—1979. "The Relocation of the Davidic Capital." *Journal of the American Academy of Religion* 47: 223-244.

—1981. "Chiefs in Israel." *Journal for the Study of the Old Testament* 20: 47-73.

—1982. "Models for the Origin of Iron Age Monarchy: A Modern Case Study." Pp. 135-156 in Kent H. Richards (ed.). *Society of Biblical Literature 1982 Seminar Papers*. Chico, CA: Scholars.

—1983a. "Succession and Genealogy in the Davidic Dynasty." Pp. 35-55 in H.B. Huffmon, et al. *The Quest for the Kingdom of God: Studies in Honor of George E. Mendenhall*. Winona Lake, IN: Eisenbrauns.

—1983b. "Social Transformation and Ritual in 2 Samuel 6." Pp. 362-372 in Carol Meyers and Michael P. O'Connor (eds.). *The Word of the Lord Shall Go Forth*. Winona Lake, IN: Eisenbrauns.

—1987. "Beyond Space-Time Systemics." *Journal for the Study of the Old Testament* 39: 22-29.

Flannery, Kent V. 1972. "The Cultural Evolution of Civilizations." *Annual Review of Ecology and Systemics* 3: 399-426.

Franken, H.J. 1960. "The Excavations at Deir 'Alla in Jordan." *Vetus Testamentum* 10: 386-393.

—1961. "The Excavations at Deir 'Alla in Jordan, 2nd Season." *Vetus Testamentum* 11: 361-372.

—1962. "The Excavations at Deir 'Alla in Jordan, 3rd Season." *Vetus Testamentum* 12: 378-382.

—1964. "Excavations at Deir 'Alla, Season 1964." *Vetus Testamentum* 14: 417-422.

—1969. *Excavations at Deir 'Alla*. Leiden: E.J. Brill.

—1976. "The Problem of Identification in Biblical Archaeology." *Palestine Exploration Quarterly* 108: 3-11.

Franken, H.J. and Moawiyah M. Ibrahim. 1977-78. "Two Seasons of Excavations at Tell Deir 'Alla." *Annual of the Department of Antiquities of Jordan* 22: 57-79.

Frankfort, Henri. 1948. *Kingship and the Gods*. Chicago: University of Chicago.

Freedman, David Noel. 1980. *Pottery, Poetry, & Prophecy*. Winona Lake, IN: Eisenbrauns.

Frei, Hans W. 1974. *The Eclipse of Biblical Narrative: A Study in Eighteenth and Nineteenth Century Hermeneutics*. New Haven: Yale.
Frick, Frank S. 1985. *The Formation of State in Ancient Israel*. Sheffield: Almond.
Fritz, Volkmar. 1975. "Erwägungen zur Siedlungsgeschichte des Negeb in der Eisen I-Zeit (1200 bis 1000 v. Chr.) im Licht der Ausgrabungen auf der Ḫirbe el Mšāš." *Zeitschrift des Deutschen Palästina-Vereins* 91: 30-45.
Frontain, Raymond-Jean and Jan Wojcik (eds.). 1980. *The David Myth in Western Literature*. Lafayette, IN: Purdue.
Fugmann, E. 1958. *Hama. Foulles et recherches 1931-1938*. Vol. II 1. Copenhague: Fondation Carlsberg.
Gadamer, Hans-Georg. 1975. *Truth and Method*. London: Sheed & Ward.
Gauthier-Pilters, Hilde and Anne Innis Dagg. 1981. *The Camel*. Chicago: University of Chicago.
Gellner, Ernest. 1969. *Saints of the Atlas*. Chicago: University of Chicago.
—1973. "Introduction to Nomadism." Pp. 1-10 in Cynthia Nelson (ed.). *The Desert and the Sown*. Berkeley: University of California.
—1981. *Muslim Society*. Cambridge: Cambridge University.
—1984. "Forward." Pp. ix-xxv in Anatolii M. Khazanov. *Nomads and the Outside World*. Cambridge: Cambridge University.
—1985. *Relativism and the Social Sciences*. Cambridge: Cambridge University.
van Gennep, Arnold. 1960. *The Rites of Passage*. Translated by Monika B. Vizebom and Gabrielle L. Caffee. Chicago: University of Chicago. Originally published as *Les rites du passage*, Paris: Nourry, 1909.
de Geus, C.H.J. 1976. *The Tribes of Israel*. Assen: Van Gorcum.
Gonen, Rivka. 1984. "Urban Canaan in the Late Bronze Age." *Bulletin of the American Schools of Oriental Research* 253: 61-73.
Goody, Jack. 1966. "Introduction." Pp. 1-56 in Jack Goody (ed.). *Succession to High Office*. Cambridge: Cambridge University.
—1976. *Production and Reproduction*. Cambridge: Cambridge University.
—1977. "Production and Polity in Voltaic Region." Pp. 535-545 in J. Friedman and M.J. Rowlands (eds.). *The Evolution of Social Systems*. London: Duckworth.
—1982. *Cooking, Cuisine and Class*. Cambridge: Cambridge University.
Gordon, Robert L. 1984. "Telul edh Dhahab Survey (Jordan) 1980 and 1982." *Mitteilungen der Deutschen Orient-Gesellschaft* 116: 131-137.
Gordon, Robert L. and Linda E. Villiers. 1983. "Telul edh Dhahab and its Environs Surveys of 1980 and 1982." *Annual of the Department of Antiquities of Jordan* XXVII: 275-289.
Gosselin, Edward A. 1976. *The King's Progress to Jerusalem*. Humana Civilitas, 2. Malibu, CA: Undena.
Gottwald, Norman K. 1979. *The Tribes of Yahweh*. Maryknoll, NY: Orbis.
—1985. *The Hebrew Bible—A Socio-Literary Introduction*. Philadelphia: Fortress.
Greenberg, Raphael. 1987. "New Light on the Early Iron Age at Tell Beit Mirsim." *Bulletin of the American Schools of Oriental Research* 265: 55-80.
Gunn, David M. 1970. "Narrative Inconsistency and the Oral Dictated Text in the Homeric Epic." *American Journal of Philology* 91: 192-203.
—1971. "Thematic Composition and Homeric Authorship." *Harvard Studies in Classical Philology* 75: 1-31.
—1974a. "Narrative Patterns and Oral Tradition in Judges and Samuel." *Vetus Testamentum* 24: 286-317.
—1974b. "The 'Battle Report': Oral or Scribal Convention?" *Journal of Biblical Literature* 93: 513-518.

—1975. "David and the Gift of the Kingdom." *Semeia* 3: 14-45.
—1976. "Traditional Composition in the 'Succession Narrative'." *Vetus Testamentum* 26: 214-229.
—1978. *The Story of King David*. JSOT Supplement Series, 6. Sheffield: JSOT.
—1980. *The Fate of King Saul*. JSOT Supplement Series, 14. Sheffield: JSOT.
—1984. Review of Robert Alter, *The Art of Biblical Narrative* in *Journal for the Study of the Old Testament* 29: 109-116.
—1987. "New Directions in the Study of Biblical Hebrew Narrative." *Journal for the Study of the Old Testament* 39: 65-75.
Hackett, Jo Ann. 1984. *The Balaam Text from Deir 'Alla*. Chico, CA: Scholars.
Hahn, Herbert F. 1954. *The Old Testament in Modern Research*. Philadelphia: Muhlenberg.
Haines, Richard C. 1971. *Excavations in the Plain of Antioch*. Chicago: University of Chicago.
Halpern, Baruch. 1983. *The Emergence of Israel in Canaan*. Chico, CA: Scholars.
Harré, Romano. 1970. *The Principles of Scientific Thinking*. Chicago: University of Chicago.
—1972. *The Philosophies of Science*. Oxford: Oxford University.
Harris, Marvin. 1979. *Cultural Materialism*. New York: Random House.
Hayes, John H. and J. Maxwell Miller (eds.). *Israelite and Judean History*. Philadelphia: Westminster.
Herr, Larry G. (ed.). 1983. *The Amman Airport Excavations, 1976*. Annual of the American Schools of Oriental Research, 48. Durham, NC: American Schools of Oriental Research.
Herrmann, Siegfried. 1981. *A History of Israel in the Old Testament*. Second edition revised. Philadelphia Fortress.
Hesse, Mary B. 1966. *Models and Analogies in Science*. Notre Dame, IN: Notre Dame University.
—1974. *The Structure of Scientific Inference*. London: Macmillan.
—1980. *Revolutions and Reconstructions in the Philosophy of Science*. Brighton, Sussex: Harvester.
Hocart, A.M. 1927. *Kingship*. London: Oxford University.
Hodder, Ian. 1982. *The Present Past*. London: B.T. Batsford.
Holden, David and Richard Johns. 1981. *The House of Saud*. London: Sidgwick and Jackson.
Holy, Ladislav and Milan Stuchlik. 1981. "The Structure of Folk Models." Pp. 1-34 in Ladislav Holy and Milan Stuchlik (eds.). *The Structure of Folk Models*. New York: Academic.
—1983. *Actions, Norms and Representations*. Cambridge: Cambridge University.
Hopkins, David C. 1985. *The Highlands of Canaan. Agricultural Life in the Early Iron Age*. Sheffield: Almond.
Horn, Siegfried H. 1973. "The Crown of the King of the Ammonites." *Andrews University Seminary Studies* 11: 170-180.
Howarth, David. 1980. *The Desert King. The Life of Ibn Saud*. London: Quartet.
Hudson, Michael C. 1977. *Arab Politics*. New Haven: Yale.
Ibrahim, Moawiyah M. 1978. "The Collared-Rim Jar of the Early Iron Age." Pp. 116-126 in Roger Moorey and Peter Parr (eds.). *Archaeology in the Levant*. Warminster, England: Aris and Phillips.
Jobling, David. 1978. *The Sense of Biblical Narrative*. JSOT Supplement Series, 7. Sheffield: JSOT.

—1986. *The Sense of Biblical Narrative: II*. JSOT Supplement Series, 39. Sheffield: JSOT.
Jobling, W.J. 1981. "Preliminary Report on the Archaeological Survey between Ma'an and Aqaba." *Annual of the Department of Antiquities of Jordan* XXV: 105-112.
—1982. "Aqaba-Ma'an Survey." *Annual of the Department of Antiquities of Jordan* XXVI: 199-209.
Johnson, M.D. 1969. *The Purpose of Biblical Genealogies*. Cambridge: Cambridge University.
Jones, Grant D. and Robert R. Kautz (eds.). 1981. *The Transition to Statehood in the New World*. Cambridge: Cambridge University.
Kasper, Joseph E. and Steven A. Feller. 1985. *The Hologram Book*. Englewood Cliffs, NJ: Prentice-Hall.
Kelly, Raymond C. 1985. *The Nuer Conquest*. Ann Arbor, MI: University of Michigan.
Kempinski, Aharon and Michael Avi-Yonah. 1979. *Syria-Palestine II*. Geneva: Nagel.
Kempinski, Aharon and Volkmar Fritz. 1977. "Excavations at Tel Masos: Third Season, 1975." *Tel Aviv* 3-4: 136-158.
Kenyon, Kathleen. 1974. *Digging Up Jerusalem*. New York: Praeger.
—1979. *Archaeology in the Holy Land*. 4th edition. New York: W.W. Norton.
Kerestes, Terry M. et al. 1978. "An Archaeological Survey of the Three Reservoir Areas in Northern Jordan, 1978." *Annual of the Department of Antiquities in Jordan* XXII: 108-135.
Khalaf, Samir. 1987. *Lebanon's Predicament*. New York: Columbia University.
Khazanov, Anatolii M. 1981. "The Early State Among the Eurasian Nomads." Pp. 155-176 in Henri J.M. Claessen and Peter Skalník (eds.). *The Study of the State*. New York: Mouton.
—1984. *Nomads and the Outside World*. Trans. Julia Crookenden. Cambridge: Cambridge University.
Klejn, Leo S. 1977. "A Panorama of Theoretical Archaeology." *Current Anthropology* 18: 1-42.
Knight, Douglas A. and Gene M. Tucker. 1985. "Editors' Preface." Pp. xii-xxi in Douglas A. Knight and Gene M. Tucker (eds.). *The Hebrew Bible and its Modern Interpreters*. Chico, CA: Scholars.
Kochavi, Moshe. 1985. "The Israelite Settlement in Canaan in the Light of Archaeological Surveys." Pp. 47-60 in Janet Amitai (ed.). *Biblical Archaeology Today*. Jerusalem: Israel Exploration Society.
Kovacs, Brian. 1978. "Philosophical Foundations of Structuralism." *Semeia* 10:85-105.
Kramer, Carol (ed.). 1979. *Ethnoarchaeology*. New York: Columbia University.
Kressel, Gideon M. 1984. "Changes in Employment and Social Accommodations of Bedouin Settling in an Israeli Town." Pp. 125-154 in Emanuel Marx and Avshalom Shmueli (eds.). *The Changing Bedouin*. New Brunswick: Transaction Books.
Kuhn, Thomas. 1976. *The Structure of Scientific Revolution*. Chicago: University of Chicago.
Lacey, Robert. 1981. *The Kingdom*. London: Hutchinson.
Langlamet, F. 1976. "Pour ou contre Salomon? La rédaction prosalomonienne de I Rois, I-II." *Revue Biblique* 83: 481-528.

Lapp, Nancy L. (ed.). 1975. *The Tale of the Tell*. Pittsburgh: Pickwick.
—1983. *The Excavations at Araq el-Emir, I*. Annual of the American Schools of Oriental Research, 47. Durham, NC: American Schools of Oriental Research.
Lapp, Paul W. 1968. "Tell er-Rumeith." *Revue Biblique* 75: 98-105.
Leach, Edmund. 1969. *Genesis as Myth and Other Essays*. London: Jonathan Cape.
—1973. "Concluding Address." Pp. 761-771 in Colin Renfrew (ed.). *The Explanation of Cultural Change: Models in Prehistory*. London: Duckworth.
—1977 [1961]. *Rethinking Anthropology*. London: Athlone.
—1982. *Social Anthropology*. New York: Oxford.
—1983a. "Anthropological Approaches to the Study of the Bible during the Twentieth Century." Pp. 7-32 in Edmund Leach and D. Alan Aycock (eds.). *Structuralist Interpretations of Biblical Myth*. Cambridge: Cambridge University.
—1983b. "Against Genres: Are Parables Lights Set in Candlesticks or Put Under a Bushel?" Pp. 89-112 in Edmund Leach and D. Alan Aycock (eds.). *Structuralist Interpretations of Biblical Myth*. Cambridge: Cambridge University.
Legg, Paul. 1980. "Arabic Topical Programs." British Broadcasting Network. July 19. Transcript.
Lemche, Niels P. 1985. *Early Israel*. Supplements to Vetus Testamentum, 37. Leiden: Brill.
Lévi-Strauss, Claude. 1955. "A Structural Study of Myth." *Journal of American Folklore* 67: 428-444.
Lewis, Norman N. 1987. *Nomads and Settlers in Syria and Jordan, 1800-1980*. Cambridge: Cambridge University.
Liebowitz, Harold. 1987. "Late Bronze II Ivory Work in Palestine: Evidence of a Cultural Highpoint." *Bulletin of the American Schools of Oriental Research* 265: 3-24.
Little, Robert. 1980. "New Book Defines Ibn Saud's Role through Court Interpreter's Eyes." *Arab News*. July 6.
Lovejoy, Paul E. 1983. *Transformations in Slavery*. Cambridge: Cambridge University.
McCarter, P. Kyle, Jr. 1980. *I Samuel*. Anchor Bible, 8. Garden City: Doubleday.
—1981. "Plots, True or False. The Succession Narrative as Court Apologetic." *Interpretation* 35: 355-367.
—1984. *II Samuel*. Anchor Bible, 9. Garden City: Doubleday.
McCarthy, Dennis J. 1965. "II Samuel 7 and the Structure of the Deuteronomic History." *Journal of Biblical Literature* 84: 131-138.
McCreery, David. 1977-78. "Preliminary Report of the A.P.C. Township Archaeological Survey." *Annual of the Department of Antiquities of Jordan* XXII: 150-161.
MacDonald, Burton. 1980. "The Wadi el Hasa Survey 1979: A Preliminary Report." *Annual of the Department of Antiquities of Jordan* XXIV: 169-183.
MacDonald, Burton, Gary O. Rollefson, and Duane W. Roller. 1982. "The Wadi el Hasa Survey, 1981." *Annual of the Department of Antiquities of Jordan* XXVI: 117-131.
McGovern, Patrick. 1980. "Explorations in the Umm Ad-Dananir Region of the Baqa'ah Valley, 1977-78." *Annual of the Department of Antiquities of Jordan* XXIV: 55-68.
McKenzie, John L. 1983. "The Sack of Israel." Pp. 25-34 in H.B. Huffmon et al. *The Quest for the Kingdom of God: Studies in Honor of George E. Mendenhall*. Winona Lake, IN: Eisenbrauns.

McKenzie, Steven L. 1984. *The Chronicler's Use of the Deuteronomistic History*. Atlanta, GA: Scholars.

McNutt, Paula M. 1983. *An Inquiry into the Significance of Iron Technology in Early Iron Age Palestine*. Unpublished Master's Thesis. Missoula, MT: University of Montana.

Malamat, Abraham. 1967. "Aspects of Tribal Societies in Mari and Israel." *XVe Rencontre assyriologique internationale*. 42: 129-138.

—1968. "King Lists of the Old Babylonian Period and Biblical Genealogies." *Journal of the American Oriental Society* 88: 163-173.

—1970. "Organs of Statecraft in the Israelite Monarchy." Pp. 163-198 in E.F. Campbell and D.N. Freedman (eds.). *Biblical Archaeologist Reader 3*. Garden City: Anchor.

—1973a. "Tribal Societies: Biblical Genealogies and African Lineage Systems." *Archives européennes de sociologie* 14: 126-136.

—1973b. "The Aramaeans." Pp. 134-155 in D.J. Wiseman (ed.). *Peoples of Old Testament Times*. Oxford: Clarendon.

—1985. "Mari and Early Israel." Pp. 235-243 in Janet Amitai (ed.). *Biblical Archaeology Today*. Jerusalem: Israel Exploration Society.

Marfoe, Leon. 1979. "The Integrative Transformation: Patterns of Sociopolitical Organization in Southern Syria." *Bulletin of the American Schools of Oriental Research* 234: 1-42.

Marx, Emanuel. 1967. *Bedouin of the Negev*. Manchester: Manchester University.

—1984a. "Economic Change Among Pastoral Nomads in the Middle East." Pp. 1-16 in Emanuel Marx and Avshalom Shmueli (eds.). *The Changing Bedouin*. New Brunswick: Transaction Books.

—1984b. "Changing Employment Patterns of Bedouin in South Sinai." Pp. 173-186 in Emanuel Marx and Avshalom Shmueli (eds.). *The Changing Bedouin*. New Brunswick: Transaction Books.

Mazar, Amihai. 1980. *Excavations at Tell Qasile*. Qedem, 12. Jerusalem: Hebrew University Institute of Archaeology.

—1985. "The Israelite Settlement in Canaan in the Light of Archaeological Excavations." Pp. 61-71 in Janet Amitai (ed.). *Biblical Archaeology Today*. Jerusalem: Israel Exploration Society.

Meeker, Michael E. 1979. *Literature & Violence in North Arabia*. Cambridge: Cambridge University.

—1980. "The Twilight of a South Asian Heroic Age: A Rereading of Barth's Study of Swat." *Man* (N.S.) 15: 682-701.

Mendenhall, George E. 1961. "Biblical History in Transition." Pp. 32-53 in George Ernest Wright (ed.). *The Bible and the Ancient Near East*. Garden City, NY: Anchor.

—1970a[1954]. "Ancient Oriental and Biblical Law." Pp. 3-24 in Edward F. Campbell and David Noel Freedman (eds.). *Biblical Archaeologist Reader 3*. Garden City, NY: Doubleday.

—1970b [1954]. "Covenant Forms in Israelite Tradition." Pp. 25-53 in Edward F. Campbell and David Noel Freedman (eds.). *Biblical Archaeologist Reader 3*. Garden City, NY: Doubleday.

—1970c [1962]. "The Hebrew Conquest of Canaan." Pp. 100-120. in Edward F. Campbell and David Noel Freedman (eds.). *Biblical Archaeologist Reader 3*. Garden City, NY: Doubleday.

—1973. *The Tenth Generation*. Baltimore: Johns Hopkins.
—1975a. "The Monarchy." *Interpretation* 29: 155-170.
—1975b. "The Conflict Between Value Systems and Social Control." Pp. 169-180 in Hans Goedicke and J.J.M. Roberts (eds.). *Unity and Diversity*. Baltimore: Johns Hopkins.
—1978. "Between Theology and Archaeology." *Journal for the Study of the Old Testament* 7: 28-34.
—1983. "Ancient Israel's Hyphenated History." Pp. 91-102 in David Noel Freedman and David Frank Graf. *Palestine in Transition*. Sheffield: Almond.
Mettinger, Tryggve N.D. 1971. *Solomonic State Officials*. Coniectanea Biblica. Old Testament Series 5. Lund: CWK Gleerup.
—1976. *King and Messiah*. Coniectanea Biblica. Old Testament Series 8. Lund: CWK Gleerup.
Meyers, Eric M. 1984. "The Bible and Archaeology." *Biblical Archaeologist* 47: 36-40.
Michalowski, Piotr. 1983. "History as Charter. Some Observations on the Sumerian King List." *Journal of the American Oriental Society* 103: 237-248.
Miller, J. Maxwell. 1979. "Archaeological Survey South of Wadi Mujib: Glueck's Sites Revisited." *Annual of the Department of Antiquities in Jordan* 23: 79-92.
—1985. "Israelite History." Pp. 1-30 in Douglas A. Knight and Gene M. Tucker (eds.). *The Hebrew Bible and its Modern Interpreters*. Chico, CA: Scholars.
Miller, J. Maxwell and John H. Hayes. 1986. *A History of Ancient Israel and Judah*. Philadelphia: Westminster.
Mohammed, Abbas. 1973. "The Nomadic and the Sedentary: Polar Complementaries—Not Polar Opposites." Pp. 97-112 in Cynthia Nelson (ed.). *The Desert and the Sown*. Berkeley, CA: University of California Institute of International Studies.
Moran, William L. 1975. "The Syrian Scribe of the Jerusalem Amarna Letters." Pp. 146-166 in Hans Goedicke and J.J.M. Roberts (eds.). *Unity and Diversity*. Baltimore: Johns Hopkins.
Mostyn, Trevor. 1980. "Books." *Middle East*. July 18: 49.
Mowinckel, Sigmund. 1962. *The Psalms in Israel's Worship*. 2 Volumes. Translated by D.R. Ap-Thomas. New York: Abingdon.
Muhly, James D. 1980. "The Bronze Age Setting." Pp. 25-69 in Theodore A. Wertime and James D. Muhly (eds.). *The Coming of the Age of Iron*. New Haven: Yale.
—1982. "How Iron Technology Changed the Ancient World." *Biblical Archaeology Review* November/December: 42-54.
—1985. "Phoenicia and the Phoenicians." Pp. 177-191 in Janet Amitai (ed.). *Biblical Archaeology Today*. Jerusalem: Israel Exploration Society.
Negbi, Ora. 1985. "Respondents [to J.D. Muhly]." Pp. 221-223 in Janet Amitai (ed.). *Biblical Archaeology Today*. Jerusalem: Israel Exploration Society.
Noth, Martin. 1960. *The History of Israel*. 2nd edition. Trans. P.R. Ackroyd. New York: Harper and Row.
—1967. *The Laws of the Pentateuch and Other Studies*. Philadelphia: Fortress.
—1981. *The Deuteronomistic History*. Trans. Michael D. Rutter. Sheffield: JSOT. Original published in 1943.
O'Neill, John P. (ed.). 1986. *Treasures of the Holy Land*. New York: Metropolitan Museum of Art.
Ong, Walter J. 1982. *Orality and Literacy*. New York: Methuen.
Orme, Bryony. 1973. "Archaeology and Ethnography." Pp. 481-492 in Colin Renfrew (ed.). *The Explanation of Culture Change: Models in Prehistory*. London: Duckworth.

—1981. *Anthropology for Archaeologists: An Introduction*. Ithaca, NY: Cornell.
Orni, Efraim and E. Efrat. 1973. *Geography of Israel*. 3rd ed. Philadelphia: Jewish Publication Society.
Parr, Peter. 1978. "Pottery, People, and Politics." Pp. 203-210 in Roger Moorey and Peter Parr (eds.). *Archaeology in the Levant*. Warminster: Aris and Phillips.
—1982. "Contacts between North West Arabia and Jordan in the Late Bronze and Iron Ages." Pp. 127-133 in Adnan Hadidi (ed.). *Studies in the History and Archaeology of Jordan, I*. Amman: Department of Antiquities of Jordan.
Peckham, Brian. 1985. *The Composition of the Deuteronomistic History*. Atlanta, GA: Scholars.
Philby, Harry St. John. 1952. *Arabian Jubilee*. London: Robert Hale.
—1955. *Sa'udi Arabia*. London: Ernest Benn.
Popper, Karl R. 1961. *The Poverty of Historicism*. London and Henley: Routledge & Kegan Paul.
Pribram, Karl. 1971. *Language of the Brain*. Englewood Cliffs, NJ: Prentice-Hall.
Price, Barbara J. 1978. "Secondary State Formation: An Explanatory Model." Pp. 161-186 in Ronald Cohen and Elman R. Service (eds.). *Origins of the State*. Philadelphia: Institute for the Study of Human Issues.
von Rad, Gerhard. 1953. *Studies in Deuteronomy*. Studies in Biblical Theology, 9. London: SCM.
—1962/1965. *Old Testament Theology*. 2 vols. Trans. D.M.G. Stalker. New York: Harper and Row.
—1966. "The Beginnings of Historical Writing in Ancient Israel." Pp. 166-204 in Gerhard von Rad, *The Problem of the Hexateuch and other Essays*. Trans. E.W. Trueman Dicken. New York: McGraw-Hill.
Rappaport, Roy A. 1968. *Pigs for the Ancestors*. New Haven: Yale.
—1979. *Ecology, Meaning and Religion*. Richmond, CA: North Atlantic Books.
—1984. "Epilogue, 1984." Pp. 299-496 in Roy A. Rappaport. *Pigs for the Ancestors*. Reprint edition. New Haven: Yale.
Rast, Walter. 1978. *Taanach I. Studies in the Iron Age Pottery*. Cambridge, MA: American School of Oriental Research.
Redfield, Robert. 1960. *Peasant Society and Culture*. Chicago: University of Chicago.
Redfield, Robert and Milton B. Singer. 1954-55. "The Cultural Role of Cities." *Economic Development and Cultural Change* 3: 53-73.
Redford, Donald B. 1985. "The Relations between Egypt and Israel from El-Amarna to the Babylonian Conquest." Pp. 192-205 in Janet Amitai (ed.). *Biblical Archaeology Today*. Jerusalem: Israel Exploration Society.
Renfrew, Colin. 1978. "Trajectory Discontinuity and Morphogenesis: The Implications of Catastrophe Theory for Archaeology." *American Antiquity* 43: 203-222.
—1979. "Transformations." Pp. 481-506 in Colin Renfrew and Kenneth L. Cook (eds.). *Transformations: Mathematical Approaches to Culture Change*. New York: Academic.
—1982. "Explanation Revisited." In Colin Renfrew, Michael J. Rowlands, and Barbara Abbott Segraves (eds.), *Theory and Explanation in Archaeology*. New York: Academic Press, 5-24.
Riis, P.J. 1948. *Hama. Foulles et recherches 1931-1938*. Vol. II 3. Copenhague: Fondation Carlsberg.
Robertson A.F. 1976. "Ousting the Chief: Deposition Charges in Ashanti." *Man* 11: 410-427.

Rogerson, John W. 1978. *Anthropology of the Old Testament*. Oxford: Blackwells.
—1985. *The Atlas of the Bible*. New York: Facts on File Publication.
Rosenberg, Joel. 1986. *King and Kin*. Bloomington, IN: Indiana University.
Rost, Leonhard. 1982. *The Succession to the Throne of David*. Trans. Michael D. Rutter and David M. Gunn. Sheffield: Almond. Translation of "Die Überlieferung von der Thronnachfolge Davids." Pp. 119-253 in Leonhard Rost. *Das kleine Credo und andere Studien zum Alten Testament*. Heidelberg: Quelle & Meyer Verlag, 1965 [1926].
Rowton, M.B. 1982. "Enclosed Nomadism." *Journal for the Economic and Social History of the Orient*. 17: 1-30.
Saha, P.K. 1988. "Metaphorical Style as Message." Pp. 41-61 in D.H. Helman (ed.). *Analogical Reasoning*. Dordrecht: Kluwer Academic.
Sahlins, Marshall D. 1961. "The Segmentary Lineage: An Organization of Predatory Expansion." *Athropological Quarterly* 63: 322-346.
Salmon. Merrilee H. 1982. *Philosophy and Archaeology*. New York: Academic Press.
Salmon, Merrilee H. and Wesley C. Salmon. 1979. 'Alternative Models of Scientific Explanation." *American Anthropologist* 81: 61-74.
Salzman, P.C. 1978a. "Does Complementary Opposition Exist?" *American Anthropologist* 80: 53-70.
—1978b. "Ideology and Change in Middle Eastern Tribal Societies." *Man* (N.S.) 13: 618-637.
Sauer, James A. 1982. "Prospects for Archeology in Jordan and Syria." *Biblical Archeologist* 45: 73-84.
—1986. "Transjordan in the Bronze and Iron Ages: A Critique of Glueck's Synthesis." *Bulletin of the American Schools of Oriental Research* 263: 1-26. (= [without bibliography] "Ammon, Moab, and Edom." Pp. 206-214 in Janet Amitai [ed.]. *Biblical Archaeology Today*. Jerusalem: Israel Exploration Society, 1985.)
Saxby, Graham. 1980. *Holograms*. New York: Focal Press.
Service, Elman R. 1962. *Primitive Social Organization*. New York: Random House.
—1975. *Origins of the State and Civilization*. New York: W.W. Norton.
—1978. "Classical and Modern Theories of the Origins of Government." Pp. 21-34 in Ronald Cohen and Elman R. Service (eds.). *Origins of the State*. Philadelphia: Institute for the Study of Human Issues.
Shaffer, Jim G. and Diane A. Lichtenstein. n.d. "Ethnicity and Change in the Indus Valley Cultural Tradition." *Wisconsin Archaeology Review* (forthcoming).
Shaw, William H. and L.R. Ashley. 1983. "Analogy and Inference." *Dialogue* 22: 415-432.
Shiloh, Yigal. 1971. "The Four-Room House, its Situation and Function in the Israelite City." *Israel Exploration Journal* 20: 180-190.
—1978. "Elements in the Development of Town Planning and the Israelite City." *Israel Exploration Journal* 28: 36-51.
—1979a. "Iron Age Sanctuaries and Cult elements in Palestine." Pp. 147-158 in Frank Moore Cross (ed.). *Symposia*. Cambridge, MA: American Schools of Oriental Research.
—1979b. *The Proto-Aeolic Capital and Israelite Ashlar Masonry*. Qedem 11. Jerusalem: Hebrew University Institute of Archaeology.
—1984. *Excavations at the City of David I, 1978-1982*. Qedem 19. Jerusalem: Hebrew University.
—1985. "The City of David: 1978-1983." Pp. 451-462 in Janet Amitai (ed.). *Biblical Archaeology Today*. Jerusalem: Israel Exploration Society.

Shmueli, Avshalom. 1984. "The Desert Frontier in Judea." Pp. 17-38 in Emanuel Marx and Avshalom Shmueli (eds.). *The Changing Bedouin*. New Brunswick: Transaction Books.
Smith, M.G. 1956. "On Segmentary Lineage Systems." *Journal of the Royal Anthropological Institute* 86: 37-79.
Soggin, J. Alberto. 1978. "A History of Ancient Israel - a Study in Some Questions of Method." *Eretz-Israel* 14: 44*-51*.
—1980. "I testi vetero-testamentari sulla conquista della Palestina." *Rivista Biblica* 28:45-57.
—1984. *A History of Ancient Israel*. Philadelphia: Westminster.
Stager, Lawrence E. 1985. "The Archaeology of the Family in Ancient Israel." *Bulletin of the American Schools of Oriental Research* 260: 1-35.
Stech-Wheeler, T. et al. 1981. "Iron at Taanach and Early Iron Metallurgy in the Eastern Mediterranean." *American Journal of Archaeology* 85: 245-268.
Stern, Ephraim. 1978. *Excavations at Tel Mevorakh*. Qedem 9. Jerusalem: Hebrew University Institute of Archaeology.
Thompson, Raymond L. 1956. "The Subjective Element in Archaeological Inference." *Southwestern Journal of Anthropology* 12: 327-332.
Thompson, Thomas L. 1979. "Conflict Themes in the Jacob Narratives." *Semeia* 15:5-26.
Turner, Terence S. 1977. "Transformation, Hierarchy and Transcendence: A Reformulation of Van Gennep's Model of the Structure of *Rites de Passage*." Pp. 53-70 in Sally F. Moore and Barbara G. Meyerhoff (eds.). *Secular Ritual*. Amsterdam: van Gorcum.
Turner, Victor. 1957. *Schism and Continuity in an African Society*. New York/ Manchester: Humanities/Manchester University.
—1974. *Dramas, Fields, and Metaphors*. Ithaca: Cornell University.
—1977. "Process, System, and Symbol: A New Anthropological Sythesis." *Daedalus* 1:61-80.
—1980. "Social Dramas and Stories about Them." *Critical Inquiry* 7: 141-168.
—1985a [1969]. *The Ritual Process*. Ithaca: Cornell University.
—1985b. *On the Edge of the Bush*. Edited by Edith Turner. Tucson, AZ: University of Arizona.
Turner, Victor and Edith Turner. 1978. *Image and Pilgrimage in Christian Culture*. New York: Columbia.
Van Seters, John. 1976. "Problems in the Literary Analysis of the Court History of David." *Journal for the Study of the Old Testament* 1: 22-29.
—1983. *In Search of History*. New Haven: Yale.
Veijola, Timo. 1975. *Die Ewige Dynastie*. Helskinki: Suomalainen Tiedeakatemia.
Verdon, Michel. 1980. "From the Social to the Symbolic Equation: the Process of Idealism in Contemporary Anthropological Representations of Kinship, Marriage, and the Family." *Canadian Review of Sociology and Anthropology* 17: 315-329.
—1981. "Kinship, Marriage, and the Family: an Operational Approach." *American Journal of Sociology*. 86: 796-818.
—1982. "Neither Alter nor Ego: An Operational Model for Social Anthropology." *Revue européenne des sciences sociales* 62: 85-104.
Waldbaum, Jame. 1978. *From Bronze to Iron*. Göteborg: Paul Åströms Förlag.
—1980. "The First Archaeological Appearance of Iron and the Transition to the Iron Age." Pp. 69-98 in Theodore A. Wertime and James D. Muhly (eds.). *The Coming of the Age of Iron*. New Haven: Yale.

Ward, William. A. and M.F. Martin. 1964. "The Balu'a Stele: A New Transcription with Palaeographical and Historical Notes." *Annual of the Department of Antiquities of Jordan* VIII-IX: 5-29.

Weber, Renée. 1982. "The Enfolding-Unfolding Universe: A Conversation with David Bohm." Pp. 44-104 in Ken Wilber (ed.). *The Holographic Paradigm*. Boulder: Shambhala New Science Library.

Weiser, Artur. 1962. *The Psalms*. Trans. Herbert Hartwell. Philadelphia: Westminster.

The White House. 1945. *The President's Trip to the Crimea Conference and Great Bitter Lakes, Egypt*. Washington, D.C.: The White House.

Whitelam, Keith W. 1979. *The Just King. Monarchical Judicial Authority in Ancient Israel*. Sheffield: JSOT.

—1984. "The Defence of David." *Journal for the Study of the Old Testament* 29: 61-87.

Whybray, R. Norman. 1968. *The Succession Narrative*. London: SCM.

Willey, Gordon R. and Philip Phillips. 1958. *Method and Theory in Archaeology*. Chicago: University of Chicago.

Williamson, H.G.M. 1976. "The Accession of Solomon in the Books of Chronicles." *Vetus Testamentum* 26: 351-361.

—1977. *Israel in the Books of Chronicles*. Cambridge: Cambridge University.

—1982. *I and 2 Chronicles*. New Century Bible Commentary. Grand Rapids, MI: Wm. B. Eerdmans.

Wilson, Robert R. 1975. "The Old Testament Genealogies in Recent Research." *Journal of Biblical Literature* 94: 169-189.

—1977. *Genealogy and History in the Biblical World*. New Haven: Yale University Press.

—1980. *Prophecy and Society in Ancient Israel*. Philadelphia: Fortress.

—1984. *Sociological Approaches to the Old Testament*. Philadelphia: Fortress.

Winder, R. Bayly. 1980. *Saudi Arabia in the Nineteenth Century*. New York: Octagon.

Wright, George Ernest. 1970. "The Phenomenon of American Archaeology in the Near East." Pp. 3-40 in James. A. Sanders (ed.). *Near Eastern Archaeology in the Twentieth Century*. Garden City: Doubleday.

—1983a [1971]. "What Archaeology Can and Cannot Do." Pp. 65-72 in E.F. Campbell and D.N. Freedman (eds.). *The Biblical Archaeologist Reader IV*. Sheffield: Almond.

—1983b [1975]. "The 'New' Archaeology." Pp. 73-86 in E.F. Campbell and D.N. Freedman (eds.). *The Biblical Archaeologist Reader IV*. Sheffield: Almond.

Wright, Henry T. 1978. "Toward an Explanation of the Origin of State." Pp. 49-68 in Ronald Cohen and Elman R. Service (eds.). *Origins of the State*. Philadelphia: Institute for the Study of Human Issues.

Würthwein, Ernst. 1974. *Erzählung von der Thronfolge Davids: Theologische oder politische Geschichtsschreibung?* Theologische Studien 115. Zürich: Theologischer Verlag.

Wylie, Alison. 1981. *Postivism and the New Archaeology*. Unpublished Ph.D. Dissertation, SUNY, Binghamton, New York. Ann Arbor: University Microfilms.

—1985. "The Reaction against Analogy." Pp. 63-113 in Michael B. Schiffer (ed.). *Advances in Archaeological Method and Theory*. Vol. 8. New York: Academic.

Yadin, Yigael. 1979. "The Transition from a Semi-Nomadic to a Sedentary Society in the Twelfth Century B.C.E." Pp. 57-68 in Frank Moore Cross (ed.). *Symposia*. Cambridge: American Schools of Oriental Research.

Ziman, John M. 1968. *Public Knowledge*. Cambridge: Cambridge University.
—1978. *Reliable Knowledge*. Cambridge: Cambridge University.
—1981. *Puzzles, Problems and Enigmas*. Cambridge: Cambridge University.
Zohary, Michael. 1982. *Plants of the Bible*. Cambridge: Cambridge University.
—1984. *An Introduction to Science Studies*. Cambridge: Cambridge University.

INDEX

INDEX OF BIBLICAL REFERENCES

INDEX OF AUTHORS

INDEX OF SUBJECTS

JOURNAL FOR THE STUDY OF THE OLD TESTAMENT

Supplement Series

1 I, HE, WE AND THEY:
A LITERARY APPROACH TO ISAIAH 53
D.J.A. Clines

*2 JEWISH EXEGESIS OF THE BOOK OF RUTH
D.R.G. Beattie

*3 THE LITERARY STRUCTURE OF PSALM 2
P. Auffret

4 THANKSGIVING FOR A LIBERATED PROPHET:
AN INTERPRETATION OF ISAIAH CHAPTER 53
R.N. Whybray

5 REDATING THE EXODUS AND CONQUEST
J.J. Bimson

6 THE STORY OF KING DAVID:
GENRE AND INTERPRETATION
D.M. Gunn

7 THE SENSE OF BIBLICAL NARRATIVE I:
STRUCTURAL ANALYSES IN THE HEBREW BIBLE (2nd edition)
D. Jobling

*8 GENESIS 1-11: STUDIES IN STRUCTURE AND THEME
P.D. Miller

*9 YAHWEH AS PROSECUTOR AND JUDGE:
AN INVESTIGATION OF THE PROPHETIC LAWSUIT (RIB PATTERN)
K. Nielsen

10 THE THEME OF THE PENTATEUCH
D.J.A. Clines

*11 STUDIA BIBLICA 1978 I:
PAPERS ON OLD TESTAMENT AND RELATED THEMES
Edited by E.A. Livingstone

12 THE JUST KING:
MONARCHICAL JUDICIAL AUTHORITY IN ANCIENT ISRAEL
K.W. Whitelam

13 ISAIAH AND THE DELIVERANCE OF JERUSALEM:
A STUDY OF THE INTERPRETATION OF PROPHECY
IN THE OLD TESTAMENT
R.E. Clements

14 THE FATE OF KING SAUL:
AN INTERPRETATION OF A BIBLICAL STORY
D.M. Gunn

15 THE DEUTERONOMISTIC HISTORY
M. Noth

16 PROPHECY AND ETHICS:
ISAIAH AND THE ETHICAL TRADITIONS OF ISRAEL
E.W. Davies

17 THE ROLES OF ISRAEL'S PROPHETS
D.L. Petersen

18 THE DOUBLE REDACTION OF THE DEUTERONOMISTIC HISTORY
R.D.Nelson

19 ART AND MEANING: RHETORIC IN BIBLICAL LITERATURE
Edited by D.J.A. Clines, D.M. Gunn, & A.J. Hauser

20 THE PSALMS OF THE SONS OF KORAH
M.D. Goulder

21 COLOUR TERMS IN THE OLD TESTAMENT
A. Brenner

22 AT THE MOUNTAIN OF GOD:
STORY AND THEOLOGY IN EXODUS 32–34
R.W.L. Moberly

23 THE GLORY OF ISRAEL:
THE THEOLOGY AND PROVENIENCE OF THE ISAIAH TARGUM
B.D. Chilton

24 MIDIAN, MOAB AND EDOM:
THE HISTORY AND ARCHAEOLOGY OF LATE BRONZE AND IRON AGE JORDAN AND NORTH-WEST ARABIA
Edited by J.F.A. Sawyer & D.J.A Clines

25 THE DAMASCUS COVENANT:
AN INTERPRETATION OF THE 'DAMASCUS DOCUMENT'
P.R. Davies

26 CLASSICAL HEBREW POETRY:
A GUIDE TO ITS TECHNIQUES
W.G.E. Watson

27 PSALMODY AND PROPHECY
W.H. Bellinger

28 HOSEA: AN ISRAELITE PROPHET IN JUDEAN PERSPECTIVE
G.I. Emmerson

29 EXEGESIS AT QUMRAN:
4QFLORILEGIUM IN ITS JEWISH CONTEXT
G.J. Brooke

30 THE ESTHER SCROLL: THE STORY OF THE STORY
D.J.A. Clines

31 IN THE SHELTER OF ELYON:
ESSAYS IN HONOR OF G.W. AHLSTRÖM
Edited by W.B. Barrick & J.R. Spencer

32 THE PROPHETIC PERSONA:
JEREMIAH AND THE LANGUAGE OF THE SELF
T. Polk

33 LAW AND THEOLOGY IN DEUTERONOMY
J.G. McConville

34 THE TEMPLE SCROLL:
AN INTRODUCTION, TRANSLATION AND COMMENTARY
J. Maier

35 SAGA, LEGEND, TALE, NOVELLA, FABLE:
NARRATIVE FORMS IN OLD TESTAMENT LITERATURE
Edited by G.W. Coats

36 THE SONG OF FOURTEEN SONGS
M.D. Goulder

37 UNDERSTANDING THE WORD:
ESSAYS IN HONOR OF BERNHARD W. ANDERSON
Edited by J.T. Butler, E.W. Conrad & B.C. Ollenburger

38 SLEEP, DIVINE AND HUMAN, IN THE OLD TESTAMENT
T.H. McAlpine

39 THE SENSE OF BIBLICAL NARRATIVE II:
STRUCTURAL ANALYSES IN THE HEBREW BIBLE
D. Jobling

40 DIRECTIONS IN BIBLICAL HEBREW POETRY
Edited by E.R. Follis

41 ZION, THE CITY OF THE GREAT KING:
A THEOLOGICAL SYMBOL OF THE JERUSALEM CULT
B.C. Ollenburger

42 A WORD IN SEASON: ESSAYS IN HONOUR OF WILLIAM McKANE
Edited by J.D. Martin & P.R. Davies

43 THE CULT OF MOLEK:
A REASSESSMENT
G.C. Heider

44 THE IDENTITY OF THE INDIVIDUAL IN THE PSALMS
S.J.L. Croft

45 THE CONFESSIONS OF JEREMIAH IN CONTEXT:
SCENES OF PROPHETIC DRAMA
A.R. Diamond

46 THE BOOK OF THE JUDGES: AN INTEGRATED READING
B.G. Webb

47 THE GREEK TEXT OF JEREMIAH:
A REVISED HYPOTHESIS
S. Soderlund

48 TEXT AND CONTEXT:
OLD TESTAMENT AND SEMITIC STUDIES FOR F.C. FENSHAM
Edited by W. Claassen

49 THEOPHORIC PERSONAL NAMES IN ANCIENT HEBREW
J.D. Fowler

50 THE CHRONICLER'S HISTORY
M. Noth

51 DIVINE INITIATIVE AND HUMAN RESPONSE IN EZEKIEL
P. Joyce

52 THE CONFLICT OF FAITH AND EXPERIENCE IN THE PSALMS:
A FORM-CRITICAL AND THEOLOGICAL STUDY
C.C. Broyles

53 THE MAKING OF THE PENTATEUCH:
A METHODOLOGICAL STUDY
R.N. Whybray

54 FROM REPENTANCE TO REDEMPTION:
JEREMIAH'S THOUGHT IN TRANSITION
J. Unterman

55 THE ORIGIN TRADITION OF ANCIENT ISRAEL:
THE LITERARY FORMATION OF GENESIS AND EXODUS 1–23
T.L. Thompson

56 THE PURIFICATION OFFERING IN THE PRIESTLY LITERATURE:
ITS MEANING AND FUNCTION
N. Kiuchi

57 MOSES: HEROIC MAN, MAN OF GOD
G.W. Coats

58 THE LISTENING HEART: ESSAYS IN WISDOM AND THE PSALMS
IN HONOR OF ROLAND E. MURPHY, O. CARM.
Edited by K.G. Hoglund

59 CREATIVE BIBLICAL EXEGESIS:
CHRISTIAN AND JEWISH HERMENEUTICS THROUGH THE CENTURIES
B. Uffenheimer & H.G. Reventlow

60 HER PRICE IS BEYOND RUBIES:
THE JEWISH WOMAN IN GRAECO-ROMAN PALESTINE
L.J. Archer

61 FROM CHAOS TO RESTORATION:
AN INTEGRATIVE READING OF ISAIAH 24–27
D.G. Johnson

62 THE OLD TESTAMENT AND FOLKLORE STUDY
P.G. Kirkpatrick

63 SHILOH: A BIBLICAL CITY IN TRADITION AND HISTORY
D.G. Schley

64 TO SEE AND NOT PERCEIVE:
ISAIAH 6.9-10 IN EARLY JEWISH AND CHRISTIAN INTERPRETATION
C.A. Evans

65 THERE IS HOPE FOR A TREE:
THE TREE AS METAPHOR IN ISAIAH
K. Nielsen

66 THE SECRETS OF THE TIMES:
RECOVERING BIBLICAL CHRONOLOGIES
J. Hughes

67 ASCRIBE TO THE LORD:
BIBLICAL AND OTHER ESSAYS IN MEMORY OF PETER C. CRAIGIE
Edited by L. Eslinger & G. Taylor

68 THE TRIUMPH OF IRONY IN THE BOOK OF JUDGES
L.R. Klein

69 ZEPHANIAH, A PROPHETIC DRAMA
P.R. House

70 NARRATIVE ART IN THE BIBLE
S. Bar-Efrat

71 QOHELET AND HIS CONTRADICTIONS
M.V. Fox

72 CIRCLE OF SOVEREIGNTY:
A STORY OF STORIES IN DANIEL 1-6
D.N. Fewell

73 DAVID'S SOCIAL DRAMA:
A HOLOGRAM OF THE EARLY IRON AGE
J.W. Flanagan

* Out of print